Writing in Public

WRITING IN PUBLIC

Literature and the Liberty of the Press
in Eighteenth-Century Britain

❧

TREVOR ROSS

Johns Hopkins University Press
Baltimore

© 2018 Johns Hopkins University Press
All rights reserved. Published 2018
Printed in the United States of America on acid-free paper
2 4 6 8 9 7 5 3 1

Johns Hopkins University Press
2715 North Charles Street
Baltimore, Maryland 21218-4363
www.press.jhu.edu

Library of Congress Cataloging-in-Publication Data

Names: Ross, Trevor Thornton, 1961– author.
Title: Writing in public : literature and the liberty of the press in eighteenth-century Britain / Trevor Ross.
Description: Baltimore, Md. : Johns Hopkins University Press, [2018] | Includes bibliographical references and index.
Identifiers: LCCN 2017058445 | ISBN 9781421426310 (hardcover : alk. paper) | ISBN 9781421426327 (electronic) | ISBN 1421426315 (hardcover : alk. paper) | ISBN 1421426323 (electronic)
Subjects: LCSH: Literature and society—Great Britain—History—18th century. | Copyright—Great Britain—History—18th century. | Democracy and the arts—Great Britain.
Classification: LCC PR448.S64 R67 2018 | DDC 820.9/005—dc23
LC record available at https://lccn.loc.gov/2017058445

A catalog record for this book is available from the British Library.

Special discounts are available for bulk purchases of this book. For more information, please contact Special Sales at 410-516-6936 or specialsales@press.jhu.edu.

Johns Hopkins University Press uses environmentally friendly book materials, including recycled text paper that is composed of at least 30 percent post-consumer waste, whenever possible.

CONTENTS

Acknowledgments vii

Introduction: Writing in Public 1

COPYRIGHT

1 Literature in the Public Domain 35

2 The Fate of Style in an Age of Intellectual Property 75

DEFAMATION AND PRIVACY

3 What Does Literature Publicize? 111

4 How Criticism Became Privileged Speech: The Case of *Carr v. Hood* (1808) 150

SEDITIOUS LIBEL

5 Literature and the Freedom of Mind 175

Epilogue: Unacknowledged Legislators 225

Notes 239
Index 289

ACKNOWLEDGMENTS

Material in several chapters has appeared in earlier forms. The first chapter is a substantial revision of "Copyright and the Invention of Tradition," *Eighteenth-Century Studies* 26.1 (1992): 1–27. Copyright © 1992 American Society for Eighteenth-Century Studies. A shorter version of the second chapter appeared as "The Fate of Style in an Age of Intellectual Property," *ELH* 80.3 (2013): 747–82. Copyright © The Johns Hopkins University Press. Reprinted with permission by The Johns Hopkins University Press. The epilogue reworks some paragraphs from "The Changing Public Functions of Literature, from Early to Late Modernity," in *Imitatio-Inventio: The Rise of "Literature" from Early to Classic Modernity*, ed. Mihaela Irimia and Dragos Ivana (Bucharest: Institutul Cultural Roman, 2010). I thank these publications for permission to reuse that work here.

Preliminary research for this study was supported through a grant from the Social Sciences and Humanities Research Council of Canada. Heather Meek provided me with valuable assistance by trawling through early trial records. I thank the anonymous reader at Johns Hopkins University Press for alerting me to several important items of recent scholarship.

This book is for Lyn.

Writing in Public

INTRODUCTION

Writing in Public

On May 3, 1695, pre-publication censorship in England came to an end when a bill to renew the Licensing Act failed to emerge from committee. From that date, Macaulay declared, "English Literature was emancipated, and emancipated forever, from the control of the government."[1] Emancipation was far from total. For decades thereafter, governments regulated the press through a mixed battery of legal and economic measures. Proceedings for seditious libel, stamp taxes, restrictions on parliamentary reporting, control of distribution through the post, and the reestablishment of trade monopolies under the Copyright Act all served to limit the extent and fervor of printed communication. Most significantly for literary production, the Stage Licensing Act of 1737 ensured that the theater would labor under censorship for more than two centuries.

We need not subscribe to Macaulay's Whig narrative of emancipation, however, to recognize that the end of licensing was as consequential for English society as the revolutionary settlement of 1688–1689 was for its political order and the financial revolution of 1694 for its economic. Despite setbacks and crackdowns, the scope of licit speech widened measurably over the next century, with a free press ever more loudly heralded as the "bulwark of the English constitution."[2] The new regime of copyright, which uncoupled anti-piracy protection from censorship, transformed authorship into a profession and publishing into an industry. The periodical press, which mushroomed in the wake of licensing's demise, revolutionized daily life by leading readers to expect a regular supply of news and commentary. And with the press enlarging under political and commercial pressures, its deep-reaching dissemination of knowledge and opinion nurtured the public sphere, a realm as centrally defining of civil society as the market is of its economy and the nation of its politics.

This book is about what the liberty of the press entailed for literary writing. Theorists of censorship have alerted us to the multiple ways that regulation, overt or tacit, has influenced speech and thought. I am concerned with an opposite phenomenon, with what happened to literature once certain forms of discourse came to be perceived as public and entitled to be free of state or private control. The liberalization of public expression, I argue, necessitated a redefinition of literature's social functions. The long revolution for free expression coincided with a broad reorganization of discourse in which, among other changes, literature was displaced as a vehicle of opinion by newer modes of public speech even as its value in expressing personal and cultural meaning was reaffirmed. The effects of these changes were not of a piece—it is difficult now to see a connection between, say, the economics of copyright and the rise of the fourth estate—but the bifurcation of these effects was itself a consequence of public discourse being reorganized.

The long-term significance of these changes for literary history has been recognized before. Habermas maintained that the rise of the political public sphere was preceded by the formation of a pre-political realm of letters, which served as a "training ground" for political debate yet remained sufficiently distinct that creative speech was in time exempted from the norms of critical reasoning that governed public deliberation. Foucault suggested that the system of authorial rights established during the period led literary writers to regard themselves as artists sufficiently independent to challenge social pieties. Derrida proposed that protections for free speech gave rise to the modern view of literature as a medium where one could say anything without being obligated to defer to beliefs about how things were. A greater influence on this study has been the work of Jacques Rancière, who has argued that, with democracy, literature was transformed from being a rhetorical instrument for imposing the will of the rulers on the ruled to being a mechanism of "self-interpretation and self-poeticization of life," whose world-making functions anyone could appropriate.[3]

My subject is the early history of these changes, how they began as discrete adjustments in cultural assumptions or as the unforeseen repercussions of political compromises. That no one in pre-reform Britain could predict how transformative these changes would turn out to be should not preclude us from understanding how these changes were set in motion in novel attempts to regulate writing in a social order increasingly beholden to the values of liberty and property. In those attempts we can see the origins of many legal and economic arrangements that society cannot now operate without. How is it, for example, that one can write a parody but not a sequel? Why is libel considered a greater offense than slander? Why are stylistic innovations celebrated but not rewarded? My aim is not to propose answers to these questions from a present perspective but rather to examine the arguments that originally gave rise to these arrangements and to suggest how choices made more than two centuries ago have shaped our thinking about literature as a public discourse.

My approach is interdisciplinary. I focus on changes made to the laws of copyright, defamation, privacy, and seditious libel, with the bulk of the evidence taken from trial records and legal commentaries, most from the period 1760–1810. Yet while I deal with legal history, I have not written a history of the law. My subject is how some discourses came to be perceived as public, and I analyze legal opinions to suggest how the public's interest in discourse was redefined during the period. Though the law may have in some instances certified a new public order, much of the time it gave formal recognition to already emerging assumptions about public speech. The legal evidence I draw on is meant to be taken as representative of broader social and intellectual changes rather than as either a record of accommodations between conflicting interests or the principal impelling cause of the changes I examine.

I develop an argument about literature, though I have not written a standard literary history. I do not set out the legal context as a prelude to a series of readings of literary texts nor do I devote much space to discussing what the changes I consider entailed for the practices of poets, novelists, or playwrights of the period. With the major exception of the repeal of a perpetual copyright, the legal changes I describe had mostly indirect effects on literary production. The effects I am interested in had to do with beliefs about literature and rationales for its value and purpose. My argument is about how, in the later eighteenth century, those beliefs began to change, such that literature would eventually perform a singular and paradoxical role in democratic society: helping to define a people while at the same time purposely serving no definable function in public life. This book is thus intended as a cultural history of ideas about literature's place in the public sphere.

Many of the most consequential of these ideas were only beginning to be formulated during the eighteenth century. Some new principles, such as liberal economic theories of copyright, were openly debated. Other ideas, like the rallying cries of "liberty" and "the people," were wildly unfixed in their meaning. Still other ideas, such as notions about the effect of words on the public mind, operated at the level of unvoiced assumptions. Only in long hindsight, furthermore, can some of these ideas be seen to contribute to the rise of democracy. For many during the period, including some reformers, democracy as a word and idea was anathema to their thinking about how society worked.[4] As my opening paragraph implies, Whig narratives of emancipation not only discount the censorship that remained in force throughout the period, but equally celebrate changes whose promulgators may have had little interest in reform. The changes were more uncertain, and their causes and consequences more complicated, than they may appear in retrospect. For this reason, my history of the law is selective and does not cover all branches pertaining to the regulation of speech. Some of these restrictions, notably the prohibitions against obscene and blasphemous libel, I deal with only in passing since challenges to their scope and rationale would not be heard until much later, when ideas about freedom of expression would be given more rigorous articulation.

A measure of how unsettled the situation was during the eighteenth century was that it was possible for commentators of all political stripes to legitimize their position by invoking the once-radical idea that the public had a right to determine its own laws. Several of the changes I consider were ratified in the midst of Old Corruption's sustained offensive against reform and the press. Implementing some of these changes actually gained state authorities a measure of public support for their efforts at suppressing dissent. The Libel Act of 1792, which E. P. Thompson called Charles James Fox's "greatest service to the common people," formally recognized the right of juries to determine what constituted libel.[5] Yet, as I relate in chapter 5, not only was the act passed less than a month after the government launched an extensive campaign of suppression against radical publications, but in the two years following the act's passage, juries frequently sided with the administration in what turned out to be a historically unprecedented number of prosecutions for seditious libel. The act, like other changes I consider, may appear modernizing from a present perspective, and I have not avoided describing these changes as such in accordance with a longer view of history. The story I tell, however, is not a conventional Whig narrative of emancipation. It has less to do, in fact, with the victories these narratives celebrate than with a host of discursive transformations the same narratives all too readily take for granted.

The chapters in this book are divided into three parts, each corresponding to a separate branch of English law governing the publication and circulation of writing. The subject of the opening pair of chapters is copyright, the first of the branches to be split off from the unified regime of regulation that had existed prior to 1695. In these chapters, I describe how the setting of restrictions on copyright protection required the envisaging of what would later be called the public domain, and how in debates over these restrictions literary writing came to be seen as at once the most private of property and the most public. The second pair of chapters, on defamation, deal with two contests involving competing claims of privacy and publicity in which older notions about the moral utility of literature and criticism were being imperfectly accommodated to emerging expectations about how public speech was to be conducted. The final part is about seditious libel and consists of the longest chapter, which focuses on political censorship. I consider how challenges to the state's control of the press led to public discourse being adjusted in accordance with new assumptions about the divergent effects and contexts of speech, and how this adjustment implied a deepening contrast between literary art and the law.

I develop several related theses. First, I contend that public speech was not liberalized so much as the nature of the constraints on speech began to change during the eighteenth century, becoming less a set of prohibitions about what could be said than a discursive order segregating legitimate from illegitimate uses of speech. In the past, censorship was practiced on the assumption that some subjects, notably radical political or religious ideas, were off-limits and to be exiled from both public discourse and private conscience. Yet once the public was believed free to make its own choices, there could be no topic that was forbidden so long as it was discussed in the appropriate language and setting and with due concern for truth, civility, and the preservation of property. There was nothing to preclude controversial matters from being publicly discussed if this discussion was conducted in the right manner, under the right circumstances, and for the right reasons. The public deemed itself entitled to know about all things but also imposed new protocols, in which speech was permitted in the public sphere only if it displayed certain formal features, produced certain effects, and was circulated under certain conditions of use and reception. The public could speak about virtually anything but limited itself as to when, where, and how it spoke.

Second, I maintain that the more public speech was liberalized, or at least assumed so, the more literature's public role seemed less easy to define. Literary writings had long been valued for both preserving traditions and transforming them. Poets kept a culture's history alive in memory just as much as they advanced learning and refined language. By the later eighteenth century, these functions were changing. Poetry fulfilled fewer instrumental uses. Many of those uses, such as in soliciting patrons or evading censors, were becoming obsolete. Poetry's ancient ties to rhetoric were reevaluated in accordance with a growing suspicion that the utilitarian and the aesthetic did not mix well. Most striking, perhaps, was how little authors by then subscribed to the old faith in the power of poetry to refine language, honor worthies, or inspire obedience to prevailing norms.

It is not that literary works had lost this power. If anything, their tradition-preserving effects were reinforced through new mechanisms of cultural reproduction: canonical works were protected as national heritage, marketed for their prestige value by large publishing ventures, and studied in programs aimed at schooling the citizenry. Yet literature's traditional and, more especially, transformative effects were also rethought, with the divergence between these two sets of effects becoming more pronounced. Literature, as much as it enabled the formation of cultural identities, could also be imagined as serving an opposing end of enabling public liberty. It could keep society plural by encouraging people to experience life from the point of view of others and keep it open to change by making it possible for people to speak beyond the protocols the public set for itself. Theorists nowadays go so far as to claim that democracy "needs" literature or that the modern ideas of "literature" and "democracy" emerged in tandem, with one idea not being possible without the other.[6] I believe these claims are insufficiently nuanced because they ignore how literary writings, transformative though they can be, also preserve traditions. In a way, though, I am exploring the prehistory of such claims. The idea of "literature," I suggest, came about as a response to a deepening ambivalence over the role literary writings were to play in democratic society.

This ambivalence, I argue finally, cannot be resolved because it is premised on an incoherent notion of the public. With popular sovereignty, the public acts with supreme authority, but in setting protocols of speech for itself, it paradoxically limits its authority in the very act of exercising it. As a result, the modern notion of the public as an agent of change is marked by irresolvable ambiguity, an ambiguity that is embedded in arguments for a free press and formalized in the law as a set of conflicting norms about the public value of writing. This incoherence has led to skepticism over the value of those discourses—namely, literature and the arts—whose form and purpose threaten to betray the inconsistency of these norms. Thus, by the late eighteenth century, some people began wondering whether literary writing lacked utility as a medium of knowledge, exhibited stylistic features too divergent from the mainstream of public debate, or purveyed beauty and affect that could be appreciated only at a remove from the distractions of public life.

The ambivalent nature of literature's role in modern society is, I suggest, one manifestation of how our democratic principles are incoherent. At the start of the eighteenth century, literary works answered to a neoclassical regime that judged them according to clear normative hierarchies—of genre, decorum, verisimilitude, and the like—that were homologous to the existing social hierarchies that literature was expected to help maintain. By the end of the period, literature, it was believed by many, was as freed from the rules as the English people were secure in their liberties. Yet much as the public was at once assigned legitimizing authority and made impervious to definition, so the new aesthetic regime, Rancière has argued, affirmed "the absolute singularity of art and, at the same time, destroy[ed] any pragmatic criterion for isolating this singularity."[7] Literature was free to make its own rules and reinvent itself time and again, which meant that it was no longer directly serviceable in the conventionalized discourse of public commerce even if it could also never be definitively distinguished from this discourse. At the same time, by its autonomy and indeterminacy literature became a model for the idea of a modern public. Poets and novelists, much like the public, were assumed to perform a centrally defining role—voicing the spirit of the people, preserving a higher knowledge, or standing above the world as its unacknowledged legislators—without contributing to the governance of society in any precisely definable way. Like the public, literature could at once remake the world and make nothing happen.

A Modern Public

What had changed was not so much literature as who or what was understood to be the "public." It is beyond the scope of this book to set out the many causes and dimensions of this change, yet since ideals of free expression make sense only in relation to publicity, I here consider a few key assumptions about what constitutes a public in modern society. Some of my conclusions are necessarily tentative because these assumptions had only begun to be worked out during the eighteenth century, just as many of the legal impediments retarding the full emergence of the public sphere would not be removed until the next century. All the same, these assumptions have informed nearly all arguments for a free press put forward since licensing's demise.

The concept of the public is central to modernity's self-understanding, and yet anyone who tries to say what the public is soon discovers that it is much easier to say what it is not—usually, though not exclusively, by setting it against the private. As commentators from Kierkegaard to Walter Lippmann have complained, the concept is so clouded in abstraction as to seem a phantom, though it is not less powerful for being impossible to identify precisely.[8] Any attempt to relate the idea to a specific referent—in eighteenth-century studies the most influential attempt has been Habermas's account of the bourgeois public sphere—is bound to seem alternately reductive and naïve, a myth belied by complex historical realities and an idealist smoothing over of multiple contradictions within liberal thought.[9]

Adding to this difficulty is the fact that the concept's indefiniteness is a direct reflection of the power wielded by the public in modern society, since it is the public that gets to decide what is public. The public is invested with supreme authority on all social matters, including the power to define its boundaries. This means that the public can maintain its authority only by refusing to settle on a positive identity since by fixing itself within boundaries, the public would be in effect positing a space outside itself over which it could exercise no authority. The concept of the public cannot therefore be made more precise because it is fundamentally unstable.[10] The public recognizes no authority other than its own, yet the clearest manifestation of this authority is the public's ability to oppose itself to forms of speech and behavior it deems either private or illegitimate.

This paradox, as Robert Post and others have pointed out, has led to much inconsistency in the law.[11] We recognize a host of freedoms—of speech, the press, assembly, artistic expression—to ensure a dynamic public sphere where, in principle, all opinions can be aired and ideas debated. At the same time, we maintain laws designed to prevent some forms of speech from entering the public sphere because we feel these violate norms of civility or rationality, endanger the peace, breach contracts of trust, or trespass on privacy and property. Our public discourse both is and is not open, in essence because our idea of the public is incoherent. The public at once enjoys supreme sovereignty and must limit this sovereignty to make possible a realm of the private against which it can be set or to define a set of exclusions through which the public can be seen to exercise its authority. This paradox is not in itself a vicious one: in limiting its jurisdiction and in setting norms for how it conducts its deliberations, the public does not thereby invalidate its own sovereignty. The incoherence that follows the paradox has nonetheless had consequences. As we know, it has given rise to many a hard case: in the modern world, public discourse has been among the sites of greatest tension that arise from a fundamental conflict between liberal and democratic principles, between the former's absolute insistence on the supremacy of the rights of individual citizens and the latter's equally absolute insistence on enshrining the supreme power of sanction in the citizenry as a whole. What I suggest is that the incoherence has also had unacknowledged consequences for how we value specific forms and features of our discourse.

In this book, I show how this incoherence was introduced into laws regulating speech and how it has informed our thinking about literature's role in public life. This incoherence may have been apparent to few in the eighteenth century, but it can be inferred from the increasingly complex ways the idea of the public was then being used. Parliamentarians and the press contended over the role of public opinion; commentators disagreed over what the "public" ought to comprise; and pamphleteers descanted on new-fashioned themes of "public credit" and "public spirit." What had been before the period a relatively stable concept had become by its end a catchall explanation for a wide variety of social phenomena. The idea of the public that emerged was arguably a modern one, in that it had become the locus of widely held beliefs about how a free society worked. And it commanded authority precisely by being serviceably abstract. I explain this by describing the two features that most sharply differentiate a modern public from its earlier incarnations.

First, as I have already said, a modern public lacks a positive or settled identity. To use a distinction that first became meaningful in the eighteenth century, a modern public is not a people who, as the ethnos, possess a positive identity, whereas the public, or demos, does not possess such an identity—or at least not *yet*, in that a modern public is always in the process of defining an identity for itself. A modern public is neither a community nor a formation linked by region, nation, class, ethnicity, religion, or any other marker. It may perceive itself as a social body, as a "general" public, but one of its main points of commonality is the awareness that in public we are not fully known to one another. It is not simply that in public locales we are usually surrounded by unfamiliar persons or, at a greater distance, by persons we will never meet. More than this, participating in public life requires us to behave toward these indefinite others in a way that acknowledges no common identity other than a mutual understanding that we will not infringe on each other's autonomy. This understanding, in turn, may reflect a deeper awareness that we rely on these indefinite others for our welfare: as Adam Smith remarked, the individual in a civilized society "stands at all times in need of the cooperation and assistance of great multitudes, while his whole life is scarce sufficient to gain the friendship of a few persons."[12]

The element of mutuality has been taken by some to imply that public life enjoins us to perceive others as equal to ourselves: Kierkegaard claimed that the "public" was an ideological fantasy designed to induce a debilitating "spirit of levelling," whereas in Habermas's account participation in the public sphere was not predicated on social status but proceeded according to a principle of universality.[13] But, as Michael Warner has suggested in his revision of Habermas's thesis, we may choose to deal with others in public as our equals and enshrine this equality as a principle of our laws, yet most of the time our encounters are merely impersonal in the sense that we do not assign any positive attribute to others. Most typically, we maintain a detached sociability that involves not denying them their otherness. The condition of strangerhood acts as a normative environment: in public we are expected not to intrude on the privacy of others or relate to them in a way that imposes an identity on them.[14]

The public can exclude anyone who violates these expectations: it seems that some are more strangers than others are. The public may, in this sense, be a democratic construct rather than a liberal one.[15] But these expectations also ensure minimal conditions for personal liberty. By restricting ourselves in public, we maintain a kind of indeterminacy in our relations with others, never presuming to know them fully. The chief function of this indeterminacy is to keep open a moral space within which individual freedom can be exercised at a relative remove from the determinations of others. Paradoxically, it is a mutual recognition of one another's desire for self-realization that makes it possible for the public to imagine itself as not wholly indeterminate, but as a body of persons who act together to defend their liberty. Formalizing this paradox in a set of laws inevitably creates inconsistency such as I have already described, but any attempt at resolving this incoherence by limiting what we mean by the public will entail exclusions and loss of freedoms.

The indeterminacy of a modern public makes possible its second salient feature, which is that it is considered the supreme arbiter of social change. By its refusal to define itself absolutely, the public ensures its members' freedom and thus their assent. A shared sense of its own indefiniteness enables the public to reinvent itself time and again, to set social priorities while being answerable to nothing except the laws and norms it enacts, and to confront no opposition except that which it posits. Self-authorized in this manner, the public may entertain any number of interests at one time or another, though in principle these remain open to question.

In this way, the notion of the public performs a similar role in a modern social imaginary as the one played by two other related abstractions, the market and the nation. These abstractions do not necessarily operate for us as foundational beliefs on the order of a doctrine of natural rights. Rather, we understand that these abstractions are convenient ways of referring to complex mechanisms by which people work out competing interests. We may doubt the efficacy of these mechanisms and recognize that there are other ways of organizing social behavior. But we may also feel that these abstractions represent as good an explanation for how society works as we currently have, and for this reason they command assent. They thus serve as legitimation stories, in that it each provides a plausible account of the dynamics of order and change by naming a corporate force that is at once transformative, self-regulating, historically variable, and even unpredictable.[16]

The public was once neither so indeterminate nor autonomous. Ambiguity has colored the concept so long as the word has been used in its familiar dual senses as a noun denoting nonprivate space ("in public") or the citizens who occupy it ("the public") and as an adjective denoting a condition of either visibility ("open to all") or access ("common to all").[17] In the late seventeenth century, however, a deeper ambiguity was introduced in its usage as a noun, specifically in terms of what was understood by the "all" the public encompassed. Before then, the *Oxford English Dictionary* records, what was public was a definable entity: "the community or people as an organized body; the nation, the state; the commonwealth." The public in this older sense was seen as fixed and knowable, so much so that the word "public" was synonymous with the nation or commonwealth—indeed, the word *publicatio* in Latin and "publication" in some early usages meant making common property through state confiscation. The public was the body politic, the union of people and sovereign, and its well-being was felt to be inseparable from the state's.

This residual sense survived into the modern age and to a degree remains the bedrock premise in conservative accounts of the social order. Yet by the later seventeenth century this older meaning of public was competing with a newer, more elliptical sense, which the *Oxford English Dictionary*'s definition strains to capture: "the community as an aggregate, but not in its organized capacity; hence, the members of the community." In this emergent sense, the public was the community in an unformed state, a loose congregation that, crucially, was not the same as the nation. This was significant, for it meant that the public signified the community in a way the state no longer did. It meant that it was possible to think of the community, as embodied in the public, existing at a relative remove from the circumstances of culture, history, and governance. A modern public was the community abstracted as an assembly of individuals able to engage in collective will formation seemingly prior to identifying themselves as a collective. A public was, in Lockean terms, the community in an ideal if unrealized state, perpetually at the moment of exercising its right of self-determination.[18]

This sense of the public as indefinite and self-generating recalled an older notion of the vox populi that designated a spontaneous popular authority whose opinion did not always coincide with official truth. Like this earlier abstraction, a modern public could be personified as a disembodied voice without origin, granting or withholding its favor to all manner of human activity. And much as ancient critics might deplore the fallibility of the people's judgment, so modern pundits might regret a public's susceptibility to fashion and manipulation. Yet whereas in the past one could spurn the popular will, a modern public commanded attention as the sole rightful authority within a vastly altered universe of belief. There was no appealing its decisions since the public was answerable to nothing except itself. Its claim to authority may have been posited on a foundation of natural rights, notably its right of consent, yet it acted solely on its own initiative in accordance with no religious or other transcendental design. Unlike the vox populi, furthermore, a modern public was not thought to behave arbitrarily. It was assumed to possess agency, since it operated through the voluntary participation of its members, and to follow more or less rational procedures for arriving at decisions and protecting its members' liberty, including their liberty to doubt its decisions and procedures. A modern public may have done little that was different from what earlier publics had done, but it was assigned far greater ideological prominence. Though its choices could still surprise, they carried the force of validation. A modern public could justify change.[19]

A modern public entrusted itself to govern the nation because it saw itself as behaving in an autonomous and rational manner. Here we once again meet with the incoherence at the heart of the idea of a modern public, since it was the public itself that decided what was appropriately autonomous and rational. A modern public's authority was most clearly manifested by its right to set the terms of its sovereignty. But since a modern public was open to constant self-revision, these terms could never be settled. Any of its members had the right to challenge the public's authority and argue that, contrary to its self-perception, the public did not behave in a rational manner according to the standards it professed or some absolute standard of objective rationality. Yet no challenge to the public could lead anywhere unless it received the public's support. Such was the force of belief invested in a modern public that, at some point, whatever problems of incoherence or circularity the concept may have posed as an explanation for social change began to seem a small price to pay for the wide serviceability and appeal of the explanation.

During the eighteenth century, the idea of the public as a metonym for social power began to be used in multiple variations to justify a broad range of activities. Most familiar was the version set out in liberal theories of civil society, where the public was both the citizenry and the site of its deliberation. Similar accounts were put forward in defense of political associations and of jurors' rights. The public in these versions was an active body, gathering to debate the common good.[20] These versions rendered change intelligible by casting the public as one of change's primary engines. In another version the public was more of an oversight body, making sense of change by containing it. This was the public presupposed in appeals for greater press freedoms. Rather than setting goals, it protected liberty by keeping things open to scrutiny. This public was commonly envisaged as a "tribunal" with the power to settle interpersonal conflicts.[21] The regime of publicity, Bentham conceded, was "a system of *distrust*," premised on the suspicion that lawmakers would commit wrongs were it not for the deterrent of public scrutiny.[22] To some, this deterrent could induce moral conformity; as one essayist crowed, "Publicity is the censor of Great Britain."[23] At the same time this version of the public was often described in terms of its independence from received dogma. Johnson had in mind such a public when, in his late criticism, he deferred to the judgment of the common reader "uncorrupted by literary prejudice."[24] Still other versions presented a public that exerted a formative influence on personal and cultural life. This was the public envisaged by theorists of sociability, for whom conversing and trading with others contributed vitally to the growth of the self, learning, and the arts. This public gave direction to change: it profited its members by encouraging them to learn from each other, while it shaped itself in progressing toward social harmony. This version inspired efforts to open museums and gardens to the public, to improve communication and travel, and to enshrine a public domain of canonical works.

That a modern public could appear in multiple versions points to some of the evidentiary difficulties the concept presents for this book. Its indefiniteness as a category is compounded by the fact that many residual ideas about the public were still prevalent throughout the eighteenth century. An example was the much-espoused ideal of "public spirit," which, though bound up with party sentiment, reflected an older classical republican vision of a social order bound by virtue.[25] The period also saw a proliferation of semi-publics, organizations that anticipated a modern public in their independence and fostering of debate yet whose membership was limited in one way or another: clubs, salons, societies, or imagined fellowships like the republic of letters. And since the idea of the public did not admit of empirical verification, politicians could easily pay court to "public opinion" while having a very narrow conception of who the public might be.

My focus is on how the public began to serve as a legitimizing story in rationales for a freer press. A modern public, unlike its precursors, functioned as an explanation for societal change rather than simply as a referent for civil society. This distinction, however, creates an additional problem of chronology for this book. It is not possible to pinpoint when the public took hold as a legitimation story since these stories must compete for our assent with other such narratives; this is what makes them stories rather than self-evident truths. British society during much of the eighteenth century was highly heteronomous, its people more apt to defer on matters of behavior to the rule of God and rank than to the vagaries of the market or the whims of public opinion. At most, we can say that the idea of the public came to be invoked more definitively during the period as justification for certain types of social activity than had been the case previously. The public had long enjoyed some formal authority, from its customary right in common land to its determinative role in the jury trial. Belief in public agency was at least implicit in attempts by Parliamentarians during the 1640s or the king's supporters during the exclusion crisis to marshal public opinion through the press.[26] Evidence for an incipient public sphere can be found in sixteenth-century humanist and reformist publishing activities. In all these early cases, however, the public's autonomy was severely limited, with officials at the ready to impose curbs on speech. They could do so because the idea of the public had not yet so taken hold of the social imaginary as to challenge the ideologies of kingship, custom, and providence. That challenge became credible only during the eighteenth century.

The Public Sphere

Before I say more about chronology, I wish to introduce a further distinction: a modern public is not the same thing as a public sphere. The latter comprises both the social spaces where persons meet to debate the common good and the organs of publicity that enable them to interact. A vibrant public sphere is a necessary if not sufficient condition for the creation of a modern public, just as the birth of the public sphere during the early modern period does not coincide with the moment of the public's ascendancy as the prime arbiter of social change. A public sphere is sustained by communication at a distance; that is, it brings together people, who may remain unknown to each other, to participate in collective deliberation through the mechanisms of print and other media. A public comes to recognize itself as a public through discourse.[27] But a modern public, one that thinks of itself as society's collective conscience, can come into being only with a shift in the social imaginary, a shift reflecting a large-scale transfer of power from traditional authorities to the citizenry. The demise of licensing in 1695 accelerated the growth of the public sphere, but this growth was only one factor among several that led to the rise of a modern public.[28]

This distinction permits us to retain the useful notion of the public sphere while setting to one side an objection commonly raised against Habermas's seminal study of the subject. Critics have faulted Habermas for glossing over the conflict that marked the public sphere's early history.[29] The charge is somewhat unfair. Habermas is concerned less with the impediments that retarded the sphere's development than with contradictions in bourgeois thinking that eventually led to the decay of civil society at the hands of commercial and bureaucratic forces. That said, he is too keen to contrast a pristine public sphere of the eighteenth century with its later degradation into a theme park of public relations and mass consumerism. Habermas makes the early sphere appear to actualize classic liberal thinking, and one of the ways he does so is by putting off the distinction between the sphere and the public until later in his argument, where it underlies his discussion of the economic barriers to civic participation during the nineteenth century. Before then, Habermas follows early proponents of the public sphere in eliding the distinction. These proponents believed they could emancipate themselves from absolutist authority simply by exercising their reason in public debate. Their faith in publicity was premised on the liberal notion that the British people enjoyed both the "right and capacity" to pass judgment on the activities of government.[30] For them, publicity was intrinsically democratic, as if the emergence of a public sphere and participation in it went hand in hand with acceptance of the public's sovereignty.

Few early liberal defenders of a free press had any inkling, however, of the radical implications of democracy. It was one thing for Addison and Steele to imagine the public sphere as a theater audience whose fashions displayed their party affiliations or as a gentlemen's club that was scarcely more representative of the electorate than Parliament was. It was quite another for Whig apologists to understand that the unfettered exercise of public judgment could lead to disagreement potentially so intense as to undermine the public's claim to sovereignty. It was only later, during the second half of the eighteenth century, that the destabilizing import of notions like popular sovereignty began to be fathomed, even as these notions were transforming the cosmos of liberal beliefs that had initially impelled the public sphere's emergence. By then, the public sphere was no longer merely a realm of civic participation. It had become a site of contestation not only about matters of public interest but about the very nature of the public itself, its judgment, and its deliberative procedures. Certainly, commentators throughout the period saw no contradiction in availing themselves of print to rail at the press or express anti-democratic sentiments. In any event, politicians could always seek publicity while remaining dead set against widening the franchise, just as the public itself could at times support calls for greater constraints on speech.

It is important to understand, however, that it is not the public sphere per se that gives rise to these conflicts. Rather, contradiction is inherent in the modern idea of the public, contradiction that the workings of the public sphere are designed to suspend if not resolve. As much as it is an abstract commons where strangers meet to talk politics, the public sphere is equally a social arrangement for managing public expression. It is supported by laws and norms for regulating how people interact in it, keeping certain speech private and outside its domain, and denying legitimacy to anyone who fails to observe these conditions. These laws and norms may well be enacted by the public itself in accordance with standards of rationality that approach what Habermas has defined as the ideal preconditions of speech. Habermas may likewise be right to suggest that the bourgeois public sphere that emerged during the eighteenth century was more open to people from diverse backgrounds than anything that had existed previously, though this still left many groups, notably women, excluded from the mainstream of public discussion. Yet even if it were comparatively open, the public sphere would already reflect choices about how best to talk politics and about the common good. To designate an arena as public, in other words, is itself the outcome of decisions as to whether and where public debate may occur. There is thus no logical way to accommodate a modern public's freedom from determination, its indefiniteness and power to reinvent itself, within the organized public sphere, which reflects a specific set of liberal, rational determinations about how the public ought to engage in debate. Any attempt to do so will create incoherence in the laws and rationales that sustain the public sphere.

Critics of Habermas maintain that the expectation that public discourse ought to obey norms of communicative rationality imposes a condition on participating in the public sphere. Such norms, they argue, inevitably regulate the heterogeneity of debate by limiting what can be discussed and how it can be discussed. This regulative ideal was actively promoted by eighteenth-century reformers, who insisted that public discourse ought to be conducted according to universal dictates of reason. More important, speech and the exchange of ideas cannot in principle proceed without preconditions of one kind or another, including the provision that the public cannot reasonably intrude upon the autonomy of persons whose freedom it aims to protect. The legal changes to discourse from the eighteenth century onward, then, represent at least attempts at arrangements for encouraging public debate to proceed in accordance with agreed-on norms while allowing enough ambiguity and possible inconsistency in their application that they could remain open to revision. It is a central contention of this book, indeed, that more than any other public discourse, literature has assumed the burden of this ambiguity to the extent that it has become valued as an enabling exception to prevailing normative arrangements.

Over and above these norms, the public sphere equally represents another, more consequential set of limits on the public's authority. Habermas, in downplaying the distinction between the public and the sphere, does not address these limits, so it is helpful to supplement his account with Rancière's investigations into democracy's radical implications. Democracy, Rancière insists, is inseparable from a principle of equality. In his view, democracy should not be understood in the first instance as a political system, such as government by elected representation. It is rather a presupposition of all regimes such that even despots can defend what they do by claiming that they are acting in the people's interests. The "power of the people," Rancière writes, "is always beneath and beyond" any given political order since it must remain available to serve the legitimation of that order.[31] More to the point, democracy consists at its most essential of nothing other than the drawing of lots, that is, the embracing of chance. It is based on the assumption that mere historical happenstance rather than an inherent right or destiny is the reason that people either rule or are ruled, and thus before this law of chance we are all equals and therefore equally entitled to draw lots. Paradoxically, this sense of equality before the law of chance is available to anyone as a legitimizing principle because it essentially denies the possibility of any absolute legitimizing principle. For Plato, this was the scandal of democracy, the fact that the drawing of lots confers a title without foundation. Yet this absence of a foundation is also the indeterminacy that makes liberty possible.

What happened in the later eighteenth century was not so much that for the first time since antiquity, democracy was seen as a sensible way of deciding who ruled. Few in Britain, at least, uttered the word "democracy" without fear or derision, and not many could imagine their cherished mixed system of governance being replaced by electoral politics at every level. But people during the period talked a lot about equality and, especially, liberty. Even if in the view of many reformers the ideals of liberty and equality were far from being actualized, these ideals had by then become powerful legitimizing principles. Earlier regimes could have invoked these principles, but none saw the value in entrusting their authority to chance when they could just as easily bind it to an anterior source, be it divine right or the obligations of kinship. Even the protodemocratic movements that sprang up during the English Revolution believed that equality was not a self-evident value but was instead promised by God or the immemorial dictates of an ancient constitution.[32] By the late eighteenth century, however, it had become possible to think of equality and liberty as self-evident values capable of justifying human activities without reference to a transcendent authority. By that point, it was felt, equality and liberty had come to be embodied in the public, understood as a self-governing body that was self-tasked with securing its members' individual rights and freedoms.

Crucially, however, this principle of equality is only ever operative within the determinable limits of the public sphere. A modern public may be the supreme arbiter, and its authority confirmed by the equality of its members, but that equality does not extend beyond their participation in public debate. Only within the public sphere, in other words, can the legitimizing principle of equality so central to democracy be asserted.[33] Equality may serve as a legitimizing principle within specific domains, such as the law or the marketplace, but this equality is granted to persons only on condition of their positive acceptance of those institutions' internal norms and procedures. In most fields of social endeavor, however, including the running of the state, the weight of equality as a normative principle is heavily counterbalanced by a panoply of other expectations about competence, educational achievement, citizenship, wealth, distinction, kinship structures, and so on. Only in the public square do persons have an equal right to speak, assemble, or be informed without any prior condition being met. Likewise, all persons are, in principle at least, free to challenge any norms the public has chosen to follow. In practice, however, participants in public debate are expected to observe ground rules about what can be discussed and how it can be discussed. Thus, both the norms of debate internal to the public sphere and the hierarchical norms that organize social relations outside of it place limits on what the public can do.

Participation in the public sphere is as much about arbitrating between competing interests as defending the public's authority against elites who stand to benefit from stricter ground rules of debate or more pervasive hierarchical arrangements. Yet the latter contests are rarely so intense as to produce wide disagreement over the validity of the commonly accepted order. Such a level of disagreement—what Rancière calls "dissensus"[34]—is unlikely to occur among those who already possess a political voice, that is, who constitute the public within an existing order. It occurs, rather, at revolutionary moments when groups that have been denied a voice seize on the principle of equality that certifies the public's authority and proclaim it on their own behalf, using it to clamor for political recognition or, more fundamentally, to challenge the legitimacy of a social order that has benefited those who have refused them recognition. At such moments, the contingency of norms governing participation becomes starkly evident to those struggling for a voice. For them, there is only contradiction between the principle of equality in whose name the public asserts its authority and the hierarchical arrangements in whose defense elites grant or refuse this equality.

The Early Eighteenth Century: Publicity without a Public

Distinguishing between the public and its sphere allows us to understand the situation that pertained during the first half of the eighteenth century. The public that occupied the vigorous public sphere of the period was not a modern one since it did not yet possess sufficient weight as a decision-making body to challenge existing hierarchies. It may have been thought to embody what Habermas termed an "abstract universality." But it was not predicated on a principle of equality nor, save for a few Dissenters and Whig radicals, did anyone believe that equality was a self-evident value. The public sphere was permitted to thrive only so long as members of the nobility felt they could derive some use from the mechanisms of publicity. The nobles' rhetorical and ideological values dominated public discourse. People from lower ranks may have been able to participate in debate, but they could do so only on the understanding that the right to participate was granted to them by those above who already possessed it.

The familiar image of the "Augustan" public sphere is one of dynamism and expansion, with myriad coffeehouses and midnight conversations, private newsletters giving way to public papers, pamphlet wars under Harley and Walpole, a vocal spirit of opposition emboldening some of the most risk-taking satire yet produced, steady improvements in roads and mail delivery, and the increasing availability of cultural goods for readers to consume. The early eighteenth-century public sphere was both sufficiently vibrant and durable to foster a culture of civic participation. People in most towns could expect a regular supply of news, could choose freely from among multiple partisan periodicals, and, above all, could express disagreement with their peers over most matters of politics, learning, and the arts. And the relative openness of the early public sphere presented opportunities for new voices to be heard, including hireling writers from the provinces, women journalists, and laboring-class poets.

At the same time, the growth of the public sphere was met with a series of regressive measures aimed at containing the political nation: successive steps taken by Tory and Whig ministries to narrow the representative system and restrict institutional opportunities for voters to register disapproval of the ruling party; the Stamp Act of 1712, which increased the cost of public information beyond the means of most everyone outside the electorate; new legal precedents extending the jurisdiction of the common courts and the government's prosecutorial powers over writing considered seditious or offensive; and Walpole's consolidation of Whig rule through corruption, the buying off of opposition voices, the patronage appointments of Whig justices in place of dissident Tories, and the muzzling of political theater with the passage of the Stage Licensing Act.

Authorities availed themselves of older measures, too, for suppressing dissent. On November 6, 1719, John Matthews became the last man in England to be executed for printing a treasonous libel. The offending work, a pamphlet entitled *Vox populi, vox Dei*, was a Jacobite tract defending the pretender's claim on the grounds of the "Whiggish Principle" of "the Voice of the People." The pamphlet's use of Whig rhetoric, culminating in a call to "rouze up the People to shake off this Arbitrary Government," may have been no more than an ironic taunt.[35] But its invoking of a spirit of popular libertarianism would henceforth be, in less incendiary form, a common strategy among opposition writers.[36] Matthews's tract was thus among the first to characterize the public in the new conception of a body of persons exercising an authority anterior to the state's.

Direct state intervention in the public sphere was supplemented by noteworthy innovations in the law that imposed indirect controls by delimiting public from private uses of speech. The most significant were a series of trade measures intended to protect native industries threatened by the unimpeded circulation of information after 1695. Only a year after it allowed the Licensing Act to lapse, Parliament forbade the export of the knitting frame, even though the invention had already been available for a century. This was soon followed by a precedent-setting case that recognized the value of safeguarding trade secrets.[37] The significance of these measures becomes clear when we recall that most newspapers at the time relied on a heavy quotient of foreign and trade news to fill their pages during periods when Parliament was not sitting. In this, they were expanding the range of public discourse into subjects that had formerly been of concern mainly to state-sanctioned guilds and charter companies. The legal changes served to limit this expansion by designating certain uses of knowledge as private even if, as in the case of the knitting frame, the content of that knowledge was already public.

This was a new way of regulating speech. Rather than proscribing whole categories of knowledge, it merely restricted what could be publicly done with the knowledge. This would be implemented most spectacularly in the case of the Copyright Act of 1710, another early piece of protectionist legislation that worked by moving the target of legal proscription from the content of speech to the conditions of its dissemination. By replacing state controls with statutory protections, the act instituted a system of private ownership that made it possible for authors and booksellers to keep writings, notably manuscript works, out of public circulation even if the writings dealt with topics of public interest. The use of these works and not their subject matter determined their private nature, which was to be protected with prohibitions against their unauthorized publication.

A similar bracketing of a private domain within the realm of publicity characterizes some of the period's most important formal innovations to discourse, namely the new genres of the novel, periodical essay, and familiar letter. These genres were essential to the public sphere's formation, Habermas suggests, because they prepared individuals for the altered relations of self and other within it by purveying representations of an intimate sphere that encouraged readers to imagine themselves governed by an autonomous subjectivity. But self-determination could not be made distinguishable from mere contingency unless it was perceived in relation to a social order that gave it value. Over the course of the eighteenth century, that order would be increasingly identified with an idea of the public that saw it performing the role of preserving individual liberty and serving as the common normative ground on which the pursuit of any goal could be sanctioned. And the more the idea of the public was abstracted from any of its identifiable components—whether political institutions, the public sphere, or the population—the more its authority appeared unchallengeable, its prerogative surpassed only by the liberty it was supposed to protect.

For the first half of the period, however, the process of abstraction remained incomplete. Political elites continued to subscribe to a premodern conception of the public. For them, the public was a body not abstracted but distinguished from the populace. As Swift's subtitle to *A Modest Proposal* made clear ("For Preventing the Children of Poor People from Being a Burthen to Their Parents, or the Country, and for Making Them Beneficial to the Publick"), the people served as the public's defining other. Political recognition was simply withheld from the populace, its sentiments dismissed as the mob's senseless braying. By contrast, the public was the political nation, whose authority derived from a moral order external to it. Thus the public was by turns the king's subjects, the nation of unified faith, the electors whose franchise was due to birth and property, and the freeborn Englishmen whom custom and ancient charter had granted inalienable rights. The public in this conception owed its legitimacy to the same immemorial order that certified the power of the elites, who were averse to seeking public approval for their actions because doing so would have undermined the authority of those legitimizing traditions.

This structure of belief was nonetheless under stress, as evidenced by how these same elites felt compelled to air their differences in public. Tim Blanning has plausibly argued that, pace Habermas, it was the nobility rather than the bourgeoisie who most exploited the potential of the public sphere during the period of its initial development, from the exclusion crisis to the first decade of the reign of George III.[38] Following the settlement of 1688, it became incumbent upon England's landed aristocracy to rely on alternative ways of affirming its right to rule now that it could no longer derive legitimacy from the representational culture of the court. The latter had become discredited by taint of association with the absolutism of the French and Jacobite enemy, and, in any event, the early Hanoverians were disinclined to exercise power through symbolic displays. The nobility needed to persuade itself that its authority rested on as sure a footing as the mythology of divine right. Yet, contending as ever for power, its members disagreed over where to locate this foundation and availed themselves of the mechanisms of publicity in the hope of winning over their brethren through persuasion. One consequence was that the traditional rhetorical values of aristocratic speech continued to pervade much of the period's public discourse even as this discourse was reaching a broader audience. As late as the 1760s, newspapers would replicate the styles of court gossip to report on the latest party intrigues.[39]

The nobility's reliance on the press to vent its disputes magnified the arguments' tone and significance, and this in turn provoked ambivalence over the role of public discourse. On the one hand, government ministers hired writers from well outside their ranks to serve as their mouthpieces, financed the publication of scores of periodicals and pamphlets, and (especially in the case of the Tories) encouraged the authors of these works to write in a mud-slinging style that was bound to appeal to a public beyond the educated elites.[40] On the other hand, the same ministers equally declared their disdain for public opinion and restrained the press through whatever means were available to them in the wake of licensing's demise. The elites' defenders, intent on shielding them from ultimate responsibility for fueling the paper wars, blamed the press for bringing politics to the commoners and distracting them from their duties. Whereas the nobility, Addison insisted, "are Politicians by Birth," the press taught persons of all ranks, ages, and sex into becoming each a "Free-thinker in Politicks" who is "qualified for modelling the Constitution."[41] The elites expected the people to perform no more than a supporting role in politics, yet the increasingly public nature of their contests implicitly accorded a measure of recognition to an idea of the public as a deliberative body that was independent of the state.

The latter half of Walpole's regime was a watershed in this respect. By then, the public was being accorded political influence, as signaled by the increasingly common use of "public opinion" as a neutrally descriptive term for the weight of popular collective thought.[42] Not everyone recognized this new authority. Pope expressed his distrust by quipping, "[T]he People's Voice is odd, / It is, and it is not, the Voice of God."[43] Political insiders may have only paid lip service to this voice, but the excise crisis of 1733 had shown that Walpole was not invulnerable. By then, his government had become less ruthless in suppressing its critics, even if it was unwilling to grant that the freedom of the press was a constitutional right. Walpole prided himself on his administration's restraint: "No Government, I will venture to say, ever punished so few Libels, and no Government ever had Provocation to punish so many."[44] Such boasting no doubt reflected the cynicism of a government confident enough in its own legitimacy that it could feign tolerance of dissent. No doubt, too, the story of the press's freedom is in part a story of how the growing power of the state permitted its officials to feel less sensitive to criticism.[45]

All the same, the government's defenders felt sufficiently pressured to begin proposing alternative rationales for social power in the face of faltering belief in traditional political pieties. The classical republican idea of the ancient constitution, for example, had been for generations a powerful sustaining mythology, called upon to justify the revolutions of 1642 and 1688, and it remained for eighteenth-century Whigs a serviceable alternative to the allure of royalty. It could be invoked in behalf of a broad range of decision-making while providing an irrefutable foundation of belief that located the origins of social authority in a time out of mind. Its only limitation as a mythology was that it was unsupported by symbols through which its ideological force could be expressed. It was an abstraction that anyone could appropriate. And, as it happened, many groups did, from the radical Whigs of the 1720s to the Country Party opposition of the next decade to later traditionalists like Burke or the American controversialists contesting monarchical rule.[46]

Hoping to regain control of the mythology, Walpole's apologists during the 1730s went so far as to dismiss the ancient constitution as a nostalgic fantasy when his Patriot opponents accused him of betraying its principles. The "so much boasted and celebrated *Magna Charta*," they sneered, had nothing to do with the people, and its defense of liberty was so vague that it could be used to justify returning "the People back to absolute Slavery."[47] This mainstay of Whig ideology could be discarded because, they claimed, the settlement of 1688 had created a government sufficiently effective at preserving liberty that it did not need defending on the basis of a feudal inheritance. In arguing this, they appeared to be endorsing two notably modern ideas: first, that liberty was grounded in nothing other than consensus, with consent being the surest evidence of liberty, and second, that governments were to be judged according to a standard of managerial competence. Since this standard had no positive justification beyond a metric of efficiency, these writers had then to embed it in a secular, present-minded mythology that naturalized self-interest as the prime motivator of conduct. Against the opposition's trumpeting of civic humanist notions of public spiritedness, they baldly declared that it was "a *Romantick Notion*" to expect ministers to "*pursue the Good of the Publick*, without any Regard to *their own particular Interest.*"[48]

Bernard Mandeville and other Whig radicals had argued for the commensurability of the public good with the pursuit of private interests. But the government's defenders took the argument further, applying the model of the market to politics, which they saw as not only driven by competing interests but, more crucially, as not necessarily tending toward ultimate social harmony. Open-ended conflict, they maintained, was the ordinary state of affairs: in Arnall's words, "Men will constantly differ with one another . . . and whilst they have different views or opinions, opposition will constantly ensue."[49] Arnall's statement signaled a change in official attitudes toward the public sphere. A measure of division and indeterminacy was henceforth accepted as not merely normal in public affairs but even necessary as a condition of liberty. Rarely before had the idea been expressed that debate in the public arena involved an ongoing process of negotiation that was not expected to end in a definitive resolution or in one side vanquishing the other.[50] Arnall's assertion marked the first time that a government in power was willing to accept that the public it served was independent of the state, various in its interests, and indefinite in its self-identification.[51]

Later generations of parliamentarians were not so ready to abandon the old mythologies, but their efforts at self-publicity confirmed that the rise of the public's authority had become irreversible. One such effort was the 1753 passage of the act establishing the British Museum. Opened six years later, the museum was instituted for the "benefit of the publick," and since it was publicly funded, it was proclaimed to be the property of the British people; it now boasts itself "the world's oldest public national museum."[52] The Whigs who had pushed for the act were motivated by the prospect of having the Magna Carta put on display. They may have genuinely believed that the physical evidence of the old constitution would attest to the immemorial nature of the rights of freeborn Englishmen, but they also clearly hoped that the act of exhibiting the charter would profit them by affirming their party's commitment to the preservation of liberty.

The display was hugely successful. The charter was the highlight for most visitors, and some were reported to have gazed upon it in a spirit approaching idolatry.[53] Yet the display's effect was more ambiguous than its promoters realized. Over the long term, it helped desacralize the constitution not only by making the charter a tourist attraction but by taking the law out of the realm of ancestral tradition and situating it instead within a changeable history of policy and discourse. More immediately, as a public relations gesture, the event granted authority to the public, entitling it to claim ownership of the constitution and to assert its influence in party politics merely by choosing to visit the exhibit. The government may have benefited politically from the event's symbolism, but what it gained was not the authority of the ages but a contemporary public's favor.

The Later Eighteenth Century: Defining Public Discourse

By then, referring to "the public" had become a credible legitimation story. It was enough for politicians, journalists, critics, and professionals to say in their own defense that they were serving the public. There was no need to buttress the public's authorizing power by referring its origin to an anterior source. By then, this power could be either affirmed or refused, but not ignored. The history of the public's ascendancy after midcentury was one of facing up to its consequences for the social order and coming to terms with the idea of the public as an autonomous, egalitarian, indefinite, changeable, and more or less rational agent of change. It also entailed contending over workable limits to the extent of the public sphere and making readjustments to the terms of public debate in hopes of arriving at a consensual understanding of how much public expression of disagreement, short of revolt, might be possible. After midcentury, then, the public was a modern one, deliberating over what was or ought to be the commonly accepted order. Yet, perhaps more than its later incarnations, the public of the later eighteenth century was also a topic of its own debate, arguing over its role and prerogatives, its speech, and its manner of proceeding.

Popular participation in the great social, political, and intellectual changes of the period varied enormously, from quiescence to rebellion, but the idea of the public made it possible to justify them all. It became possible to use "the public" as a metonym for "democracy" and to uphold the equality implied by the idea as a self-evident value that overrode all other forms of authority. It became possible to shame authorities by accusing them of failing to heed public opinion, and to insist that political ideas be tested in the public tribunal. It became possible to think that the number of signatories to a petition submitted to Parliament was more compelling evidence of its importance than the identity of its signatories. It became possible to suppose that behavior in public settings, in which people suppress to a degree their passions for the sake of getting along with others, was paradigmatic of all forms of experience, including the impartial spectatorship of the sympathetic moral subject, the impersonal rationality of the marketplace, and the disinterestedness of the aesthetic experience. It became possible to believe that the ability to speak on public matters did not require the recognition of those already possessing a voice but could instead be self-asserted as an inherent right. It became possible for a phrase like "we the people" to be deemed wholly sufficient to justify the creation of an entirely new political constitution.

It also remained possible for lawmakers to defer to the public's authority without committing themselves to popular sovereignty. The idea of the public as a legitimizing body continued to compete with older accounts of social order and would never take hold in some areas—religion, most obviously. It had also to compete with newer operative norms that were developed to circumscribe its jurisdiction: standards of competence, professional expertise, scientific protocols, educational attainment, aesthetic judgment, artistic genius, and social and psychological normality. The equality that the public was assumed to embody would never cease to conflict with determinants of class and wealth or with beliefs about race and gender, though these conflicts were often deeply ambiguous, coming to the fore only at moments of fundamental disagreement, such as during the campaign to abolish slavery. And, as I have already suggested, the idea of the public could never transcend its incoherence, given that the public had at once to be free to fulfill its task of preserving individual liberties and to forsake some of its freedom to permit these liberties to exist.

The newer sense of the public required adjustments to the modes of public expression. Some of these adjustments may be apparent only by virtue of comparison with what had gone on before. For example, the centralized structure of power that was in place a century earlier made for debate that was often intensely animated and conducted through all manner of oral and written performances, often ranging well beyond matters of policy to include the interests of national institutions from the claims of the church to the ties of dynastic families. In this context, all discourse, from personal papers to coffeehouse conversations, could be subject to prosecution, while all media, from songs to sermons and plays to prints, could serve to disseminate this knowledge. This was the era when almost everyone seemed to write poems on affairs of state, verse as scabrously personal as it was politically partisan. In this context, all knowledge had the potential to be politicized in whatever form it was expressed, and all discourse was in some sense public.

With the end of licensing came the potential for broader dissemination of knowledge but equally for a public discourse that was no less politicized in degree but gradually less so in the range of forms and styles that commentators used to address this broader public. While the next decades would see some of the greatest political poetry produced in English, collections called *Poems on Affairs of State* quickly fell out of favor. The genre's last major anthology bearing the name appeared in 1716 and included no poems written after 1707—despite being published at the height of propaganda battles over the Hanoverian accession, the Septennial Act, and the first Jacobite rebellion.[54] Journals throughout the century included political verse, but prints and pamphlets soon overtook ballads as the preferred media for partisan opinion. After midcentury, prints were often issued without explanatory verses, which became redundant once cartoonists adopted a less emblematic, more accessible style of caricature.[55]

Making their publications easily understandable was a commercial necessity for newspapers, whose growth in numbers not only increased readers' access to news but encouraged them to expect information about current events on a regular basis. One historian has argued that this change in expectations represented a "politicization of consciousness" in English society.[56] The periodical press certainly encouraged the public to be conscious of itself as a social body, yet arguably newspapers did not politicize public consciousness any more than it already was. What happened, rather, was that politics came to be regarded as the topic of public debate at its most public. This explains the change in usage of the phrase "liberty of the press." At the beginning of the eighteenth century, the phrase encompassed all printed material, just as the "press" denoted both the printing machine and the trade that depended on it. A century later, the phrase was used most often with reference to newspapers and political tracts, even though other genres remained no less subject to prosecution than journalism was. In the defense of a free press, political reporting and commentary took precedence over other writings because politics had become unequaled among the subjects of public discourse. Just as the liberty of the press was the palladium of all other liberties, so the press appeared to serve the public to a greater degree than other genres because it helped to keep debate open and to preserve freedom.

Journalism also altered the nature of publicity. It hugely increased the degree of market penetration, yet equally decontextualized current events by presenting its reports in terms of localized facts detached from beliefs, traditions, or wider social or historical perspectives.[57] Being unsigned, newspaper editorials also usurped the rhetorical advantage of anonymity while neutering its impudence. Above all, journalism helped render any subject suitable for public discussion by regularizing the language of public debate, using an impersonal, expository prose that purveyed univocal meaning with determinate applications. The reporting of political and economic news in such prose would epitomize public discourse from the mid-eighteenth century onward, though in actuality it was one of many forms of generalized speech either developed or standardized during the period to facilitate comprehension of the increasingly complex nature of public experience: advertising, price tags, bills of fare, tax tables, city directories, road signs, and public notices, not to mention the small talk that made it possible for strangers to interact in public.

Several of the discursive changes of the kind that are the focus of this book were debated at the time, with several affirmed by Parliament or the courts. Their possible consequences were also extensively mooted with rationales for and against their implementation. But the assumptions propelling the changes remain so ingrained in modern thinking that it is difficult even now to grasp how dramatically these innovations altered the shape and texture of public speech. For example, Wilkes and his supporters are nowadays credited with leading several progressive efforts on behalf of a free press. In 1771, Alderman Wilkes used the privileges of the City to hinder Parliament from prosecuting the daily papers for reporting its debates.[58] A few years later he worked behind the scenes to allow regular publication of trial proceedings at the Old Bailey.[59] These measures, it was believed, would ensure accountability in the legislature and the courts.

In a similar if less high-minded spirit of openness, Wilkesite newspapers were notorious for muckraking into the domestic lives of peers. No doubt they wished to insult those in power by exposing evidence of corruption, much as satirists had always done. But their scandalmongering did not stop at embarrassing people but served to promote a self-professed ethic of "candor." Nothing, they felt, ought to be off-limits. Arguably, they invented the modern public figure, a person whose private life is considered fair game for investigation because he or she has chosen to court publicity in the pursuit of power and fame. And none was fairer game, it turned out, than Wilkes himself, as he discovered when the government prosecuted his privately circulated *Essay on Woman* for obscenity. Whether a person's private life had any bearing on his or her conduct in public was something that only the public could decide. The public could not exercise ultimate decision-making authority unless it also enjoyed the right to determine for itself whether private matters were relevant to its decision-making.

The most celebrated of the Wilkesites's legal campaigns ended, however, in a victory for the right of privacy in the decision in *Entick v. Carrington* (1765) against the government's use of general warrants, which had enabled it to conduct sweeping searches and seizures of the private belongings of anyone suspected of writing libels on the ministry. The Wilkesites won their case by arguing that governments could not override the law of trespass without adequate justification. Personal documents, they contended, were private property, and no state official could confiscate them on the mere suspicion they might be used to stir sedition. Going against precedent, Chief Justice Pratt, later Lord Camden, did not merely agree but held that private manuscripts, whatever their subject matter, merited special protection because they were an individual's "dearest property."[60] At the same time that they were pressuring politicians to be more responsive to public opinion, the Wilkesites were setting limits on the public sphere by affirming a division between public and private based not on the content of writings but on their ownership.

To say this is neither to laud the Wilkesites for their forward thinking nor to accuse them of hypocrisy in campaigning simultaneously on behalf of greater transparency and greater protection of privacy. Nor is it simply to reaffirm the banal truth that meaningful speech is not possible without some form of constraint. I state this, rather, to give an example of the incoherence that troubles modern notions about the public. It troubles because it leaves unresolved the question of how a modern regime of constraint—based on the use, form, and context of speech rather than on its substantive content—can be made compatible with an ideal of free speech. The Wilkesites, like jurists and legislators ever since, believed they could translate their principles of public liberty into workable legal arrangements while still leaving the idea of the public sufficiently undefined to enable the public to change its mind about what it considered a legitimately public use of private information. Yet the more these arrangements were put in place, the more difficult it was to recognize inconsistency across various branches of the law or to see what this inconsistency entailed for the character and function of the various forms of public discourse.

By the end of the eighteenth century, the regime of publicity that the Wilkesites had fought for was so firmly in place that judges were insistent that its public benefits outweighed any damage done to the reputation of individual citizens. In a 1799 case against a bookseller charged with publishing a speech uttered in Parliament that appeared to slander John Horne Tooke, Justice Lawrence maintained that the "general advantage to the country in having [court] proceedings made public, more than counterbalances the inconveniences to the private persons whose conduct may be subject to such proceedings. The same reasons also apply to the proceedings in Parliament." In what this general advantage consisted Lawrence did not say, nor did he feel any need to suggest why this advantage took precedence in this instance, in which a conservative Court of King's Bench was effectively permitting a libel on a well-known reformer to be publicly circulated. It was by then enough for Lawrence, who was otherwise no friend of the press, simply to declare that the public was entitled to know about private matters if these were discussed in the context of public deliberation and in an appropriately public setting.[61]

Yet even as reformers and conservatives alike were speaking up for openness, they were also voicing new concerns about how public deliberations were to be conducted. It had long been thought that jurors ought ideally to have prior knowledge of the circumstances of a crime; by the late eighteenth century, judges were rejecting the idea because of dismay over the prejudicial influence of pre-trial publicity. Similar fears were felt in relation to parliamentary debates. Bentham, the champion of publicity, believed that disseminating the debates in print lessened the effect of "passionate harangues" on the public; people read them, he said, only "after they have passed through a medium which cools them." This left the problem of what to do about the unmediated effects of speech on parliamentarians. Bentham, in mocking imitation of elite attitudes, suggested that the presence of women in the galleries might turn lawmakers into poets. "Admit females," he wrote, and the debates "would take an exalted tone, brilliant or tragical—excitement and tropes would be scattered everywhere; it would be necessary to speak of liberty in lyric strains, and to be poetic with regard to those great events which require the greatest calmness."[62]

Public speech could be free but not lyrical, it seems. Literary works could produce effects or deal in subjective experiences and perceptions that rendered them problematic as public speech. Since the eighteenth century, as evidenced by what Bentham said about "lyric strains" undermining political debate, poetry has been perceived as the opposite of the prosaic modes of public address.[63] Literature may affect or transport private readers in ways that appear to compromise its public utility as a medium of knowledge. Other genres may also deploy fictions and passionate speech, and the ability to inspire remains prized in some forms of moral, religious, and political argument. But since the eighteenth century most discourses other than literature have undergone extensive modifications to facilitate, or so it is assumed, the circulation of knowledge and to do so with minimal recourse to the devices of artful and fictive speech. In fact, literature may work pretty much the same way it always has, but its public role has changed because all other public discourses have changed.

Literature and Nation

One caveat is in order. I rely on a modern idea of "literature" to explain a long-term transformation in the public functions of literary writing since it is my contention that the change led to "literature" becoming widely accepted. My use of this modern category, however, may obscure how literary genres since the eighteenth century have overlapped with other discourses, how aspects of modern literary production are continuous with older practices, and how some authors since the eighteenth century have been no less fervent in their public commitments than were earlier writers. My caveat is that I should not be mistaken for adhering to any particular determinate conception of literature other than the idea that, like the public, literature in the modern world is indeterminate to a degree and in ways that could never have been imagined in earlier ages.

In the modern world, literature's purpose is as undefined, its forms as open to revision, and its constituent genres as subject to debate as a democratic public is believed to be free to reinvent itself and the laws it lives by.[64] So makers of agitprop will denounce claims like Auden's that poetry makes nothing happen, challenge what they see as dubious distinctions between art and polemics, and insist that literature can change the world. In turn, Auden will dismiss his former colleagues' manifestos as the productions of a low, dishonest decade and agree with someone of a different political inclination, like Orwell, about the need to maintain a "frontier" between art and propaganda.[65] Both sets of belief about literature, and many more, are at once tenable and contestable in the modern world in a way that was not so before the liberalization of speech.

By the end of the eighteenth century, I argue, literature was becoming more indeterminate in the purposes it served. This is not to suggest that literature was becoming either less or more important to public life than it had been previously. Nor is it to propose that literature in the modern world is *always* indeterminate. On the contrary, it is a logical inference from its indeterminacy that literature can at times serve determinate purposes. For example, as I consider in chapter 1, it is possible to think of literary works as expressing national identities in a way that counterbalances the effects of marketplace competition and the ceaseless exchange of capital, two of the more potent conceptions of indeterminacy in the modern world. Likewise, it is possible to believe that literary works with no obvious political import, whether representations of subjective experience or formalist experiments with language, can have emancipatory effects by helping people transcend common perceptions. Literary works can serve continuity as much as change.

The public can similarly embrace either. It may not have a positive identity, but it is always in the process of positing one. Every time the demos forms an opinion and makes a decision, it becomes an ethnos, though it may revise that judgment in its very next set of opinions. The public is always defining itself as a people that is at once evolving from and becoming. Any time the public patronizes efforts at cultural or intellectual progress, such as programs of scientific research, it is projecting a more or less hypothetical identity for itself that it assumes will result from this progress. More commonly, a modern public defines an identity for itself retrospectively, in relation to its members' history, achievements, and accustomed points of commonality, or comparatively, by contrast with the history and accomplishments of other peoples.

Nationalism, the dominant form of cultural identity in the modern world, is an outgrowth of democracy.[66] It differs from earlier sentiments of commonality in presupposing that a people's identity is not fixed and immutable but something to be created and reproduced.[67] During the later eighteenth century, literature was the focal point of multiple endeavors to define a national cultural past and perpetuate its memory through multivolume editions, tourist attractions, and comprehensive histories of English poetry.[68] These efforts at positing traditions took place amid a tide of nationalist sentiment and John Bull stereotypes that seemed a more or less spontaneous public response to war, the growth of empire, and revolution abroad. Yet arguably the rise of British nationalism was concomitant with the spread of democratic ideas, serving as it did a felt need to assert unity in the face of the modernizing transformations these ideas augured: the weakening of the old social order, the displacement of custom by the rule of law, the ascendancy of capital, and the increasing ubiquity, impersonality, and variousness of public discourse.[69]

Nationalism is an emotional rejoinder to the indeterminacy of public debate. In affirming a people as an imagined community standing atop the community in formation of the public, it essentializes the former as the source of social authority. In actuality the public and the people are one and the same body, though it is performing a different role in each capacity.[70] If a public deliberates, a people is a public's self-image in time, what it sees itself becoming or having become in accordance with its own determinations. The degree of divergence between these roles is highly variable, and indeed the incoherence of our modern conception of the public is obscured by the interchangeable way we use the phrases "the public" and "the people." All the same, there is enough connotative divergence between the phrases that together they represent a range of possible audiences that are served by specific discourses. Journalism, for example, provides knowledge essential to the public's ongoing debates. Most history, though allied with journalism, provides a people with a retrospective sense of itself. Politics is usually the domain of the public, as religion is of the people. These are facile distinctions, to be sure, but they do give a sense of the different functions that public discourses are expected to serve.

The distinctions did not exist in earlier cultures. Continuity being valued more than change in these cultures, no one could have imagined that poetry's power to teach and delight a contemporary public was not the same as its power to give enduring life to a people's stories, hopes, and faiths. The distinctions only took hold during the later eighteenth century. By then, literature was being contrasted to the presentist preoccupations of journalism, trade, and politics and being loudly celebrated as the living record of a British national identity. For a poet like Wordsworth, the people were the ideal audience for literary works because they personified the time-defying identity that the public lacked: "Towards the Public, the Writer hopes that he feels as much deference as it is entitled to: but to the People, philosophically characterised, and to the embodied spirit of their knowledge, so far as it exists and moves, at the present, faithfully supported by its two wings, the past and the future, his devout respect, his reverence, is due."[71] Wordsworth's mythmaking would have made little sense to earlier writers who, even if they could envisage a public that was not the people, would not likely have felt any deference toward this public or even the people. To believe that literature serves to express a positive identity without also contributing to ongoing deliberations about that identity not only bespeaks anxiety about the author's role in public life. It also places literature in the ambiguous position of being a public discourse that can be properly appreciated only when a public defines itself as a people. Yet for many other writers during the late eighteenth century and beyond, literature's position as both inside and outside the public sphere—at once public and not, determinate and not—could paradoxically make possible its most vital public functions.

# COPYRIGHT

CHAPTER ONE

Literature in the Public Domain

The Statute of Anne, the first copyright legislation, was passed in England on April 4, 1710.[1] It was intended to promote the "Encouragement of Learning" by vesting the right to print copies of books in their authors or assigns and by enforcing the right with protections against piracy over a limited term: twenty-one years in the case of old books and fourteen for new works with the possibility of an additional fourteen years if the author survived the initial term.[2] However, London booksellers, who had originally petitioned for the act, ignored its statutory limits and claimed instead that intellectual property, like real property, was recognized in the common law and was therefore a right held in perpetuity. Their claim did not go unchallenged: provincial booksellers, eager to publish their own editions of canonical works, repeatedly confronted the London monopoly on the notion of perpetual copyright, both in the courts and in scores of pamphlets. The ensuing literary property debate, as it was then called, was not resolved until February 22, 1774, when, in the historic case of *Donaldson v. Becket*, the House of Lords rejected arguments for perpetual copyright and upheld the statute's term limits. The debate was a momentous one, engaging several of the period's most prominent authors, from Defoe, Swift, and Addison to Johnson, Hume, and Wordsworth. As one contemporary put it, "No private cause has so much engrossed the attention of the public, and none has been tried before the House of Lords, in the decision of which so many individuals were interested."[3]

The decision in *Donaldson v. Becket* has been celebrated by legal historians as "the Magna Charta of literary property" since, in affirming statutory limits on copyright protection, it established the principle of a public domain for printed works.[4] More recent literary critics, inspired by Foucault's interrogation of the author function, have also examined how the copyright debate, while ultimately being settled in the public's favor, served as a kind of conceptual nursery for such doctrines as genius, originality, and the modern proprietary author.[5] Yet what all of these scholars have taken for granted is the very idea of a public domain, an idea so basic to democratic culture that its authority is now virtually uncontested, despite persistent efforts by authors' estates and corporate interests to encroach on the domain's scope.

In an earlier version of this chapter, I tried to show that the idea's emergence during the eighteenth century was not inevitable.[6] The idea of the public domain was nowhere set out in the statute, but was merely implied by the limits the act placed on protection and by its stipulation that booksellers could not claim ownership of works in Greek, Latin, or "any other foreign Language printed beyond the Seas."[7] By 1774, however, the idea had come to the fore in arguments against perpetual copyright, as it was felt by many that rewarding creative work ought to be balanced against providing the public with ready access to inexpensive editions of canonical writings. In this way, the public's interest in the "Encouragement of Learning" was dramatically redefined. The statute was designed to promote learning by deterring piracy and ensuring stability in the trade while restricting the political power of the booksellers' monopoly by keeping the period of its enforcement temporary. By 1774, lawmakers had come to believe that learning was best encouraged by providing financial incentives to creativity, yet equally by restricting the scope of these incentives to allow the public to benefit even more widely from the learning already available from the nation's most esteemed works.

So valuable were these works, lawmakers believed, that the public was felt to occupy them by right of eminent domain, a right that eclipsed any private claim to these works. Never before had it been possible for anyone to express the idea that the nation's literature ought to be the possession of its people. Yet once it was articulated, the idea seemed to command considerable assent. In effect, the literary property debate forced its contenders to provide answers to questions that had never been previously posed, questions such as, to whom does literature belong? Was learning best served by encouraging its production or by facilitating its dissemination? We may still be contending over these questions, though it is by now difficult to imagine a circumstance where the right to publish the works of Shakespeare or Milton would be vested in a single bookseller. That situation might have been today's reality were it not for the defeat of perpetual copyright. As the provincial booksellers declared following their victory, "the Works of *Shakespeare*, of *Addison*, *Pope*, *Swift*, *Gay*, and many other excellent Authors of the present Century, are, by this Reversal, declared to be the Property of any Person."[8] The reversal in effect institutionalized the belief that the formation of a literary culture ought to take precedence over the pecuniary rights of authors and booksellers.

I here revisit my earlier argument to investigate more closely the reasoning behind the 1774 decision and how it reflected changing assumptions about the social function of literature.

Literature as Property, Property as Literature

The idea of legal protection for booksellers' "copies" greatly antedates the Statute of Anne, as do notions of authorial rights.[9] However, private copyright as such was not recognized during the first two centuries after the coming of print except in rare instances when an author received an exclusive royal license to print his own work. In principle, control over all books and their reproduction lay with the Crown, which sometimes exercised its prerogative directly when it sought to censor the press by restricting the supply of new books.[10] Otherwise, the Crown normally asserted its privilege over the publication only of works it deemed publicly important or for which there was no particular author: Bibles, Books of Common Prayer, almanacs, law books, and anything having to do with "[m]atters of state and things that concern the Government."[11] The trade in all other books, at least until licensing's demise in 1695, was regulated by the domestic monopoly of the London booksellers who formed the Stationers Company. The notion of an author's copyright, then, was never actually declared as a right in the common law before the eighteenth century; this was despite the customary assumption that one ought to be entitled to the fruits of one's labor and be therefore legally protected against the unauthorized appropriation of those fruits.[12]

This ambiguity in the law was the locus of contention for much of the literary property debate. The defenders of perpetual copyright, including for a time Samuel Johnson, could reasonably claim that authors enjoyed a natural right in their works. "There seems," Johnson argued, "to be in authours a stronger right of property than that by occupancy; a metaphysical right, a right, as it were, of creation, which should from its nature be perpetual."[13] Yet equally reasonably the British judges who surveyed the legal history could conclude that copyright came into legal existence only after the coming of print and thus had no immemorial foundation in the common law. As the lord justice clerk of the Scottish court remarked in dismissing arguments for a perpetual copyright, "our statutes, the Roman law, the ancient customs of the kingdom, the doctrines of our lawyers, and the decisions of this court; all these have been investigated, and no trace or vestige is to be found of this idea of a *copy-right*."[14]

The Statute of Anne had intensified this ambiguity by proposing two conflicting accounts of authorial rights. On the one hand, by both defining those rights and limiting the period of protection, the act appeared to have made copyright a purely statute-dependent privilege. On the other hand, by referring to authors as "proprietors" in their works, the act seemed to clarify rather than supersede the common law, providing it with the legal mechanism for enforcing penalties against piracy. In this way, the growth of publishing and piracy, so the argument went, may have necessitated the statutory declaration of copyright in the 1710 act, but the privilege itself was founded on a customary principle of property rights, which predated the new technology. As any common lawyer will tell you, lawmakers do not protect something because it is property, but rather call something property in order to protect it. Indeed, it was later routinely acknowledged that the term "property," which appeared only once in the statute to characterize a right of consent over a book's printing rather than ownership of the physical copy, was to be understood entirely in a figurative sense. But the trope had considerable force in the law, which may explain why most justices before 1774 ignored the statutory limits of the act, preferring instead to support the notion of an author's perpetual copyright. That almost all of the many contests over perpetual copyright involved booksellers and not authors (who invariably sold their rights to the trade prior to publication) did not seem to matter. Even in the case of older works, such as Shakespeare's, the natural rights of the author continued to be proclaimed, despite the fact that Tonson's "ownership" of Shakespeare was based in a de facto occupancy and not in a right assigned by the playwright's estate.

The authority of the term "property" meant that much of the debate focused on the nature of intellectual property and on the question of whether the ideas, sentiments, and style of a given work could be awarded the same protection as that assigned to an estate or invention. The London booksellers, with the support of Blackstone, among others, argued that the identity of a text was secure enough to permit its ownership as property: "the same conceptions, clothed in the same words, must necessarily be the same composition; and, whatever method [the author] takes of conveying that composition to the ear or eye of another, by recital, by writing, or by printing, in any number of copies, or at any period of time, it is always the identical work of the author which is so conveyed."[15] Said another advocate, a text retained an integrity in perpetuity however variously it might be reproduced: "a literary work . . . may subsist in various forms: it may remain lodged in the author's memory; it may be recited *vivâ voce*; it may be written, or it may be printed: but in all these forms it is still the same work; and these are only incidental circumstances which do not at all change its nature, or affect its identity. Literary property... is indeed a kind of property invisible and untangible; but it is not on that account the less real."[16]

The opponents of perpetual copyright countered by saying that something invisible and intangible could be, at best, considered only "*quasi* property."[17] Property and corporality, argued Henry Home, later Lord Kames, "are relative Terms which cannot be disjoined, and *Property*, in a strict Sense, can no more be conceived without a *corpus*, than a Parent can be conceived without a Child."[18] Yet the argument was too abstract to compel a change in the law, and at any rate, even critics of copyright were reluctant to deny authors a proprietary right in their unpublished manuscripts.[19] The key therefore for the provincial trade was to demonstrate how, by the terms of the Statute of Anne, publication transformed private property recognized in the common law into public domain regulated only by statute. The provincial booksellers were willing to grant authors the rights of first publication and of financial reward for their labor. But, they added, once a work was published, the owner of its copyright could enjoy only temporary protection from piracy while the work's ideas and sentiments, once disseminated, could not but be held in common. As it was impossible for an author to own ideas once they had passed into a reader's mind, the booksellers reasoned, publication rights could not be granted the same legal status as rights to real property.

The most memorable articulation of this position was by Justice Yates, who cast the only dissension in a rare split vote of the Court of King's Bench in the landmark case of *Millar v. Taylor* (1769). Publication, Yates argued, was a gift of ideas to the public: "the very matter and contents of... books are by the author's publication of them, irrevocably given to the public; they become common." Ideas in print, according to Yates, could not be owned or recalled by the author. Once a work was published, its contents became part of every reader's body of learning. Upon publication, Yates insisted, "ideas are free."[20] Yates understood that the advocates of perpetual copyright did not pretend that an author retained ownership in a work's ideas following its publication. A work's substantive content was not copyrightable; only its arrangement of words could be protected in accordance with the idea–expression dichotomy, which the courts were then beginning to work out as the most practicable way of resolving contests over infringement. Yates's point, rather, was that copyright should be treated as a trade regulation and not a form of property. But the other three judges on the bench, including Lord Mansfield, disagreed and ruled in favor of recognizing copyright as a right under the common law.

Millar v. Taylor was notable in several respects. First, it was the Stationers' most significant legal victory in their campaign to preserve perpetual copyright; however, Yates's lengthy dissent, along with a number of decisions by the Scottish courts, proved influential five years later when the House of Lords reversed the ruling in the case. Second, since both the case and its later appeal involved disputes over the ownership of Thomson's *The Seasons*, the judges and lords who decided on the matter were primarily concerned with the social and economic functions of literary writings and, just as important, with their value as heritage within English and Scottish cultures. Third, the opinions expressed in the case revealed how newer conceptions of value were colliding with older assumptions about the social order, with elements of both old and new thinking contributing in surprising ways to arguments on either side of the question. These ideas, having to do with the value of property and the consequent value of literature as a form of intellectual property, I outline below before addressing how these views were used in arguments about the scope of copyright protection.

Yates's plea was essentially a restatement of the traditional case against monopolies. His was an older view of the public order, which the regime of property was designed to safeguard rather than enrich. "The principal end for which the first institution of property was established," he insisted, "was to preserve the peace of mankind, which could not exist in a promiscuous scramble." Monopolies threatened this order by investing private persons with the power to suppress writings—the very scenario that the statute's term limits were designed to prevent. Yates was not opposed to a limited copyright and acknowledged that "the labours of an author have certainly a right to a reward." Yet, he insisted, once authors had been compensated for their intellectual labor, the fruits of that labor should "revert to the common mass" so that all booksellers might have the opportunity to publish them. Labor, no matter how valuable its result, did not entitle authors to perpetual ownership over their writings because "mere value does not constitute property."[21]

The other three judges on the bench, who upheld a common-law copyright, took a different view of property. They could not dispense with a labor theory of value since without it, there was no basis in natural law for authors owning rights to their published work. Labor established title. "[I]t is just," Mansfield insisted, "that an author should reap the pecuniary profits of his own ingenuity and labour."[22] Yet by speaking in terms not of the fruits of labor but of its possible profits, Mansfield was also relying on a newer conception of property's value, one set out at greater length in the concurring opinion of his colleague Justice Aston. The word "property," Aston argued, could apply to anything that had both "a distinguishable existence" and potential commercial value for its owner. Intellectual property was "personal, incorporeal property," but it was no less "saleable and profitable" for being so. Authors might consider their writings the precious "effect and produce" of their labors, but an unpublished work possessed value as property only in the expectation of its future sale. Publication was necessary to transform a work into "a distinguishable subject of property" that could be bought, sold, and circulated for profit. Without publication, a work is "useless to the owner; because without profit: and property, without the power of use and disposal, is an empty sound. In that state, 'tis lost to the society, in point of improvement; as well as to the author, in point of interest."[23] Intellectual property was, in this account, nothing other than a work's exchange value as measured in either actual or potential profit. And exchange, the justices believed, was no less natural law than labor, and it was therefore compelling as a rationale for a common-law copyright.

Though Aston did not say what he meant by the improvement that society stood to gain from published works, the fact that he believed this improvement merited a profitable return to authors suggests how modern ideas about exchange value were by then beginning to challenge older perceptions of the social order. For conservatives like Yates, property was a defining pillar of "the fixed constitution of things."[24] A credential of power within a social hierarchy founded on landed interests, property was to be respected as a right so absolute as to appear, in Blackstone's account, as the "sole and despotic dominion which one man claims and exercises over the external things of the world."[25] In this order, learning served the unchanging norm of the "good of mankind," while the public was neither an agent in its own improvement nor a body independent of the state. Hence Yates, though distrustful of private monopolies, believed that the Crown ought to retain its prerogative over the reprinting of the most important works of "national and public concern" since correct editions of these works were required to ensure that "uniformity and order be duly observed, and the subject informed with precision, how to regulate his conduct."[26]

As a system of perpetual ownership accorded with belief in a fixed regime of property, a similar conception of social order could equally inform arguments in support of a common-law copyright. For Blackstone, serving as counsel for the London booksellers in the earlier case of *Tonson v. Collins* (1761–1762), "universal law" decreed that manual or mental labor established not merely ownership but "a permanent, perpetual property" in a man's own productions. And while the resulting monopolies might be detrimental to the common good in the case of mechanical inventions, which, Blackstone allowed, "ought to be cheap and numerous," a perpetual copyright on published writings harmed neither society nor the trade since the reading public was so small and exclusive: learning "can, and ought to be, only the employment of a few. And one printing house will furnish more books, than any nation can find able readers."[27] In supposing a market too small to support competition, this argument threatened to moot the case for copyright. But the size of the market was beside the point. The value of learning was determined by the interests of a propertied elite that deemed itself fit to rule by dint of its virtue, which learning could confirm but not change.

Under a theory of exchange value, by contrast, property was understood to exist within a historical process and to accrue value from its circulation in an expansive market economy. Change characterized the social world, itself perceived not as a hierarchical order but as a dynamic structure of productive relations. And, as J. G. A. Pocock has explained, once "property moved from being the object of ownership and right to being the subject of production and exchange," there occurred a corresponding transformation in prevailing notions of the human personality. "We are contrasting," Pocock writes, "a conception of property which stresses possession and civic virtue with one which stresses exchange and the civilisation of the passions."[28] With the emergence of this commercial ideology, personality was no longer the aim and function of moral discipline, but was instead the product of experience, circulation in society, and self-improvement through education.

As with any ideology, this understanding of personality was premised on a normative equivalence, in this case between economic profit and moral or intellectual benefit, an equivalence that followed plausibly from the assumption that value of whatever kind could not exist outside relations of exchange. This equivalence made it possible to treat all forms of value as transferable capital, as one exchangeable for another. The improvement readers obtained from the publication of an author's work may not have been the *same* value as the financial profits the author might gain from publication, but the latter seemed to Aston a fair trade for the former. The transfer could likewise go in the opposite direction, with property and its ceaseless exchange gradually assuming the didactic functions traditionally ascribed to literary works: "Commerce, and the complexity of exchange which it generates, teaches both rulers and subjects the conventions according to which government must be conducted."[29] In effect, literature was being proclaimed as intellectual private property at the very moment when the circulation of property was becoming intellectual capital.

This change in the perception of property was reflected at various levels of the literary property debate. One question that was hotly debated was whether perpetual copyright could be considered a monopoly. The London booksellers maintained that theirs was not a monopoly because, first, a monopoly was strictly speaking a grant of the Crown, and second, perpetual copyright was not a monopoly because it did not restrict the public's access to any work that had *previously* been widely available. As Warburton explained, "[A] *Monopoly* is an exclusive *Privilege* by *Grant* of doing that, which all Men have a Claim to do; not an exclusive *Right* by *Nature* of enjoying what no one else has a Claim to."[30] Thus the London booksellers subscribed to the older view of property as an object of rights and privileges, bestowed by either nature or a grant of the Crown.

Their opponents countered by asserting that copyright operated like a monopoly since it precluded other booksellers from sharing in the fruits of an author's labor. The retention of perpetual copyright, in Yates's version, would "exclude all the rest of mankind from enjoying their natural and social rights."[31] This opinion equally presumed an older view of property, however, and was therefore soon supplemented by newer exchange-based objections to monopolies, according to which a perpetual copyright inhibited the growth of the book trade and of learning more generally. Any publishing cartel, later critics charged, that hindered the full circulation of property and knowledge ultimately threatened England's liberty and the proper ideological development of its citizenry: "In every kind of commerce, and in every art, there ought to be a competition. Without this, industry will not prosper; and any monopoly or restraint must nourish tyrants, to oppress the country, and to annihilate ingenuity."[32] Unrestricted private control over "the Channel of public Information" posed no less of a danger to "the constitutional Rights of the People" than did official censorship.[33] The London booksellers, their Scottish rivals charged, had taken advantage of the law's ambiguity with "the Genius of a *Spanish* Inquisition" to stifle competition and grow powerful at the expense of readers and public reason.[34] The London publishers strenuously denied these charges, though their case was considerably weakened by the discovery that they had conspired to undermine the provincial trade's efforts to expand its market.[35]

At a more profound level, the change in the way property was perceived altered the way the value of literature was defined. If the commerce of property was gradually assuming the didactic functions of literature, then literature's own functions had to be reconceived in accordance with the new emphases on circulation and exchange. In place of the old pragmatic claim that literature teaches as it delights, literature began to be seen as operating within a complex of human activities, and if properly disseminated, it contributed to the formation of a national culture. The distinction may have merely been a matter of emphasis, where an older perception of literature, which openly stressed literature's function as a fount of sociable pleasure or moral instruction, was rendered less patrician with the suggestion that literary works were phenomena freely shared among all members of a community. Yet however ideological the distinction, the perceptual shift it identified was significant since it meant that a work's value was measured less by its direct effects on an audience than by how widely and profoundly it helped shape a culture. A literary work, much like property, had to circulate in society for it to become valuable: it had to be read over multiple and divergent generations of readers before it could be treated as a canonical legacy. In this perceptual shift can thus be located the legal and economic origins of one of the public sphere's most important legitimizing metaphors, the marketplace of ideas.[36]

This perceptual shift operated decisively in the copyright debate. The older, didactic view was that of Lord Camden in the decision of 1774. "Why did we enter into Society at all," he asked, "but to enlighten one another's Minds, and improve our Faculties, for the common Welfare of the Species?" The assumption here was that society provided a structure of collective norms of virtue and discipline, in the absence of which, Camden claimed, humanity would lapse into the chaos to which its "irregular and uncertain and various" temperaments were naturally prone. By extension, the function of literature could be understood only in relation to this structure of norms, such that, for Camden, any author deserving of the title could have no other motive for writing than to strive for the glory of bringing light to truth: "Those great Men, those favoured Mortals, those sublime Spirits, who share that Ray of Divinity which we call Genius, are intrusted by Providence with the delegated Power of imparting to their Fellow creatures that Instruction which Heaven meant for universal Benefit."[37]

Though the House of Lords was not voting on whether to repeal the 1710 statute, Camden was effectively calling for a rejection of its principles. Limited or permanent, copyright, in his view, enervated rather than encouraged learning. A system of cash rewards for authors was undeserving of legal protection because it debased the art: "It was not for Gain, that *Bacon, Newton, Milton, Locke*, instructed and delighted the World; it would be unworthy [for] such Men to traffic with a dirty Bookseller." For Camden, as for Yates, treating literature as intellectual property did not make sense because it contravened writing's moral purpose. In their minds, property was not something that circulated, while truth had no force unless imparted: "Knowledge has no Value or Use to the solitary Owner: To be enjoyed it must be communicated."[38]

The newer view of literature's function was that of Lord Kames, articulated during a 1773 decision of the Scottish Court of Session. A limited copyright, Kames argued, "excites men of genius to exert their talents for composition; and it multiplies books both of instruction and amusement. And when, upon expiration of the monopoly, the commerce of these books is laid open to all, their cheapness, from a concurrence of many editors, is singularly beneficial to the public." Enshrining a perpetual right in the common law would, he added, "unavoidably raise the price of good books beyond the reach of ordinary readers. They will be sold like so many valuable pictures. The sale will be confined to a few learned men who have money to spare, and to a few rich men who buy out of vanity as they buy a diamond or a fine coat." Kames was not merely objecting to canon making by wealthy elites, but making clear that the value of literature ought to be determined within a dynamic scheme of productive relations. As ever, literature provided instruction and amusement, but its benefits were to be understood in quantitative terms, in the multiplicity of books and in their wide diffusion and "commerce" among a broad audience. By this logic, the commodification of literary works was something to be welcomed rather than feared, so long as their consumption was not restricted to a small sector of the market. Hence the true extent of literature's social value was apt to be forgotten in a society that, through its economic monopolies, denied reading to all but its richest members. In time, the concentration of ownership in a select few would, Kames concluded, "put a final end to the commerce of books in a few generations."[39]

Kames prefaced his argument for the circulation of ideas with a sociology of reading that did not presuppose the essential volatility of human nature. Instead of virtue and self-possession, we read in Kames's argument the newer codes of refinement and progress, of individual identities being formed by social relations and the exchange of material and cultural goods: "Why was man made a social being, but to benefit by society, and to partake of all the improvements of society in its progress toward perfection? At the same time, he was made an imitative being, in order to follow what he sees done by others. But to bestow on inventors the monopoly of their productions, would in effect counteract the designs of Providence, in making man a social and imitative being: it would be a miserable cramp upon improvements, and prevent the general use of them."[40]

Just as Kames was substituting the modern theme of progress through innovation for the older dogma of duty staunchly defended by Yates and Camden, so was he rejecting the latter's didactic theory of literature. In his view, the theory was reductive in that it located literary value in each work's instructiveness to readers on their fixed role in society. For Kames, socialization was an extended process that involved the "general use" of many literary productions. The ultimate value of literature was an aggregate measure: in an exchange economy, the size of the market was the point. Reading yielded not a pot of sweetness and light, but a fund of acculturation. Thus the law, according to Kames, had to recognize that the unrestricted reproduction of literary property ensured the upward intellectual and economic mobility of society as a whole. The concept of property held as much authority for Kames as it did for Camden and Yates, but for Kames the *value* of property, including literary property, was to be measured within a system of progressive exchange and general utility and not according to a rigid hierarchy dominated by landed or moneyed interests.

Alexander Donaldson and his colleagues, fresh from their victory in the Scottish court, happily drew on Kames's opinion in their 1774 appeal to the English lords. "*Public Utility*," they declared, "requires that the Productions of the Mind should be diffused as wide as possible."[41] The argument did not so much resolve the ambiguity at the heart of the 1710 act as update its assumptions. Intellectual property may have been a right under the common law, but public utility dictated that property serve, through its commerce, to enrich society as a whole. Remarkably, this account of value as deriving from exchange was virtually identical to the one that, just a few years earlier, the Mansfield court in *Millar v. Taylor* had used to defend a common-law copyright over moral objections like Yates's to the power of monopolies. Kames and the Scottish appellants were invoking the theory in the service of the case against permanent authorial rights, a case that was also being argued by conservatives like Camden, who felt a gentleman's abhorrence for the commercialization of letters that the theory promoted. To the puzzlement of later critics of the 1774 decision, Camden's florid speech was widely touted in the press as having done the most to turn the lords against perpetual copyright.[42] The questions that remain to be answered, then, are how an economic theory of exchange value that had initially been introduced in defense of perpetual copyright could be very quickly appropriated in arguments for its defeat, and why these arguments had to be combined with a seemingly incompatible account of the antipathy of genius to commerce in order to affirm the rightfulness of retrenching copyright protection to its statutory limits.

The Exchange Value of Genius

Adding to the puzzle was the fact that the advocates of perpetual copyright argued for its retention with assertions very similar to Camden's about the sublimity of genius and the threat posed to literature's high calling by the Grub Street menace. The end of permanent authorial privileges, they declared, would undermine the integrity of the canon by encouraging the production of short-lived hackwork, reducing the value of all writing, and even rendering literary theft unprofitable. "Scarce any production," one commentator predicted, "will issue from the press, but hasty, fugitive pieces, calculated to serve the run of the day, and which will excite as little temptation, as they afford opportunity, for piracy."[43] In answer to those like Camden who rejected copyright outright as unworthy of the greatest authors, the law's defenders conceded that the profit motive was not as noble an incentive for writing as the quest for immortality but, they warned, without financial support genius might lie forever mute and inglorious. Lord Lyttelton made the point in responding directly to Camden. Genius, he reminded his fellow peer, "is more frequently found in the Cottage than the Palace; it rather crawls on the Face of the Earth than soars aloft; when it does mount, its Flight should not be impeded. To damp the Wing of Genius is, in my mind, highly impolitic, highly reprehensible, nay, somewhat criminal."[44]

The mythology of genius lent emotional appeal to several dimensions of the London booksellers' case. It made it easier to elevate copyrights as a class of intellectual property superior to statute-dependent arrangements like patents; authors of genius, Catherine Macaulay proclaimed, should not be "levelled with the inventors of a very inferior order."[45] Likewise, the idea of genius accorded with a labor theory of value, naturalizing it by locating the source of creativity in providential talent and supplementing it by providing additional rationales for keeping authorial rights permanent.[46] An indefinite copyright, William Enfield maintained, permitted the author to improve his writings over his career and thereby "give them all the perfection he is able."[47] It might also, Macaulay noted, take more than fourteen years before genius was properly recognized: "it is a length of time before the value of a literary publication is discovered and acknowledged by the vulgar," especially if the work in question "teaches an offensive doctrine, or tells disagreeable truths to the public."[48] In effect, the ancient belief that the genuine value of literary endeavors could be revealed only in posterity was being recycled in defense of an economic monopoly.

The idea that value emerged only over time also made it possible to accommodate the mythology of genius to newer exchange theories of value and their full-scale modeling in the discourse of political economy. What was deficient about the existing mechanism of copyright, it was suggested, was that it devalued genius by treating its productions no differently from other publications, and by setting limits on protection, it made it impossible for the market to correct the devaluation over time. A temporary copyright, Enfield explained, was insufficient to reward a work of lasting merit because those rewards expired before its author could earn more than "the Ephemera of Literature who are born and die in a day."[49] Only a system of perpetual ownership, it seemed, could do justice to the immortality of genius.

On the face of it, the mythology of genius was irrelevant to exchange theory, according to which the value of property derives from its circulation rather than inheres in the labor or talent required to produce it. As Adam Smith made clear, neither the abilities of individual persons nor the fruits of their labors necessarily increase a society's wealth. Prosperity, as well as social and material improvements, result from the division of labor and the human "propensity to truck, barter, and exchange one thing for another." Smith was willing to grant that the labor of "men of letters of all kinds" is as deserving of "its reward" as the work of manufacturers is of their profits. Yet since most literary activity generated insufficient capital to cover its cost in intellectual resources, it was for him among the varieties of "unproductive labour," a view that appeared to validate the conservative belief that genius could have no commercial value.[50]

The theory likewise appeared to promise the mythology little in return. Crucially, it offered no way to indicate what made works of genius worthy of greater profit. The theory left such determinations to the market but, as Enfield lamented, this could not be verified so long as the market was impaired by copyright's statutory limits. Justice Willes, the third concurring judge in *Millar v. Taylor*, had made a similar point in his opinion. A work of genius, Willes explained, possessed an authentic value that was not necessarily reflected in its initial selling price. Only the passage of time could ensure that pecuniary profits were a fair trade for an author's labor: "a good book may be run down, and a bad one cried up, for a time; yet sooner or later, the reward will be in proportion to the merit of the work."[51] Willes was essentially allowing that a price could be put on genius to the degree that time rendered a work's sales commensurate with its moral, intellectual, or artistic worth. Commensurate but not identical: financial remuneration remained distinguishable from a work's merit. In acknowledging the distinction, Willes appeared to be resisting the full force of the principle of equivalence that the theory of exchange value presupposed, or at least deferring this equivalence to a time "sooner or later" when a work's merit had transcended any distorting influence on its author's financial return. Genius might be transferable, but its value could not be reliably measured within the existing period of statutory copyright protection. Thus, whereas market price could at any time be taken as a plausible measure of the value of real property, the tradable value of intellectual property was liable to remain a doubtful indicator of genius until such time as a work's genuine value could be otherwise revealed.

The trouble was that the discourse of political economy had little to say about this genuine value. Unlike the old labor account of value, which presupposed an unchanging normative order, the theory of exchange value appeared to treat all forms of tradable activity as conducive to prosperity. The idea of genius, by contrast, assumed that not all writing, no matter how financially profitable, aided the progress of learning. Many of the old complaints about the deleterious effects of bad writing could be expressed in exchange terms: it wasted intellectual resources, depressed the market by flooding it, and detracted consumers' attention from deserving work. But an exchange theory offered few means of acknowledging the qualitative benefits that works of genius rendered to society, and it provided no obvious rationale for an indefinite monopoly on the reproduction of these works other than the assertion that the Statute of Anne had caused market failure.

The one benefit that political economy did recognize was improvement, a purposefully open-ended category that was meant to encompass known advancements in technology, labor efficiency, and the extension of trade markets, as well as any form of social or economic betterment that had yet to be dreamed up. So abstract was the category that contestants on either side of the literary property debate made liberal use of it. It was meant to be widely serviceable, though it was not without referent or force. It suggested a more or less extensive process of melioration that, for Kames, could stretch into a teleological "progress toward perfection." Improvement could be either a change caused by society to its members and their "faculties," as Camden believed, or one caused by great writing to society or, as Enfield would have it, "to distant ages." The word "improvement" itself had special applicability to the value of property, being commonly used to denote the act of making unoccupied land more profitable through enclosure.[52] In the discourse of exchange, the idea of improvement nonetheless remained sufficiently impervious to specification that it could seem an adequate modern substitute for as traditional a concept as the encouragement of learning.

Beyond that, it was not clear how the idea could help the London booksellers to identify the enduring value in works that might entitle them to an indefinite term of protection. The Statute of Anne had intended copyright to advance learning by preventing its unauthorized reproduction. Yet the substantive content of learning was not subject to protection. It was not an infringement on its owner's rights for someone else to reproduce a work's ideas and sentiments in different form. Though an abstract of a previously published work might fail to do justice to the profundity of its argument, it was hard to see how multiplying the available renditions of its ideas did not contribute to its reputation or the dissemination of knowledge. If anything, the London booksellers, whose business typically included derivative works, such as abridgments and translations, were only too happy to grant that such publications helped to make an author's "work more known and attended to, and therefore are in reality beneficial to him."[53] Yet if ideas could not be protected, they could not constitute the durable property for which a limited copyright failed to provide adequate compensation.

That left "expression" as the one feature in a work that could potentially distinguish timeless genius from perishable verbiage. No one disputed that works were to be differentiated by their "use and arrangement of words."[54] Expression was the ontological basis for a work's copyright. Whether expression could equally perform the normative function of justifying an indefinite term of protection was another matter. It had not been required to do so in the defense of copyright under a labor theory of value. Prior to value being redefined as the outcome of exchange, it was enough to say that replicating the language of other writers' published work was theft of the reward for their labor, regardless of whether their work had contributed to learning. Expression was a lasting record of their labor though not necessarily what made their work valuable.

Under the theory of exchange, by contrast, replicating the language of other writers' published work was theft of their reward for the improvement that resulted from the circulation of their work. For advocates of perpetual copyright, like Willes, an indefinite monopoly was necessary to ensure adequate compensation over time for works that produced continuous improvement of one kind or another. This enduring power of improvement, they contended, was the true value of genius. At the same time, for a work to be copyrightable, it had to be distinguishable on the basis of its expression, whose unauthorized replication the law was designed to prohibit. Hence the enduring value of a work of genius, what enabled it to effect unending improvement and to merit indefinite protection, had to be inseparable from the work's expression. Genius could not be reproducible in any other form. For its true value to be at once effective, recognizable, and properly compensated, the work had to be endlessly circulated without its words ever being changed.

Booksellers eager to preserve their rights over a canonical work were thus given an incentive to rely on authentic versions of the work, those copies that were verifiably approximate to the original language through which its author had expressed his or her ideas. One of the standard charges against pirates was that they cared little about producing accurate editions of the works they reprinted. After the lords' decision, Burke was reported to have inveighed that were the London stationers' monopoly not restored, "anarchy and confusion among the trade must be the consequence, and a multitude of incorrect, wretched editions would pour in upon the public."[55] The alarmism of such warnings notwithstanding, it was not obvious how most readers stood to benefit from authentic editions of writings that had already long been subject to redaction and appropriation. Prior to the mid-eighteenth century, few categories of books were felt to be so important as to require some measure of accuracy or uniformity in their editions, and none of these books was subject to private copyright: Bibles, acts of Parliament, almanacs, and other "prerogative copies" whose reproduction the Crown controlled, and the classics, which the Statute of Anne had excluded. Most other well-known writings in English were routinely republished in altered versions and often seen as requiring emendation to suit contemporary expectations. Dryden modernized Chaucer, Bentley corrected Milton, and virtually everyone adapted Shakespeare to the taste of the age.

There were likewise no received critical principles that advocates of copyright could use to explain why modifying the expression of older works would hurt their value. Under the rhetorical tradition, expression and its many components of invention, disposition, and figures could serve a range of instrumental functions, though few required that a work's particular arrangement of words be irreproducible. Older writings might be prized as models for composition, but this use could hardly seem appealing to owners of copyrights because it invited replication of an author's words; besides, writing extracts suitable for student imitation could be freely reproduced in anthologies. Older writings might also be valued for the socially beneficial effects of their expression: English poets since Chaucer had been celebrated for improving their native language, polishing its numbers, and enhancing its rhetorical efficacy. But the idea that great works refined language presupposed that, as in the obvious case of Chaucer's writings, a work's expression would eventually grow obsolete and in need of updating to preserve the value of the work's other features. The idea was therefore not merely unhelpful to advocates of a perpetual copyright, but it had to be repudiated in order to justify preserving a work's expression in perpetuity—a development I consider in chapter 2.

Originality and the Division of Labor

A more promising idea was originality, an old notion that the mythologizers of genius were enthusiastically attempting to revive. Historians of authorship, taking up Foucault's suggestion about the modern individuation of discourse, have argued for a direct correlation between the emergence of copyright law and the increasing use of "originality" as a term of critical approbation. In actuality the idea was not initially pertinent to the literary property debate. The Statute of Anne had made no mention of originality since the idea had not been required under a labor account of value. The fruit of an author's labor had to be merely differentiable from other works, regardless of whether that labor had been expended on producing new material or adapting existing material.

The theory of originality became relevant to arguments over perpetual copyright only when critics began to deploy it in response to newer exchange notions of value. The theory's best-known manifesto, Edward Young's *Conjectures on Original Composition* (1759), has been cited by Martha Woodmansee as evidence of an increasing tendency to treat a work's ownership as "contingent" upon its originality.[56] Yet what is most remarkable about the specific passage that Woodmansee quotes is less the connection Young drew between originality and property than his metaphoric slurs on the exchange of creative material:

> Thyself so reverence as to prefer the native growth of thy own mind to the richest import from abroad; such borrowed riches make us poor. The man who thus reverences himself, will soon find the world's reverence to follow his own. His works will stand distinguished; his the sole Property of them; which Property alone can confer the noble title of an *Author*; that is, of one who (to speak accurately) *thinks*, and *composes*; while other invaders of the Press, how voluminous, and learned soever, (with due respect be it spoken) only *read*, and *write*.[57]

Labor remained the basis of property, but not all writing, however copyrightable, involved genuine labor. More important for Young, borrowing from even the richest fruits of authorial labor led to trade imbalances that ultimately impoverished literature.

His use of the property metaphor aside, Young was not discussing copyright. Though he addressed his *Conjectures* to a bookseller, Samuel Richardson, who was plagued by pirates, Young was not concerned with the unlawful reproduction of published works. Young's aim was to overturn the centuries-old rhetorical doctrine of imitation; that is, he was campaigning for originality in new writing rather than arguing for the preservation of canonical works in their original language. He believed that original genius individuated discourse in the sense that the greatest authors, by owing nothing to others, impressed their unique selves upon their writings: "*Shakespeare* gave us a *Shakespeare*."[58] Yet in good neoclassical fashion, he willingly allowed that even a genius like Shakespeare was not above committing faults that needed to be corrected for presentation onstage.

The idea of originality nonetheless seemed promising to the London booksellers because it appeared to provide a normative basis for keeping a work's expression unchanged in perpetuity. Originality, they claimed, was the sign of an author's individuality: "a literary work *really* original, like the human face, will always have some singularities, some lines, some features, to characterize it, and to fix and establish its identity."[59] Pirates who tried to evade the law by publishing altered versions of an important work were guilty of stealing an author's identity and its market value by attempting to pass their versions off as the original. A perpetual copyright, the argument supposed, was the only way of forever preventing an author's identity from being misrepresented and the public from being misled by inferior knockoffs. Then again, under the statute there was nothing to prevent provincial booksellers from exactly reproducing a work upon the expiration of its copyright.

As it happened, the idea of originality played a somewhat different role in the literary property debate, one that was ultimately unfavorable to the case for perpetual copyright. To understand this, it is necessary to consider how the theory of originality was revived as a response to exchange-based conceptions of value. At one level, the theory seemed a reaction to these new ideas. The concept of imitation, if not its rhetorical practice, was central to claims for the value of exchange: circulation, as Kames suggested, enabled a naturally imitative human species to partake of improvements. For Young, this assumption was unacceptable because it ran counter to the individuation of discourse. Yet as an argument against the discourse of political economy, his theory of originality was a nonstarter because it provided no alternative account of the benefits to society of literary production. At most, it presented an obscurantist refurbishing of a labor account of value that attempted to reconstitute in the literary system the old normative hierarchy that had formerly upheld ideological assumptions about the role of property in a fixed social order.

Without this supporting structure of belief, Young and his fellow mythologizers had little to say about the social function of genius. Unable to explain why genius was worth promoting in a modern world, they indulged in primitivist fantasies about how original genius is "displayed in its utmost Vigour in the early and uncultivated Periods of Society which are peculiarly favourable to it."[60] Or, as Young did, they championed genius for its privatization of improvement: "How independent of the world is he, who can daily find new Acquaintance, that at once entertain, and improve him, in the little World, the minute but fruitful Creation, of his own mind?" Composition withdrew the poet-genius from "the thronged Walks of public Life, it gives us a respite, at least, from Care; a pleasing Pause of refreshing Recollection."[61] Under the old order, writing was produced for clear purposes: as moral or religious instruction, for career advancement and the memorializing of patrons, and in the service of state and commonwealth. No such outward-looking considerations entered into Young's idealizing of originality. His unique genius wrote only for himself, rejecting even the lofty didactic aims endorsed by Camden and Yates.

To see the mythology of genius as merely a rejection of exchange, however, is to miss its real historical significance for the cultural field and, within it, the literary property debate. The mythology represented as much a reaction to the discourse of political economy as its confirmation. In celebrating the act of writing as a refuge from public life, Young appeared to be stoically making the best of a situation in which poetic activity was being denied its former centrality in the moral economy of civil society. What he was really doing, though, was redefining literature as a modern profession, one whose practice required *specialized* labor. Poetic genius may have seemed to him the most exclusive of gifts, "the Key of which is denied to the rest of mankind."[62] But, as Smith demurred, "the very different genius which appears to distinguish men of different professions, when grown up to maturity, is not upon many occasions so much the cause, as the effect of the division of labour." Vanity, Smith supposed, prompted those in more exclusive professions to attribute their success to natural talent. But just as occupations grew more diverse and specialized as populations increased and markets expanded, so certain professions seemed more exclusive than others not by virtue of their specialization but as a consequence of scarce opportunities for success in an overcrowded market. The fewer the opportunities, the more these professions measured success not in financial terms but in degree of prestige: "To excel in any profession, in which but few arrive at mediocrity, is the most decisive mark of what is called genius or superior talents. The publick admiration which attends upon such distinguished abilities, makes always a part of their reward; a greater or smaller in proportion, as it is higher or lower in degree. It makes a considerable part of it in the profession of physick; a still greater perhaps in that of law; in poetry and philosophy it makes almost the whole." In these last professions, Smith added, public esteem comprised so great a portion of their reward as to make financial self-interest seem unworthy of genius, as if exercising literary talent for the sake of gain were "a sort of publick prostitution."[63] So rare was success in literary authorship, it seemed, that the profit motive had to be imagined as too poor an incentive for anyone to pursue it.

It became incumbent on Young and others to characterize authorship as specialized labor once a corresponding transformation was felt to have affected all other occupations, especially other activities in the literary system. I have argued elsewhere that the eighteenth century saw a change in perspective in how literature was valued: from valuing the instrumental benefits that poets produced to valuing the beneficial aesthetic effects that literary works had on readers.[64] The causes of this change were many and complex, but it may be helpful in this context to see it as consequent upon the division of labor and, by extension, as reflecting newer ideas about social order being set out in theories of political economy—and, at a longer distance, in appeals for liberty and popular sovereignty. For conservatives like Blackstone, the literary system was too small to be diversified and needed to be kept small so that learning would remain the employment of only a few. In such a system, as in the coterie worlds of the early modern period, it was less important that the roles of author, reader, patron, or bookseller be distinguished as that all writing be understood to contribute productively to the maintenance of virtue, hierarchy, and the fixed constitution of things.

By contrast, in an expanding market these same roles were sharply differentiated in the competencies required to perform them and in the nature of their obligations to society. Whereas in the past poets claimed to have been inspired by their gods, heroes, and patrons, the mythology of genius attributed the source of poetic authority neither to an external origin nor to the service that poets rendered. Genius was an innate disposition, one so determining, it was claimed, that it left poets unfit for other occupations or even normal conversation. Their authority was thus correlated to the degree that they heeded no inducement to write except their own highly individualized nature, whether imagined as the elusive poetical character, a bardic self-absorption, or, in Wordsworth's version, a "more than usual organic sensibility."[65] "A man of Genius," William Duff alleged, "is really a kind of different being from the rest of his species. The bent of his disposition, the complexion of his temper, the general turn of his character, his passions and his pursuits are for the most part very dissimilar from those of the bulk of mankind."[66] Solitary and self-taught, an original genius obeyed an inner compulsion to write, and he did so without regard for civic duty or for any reward except public esteem: "Admiration hath ever been the idol of Genius."[67] Other constructions of authorship during the period likewise made a virtue out of the writer's freedom from obligation and external authority, most notably the professional hero of Boswell's *Life of Johnson*, who spurned patrons and would not write except for money.

Booksellers, meanwhile, were as ever blamed for having commercialized the literary system out of self-interest and without regard for the greater good. But they were also viewed favorably by Johnson and others as the new "patrons of literature" whose business sense had prompted them to invest in large-scale undertakings, like Johnson's own dictionary.[68] Said one commentator, booksellers have become "for authors, what the monied capitalist is to the manufacturer." Writing after the decision of 1774, this commentator noted how relations within the literary system had been changed "by a sort of *division of labour*," whereby booksellers had interposed themselves between authors and readers, disrupting their formerly close connection to the point where their interests diverged. Inasmuch as they "facilitate the dispersion of literary produce," booksellers "*lower the market* of knowledge, and perhaps, in some degree, diminish the importance of authors, as they diffuse information more widely among men."[69]

The figure that underwent by far the most dramatic transformation was the reader. The rhetorical tradition had identified numerous effects that eloquent speech could have on audiences, but it had said little about what reading involved, the abilities it required, or its cognitive benefits beyond the pleasurable instruction that eloquent speech ideally provided. By the later eighteenth century, in contrast, an entire new discourse emerged to instruct the public on how to read and judge literary works. At readers' disposal was a huge array of publications designed to facilitate various aspects of their experience: reviews to help them select books, critical editions to aid their understanding, elocution handbooks to train their verbal mastery of literary works, and literary histories and biographies to deepen their knowledge. Each of these genres was seen as the product of specialized labor, but all of them presupposed that reading was itself an activity requiring a certain level of competence. Like genius, competence at reading was internalized insofar as it was assumed to depend on natural faculties of taste and judgment. Yet these faculties were seen as fundamentally unlike the imaginative powers needed to produce literature, innate to many more persons than creative talents were, and, most important, in need of cultivation through an ongoing course of study in literature and criticism. Reading became specialized work.

With discipline came agency and responsibility. Of all the newly specialized laborers in the literary system, readers assumed much of the burden of bringing to fruition the work of personal and social improvement. They were expected to refine their tastes and sensibilities, to form their moral being through immersion in the best works, and to transcend their own narrow views by transporting themselves imaginatively into the literary past and its fictive worlds. As Hugh Blair advised in his hugely influential *Lectures on Rhetoric and Belles Lettres* (1783), study might at best "assist and direct" genius, whereas "the exercise of taste is, in its native tendency, moral and purifying." Exercising the critical faculties individuated readers by teaching them "to admire and to blame with judgment, and not to follow the crowd blindly," while a failure to cultivate an early taste for reading could have negative consequences as much for society as for the unfortunate students: an inability to appreciate poetry was evidence "of their being prone to low gratifications, or destined to drudge in the more vulgar and illiberal pursuits."[70] Whereas in the past, it was the practitioners of eloquence and poetry who were tasked with providing youth with moral guidance, now it was readers who were responsible for educating themselves.

Readers similarly assumed much of the labor that authors had formerly undertaken during years of rhetorical training yet now avoided as harmful to their development. It was readers more than authors who stood to gain from educating themselves in the great books and, more especially, from confronting them in their authentic and most demanding form. Whereas for Young imitating canonical works inhibited writers from being original, for educators like Vicesimus Knox the originality of great books presented readers with a welcome hermeneutic challenge. Students, he advised, ought to study each discipline's founding documents in as close to authentic versions as possible: "One rule of the greatest consequence is, to read only or chiefly the original treatises in all the various departments of science, and of literature." Abstracts, compilations, and digests of important books "detract from the respect which is due to real knowledge and original compositions." But, Knox believed, students owed this respect as much to knowledge as to themselves. Their own individuation depended on an awareness of past writings, from which they could differentiate themselves by learning to express an author's sentiments in their "own words. In this exercise, the memory is exerted, and the style improved. We make what we write our own."[71] By doing precisely the kind of imitative exercises that authors had been doing for centuries, students could learn to become if not original creators then at least better readers and writers.

The idea of originality thus provided a rationale for keeping works unchanged in perpetuity, though this had to do more with readers than authors. Originality was the mark of an author's genius, but its preservation in a work's expression benefited readers in a way that a mere redaction of the author's ideas could not.[72] This shift from authors to readers as the foci of value had already been recognized by London booksellers who, increasingly during the period, commissioned authoritative editions of English writings to fuel a demand for authenticity and to reinforce their legal claim to these works. It is one of the ironies of literary history that Johnson, a champion of the common reader, wrote his *Lives* as prefaces to an edition that was deliberately designed to divert attention from the one reprint series, Bell's, that the common reader could afford.[73] Johnson's was the prestige edition. The London booksellers believed that Johnson's name before their "elegant and accurate edition of all the English Poets of reputation" might help them preserve at least a symbolic hold on their literary property following the defeat of 1774.[74] Yet even prior to their defeat, they had sought to retain their property in canonical works by surrounding them with scholarly apparatus in much the same way as landowners during the period were enclosing common property by improving its productivity. As Donaldson's lawyers protested, the notes and emendations supplied by a hireling editor "carry along with them a property in the book thus manufactured, and each critic becomes proprietor of a work which he was never capable of writing. In this way, not only the works of Shakespear, but those of Spenser, Ben Johnson, Butler, Milton, &c., have been appropriated by different commentators."[75]

All this scholarly activity had the effect, however, of elevating the value of these writings in a way that was counterproductive to the London monopoly's cause. In magnifying the aura of canonical English writings, authoritative editions made them appear as a cultural heritage whose enclosure seemed an affront to the people of Britain. They also heightened the sense that, as in the case of Johnson's Shakespeare and the later *Lives*, these writings ought to be preserved as prestige items, as works of genius that were to be rewarded with esteem rather than money. As Smith noted, excellence in any given profession seemed less vendible in direct proportion to how rare it was made to appear. By commissioning the production of prestige editions designed to enhance the aura of original genius, the London booksellers were effectively feeding the prejudices of those like Camden for whom financial gain was morally incompatible with genius. But whereas Camden objected to copyright on principle, the fact that editorial labors like Johnson's were being lavished on older English writings had the additional effect of strengthening the case for a limited copyright since it made these works seem less vendible and more deserving of admiration than contemporary publications that were currently covered by statute. As Enfield pointed out, a limited term of copyright provided no greater financial reward for enduring works of genius than it did for perishable ephemera. But if esteem was the appropriate reward for genius, it was difficult to see how honoring these works with special critical attention was not only a sufficient additional reward but a better one than an indefinite copyright.

Contrary to what Woodmansee and other Foucault-inspired historians of copyright have contended, the mythology of original genius undermined more than it strengthened the case for perpetual copyright. On the one hand, it offered the London booksellers a plausible justification for reproducing textually authentic versions of English works, versions over which they claimed exclusive ownership. It did so by characterizing original authors as specialized laborers who individuated discourse to such a degree that only authoritative editions of their writings could furnish readers with a true sense of their uniqueness. On the other hand, it was a mythology, a set of beliefs that derived its force from the sense that what it described lay outside conventional experience: if ideologies operate by creating chains of equivalence between disparate beliefs and practices, mythologies work in an opposite direction by presenting fictions of sublime exceptionality, of the extraordinary, heroic, or freakish. What

Young, Duff, and other proponents of the mythology hoped to accomplish was the establishment of a new standard of excellence in a literary system that was becoming increasingly commercialized and less beholden to old rhetorical notions of poetic value.

In their view, original authors were not merely better writers than most but exceptional beings who stood apart from a social world where personalities were formed on the basis of exchange and experience. Whereas ordinary mortals were to seek self-determination in public life and cultivate a taste for the civilizing power of great books, anyone with a spark of genius was told to remain aloof from mundane concerns and draw inspiration from no source other than his own preternaturally unique self. Far from pretending to advance a moral or economic rationale for literary writing, the mythology of original genius valorized the authorial profession by exempting it from the commercial ideology then being promulgated by the prophets of political economy. In portraying authors as immune to this ideology, the mythology refused the principle of equivalence by which, as the Mansfield court had supposed in *Millar v. Taylor*, a work's value to society was estimable by its sales. The work of original authors, according to the mythology, was of incalculable value, the more so for not being produced out of a desire for profit. And the more that authoritative editions of a work added luster to its uniqueness, the less it seemed right to treat it as alienable and exchangeable property.

The Invention of Tradition

The mythology's sentimental appeal was nevertheless not enough to clinch the defeat of perpetual copyright. The London trade's defenders were willing to concede that a work's cash value was an inadequate indicator of its merit or its author's original genius, although the problem, Justice Willes maintained, was the result of market failure under the existing limited term of copyright. In his view, a work could eventually earn as much money as its merit deserved were its copyright held in perpetuity. The thought may have been unpalatable to those who felt genius was priceless, but aristocratic prejudices like Camden's were not enough to dissuade copyright's defenders from thinking that a work of original genius ought to be entitled to both esteem *and* profit. They may not have been the same reward, just as a work's merit was not the same as its market price. Yet while not identical, profit and esteem could become commensurate over time. And while esteem might be preferable as a reward, it did not follow that one reward should necessarily preclude the other.

To counter this argument and win their case, the provincial booksellers had to argue that the greatest books enriched society in inestimable ways beyond the rewards they returned to their authors and publishers. This was not a straightforward argument to make, since it was not demonstrably clear how a monopoly on publications had a deleterious effect on the national economy in the same way that a cartel on commodities, like silver, impeded the growth of industry. Monopolies on goods and inventions, Smith maintained, hindered overall prosperity by limiting their supply: "the great loss is to the public, to whom all things are rendered less comeatible, and all sorts of work worse done."[76] Yet with books, which were already under monopoly control, the public did not stand to lose anything from the extension of copyright privileges into perpetuity, nor was it obvious what it stood to gain were those privileges kept to their statutory terms.

Anti-monopolists, like Yates, may have believed that an open market in publishing would allow new booksellers to expand their business, but it was not clear whether the demand for books could be sustained at a level high enough to support competition over the long term. There was some evidence for this demand: the trade in pirated books from Ireland and America was flourishing, and the London booksellers obviously felt that their control over older writings was well worth defending in court. But the evidence was not conclusive. As the book trade had never been unfettered, there was no historical precedent for believing that open commerce in canonical works was as economically desirable a policy as the free circulation of industrial goods. And there were many, like Blackstone, who supported that free circulation of manufactures but opposed the open commerce in publications on the grounds that the market for learning needed to remain small in order to preserve social order.

The provincial booksellers could always assert that it was impossible to gauge the market's potential for growth so long as the existing monopoly restricted its size. In this vein, they challenged the claim that copyright's statutory limits had caused market failure by arguing that if anything had distorted the market, it was not the law's term limits but its restraint on competition. A monopoly right enabled the London booksellers to set their own prices and reward authors as they saw fit, no matter how lengthy the term of copyright.[77] It was thus disingenuous of them to claim that their prices were unavoidably at variance with the quality of the books they published, or that meritorious authors were not properly compensated within the existing period of protection. The London publishers answered the charge by saying that they had no control over the demand for most books. In the case of most publications, Macaulay noted, it was in a bookseller's interest "to sell off at the most moderate price, as many editions as with all his art and industry he can dispose of."[78] And in the case of more expensive productions, Enfield added, their owners typically put out cheap editions "after a few years" to meet any ongoing demand "since the booksellers can never find it in their interest to preclude by far the most numerous class of their readers from purchasing books, by publishing only such editions as do not come within their compass."[79]

The copyright debate was not about new works whose popularity over the long term was difficult to predict, however. It was a contest over older works for which the demand had remained high for years after the expiration of their statutory copyright. These books, known collectively as the "English stock," were among the trade's most lucrative intellectual properties. In making their bid for an open market, the provincial booksellers assumed that demand for these books would remain robust even as their supply increased. The market, they believed, was not being exploited to its fullest, despite the London publishers' claims to the contrary. Though it could be subject to distorting influences, including the publication of prestige editions that inflated a book's merit, demand over time was a credible manifestation of the esteem that was due to a work's author. Said Kames, "The best authors write for fame: the more diffused their works are, the more joy they have."[80] Though Camden and other deifiers of genius might balk at the thought of valuing great works by numbers of copies sold, the idea of an open market for great books was at least compatible with their belief that genius was best rewarded with public admiration.

In making suppositions about what this market could bear, the provincial booksellers went much further than the Mansfield court in stressing the role of speculation in an exchange economy. Justice Aston had suggested that an unpublished work possessed value as property in the expectation of its future sales. But there was no reason to conclude from this, the provincial booksellers surmised, that the expectation of profit ended at the point of a volume's initial sales. If value was a function of expectation, a work of enduring popularity remained valuable so long as it was expected to sell or to generate improvements. By this logic, prosperity was not merely the sum of all individual profits at a given time, but encompassed both the existing and potential size of the market in terms of any real and projected opportunities it allowed for financial gain and personal betterment. The London booksellers were well aware of this: their intellectual properties were investments as much as they were assets, and they were willing to pay dearly for shares of the English stock whenever those works came up for sale in their Stationers Company. Yet even if they believed they were already reaching as many readers as possible, their monopoly blocked the market's potential for growth by constraining expectations for its products—by limiting their capitalization, as it were.

The key to the provincial booksellers' case, then, was to take exchange thinking to its logical conclusion by projecting expectations about the value of literature over time, into the perpetuity that their opponents claimed was the rightful term of common-law ownership. "Our booksellers," Kames remarked acerbically, "aiming at present profit, may not think themselves much concerned about futurity. But it belongs to judges to look forward; and it deserves to be duly pondered whether the interest of literature in general ought to be sacrificed to the pecuniary interest of a few individuals."[81] Only in a free market, the provincial booksellers maintained, would it be possible for society to take fullest advantage of the enduring investment that the greatest works represented.

As a corollary to their sense of exchange's boundless momentum, the opponents of perpetual copyright happily embraced the principle of equivalence that exchange thinking presupposed. A monopoly on books, they claimed, harmed all aspects of literature equally—the dissemination of learning, the vitality of public discourse, the refinement of manners, and the rise of British letters—and no less than the growth of the print trade. Perpetual copyright, according to Edmund Law, enabled the London booksellers to occupy "several Classic, or capital writers in our Language, ancient and modern" and to "secrete them from common use, and traffick with them among some of the combination everlastingly; to the no small detriment of the commonwealth of letters, which is hereby deprived of all the benefits arising from that grand source of Improvement, the emulation of various artizans; who would constantly be striving to surpass each other in the usefulness, elegance and cheapness of such works, had they all an equal, incontested right to the fabrication and disposal of them."[82]

Law was evidently referring to booksellers, but his argument makes virtually no distinction between their commercial activities, the cultural roles played by authors and readers ("the commonwealth of letters"), and the divergent criteria of literary value ("usefulness, elegance and cheapness"). Their equivalence is further underscored by the financial metaphors of "benefits" accruing from "capital" authors and by the implication that exchange rates and aggressive competition ("constantly . . . striving to surpass each other") in an open market ought to dictate the artisanal value of works in print. The argument's most striking implication, though, is that the literary system itself ought to be viewed as an economy that thrives on exchange: for a healthy level of literary production to be maintained, Law suggested, there must exist conditions adequate to ensure the commercial and cultural *re*production of works, their ongoing reintroduction and circulation among generations of authors and readers. In restricting such reproduction, perpetual copyright discouraged new writing, obstructed the socialization of the public, and undermined the survival of the very canon the London booksellers had so long claimed as their own.

Exchange is wealth. This belief, a central tenet of political economy, provided the provincial booksellers with an argumentative advantage over the London stationers. The latter needed to exempt canonical writings from the principle of equivalence in order to justify keeping their intellectual property from circulating outside their company. But in arguing for this exemption, they faced the impossible task of identifying the improvements that these works could ostensibly produce only under circumstances of monopoly control. Their opponents, in contrast, had only to insist on the utter equivalence of all value, whether it involved utility, beauty, or property ("usefulness, elegance and cheapness"). To them, improvement designated simply any appreciable advance in an economy's capacity for growth, so any consideration of the specific improvements that resulted from literary commerce was immaterial to their argument. All that mattered, they believed, was that exchange be permitted to happen without impediment.

Crucially, it was possible for the anti-copyright pamphleteers to envision the dynamic work of exchange extending prospectively into a distant futurity as well as retrospectively to the beginnings of culture itself. Responding to the claim that originality deserved permanent royalties, the author of *An Enquiry into the Nature and Origin of Literary Property* (1762) said that he found "very few Productions of modern Authors . . . whose Sentiments are new or original." Contemporary works, he believed, were inescapably intertextual, and if perpetual copyright were upheld, the courts would eventually be swamped by lawsuits brought by authors eager to fix their uniqueness: "Poet would commence Action against Poet, and Historian against Historian, complaining of literary Trespasses. . . . The Courts of Law must sagely determine Points in polite Literature, and Wit be entered on Record."[83] Echoing the sentiment, Lord Gardenston of the Scottish court averred that if the principle of literary property were taken to an extreme, quotation alone could be considered "literary theft." Worse, the canon would be off-limits to new poets seeking inspiration. "Who steals from common authors," said Gardenston, "steals trash; but he who steals from a *Spencer*, a *Shakespeare*, or a *Milton*, steals the fire of heaven, and the most precious gifts of nature."[84] Where Young spurned "borrowed riches," Gardenston inherited the gifts of the canonical gods. Gone were the dwarves on the shoulders of giants; here were authors building on a tradition. "The Interest of Literature," the *Enquiry*'s author insisted, demanded the free exchange of ideas, sentiments, and techniques among all authors. "The Learning of the present Age," he proposed, "may be considered as a vast Superstructure, to the rearing of which the Geniuses of past Times have contributed their Proportion of Wit and Industry; to what Purpose would they have contributed if each of them could insist that none should build on their Foundations?"[85]

The classical trope of writers building on foundations no doubt recalled the old rhetorical doctrine of imitation. But the image of a superstructure to which geniuses contribute with the aim of inspiring others suggests a dynamic mechanism of exchange that can produce value only if it is accessible to all.[86] What was most deplorable about a monopoly on books, the anti-copyright critics insisted, was that it claimed retrospective control over canonical works that were integral to the formation of British culture. The canon was heritage, and the London booksellers were no more entitled to own it than to possess the culture that produced it. Harry Levin noted that the idea of a national literary tradition emerged only in the last 250 years.[87] Its origins, I would suggest, can be traced to the great literary property debate of the eighteenth century. The anti-copyright pamphleteers relied on the idea of tradition for its symbolic power, for its enabling sense of social and historical continuities that could never be contained despite the efforts of a few wealthy booksellers. In this way, the idea was as much a fabrication of the period as other important traditions that were then being "invented," from the national anthem and the British flag to the forged folklore of Ossian and Rowley.[88] Ossian, indeed, was cited by Lord Auchinleck of the Scottish court as an example of a canonical figure whose works had been so deeply absorbed into the cultural fabric as to transcend questions of ownership: "Let us consider, that anciently very valuable performances were preserved only by the memory. It is said *Homer* was so, and *Ossian*.... The poem of *Chevy-chace*, so much celebrated, and upon which we have a criticism by Mr. *Addison*, was, in my remembrance, repeated by every body.—Was there a *copy* of this little heroic poem? What privilege could the author have in it, after he had let one man get it by heart?"[89]

The provincial booksellers arguably won their day in court as much on the strength of their economic arguments about the benefits of free trade as on the emotional force of the idea of a literary tradition. Conceivably they could have argued merely to have shares in the English stock opened for sale to booksellers like themselves who were not part of the London cartel. Doing so might have presented financial advantages to cartel members, who would have seen the value of their investments grow as a result of increased competition for their shares, and it would have accorded with the marketplace assumption that wealth accrues from the exchange of property. Yet quite apart from there being no legal grounds for compelling the London monopoly to expand its membership, the provincial booksellers would likely not have been able to persuade the British judges and the House of Lords to support their cause if they were seen as acting purely out of self-interest, as their London rivals clearly were. By tying their interests to a grander vision of a cultural heritage whose value transcended any profits it might yield to individual owners, they made their commercial hopes seem at one with the aspirations of the nation.

The economic and emotional claims of the provincial booksellers were not strictly compatible. The London booksellers, as I already noted, tried to exempt works of genius from the principle of equivalence so as to justify their own monopoly's exception in a regime of open commerce. The critics of copyright did not face this problem and could tout the wealth-creating benefits of exchange without having to distinguish between financial profit, literary merit, public knowledge, and any other value in which this wealth might consist. But in presenting themselves as the champions of the literary tradition, the provincial publishers were themselves resisting the full implications of equivalence by positing a determinate if transhistorical value that was antecedent to any wealth its exchange might produce. For the purposes of their argument, a belief in the importance of tradition did not have to be made consistent with faith in the market. But this inconsistency meant that canonical works played a paradoxical role in their rationale for a free trade in books. These works, the provincial booksellers suggested, ought to be exchanged among a present and future reading public to ensure social prosperity, yet at the same time these works constituted a tradition that could not be privately controlled because it was already the possession of the people.

The inconsistency was especially evident whenever the provincial booksellers attempted to exploit nationalist sentiments, which were inevitably bound up with the appeal of invented traditions. Donaldson, in his case before the Edinburgh court, played to Scottish feelings of being politically and economically marginalized by English interests. A London-based monopoly, his lawyers averred, was "extremely injurious" to "the public, and particularly to Scotland," and they cited as evidence the fact that English publishers had hiked prices on books destined for resale through Scottish retailers, including books "composed by Scotchmen." The English people, they added, would not tolerate a situation in which the tables were turned and a Scottish bookseller was fortunate enough to purchase "the pretended copy-rights of Milton, Shakespear, Locke, Newton, and all the best authors presently claimed by the London booksellers." Not only was it unlikely that London booksellers "would trust to the Aberdeen or Orkney bookseller for supplying the English market," but more important, Donaldson's counsel supposed:

> It would certainly appear hard to every Englishman, to see his country deprived of the right of printing her best authors. It would be said that these great men did not write merely to get a little pittance to themselves or their families, but to enlighten mankind; and that the race of booksellers, after being indemnified a hundred times over, had no right to deprive their country, or prevent the public, from having the full benefit of such useful works; that England had the best right to possess and enjoy the writings of those great men to whom she had given birth, education, and protection, and was not for ever to be at the mercy of a Scotch bookseller.[90]

The statement was a caustic rebuke of English arrogance, but as an expression of nationalist sentiment, it was not an argument that Donaldson could push very far without undermining his case for free trade. That a nation "had the best right to possess" its canonical writings argued not so much against monopolies as in favor of transferring the monopoly on Scottish works to Edinburgh. But Donaldson, who a decade earlier had set up his own shop in London, was fighting for an open market in all English-language publishing, not for control merely of books written by fellow Scots. Perhaps not surprisingly, Donaldson did not dare repeat his argument before the English lords, nor did the Scottish judges evidently see fit to respond to it directly.[91]

Donaldson's curiously quibbling assertion that unfair laws can deprive a country *or* prevent a public from enjoying canonical writings nonetheless suggests something important about the idea of a public domain. What the concept does is suspend the often contentious relation of nationalism to free trade by setting at intervals the positiveness of nationalist sentiment, which emphasizes an enduring cultural identity, and the speculative indeterminacy of political economy, which presupposes a dynamic system of exchange stretching into futurity. In a public domain any conflict between the right of a people to define its own traditions and the public's interest in constantly striving for improvement is held off by virtue of these desires being projected in opposite temporal directions. A literary tradition is a retrospective construct. While the works it comprises may have long been esteemed, a tradition essentializes these literary works as a legacy, treating it as a people's shared possession, the preserve of its identity, and even as its creation. A tradition cannot be altered without changing the culture. The national literary tradition, implied copyright's critics, was a cynosure of Englishness or, as Donaldson would have it, of Scottishness within Britishness.

At the same time, a public domain also designates those writings that have yet to enter the tradition, including those yet to be written whose value can nonetheless be prospectively envisioned as investments that will benefit later generations. These writings are neither canon nor heritage, at least not yet, and therefore bear only a hypothetical relation to a people's current sense of itself— though, in theory, this cultural identity will eventually be modified under the influence of these writings. Accordingly, the potential body of work they represent is said to belong to the public and not a people, to a public domain rather than a nation. It might be more precise to say that these writings belong to the people that a public sees itself becoming, since it is likely that the works themselves, if they exist at all, are currently under private control. But it is extremely difficult to conceive of the potential value of this work without analogizing it to the importance of canonical works whose copyrights have long since lapsed. Hence Johnson could refer to this hypothetical canon only as if it were already public property. "For the general good of the world," he told Boswell, "whatever valuable work has once been created by an authour, and issued out by him, should be understood as no longer in his power, but as belonging to the publick."[92]

The idea of a public domain makes it possible to make economic arguments for change seem reconcilable with ideological arguments for cultural continuity.

But these arguments are not in fact reconcilable, which is to say that the idea of a public domain is incoherent. From a cultural point of view, works in the public domain belong to all, whereas from an economic, they belong to none. And even if these propositions are tenable from different perspectives, that still leaves the rationale for a public domain founded on a circular argument that conflates *is* with *ought*. Some works, according to the cultural argument, are so deeply part of our identity that they ought to belong to all of us. To cite one modern jurist, "works are relegated to the public domain *to become* the heritage of all humanity." Yet, to cite another, "the public must be able freely to copy, modify, and reformulate the works that *have become* a part of its cultural matrix."[93] It is impossible to infer from these two statements whether works become heritage before or after a copyright's expiration. If works become part of a cultural matrix only after protection lapses, the term of copyright can conceivably be extended indefinitely without harming this matrix. Yet if works become part of the culture before protection ends, temporal limits are irrelevant. The public domain is justified on the basis of arbitrary assumptions about how and when works become heritage, though none of these assumptions has a direct bearing on the actual scope of the public domain, which encompasses all works that have fallen out of copyright, at present and in the future, and not just the ones that have been celebrated for their formative influence.

Similarly, from an economic perspective, improvement is at once the ground and the effect of the law; it justifies copyright legislation and serves as its measure of success, which means that there is no way of establishing whether success has been achieved. This circularity is not a problem so long as improvement is seen as open-ended progress, always encouraged and always achieved. However, there remains a deeper ambiguity, since the improvement that learning provides is also the condition of the public sphere where individuals meet to decide what counts as a sufficient good. Learning is the public sphere's eligibility requirement: people must be educated in order to participate disinterestedly. In Habermas's account, the public "from the outset was a reading public."[94] Copyright regulates the learning that is seen as a prerequisite for taking part in public debate. Yet copyright involves a trade-off: it encourages learning's production by restricting some of its uses. This raises a difficult question, one that is by turns epistemological and ideological: how can the public decide which uses of learning are more conducive to its identity, prosperity, and deliberations if legal restrictions on these uses must already be in place before the public can make this decision? Attempting an answer to this inevitably entails envisioning an ideal public, one that negates the trade-off by being effectively both *is* and *ought*, at once the ground and the effect of the law, the people that a public simultaneously imagines itself to be and hopes to become.

Despite the incoherence of its rationale, the public domain remains an enormously appealing legal abstraction, being part and parcel of a modern democratic conception of the public whose function it is to certify value itself. Prior to the advent of statutory copyright, the value of any printed work was underwritten by the Crown, under whose authority the print trade was allowed to operate, the Stationers Company was protected from competition, books were licensed for publication, and works that disseminated essential political, religious, or customary knowledge were published in correct editions. With the end of licensing and the passage of the Statute of Anne, the Crown formally ceded control over commercial aspects of the trade to the stationers, who were to defend their interests through the courts. In doing so, it confirmed what was fast becoming apparent, namely that the market was determining the value of most books other than censurable publications over which the state still exercised moral authority. By 1774, the rationality of political economy, which was beginning to inform decisions at the highest levels about the general good, had revealed that in fact the market estimated value only at the point of exchange and that its estimations constantly changed as they followed the ceaseless movement of capital. The market therefore promised prosperity and freedom from state control at the cost of precluding any fixed norm that might guide far-reaching decisions about the common good.

To conservatives, like Camden, it was bad enough that the market reduced all value to its cash equivalent, yet worse was its indeterminacy, which they saw as a fundamental amorality and lack of customary standards for judging literary excellence. But even economic liberals recognized that the open trade in printed books promised greater prosperity through their ongoing exchange without offering any security as to the value of literature to the social order as a whole. Mansfield tried to address this problem by grounding the ownership of property in an older account of labor value but, as he eventually came to realize, doing so impeded the market's capacity to produce wealth; copyright, he conceded a decade after the 1774 decision, ought to be limited so "that the world may not be deprived of improvements."[95] The mythology of original genius similarly represented an attempt to supply the market with a providential source of value, but this source was irrelevant to decision-making about the common good since whatever authority it possessed was contingent on its utter exemption from public discourse and the world of commerce.

A realm of public intellectual property, with the canon serving as its nonmonetary reserve and any projected social benefit of writing as its credit, had therefore to be envisioned to make moral and conceptual sense of the private ownership of intellectual activity. The idea of a public domain made it possible to imagine that there could be a source and a standard of literary value even as this value remained susceptible to fluctuation in an exchange economy. Any contradiction between the absoluteness of the standard and the relativity of the market could be deferred to a history or futurity where it no longer seemed to matter. The idea of a public domain enabled the provincial booksellers to win their case because the concept appealed to both conservatives, for whom the value of learning transcended its cover price, and liberals, for whom this value was inestimable from the perspective of the present. For Camden, a public domain was a commons as natural as the elements: "If there be anything in this World, my Lords, common to Mankind, Science and Learning are in their nature *publici Juris*, and they ought to be free and general as Air or Water."[96] For free marketeers, through that same domain lay the high road to Britain's commercial and imperial triumph: "It is therefore the Interest of the Public to take off all Restraints that Statute has not laid on, that a more free and generous Emulation may be spread over the Nation; that Knowledge and Virtue may be more universally diffused, and English Authors, by an Export-trade, spread over the World."[97] For both groups, the idea of the public domain functioned as both copyright's defining opposite and its guarantee. Not only was the idea needed to justify why private persons ought not to have indefinite control over works of learning on which both prosperity and identity depended, but more than this, it represented the very learning, prosperity, and identity that copyright was ultimately intended to encourage.

For this reason, the idea was more than a latter-day version of the old Roman category of *res extra commercium*. Just as the public had displaced the state as the steward of the common good, so the public domain was the standard that replaced the Crown's former authority over all books. This was soon confirmed in the aftermath of another legal contest, begun just a few weeks before the lords were to rule on perpetual copyright. The bookseller Thomas Carnan was accused by the Stationers Company of invading the Crown's prerogative copyright in almanacs, the printing of which, the stationers claimed, had been granted to them by James I as a monopoly right. In reply, Carnan claimed that the stationers' editions of these works failed to meet the standard of correctness on which the prerogative was based and, besides, almanacs could only get better were they produced in response to market pressures. "The way to make them correct," he declared, "is to permit an emulation and rivalship."[98] Ignoring the economic argument, the judges, among them Blackstone, ruled for Carnan on the grounds that the Crown's copyright covered only editions it had officially authorized. In a subsequent bid to save this profitable part of their business, the stationers lobbied to have their monopoly recognized by statute. Acting as Carnan's counsel, Thomas Erskine told the Commons that monopolies were an anachronism that, if restored, would rise up "like a tare among the rich fields of trade, which the wisdom of your laws has blown into a smiling harvest all around the globe." Worse, passage of the proposed legislation would be a "dangerous infringement of the general freedom of the press" since it would effectively reinstitute state control over the reproduction of learning. In denouncing it, he said, "I lose sight of my client, and feel that I am speaking for myself,— for every man in England."[99] The legislation failed to pass, and *Stationers Company v. Carnan* would go on to receive far less attention from commentators than *Donaldson v. Becket*, perhaps because, unlike the question of literary property, its outcome quickly came to seem a foregone conclusion.

Some Consequences

With the defeat of perpetual copyright, all works first published in England and Scotland before 1746 entered the public domain. There followed a publishing boom on a scale far greater than anyone could have anticipated. As William St. Clair has extensively documented, the boom had multiple seismic effects throughout the industry and society at large, which dramatically altered the conditions for literature's production and reception: a race to produce comprehensive anthologies of canonical texts, a steep increase in the number of titles produced annually, longer print runs and falling prices for old books, unprecedented profits and bankruptcies in the industry, many new publishing firms and venues, major innovations in printing technology and lower costs of manufacturing, scores of bestselling miscellanies, abridgments, and textbook anthologies aimed at children and new readers, and an "explosion" in reading throughout the nation.[100]

The defeat led to other, less material changes, a few of which are worth mentioning since they involved public perceptions of literary value. First, the massive expansion of the public domain heightened the sense that the national canon was made up primarily of *old* works. Prior to the defeat, the canon included works by Shakespeare, Milton, and other authors from previous centuries, though equal pride of place was given to recent writers, whether standard-bearers of neoclassical correctness, like Pope, or new voices of sensibility, like Gray. Perpetual copyright helped to maintain the canon's modernity. Reprints of older works were infrequent and expensive, while leading miscellanies like Dodsley's showcased new writing whose ownership was easier to secure. That the canon was both old and new helped sustain two divergent accounts of literary value. Despite noisy quarrels over ancients and moderns, it was possible to cherish older works for their enduring truths and the continuity they provided with an antique past, and equally possible to celebrate living authors for improving the nation's literary culture. Dryden could look back on England's literary history and see something like a tradition forming through the "lineal descents and clans" that linked him to literary fathers like Chaucer and Spenser, while also believing that the writers of his generation had refined the language and its numbers, as well as the taste and manners of their day.[101]

Literary collections produced after 1774, by contrast, contained a significantly higher quotient of older writing and were often sold on the strength of their selections from big names like Milton or Dryden. Moreover, these collections were greatly outnumbered on bookstore shelves by a growing array of newly available reprints and multivolume anthologies of classic English texts, their canonicity enhanced by the accompanying annotations, illustrations, and critical introductions. The ubiquity of this old canon attested to its authority, as did its stability. Its core, stretching from Chaucer to Cowper, stayed largely unchanged for a century.[102] A number of midcentury authors were eventually dropped, but none from the distant past were added since publishers saw little commercial point in reviving the work of forgotten authors, like Donne. More important, thanks to a series of successful campaigns beginning in 1808 to lengthen the copyright term, the public domain would not be significantly enlarged until the second half of the nineteenth century, when writings from the Romantic period began to fall out of copyright. As a result, the work of the most esteemed writers after Cowper would not appear alongside the old canon until updated anthologies of English literature began to be produced in the 1870s. The extensions to the terms of copyright were also accompanied by sharply escalating prices for new books, which put them beyond the reach of most consumers, who had to stick with the old works they had likely been reading since their youth. With these old works getting older by the year, the gap between the canonical past and the literary present grew ever wider for much of the reading public. For these readers, canonical literature performed the role of preserving cultural traditions more than it did a modernizing function in remaking those traditions.

Second, the copyright debate convinced many that the value of literary works could not be reliably established during the period of statutory protection. In effect, the test of time was keyed to the terms of copyright legislation. "A period of fourteen Years is a sure Test of every book," Donaldson's lawyers insisted. "The term of legal protection," Gardenston concurred, "outlives the great bulk of books that are published. Nine hundred and ninety-nine of a thousand have little merit but their novelty. . . . How few books published in the last century are re-printed in this? How few books of this will be re-printed in the next?"[103] Johnson, who is credited with reintroducing the Horatian test of a century, initially endorsed a perpetual copyright, but later reversed his view and favored a limited though lengthy term. Perhaps the protracted legal wrangling with Tonson over the Shakespeare copyright led to his change of heart. Boswell reported that in 1763 Johnson advocated a term of sixty years. A few years later, during the period of his "Preface" to Shakespeare, Johnson extended this limit to a hundred years.[104] By the decisive year 1774, Johnson had reduced his test by half. "In fifty years," he told Strahan, "far the greater number of books are forgotten and annihilated, and it is for the advantage of learning that those which fifty years have not destroyed should become *bona communia*, to be used by every scholar as he shall think best."[105]

That Johnson repeatedly revised his estimate of how long the test of time might take, and did so in the context of discussing the optimal duration of copyright, was indicative of how exchange thinking was already informing assumptions about literary value. Few critics before Johnson, including Horace, had taken the idea of a test of time seriously: better to trust men of learning, they advised, than to follow obsolete tastes. It was only once value began to be estimated on the basis of market expectations rather than notions of intrinsic worth that the test of time could begin to seem a credible empirical check on any undue critical bias or enthusiasm that might attend the reception of new books. As Johnson made clear in his "Preface" to Shakespeare, the reputations of contemporary writings could be sustained by "the modes of artificial life" for years before their genuine merit might be verified by "length of duration and continuance of esteem." Or, in market terms, the value of new publications was susceptible to inflationary bubbles that could be corrected only when evidence of long-term demand for these products became available. Only then, following a series of "gradual and comparative" estimates of their investment value, was the risk to booksellers sufficiently lessened to permit a stable consensus to emerge as to the works' profitability, a consensus that was reflected in the high price of shares in the English stock.[106] How soon consensus would form in relation to new books could be to a degree inferred from experience. But the test of time remained an empirical measure of consensus, a retrospective confirmation of a work's staying power, and had no determinative force on when new works could be expected to become canonical. Applying the test prospectively to decide when works ought to enter the public domain was as speculative an exercise as making predictions about the market.

One upshot of this indeterminacy was that owners of intellectual properties would henceforth make emotional pleas for longer terms of protection by playing up the contingent nature of authorial fortunes. In 1814, the term for all works was set at twenty-eight years or the life of the author, since it was felt that the original legislation took no account of the hardship that might befall an author's family in the event he or she died before the expiration of the initial fourteen-year term.[107] Thomas Talfourd's 1837 bill to extend the term to sixty years met with considerable opposition, yet a compromise was reached five years later whereby authors were for the first time granted postmortem protection: copyright was extended through the author's lifetime plus seven years or was forty years from a work's publication, whichever was longer. Speaking against the bill,

Thomas Babington Macaulay pointed out the fruitlessness of arguing over incentives that would be "enjoyed more than half a century after we are dead, by somebody, we know not by whom, perhaps by somebody unborn, by somebody utterly unconnected with us."[108] Yet acknowledging the uncertainty over what, if any, impact copyright might have on later generations was hardly an objection to extending its term. Talfourd suggested as much in characterizing his opponents as "mere speculators, like ourselves, on the probabilities of the distant future."[109]

A third consequence, widely noted at the time and since corroborated by St. Clair and others, was a gradual yet significant shift in publishing priorities. Their shares in the English stock having been rendered worthless by the repeal of perpetual copyright, the London booksellers tried at first to retain the old canon as a tentpole of their business by co-investing in editions of the English classics and then by copying from each other's lists. The demand thereafter for reprints and remainders would remain strong, though the old monopoly firms would eventually find their control of this market being usurped by specialist booksellers, like Lackington and Tegg. The trade was by then seeking profits elsewhere: in new literary properties, exclusive contracts, and publications that promised quicker returns on investment. By 1818, John Murray, Byron's publisher, was telling Parliament that he was much less concerned than authors were about the duration of copyright since he could expect only 1 percent of new properties to continue selling beyond fourteen years.[110] Established houses like his were thriving, but their focus was now squarely on forms of writing designed for ready consumption by a wide reading public. These presses continued for a time to court an elite market by issuing thin volumes of poetry in small print runs, but poetry's share of the market had already shrunk dramatically. By the 1820s, novels were the most profitable genre among stand-alone literary publications, while most publishers had long since come to rely on magazines, reviews, and newspapers for the bulk of their revenues. Periodical publication offered more venues for new writing, though most of it took the form of critical reviews and essays. "Prose," as Lee Erickson has suggested, "became the currency of the day."[111]

Given this shift in priorities, literature's role in public life became ambivalent. On the one hand, the literature of the past dominated the national culture as never before. Readers at all social levels were at least aware of *Paradise Lost* and *The Seasons*, and more than likely they had become acquainted with them in school or through sermons and public readings. Canonical works circulated in a broad range of editions and formats and were a frequent subject of adaptations, commentaries, and pictorial representations. Canonical authors were treated as public icons and communal property, their birthplaces and tombs turned into tourist attractions, their manuscripts and personal effects housed in public archives, and their portraits made to grace monuments and institutions. They had already been celebrated for some time as a common legacy and as the emblems and ornaments of national identity. But more and more they were equally seen as public goods that were essential to the continuance of this identity. As Carlyle said, Shakespeare's writings were "a real, marketable, tangibly useful possession" precisely because they enabled people throughout Britain's empire and former colonies, both now and "a thousand years hence," to "say to one another, 'Yes, this Shakespeare is ours; we produced him, we speak and think by him; we are of one blood and kind with him.'"[112]

On the other hand, following the ferment of the 1790s, literature seemed to recede somewhat from the currents of public debate. Literary writings that addressed social concerns increasingly did so from a position outside the mainstream, as expressions of radical or plebeian protest that demanded political recognition for groups heretofore excluded from decision-making. Within the mainstream, there were plenty of periodical outlets where writers could discuss public topics, yet many authors felt that the success of the reviews, which by commercial necessity were written to appeal to a broad readership, augured the decline of serious literature.[113] Much new writing in romances and verse narratives played to a sense of cultural heritage by dealing with the national past while engaging little with the present. New aesthetic theories stressed literature's effects on the private sensibility but said little about its social function. Authors like Wordsworth may have spoken fervently of the benefits that literature promised to language and knowledge, but none of these benefits, they felt, was readily appreciable by a contemporary public.

This was one reason that Wordsworth fought throughout his career for the reinstitution of perpetual copyright. Like its earlier defenders, he insisted that only permanent rights could adequately reward immortal genius. "The law, as it now stands," he wrote in 1808, "merely consults the interest of the useful drudges of Literature, or of flimsy and shallow writers, whose works are upon a level with the taste and knowledge of the age."[114] However, much as Kames and other advocates of a public domain had supposed, he also insisted that the value of new literature could scarcely be imagined from a present perspective. A great and original writer could be recognized as such only once he had created "the taste by which he is to be enjoyed."[115] Accordingly, copyright had to be extended because under the current terms the improvements that new works could produce were likely to be recognized only after their copyright had expired. Like Kames, then, Wordsworth projected literature's value into an ideal future fundamentally unlike the existing public sphere. Yet such was the incoherence of the public domain that whereas Kames believed this future would happen as a result of literary works becoming widely available, for Wordsworth it would come about regardless of copyright's term. As Talfourd, his ally in Parliament, put it, copyright was payment for benefits the public could contemplate but had yet to receive: "I call on those who anticipate successive changes in society, to acknowledge their debt to those who expand the vista of the future, and people it with goodly visions."[116]

The distinction between public ideas and private invention greatly antedated the literary property debate of the eighteenth century. Horace used the conceit in his *Ars Poetica* when he advised young writers on how to revitalize well-worn subjects: "The common stock will become your private property [*publica materies priuati iuris erit*] if you don't linger on the broad and vulgar round, or anxiously render word for word."[117] The copyright debate, however, made the distinction a matter of legal and economic purport. More than this, the defeat of perpetual copyright resulted in very altered conditions for literature's production and reception, conditions that in turn helped to intensify the ancient belief that literature could be at once traditional and transformative. That a public domain of canonical writings was discernible only in long hindsight or distant posterity meant that new works were perceived to have at most the potential to perform literature's supreme social functions of both preserving and remaking the national culture. Despite its economic origins, this idea of literature's potential value would eventually form the basis of modern theories of the avant-garde, wherein it would serve as a credible justification for keeping art out of the commercial mainstream, resisting its commodification, and granting cultural distinction to artists who refuse, as Wordsworth put it, "to court the living generation."[118] A new work, much like new property, might be greeted with great expectations of its possible value, but its worth in helping to unify and revolutionize society could not be publicly ascertained until after it had gone through an extended process of exchange and circulation. It had to be read by multiple and divergent generations of readers before it could become heritage and turn the public into a people.

CHAPTER TWO

The Fate of Style in an Age of Intellectual Property

The decision of 1774 upheld limits on the term of copyright, but jurists at the time also debated other restrictions on the law's scope. The subject of this chapter is the idea–expression dichotomy, the legal principle that copyright does not protect a work's ideas and sentiments but only the arrangement of words through which they are expressed. The principle represents the most important restriction on the scope of protection afforded to works whose copyright has not yet expired. While not set out in early copyright legislation, it was recognized throughout the eighteenth century as a check on the private control of public discourse. The London booksellers invoked the principle at the height of the literary property debate to defend themselves from the charge that their monopoly impeded the circulation of ideas. More generally, both sides of the debate argued over whether it was in fact possible for property rights to inhere in a work's verbal form but not its content. And decades before the debate began, the principle was cited in at least one early infringement case, which may suggest that it was already a working guideline within the trade.[1]

Most early contests over infringement involved unauthorized abridgments of previously published works, which courts during the period usually permitted on grounds of public utility.[2] Only toward the end of the eighteenth century did judges begin to rule on more specific forms of infringement, such as the copying of maps, charts, and other nontextual material. Thereafter, in a disorderly history of decisions, courts in Britain and America declared that copyright did not protect methods, facts, titles, themes, plots, or idioms, not to mention the law and ultimately the entire cultural vocabulary of words, conventions, and beliefs that are the raw ingredients of writing. This realm of the uncopyrightable, now called the "commons," remains deliberately vague at its edges and open to challenge for the simple reason that, unlike the public domain of works that have fallen out of copyright, courts have found it easier to define copyright in negative terms—by limiting its scope—than to identify the many components of discourse that it ought to encompass.

The specific discursive feature I am concerned with here is literary style. Style can be a point of contention in disputes over forms of nonliterary intellectual property, like trademarks or designs. In a number of US decisions involving printed ephemera, such as greeting cards and film posters, style has been granted protection as part of a work's "total concept and feel" in instances where an offending work replicated an earlier work's style in relation to the same subject matter.[3] Most significantly, literary style can be taken as evidence of originality in the case of factual reports that demonstrate no other sign of creative input. A 1921 decision ruled that while news was not protectable, a newspaper article could be awarded protection because it had "a peculiar power of portrayal, and a felicity of wording and phrasing, well calculated to seize and hold the interest of the reader, which is quite beyond and apart from the mere setting forth of the facts."[4]

Apart from these exceptions, copyright protects the expression of a style in a given work, but not style itself to the degree that it can be abstracted from expression. Courts have treated literary style as a set of formal techniques—a UK decision in 1999–2000 cited Hopkins's sprung rhythm as an example—that is equivalent to an unprotectable idea rather than to protectable expression.[5] A style can certainly be replicated in other contexts without thereby rendering it unrecognizable. If styles cannot be copied, then forgers, hoaxers, and many ghostwriters would be out of business, journals would not have their house styles, professions their discourses, or parodists their targets. The range of familiar stylistic imitations is vast, from ersatz medievalisms to the stock verbal mannerisms of pulp fiction. Much smaller may be the number of styles that have come to be identified with certain authors, but they too can be imitated, although not plagiarized.

The law may consider literary style for all intents and purposes equivalent to ideas but, crucially, it accords less importance to a work's formal features than to its content. It recognizes no possible competition between stylistically similar works on different subjects because it operates on the assumption that no two works on different subjects can be identical. Though copyright disputes may be decided on the basis of differences in expression, such disputes have arisen only in relation to works on similar subjects or of strictly factual matter. The law assumes that the value of intellectual property can be determined only on the basis of a work's content, even if that content is itself not protectable. The law rewards creativity in ideas by protecting their expression in a work, but it rewards creativity in expression only if there is otherwise no creativity at the level of content. Content has priority. With respect to most types of writing, the law presents no incentive or disincentive for pursuing either stylistic imitation or originality. A work's expression may represent a particular manifestation of its author's style, but the law does not encourage authors to define their own styles any more than it prevents anyone from riding on an author's coattails by mimicking his or her style. Copyright treats style the same as an idea insofar as it attributes a right of property on the basis of the expression of either, but it is indifferent to the value of style as a mode of creativity except in rare instances where style represents a work's sole original feature.

The law's indifference is surprising in view of the value that early rationales for copyright attached to literary style as evidence of authorial uniqueness and thus as justification for granting authors a monopoly privilege in their own writings. Yet it is precisely because copyright's proponents treated style as a particularized mode of discourse through which authors defined their identity that there was no felt need to use the law to encourage it. Indeed, some defenders of perpetual copyright worried that the law as it stood might unduly favor works of stylistic merit over those whose originality lay in their ideas and doctrines. Their opponents essentially agreed with them on this point by noting that most writings were not stylistically distinctive, but they concluded from this that copyright protection could not be universally extended to all works if stylistic indexes of ownership were discernible only in a few. Both sides thus took the view that style, if it graced a work at all, was a private feature of discourse, the product of an author's skill and sensibility. Stylistic creativity, unlike creativity in ideas, did not require legal or commercial encouragement, they believed, since it would naturally come about as a verbal reflection of an author's unique self. The law could be indifferent to style, neither protecting nor promoting it, because stylistic innovation could be expected to happen regardless of legal regulation or economic incentive.

In thinking of style in terms of an author's distinctiveness, the contenders in the literary property debate were helping to enshrine into law a set of emergent assumptions about the role of style in public discourse. I say "emergent" because these assumptions were not yet so widely embraced as to overturn the still-prevalent rhetorical principles that put great store on the social uses of verbal forms. Most participants in the debate, having been drilled in these principles during a decade or more of training, were guided in their attitudes toward language by these older habits of thought. Yet as the debate was nearing its climax in the decision of 1774, newer ideas about the value of a personal style, which had been circulating for some time though only just then receiving pedagogic certification in the period's "new rhetoric," began to be cited by copyright's defenders as a way of supplying a vital link between a work's expression and its author. What these commentators could not see, however, was how their individuating of style as an author's unique mode of address was inconsistent with rhetorical principles. Their arguments thus reflected an ongoing trend during the period that saw literary style being increasingly bracketed off, although never fully segregated, from rhetoric. Style in this newer conception was the manifestation of the private sensibility, while rhetorical norms continued to govern the modes of public speech.

Yet whereas rhetoric was supported by a panoply of age-old beliefs about the persuasive force of eloquence and the role of poets and orators in helping to sharpen its power, it was not obvious how these beliefs pertained to literary style. The "refinement" of speech, it had long been felt, benefited society by helping to enhance political, religious, and moral signification. By contrast, authorial style could be imitated but not improved for the use and benefit of others. As a consequence, from the mid-eighteenth century onward intellectual property in written works would be delimited in such a way that it would not reward the development of style and, by extension, the contributions of poets and other verbally inventive writers in helping to refine public discourse. The law's indifference to style was thus institutional confirmation of the increasing irrelevance of one of literature's oldest social functions.

Refinement and Its Uses

To explain this change, I will suggest how style was traditionally defined before I contrast these older notions with their later transformation into suppositions about the private ownership of works. In the past, style involved not self-expression but the application of recognized sets of rhetorical, lexical, and syntactic options aimed at achieving certain effects. Style was highly conventionalized, and any innovation in style had to be amenable to codification in its effects and purposes. Styles were classed according to scales of address (the Roman categories of high, middle, and low), characteristic patterns of construction (periodic, curt, loose, etc.), or their classical and modern prototypes (Senecan, Ciceronian, Attic, Spenserian, etc.). These categories were quite permeable; writers were free to come up with their own variations on an existing style or a combination of several; and in principle all styles were available for use by anyone, regardless of rank or temperament. At the same time, no manner of expression, even one that had come to be identified with its originating orator or author, could be acknowledged as a style unless it was imitated by others and gave rise to a school or movement.

In choosing a style, writers were guided by an established regime of public expression. Some styles were thought to articulate class identities or specific political or theological allegiances.[6] More generally, the exercise of style had to observe principles of both harmony and hierarchy. While form could be considered separately from content, the style of an utterance had to be in harmony with its sentiment, suited to its subject, appropriate to its purpose, and closely adjusted to the ethos and social standing of its audience.[7] This harmony of form and signification, in turn, accorded with a corresponding set of normative hierarchies. There were agreeable topics and base ones, serious and ignoble sentiments, formal and intimate occasions, and many other such divisions, each of which commanded its own range of rhetorical options. In this way, all styles had to be deployed with the overriding goal of heightening belief in the social structure, whether by sharpening the force of accepted moral truths or by polishing speech according to class-based norms of decorum. Though any homology between the "rules" of address and the rigidities of the social hierarchy was more asserted than precisely drawn, writers were expected to make stylistic decisions in accordance with what Rancière has called "a determined order of relationships between bodies and words, between ways of speaking, ways of doing and ways of being."[8]

This order, though fixed in an ideal sense, allowed considerable room for individual contributions to its "refinement." England's canonical authors, and in particular its poets, were celebrated for having enriched the language, classicized its grammar, smoothed its numbers, polished its wit, methodized its literature according to antique rules and practices, and led the progress of the arts. As no one since antiquity was felt capable of attaining absolute perfection in plying a given style, the contributions to refinement made by authors were measured in terms of their proficiency at using the available means. Chaucer was hailed by his followers as the first "perfecter" of poetic rhetoric in English, but by the seventeenth century his language had grown so obsolete that there were calls to drop him from the canon in order to restore its modernity.[9] An author's achievement might set the standard in his own day and for a time exhaust a style's eloquent potential, but it possessed little value unless it could be copied, built upon, and eventually surpassed by the work of later authors. Refinement involved a dynamic process of literary and moral production, an unfinished cultural project pursued at both an individual and a collective level, and a determining order of words and bodies that could always be strengthened.

Refinement was a service that writers rendered to the state. It presented them with a recognized role by which they could believe themselves to facilitate the circulation of linguistic and symbolic capital vital to the integrity of the social order. Refinement accordingly held strong normative appeal for a low-born poet like Ben Jonson, since it offered both an enabling revisionist narrative by which to define his modernity and the prestige of being able to contribute to the nation's cultural enrichment as fully as any peer. The more productive these contributions seemed, the greater literature's role in public life. With "the English language arising daily to greater perfection and purity," one neoclassicist wrote in 1657, "Poesie must needs accordingly extend to all subjects and occasions, incident to humane life."[10] At the same time, performing the role of refiner within a fixed order of address rendered poets directly subservient to political and religious authority. The perfecting of the language, as much as it represented a writer's highest service to the nation, had equally to be attributed to the sovereign's polite influence on his subjects. As late as 1672, Dryden could still ascribe the source of refinement "to the Court; and, in it, particularly to the King, whose example gives a law to it."[11]

By then, however, the expressive regime that had been premised on a normative hierarchy of styles and subjects had proven ineffective at maintaining social order. It retained its traditional authority, but the project of refinement—and with it the principle of harmony that writers were to follow—began to be redefined in accordance with a new modern division of discourse. On the one hand, there was a loudly promoted, successful campaign to institute a greater rhetorical plainness in public genres. It was not the first such campaign, and like earlier ones, this movement toward an isomorphic plain style, a development commonly associated with the language schemes of the Royal Society, did not involve a full-scale rejection of rhetoric so much as a retreat from extravagant and affective figuration. Like earlier campaigns, too, this one was propelled by the belief that verbal directness—"a close, naked and natural way of speaking," as Thomas Sprat put it—was a more ethically responsible mode of address than were overt displays of eloquence.[12] Yet whatever its moral import, the plain style had remained till then one rhetorical option among many.

What made this particular campaign influential was the promise it held of rationalizing public speech. Sprat, notoriously, called for a return to a "primitive purity" where "men deliver'd so many *things*, almost in an equal number of *words*." But the campaign's true focus, as he went on to suggest, had less to do with economizing on words than with promoting a common, depersonalized vernacular standard based on the language of trade and social interchange: all writers, Sprat urged, ought to prefer the "language of Artizans, Countrymen, and Merchants, before that, of Wits, or Scholars."[13] Its use no longer dictated by subject matter, the plain style could be applied uniformly to a variety of topics whose treatment had formerly been codified according to fixed scales of address. Its appeal lay not in its alleged economy but in the prospect it held of containing rhetoric's agonistic energies so that stylistic conformity might be achieved in public speech. Such conformity, in turn, could seem a credible alternative to an age-old hierarchical order of expression and potentially more efficacious at maintaining political harmony, because it would ostensibly enable a rational consensus to emerge across a broad social stratum. This new regime of expression would not be fully worked out for some time, and writers over the next century would continue to be taught how to employ different styles for different purposes. But henceforth the range of available styles was increasingly narrowed as the goal of standardizing public genres according to new norms of verbal correctness gradually displaced the social ideal of achieving cultural and linguistic perfection through refinement.

On the other hand, adopting a common style for most forms of public speech could seem a meaningful choice for writers only if the possibility remained open to them of making individual contributions to verbal art. Significantly, writers expressed a will to distinction in response not to the ascendancy of the plain style but to a redoubled critical effort to tighten up the "rules" for literary writing. As I have argued elsewhere, the comparative weakness of monarchical rule in Restoration England made for a corresponding doubt about the ideological value of neoclassical refinement as practiced in its stricter French form. Though critics strenuously enforced the rules in hopes of sustaining an enabling relation of cultural to political order, many working authors balked at complying fully with neoclassical doctrine as a way of asserting a measure of independence for their art from subservience to the state.[14] Most familiarly, this resistance took the form of defending Shakespeare's violations of the unities and, later, of proclaiming a greater poetic license in accordance with a greater English liberty in the political sphere.[15] Literature had always been prized as a genre in which authors could move the work of refinement forward, yet in the face of neoclassical prescriptions so loudly proclaimed as to acquire the force of law, it was also more and more seen as a means of expressive release from stylistic and ideological conformity.

Among the most prescient gesture of resistance in this regard involved resituating value in the subjectivity of the author. A notable example was Dryden's dismissal of Cowley's loose imitations of Pindar on the grounds that his "libertine way of rendering authors" had failed to respect the "sacred and inviolable" nature of the classical poet's work. From a rhetorical perspective, imitative practices like Cowley's were worthy contributions to refinement because they appropriated ancient forms on behalf of an aristocratic poetics—a view that Cowley, to judge from his exalting of the ode as "the highest and noblest kind of writing," was happy to endorse. There was nothing wrong from this perspective with Cowley substituting his own meaning for Pindar's while retaining only the structure of the ode, even if the result abstracted the Greek poet's style beyond recognition. But to Dryden, what Cowley had done was "the greatest wrong which can be done to the Memory and Reputation of the dead" because it undid the original odes' harmony of style and subject, which, Dryden believed, was not simply an achieved quality of the poetry but Pindar's distinguishing property. Translators, he declared in one of his most startling statements of principle, must attend to not only "the language of the poet, but his particular turn of thoughts and of expression, which are the characters that distinguish and, as it were, individuate him from all other writers." Abstracting the style of classical authors may have accorded with past practice, but the resulting imitation was "no longer to be call'd their work."[16]

The implications of what Dryden was arguing were radical. He could have simply said that Pindar had developed something like a poetic brand by cultivating an original set of phrases and figures. The claim would have accorded with rhetorical precepts, since writers had long been praised for having come up with their own variations on existing styles. At the same time, students were advised not to embrace the idea as a guiding principle of composition since it could easily be taken as license to apply the same style to different subjects, which was discouraged under the prevailing regime of expression as a violation of the regime's customary norm of harmony. As one rhetorician early in the next century lamented, "the greatest, and yet the common mistake" among young writers "is still imitating the same Style in all different subjects, whereas each has its proper beauty and rules."[17]

What Dryden appeared to be suggesting, however, was a mythology of exception to those rules. The notion that a poet like Pindar could fuse thought with expression in a manner so distinctive as to "individuate" him from all other writers implied a conception of harmony very different from either the traditional standard, which required that an author's style be appropriate to a subject or occasion, or the new conformism of a plain style that could be uniformly applied to any subject. Harmony in this new conception resulted not from following convention but from an author making a discourse his own by applying "his particular turn of thoughts and of expression" to any subject. Form and meaning, Dryden was proposing, corresponded at an organic level and were actualized in a text as a singular consciousness that evinced a distinct authorial presence. This ability to stamp a work with a unique stylistic signature could, in turn, serve authors as the basis for a moral if not legal claim to ownership in "their work," at least insofar as it precluded other writers from passing off imitations as the original author's work. Individuation established property.

That writings might be differentiated by an author's peculiar manner of alloying words and thought undoubtedly appealed to professionals, like Dryden, who were keen to differentiate their work in both an increasingly competitive print market and a still-vibrant coterie culture where manuscripts circulated often with no record of their authorship. Practicing a unique style could purchase authors a measure of distinction. Yet while the idea helped to raise authorship's prestige, it was not immediately clear how society stood to gain from a system of writerly proprietorship founded on the individuation of discourse. An individuated style limited a work's utility as a model for composition. The less an author's style could be subject to imitation and improvement by others, the less his writing could serve to enhance the efficacy of discourse and advance the larger project of cultural and linguistic refinement.

Over the next century that project was not so much abandoned as its script was rewritten. Rhetoricians continued to produce sizable guidebooks describing styles by category—concise, dry, florid, and so on—and analyzed scores of examples in each. They did so, however, less to introduce students to a hierarchy of options than to instruct them on attaining a consistent manner of expression, which they variously designated as a just, accurate, or correct style. Though advising young writers to modulate their style to suit different occasions, they placed little emphasis on the traditional rule that a work's style be appropriate to its subject; Henry Felton scarcely mentioned it in his 1709 treatise on "forming a just style." As ever, students were encouraged to improve their skills by imitating classical and, increasingly, English models. Yet the ultimate aim of their training was no longer to build on those models to open new rhetorical pathways for others. Imitation was instead a first step toward individuating discourse. "Your own Wit will be improved" by following ancient models, Felton told his addressee, Lord Roos, but no matter how faithful the imitation, "the Spirit, the Thought, the Fancy, the Expression which shall flow from Your Pen, will be entirely Your Own." Nature had made it simply impossible for authors of genuine merit to imitate the work of others without translating it into their own style. Roos's training in the classics, Felton assured him, would give him the tools to become a writer "equal in Rank, tho' different from them all."[18]

Refinement remained a normative ideal, though the point of it had less to do with sharpening the efficacy of discourse than with enforcing measures of social distinction. Students were taught to perfect a style with the same deference to codes of politeness they were expected to observe in polishing their taste and manners. And whereas refinement had previously entrusted writers with the supreme duty of leading the progress of language and letters, its appeal now lay in the opportunity it offered them to achieve distinction by demonstrating a singular yet correct manner of self-expression. The more codes of politeness were pressed on students, the more stylistic refinement was presented to them as a course of self-improvement that would enable them to join the rank of accepted authors yet equally, as Felton would have it, to be different from them all.

The parameters for expression were more tightly patrolled than ever, yet the quest to be different entailed one major change to the prevailing regime, which is that within these narrow parameters the writer's character rather than a work's topic determined the choice of style. The writer was now the source of harmony. No one took greater advantage of the opportunity for distinction presented by this change than Pope. At William Walsh's urging, he made it his aim to be the "one great poet that was correct," as if correctness could only be an isolated achievement.[19] Pope may have believed that his mastery of correctness, in addition to elevating him above earlier poets, might never be surpassed. Mastery of the middle style, if not the style itself, was what made him different. The style was not his to monopolize since treating it so would have undermined correctness as a universal prescription. One reason, indeed, that the style was so appealing was that it could be readily methodized; Pope's collaborators on the *Odyssey* (1720–1726) copied it so effectively that the translation appeared seamless to most readers. Yet while the style could be copied, Pope had polished it to the point where his refinement marked him within his work; "there is certainly nothing in his style or manner of writing, which can distinguish or discover him," he teased readers of the anonymous 1728 *Dunciad*.[20] Anyone could use the style, but Pope's supreme virtuosity individuated it. This lent his poetry a new kind of rhetorical authority, derived from the seeming unity of a persona that could, as Susan Staves remarked, take up with an unwavering equanimity "subjects ranging from a pissing contest (in *The Dunciad*) to the theodicy problem (in the *Essay on Man*). The style assumes a form of universality."[21] Unmooring the style from any particular purpose or occasion, Pope tied it instead to an original textual self in a way that made it seem like the same precisely controlled sensibility was being brought to bear on any moral or social concern. In doing so, Pope won the distinction of being able to claim his unwavering commitment to correctness as evidence of his personal integrity.

The figure of the author gradually displaced the rule of subject matter as language's central harmonizing force in direct correlation to the increasing standardization of discourse. Without this change, there could be no distinction in verbal art. Yet there was arguably a more fundamental reason for the change, which had to do with the ascendancy of a modern reading public as the anonymous arbiter of value. Harmony as a rhetorical principle had formerly presupposed an external order to which all writers owed their power of discourse. Harmony of style and subject, it was believed, lent writing affective force because the work was directed at a defined audience, a homogeneous assembly of people who shared the writer's faith in the power of language, who could appreciate the particular ethos the writer aimed to convey, and whom the writer could confidently address in a manner appropriate to their position in the social hierarchy. In the eighteenth century, that hierarchy was still firmly in place, but it had become painfully clear to authors that they were no longer writing for an audience they believed they could either know or control. A modern public was both unquestionable in its authority and indefinite in its composition. Writers, Blair advised, must accept that "the Public is the supreme judge to whom the last appeal must be made in every work of Taste."[22] But there could equally be no predicting the general public's decisions since it was physically and emotionally removed from the contexts in which authors wrote, too diverse for them to address in any particular key, and too indeterminate in size and skill to respond uniformly to the effects that stylistic choices were intended to produce.

Writers tried plenty of rhetorical expedients for dealing with this indefinite public, not least the widely used device of projecting an ideal audience by directly addressing a work to a patron or a friend in the country. A popular option among poets was to write verse openly billed as "in the style of" a canonical author, like Milton, without actually imitating a specific work, as if this style were a known quality whose features could be applied to any subject. These impersonations presupposed a readership familiar enough with English literary history to recognize these styles and their import. But their popularity was short-lived since they soon seemed an inadequate compromise between an older ideal of refinement and a newer emphasis on the harmonizing power of the author. On the one hand, the impersonations appropriated an existing style without doing anything new to it, and by applying the same style to diverse subjects they threatened to disrupt the traditional principle of harmony that lent discourse its authority. On the other hand, in advertising style as an author's characteristic mode of expression, these works appealed to an emergent sense of harmony as residing in a power to individuate discourse; yet the more prevalent this conception became, the more the act of impersonation seemed a pointless exploit. By contrast, later medieval and Shakespearean forgeries that claimed to uncover a lost individuality seemed at their exposure to be an affront to the public because, no matter how creative they were as poetic documents, they violated readers' expectation of an essential unity of writer and work, the self and its expression.

This new conception of harmony, as inhering in the script that genius writes from itself, elevated authorship's stature by making the work of writing seem more difficult. Writers, according to the proponents of the new rhetoric, could no longer rely solely on convention to win readers over or gain distinction. Faced with a reading public they could not know, authors had instead to rely on style to make themselves known to readers.[23] In effect, once authors could no longer count on an external order of discourse to enable their exercise of verbal power over a defined audience, it became imperative for them to internalize this order by attempting to harmonize style with sensibility in a way that was sufficiently consistent so that readers could recognize their peculiar manner of thinking and writing. As Blair explained, a writer might take up any number of different subjects and sentiments, but "amidst this variety, we still expect to find, in the compositions of any one man, some degree of uniformity or consistency with himself in manner; we expect to find some predominant character of Style impressed on all his writings, which shall be suited to, and shall mark, his particular genius, and turn of mind."[24] Adam Smith, in his lectures on rhetoric (1762–1763), similarly claimed that, ideally, style "not only expresses the thought but also the spirit and mind of the author." More surprisingly, he went so far as to suggest that the best English prose writers had always followed their natural inclinations with no concern for refining style to benefit society or language. "These authors," he insisted, "did not attempt what they thought was the greatest perfection of stile but that perfection which they thought most suitable to their genius and temper."[25] Authors perfected *a* style, not style in general.

Significantly, neither Blair nor Smith indicated what role this harmony of genius and style played in discourse or why readers ought to attend to it. Of the many tenets of the new rhetoric—its rejection of grandiloquence for the plain style, persuasion for the truth of experience, authorities for inferential reasoning, and topoi and commonplaces for fact—the idea that style should not be based on formulaic arrangements but rather reflect an author's character was perhaps the least clearly expounded or justified in terms of how it might render writing either conducive to the pursuit of truth or agreeable to the public taste. For these purposes, it was sufficient for most writers to follow the vernacular standard of the day. Blair identified several kinds of style for addressing the public, though he believed that English syntax and other components of prose had by his time come to express a plainness well suited to the national temperament. "Our arrangement of words has become," he averred, "more plain and natural: and this is now understood to be the genius of our Language."[26] Smith was even more insistent that the "naturall order of expression" provided by the plain style made it the only defensible option for anyone seriously committed to communicating to a modern public. He was strongly opposed to what he believed was the prevailing view that "the farther ones stile is removed from the common manner it is so much the nearer to purity and the perfection we have in view."[27]

In encouraging the use of the plain style for any subject, the new rhetoricians were rejecting an older determining order of words, persons, and things. They could not abide the breaking of that order, of course, since nothing for them could have value without a firm footing in nature. But if style was to have this footing without being governed by an external world of subject matter, its normative foundation had to be located elsewhere, in an internal sphere of subjectivity. Authors, the new rhetoricians proposed, had to learn to bridge the gap between themselves and language by making their style so closely follow the flow of their thinking as to seem determined by it. A perfect personal style was the ultimate refinement of the plain style. It disclosed the author's sensibility as much as it did truth, yet did so without calling attention to itself. The perfect stylist did not flaunt his creativity, Smith declared, but instead wrote "in the manner which best conveys the sentiment, passion or affection with which it affects or he pretends it does affect him."[28] In this account, style performs the rhetorical functions of concealing itself while persuading readers that authors feel things they might only pretend to feel. Anyone could write differently, but perfect stylists made it seem as if they wrote differently because they thought differently.

This notion of a personal style, available to anyone though perfected by few, offered individualism a loophole to slip through at the historical moment when language's ongoing standardization was being extended well beyond metrics and figures to the levels of usage, pronunciation, and spelling. Yet this idea did more than naturalize the possibility of personal distinction within a new regime of correct, plain English. It also anchored style to subjectivity in a way that rendered a writer's style out of reach for others to use. A personal style was not simply an author's property to defend with a moral argument against its infringement. It suggested an internal order of mind that was anterior to language and therefore immune to dispersal, however diverse the subjects an author took up or how widely his work circulated. Style provided writers with authority to the degree that it was incontestable, their natural manner of thinking and speaking. It likewise made that manner seem inviolable to readers, who could not presume to impose their own identity on another's voice in much the same way as they could not, as members of the public, intrude on the autonomy of the strangers who surrounded them without inviting corresponding intrusions on their own. The idea of a perfect style made authors appear as strangers, whose order of mind could be discerned but not appropriated. Others might copy elements of a writer's style or thinking, but any attempt at imitation would fail to replicate the singularity of its source while either betraying or occluding the imitator's own way of thinking.

All of this signaled a profound change to the social function of style. In the past, style had clear social utility in helping orators and poets to enhance language's power to signify, persuade, and inspire belief in the prevailing order. Beginning with the new rhetoric, style was no longer thought to influence audiences in a direct instrumental fashion. The old structure of conviction, which had at its center a belief in the powerful persuasive force of words, was breaking down. It was simply incompatible with a newer universe of belief, which presupposed a fundamental freedom of mind. Language was to be used to communicate knowledge, ideas, and opinions among a diverse public whose members treated each other as equals capable of reason and independent judgment. Anyone seeking to engage this public was expected to observe standards of verbal competence and to address its members in an impersonal plain style or at least one not so remote from the norm or coercive in its effects that it undermined judgment and the pursuit of truth.

A perfectly individuated style, however, met the ends of truth while also imparting a sense of its author's particular manner of thinking. Style in this new conception, Fredric Jameson suggested, is prized as "the very element of individuality itself, that mode through which the individual consciousness seeks to distinguish itself, to affirm its incomparable originality."[29] Yet this argument underplays the crucial point that an affirmation of individuality is nothing if not public in its orientation; it is a deeply rhetorical exercise in that it deploys the force of words on behalf of individuality. The figure of the author whose genius created its own style was in this way a representation of the self's freedom from determination. Just as crucially, a personal style was to be read as an inalienable form of public knowledge about its author's sensibility. A writer's singular style mediated meaning in a way that suggested something about the author's peculiar turn of mind, and this knowledge was valuable since it permitted the public entry into the subjective realm so that its members might confirm that they were doing their job of preserving personal liberty. Yet this knowledge also came in a form that neither permitted others to encroach on a person's autonomy nor erased the otherness of subjectivity with impersonal language. Though a personal style might rely on all manner of sensuous, emotive, and cognitive effects, it benefited society chiefly as a kind of signification rather than as an instrumental aid to discourse. It made it possible for persons unknown to one another to exchange knowledge about themselves in a form that preserved their individuality. By refining their own personal styles, they could reveal and perhaps distinguish themselves in the very act of communicating as equals.

The refinement of style thus became a project conducted solely at the individual level, which principally served to renew the content if not the form of public speech since its specific achievements could not be codified, duplicated, or improved. No form of writing was seen to advance this project more readily than any other because style was not transferable from one writer to another. As a consequence, poets had by the mid-eighteenth century begun to disavow any obligation to polish public speech. "[T]he language of the age," Gray declared, "is never the language of poetry. . . . Our poetry, on the contrary, has a language peculiar to itself."[30] Poets had always been heralded for spearheading refinement, but with verbal innovation being perceived as an affirmation of individuality, the special opportunities for creativity that poetry allowed were thought to render it the antithesis of conventional discourse. As Edward Young put it, "There is something in Poetry beyond Prose-reason; there are Mysteries in it not to be explained, but admired."[31] Indeed, it has been suggested that there has occurred since the 1800s a "polarization of poetic genres from the prosaic modes of public address" in part because poetry has come to be epitomized by the lyric, which presents the personal in both content and expression.[32]

Wordsworth, of course, rejected the division between literary and ordinary language. In his view, it threatened to deny poetry its power to revivify public speech. But his efforts to bridge the division merely confirmed the changes that had already taken place. He may have believed that "language really used by men" ought to be the standard by which poetic language was to be refined. But the perfecting of a personal style no longer followed standards and models, and writing poetry in a style reminiscent of ordinary speech served only to individuate Wordsworth's own art. Likewise, it was possible for him to claim that the language of good poetry must "in no respect differ from that of good prose" only because there no longer existed any pragmatic criterion—except meter, in his account—for differentiating poetry from other public genres. Innovation and differentiation could now happen only at an individual level. Finally, he may have felt that the value of poetry lay in its ability to convey truth with greater feeling and vividness than was possible in other discourses: "Poetry is the breath and finer spirit of all knowledge; it is the impassioned expression which is in the countenance of all Science."[33] But as his own practice attested, whatever subject a poet might take up, poetry's "impassioned expression" was henceforth to be read as knowledge that no science could provide of the poet's own mind.

A Mark of Ownership

The literary property debate brought into conflict old and new beliefs as much about style as property, with elements of each being cited in support of positions on both sides of the argument. Unlike theories of property, however, neither traditional rhetorical nor modern author-centered assumptions about style had a decisive influence on the debate's outcome. Older pragmatic notions of language's utility, shorn of much of their supporting ideological apparatus, informed decisions in infringement cases throughout the period since they offered judges a workable framework for distinguishing ideas from their expression. Newer notions about stylistic individuation were introduced late in the debate with arguments for treating copyright as an inherent right of property. In tying a work's protectable expression to its author, these arguments appeared to provide a strong rationale for the law. Yet the detractors of a common-law copyright could reasonably claim that these notions favored certain kinds of writing over others and were therefore inadequate justification for extending the law to all publications. No compromise could or would be worked out between these two sets of beliefs, as a consequence of which aspects of rhetorical thinking continued to guide legal practice while newer ideas about style were increasingly invoked in defense of the principle of copyright. Next, I identify some of the specific legal implications of each set of beliefs before going on to suggest what these conflicting beliefs entailed for the value of style.

The legal distinction between ideas and their expression was an inheritance from the rhetorical tradition. In Mansfield's account of the distinction in *Millar v. Taylor* (1769), copyright protected the "right to print a set of intellectual ideas or modes of thinking, communicated in a set of words and sentences and modes of expression." According to this argument, there existed no necessary connection between an author and a work's arrangement of words. A work's expression was primarily determined by its subject matter and by prevailing conventions of expression. This meant that it was possible to imagine authors of diverse temperaments using similar styles to write on the same subject. It was even conceivable that two authors could produce identical works. Mansfield noted this possibility in arguing that literary property, being incorporeal, differed from real property in possessing no outward sign of ownership: "There are no indicia: another may have had the same thoughts upon the same subject, and expressed them in the same language verbatim."[34] An author owned a work by virtue of having published it first and did so, Blackstone conceded, "without stamping on it any marks of ownership."[35] A literary property might be valuable for its ideas, its style, or both, though neither was linked in any essential way to the work's expression. It was sufficient in legal practice to tell one work from another by their arrangements of words, but those words were merely the vehicle that conveyed the work to the reading public.

Property in this account inhered in a work's ideas and style, whereas putting them into words made them public. As Yates insisted, "[I]n every language, the words which express a publication of a book, express it as giving it to the public."[36] Works may be distinguishable by their expression, but expression has no worth other than its utility in facilitating the circulation of value.[37] It enabled readers to profit from a work, whose style no less than its substance they could abstract for their own purposes as a model worthy of imitation—"if, by reading an epic poem," Willes averred, "a man learns to make an epic poem of his own, he is at liberty"[38]—or as a set of expressive options worthy of refinement.

Accordingly, under rhetorical precepts, variations in expression were acceptable on grounds of utility. These variations, as Johnson acknowledged in his defense of abridgments, might cut into the original author's profit, but any cost to the author was more than compensated by the benefit to the public of having important ideas and styles rendered in accessible versions.[39] This attitude explains why courts in the eighteenth century gave wide latitude to derivative works, including abridgments, sequels, and translations. Only late in the period did this view begin to be displaced by newer notions, in which a condensed version of a previously published work could be permitted only on the very different grounds that it evinced sufficient creativity to qualify as an original work. By then, only part of a work could be appropriated verbatim by another on condition of fair use; otherwise, works that presented less than a "totally new arrangement" of existing material failed to meet the minimal acceptable threshold of creativity.[40] Thereafter, judges would interpret this new standard ever more strictly, with derivative works becoming increasingly viewed as unlawful trespasses on authors' original properties.

Compared with these later notions, rhetorical principles had at least the virtue of being easy to apply in infringement cases. They were nonetheless vulnerable to theoretical challenge since they recognized no basis or indicia other than priority for assigning a work's ownership to one author or another. Rhetorical arguments divided what Blackstone called a work's "identity" into two components: its style and substance, which served as the legal and moral grounds for establishing the work as its author's intellectual property, and its expression, which served as the ontological grounds for differentiating it from other publications even as it also conveyed its contents in a form accessible to the public. Copyright's defenders no less than the courts recognized that a work's expression was the object of piracy. Yet it made intuitive sense to them to identify property with a work's most profitable features: its ideas and style. "Style and sentiment," said Blackstone, "are the essentials of a literary composition. These alone constitute its identity."[41] If property were not secured in these features, they feared, then authors would profit from the mere rewording of old material, and copyright would fail in its declared purpose of encouraging learning. Enfield even suggested that in the case of works whose ideas could be easily restated in other words, their authors ought to be entitled to "an immediate grant of some equivalent from the state" to compensate them for any lost profits they might suffer at the hands of redactors.[42]

For the opponents of a monopoly copyright, many of whom also subscribed to rhetorical principles, this division between property and expression made for a disabling ambiguity in the law, in which the value of a work was said to inhere in aspects that were rendered public by a work's language. Most of these critics, notably Yates, focused on what this ambiguity entailed for the ideas in a work, which, they argued, could not conceivably be subject to ownership once they had been disseminated in print. The London booksellers, as noted earlier, loudly denied that copyright granted authors ownership in their ideas and were only too happy to declare that since their monopoly did not extend to ideas, it could not impede their circulation. Copyright, said one of the booksellers' defenders, did not "confine the powers of genius: for he who obtaineth my copy may appropriate my stock of ideas, and, by opposing my sentiments, may give birth to a new doctrine" and in so doing "acquireth an exclusive title to his copy, without invading my property."[43] Yet the claim intensified the underlying ambiguity. If reworking a stock of ideas could produce a new exclusive title, then the words used to make ideas public had also to serve as the markers of property. Ideas were free, as Yates protested, but it was difficult to see how expression made them free without itself being free.

This ambiguity, a few critics noted, was most apparent from the conflicting rationales for original and derivative publications. The author of *An Enquiry into the Nature and Origin of Literary Property* (1762) claimed that writers ought to "derive a Property from the Ideas of others not only by improving and adding to them, but meerly by employing more Labour on them." Yet it was puzzling to him why, under the law, restating those same ideas in different words constituted productive labor, such that an author, editor, and translator could all lay claim to "many original exclusive Properties all existing in the same Subject." In accordance with rhetorical principles, this critic felt that expression could not constitute a work's identity. Its "Form and Composition," he insisted, were merely "an Accident which never can be the Subject of Property." Besides, he added, lawmakers ought not to waste their time protecting style if its expression produced nothing useful. "Meer Pleasure is not the Object of the Legislature," he sneered.[44]

Directly answering the *Enquiry*, the author of *A Vindication of the Exclusive Right of Authors* (1762) maintained that expression was a form of labor: "being the author of the language only, is a good ground for maintaining an exclusive right in a copy, though the ideas belong to another. Thus a translator, may claim such a right, being, in respect to those who are not skilled in the original, the parent of a new doctrine." Far from resolving the ambiguity over the legal basis of ownership, this argument laid bare its intractability by treating the "right" separate from "ownership." The right to copy could be vested in a translator, even if a work's ideas might "belong to another" or might even appear to the untrained reader as originating with the translator. Under the idea–expression dichotomy, the question of who originated a work's ideas was irrelevant to an author's claim of copyright. The author of the *Vindication* could have simply said that literary property in any work was vested in the "author of the language." This would have removed all ambiguity by locating the ground of ownership solely in expression. But he, like the writer of the *Enquiry*, subscribed to rhetorical principles, according to which a work's expression was dictated by the subject matter that gave it value. Thus, within a few pages of the above passage, he insisted on the primacy of subject matter. An author, he declared, "hath certainly a perpetual exclusive dominion over that subject which he can use in public, and which nevertheless another cannot imitate against his will."[45]

The ambiguity could be forestalled by sidestepping the issue of ownership altogether. Lord Monboddo of the Scottish court, dissenting from the majority ruling that perpetual copyright was not recognized under Scottish law, argued that literary property ought to be defined solely as a condition of use. "[E]very right of property," he proposed, is "the right of using a thing exclusive of others.... If I purchase a book, I may use it for my instruction or amusement, or I may employ the paper or binding of it as I think proper; and so far I may be said to have the property of it. But, I cannot re-print it, because that use belongs to the author or his assigney, and so far he is proprietor."[46] This argument put aside some of the conceptual problems earlier commentators had faced in trying to specify the nature of literary property, and to this extent it anticipated how later courts would equate copyright with a set of legal rights and privileges rather than seeing it as a definable asset. Yet Monboddo's respondents did not find his clarification of the matter compelling since it appeared to give rise to two new problems, one technical and the other philosophical. First, the argument appeared to turn copyright into an entirely contractual arrangement between author and purchaser. If authors by this agreement were guaranteed only certain privileges of use, then by the law of contract copyright claimants had to specify these privileges within the publication as a condition of sale—which, in fact, they would eventually be required to do. Without a clear indication as to what constituted a legitimate or illegitimate use of a publication, Donaldson's lawyers responded, a "prohibition to multiply copies can no more be *inferred*, than a prohibition to lend to a friend, or to keep a circulating library; by which, as well as by multiplying, the profits of the first publisher may be abridged."[47]

More significantly, in the view of his respondents, Monboddo's division of privileges between author and purchaser could not be reconciled with a rhetorical understanding of language's utility as a vehicle for conveying a work's form and content to the public. It did not make sense to them why anyone would put sentiments or poetic images into publishable language if not to make them available for others' use. Language and publication made ideas common. More to the point, from a rhetorical perspective the concept of expression implied no direct link between authors and the language they employed. Authors were guided in their selection and arrangement of words by rhetorical conventions and the primacy of subject matter. Nothing about the written expression of an idea or style was thought to derive from authors in a way that entitled them to its exclusive use. Even in the case of a private code, Donaldson's advocates supposed, there could be no justification for preventing others from replicating it: an author may retain exclusivity over his ideas "if he writes in an unknown language, or character invented by himself, and which he alone can decypher. At the same time even there, supposing any person into whose hands the book has come, should take a fancy to reprint it, what power has the author to hinder him?"[48] A work's expression might differ from that of other publications, but difference in itself provided no normative basis for assigning the author a right of property in the work, whether this right pertained to the work's use or ownership. Difference, at least within a rhetorical cosmos of belief, was not a mark of ownership.

Origins of Expressive Diversity

In a key strategic move, the London trade's defenders sought to supply difference with a normative foundation by taking up the idea of individuation. That idea, only recently affirmed as a doctrine of the new rhetoric, posited an organic correspondence between some authors and the particular selection and order of words in their writings. That not all authors managed to craft a personal style meant that a work's expression could not be read as conclusive proof of its ownership. Yates dismissed as irrelevant Blackstone's claim that a work's identity inhered in its style and sentiment since, according to the judge, only in exceptional instances could a work's style be traced to a specific author: "Some few may be known by their style; but the generality are not known at all."[49] Were all writers known by their style, of course, there would be no risk of their works being infringed. Yet if the idea of individuation could hardly help judges to decide infringement cases, it nonetheless appeared to present a strong moral rationale for treating copyright as a legal principle consonant with the principles of natural justice. Individuation rooted difference in nature and the mind: if few authors managed to perfect a style that could be discerned in their every utterance, all persons had at least the potential to develop a personal style that accorded with their sensibility and thought. Language made ideas public, but expression always carried the possibility of communicating something intrinsic and inimitable about its author. Copyright, by this logic, encouraged self-determination and the renewal of public discourse through diversity by protecting the natural tendency of all persons to distinguish themselves in expression.

The most forceful application of the idea of individuation to the defense of a common-law copyright was set out in a speech prepared by one of the advocates for the respondents in *Donaldson v. Becket*, Francis Hargrave. Not given a chance to deliver his speech before the House of Lords, Hargrave rushed it into print just days before they were to rule. His pamphlet, *An Argument in Defence of Literary Property* (1774), had no influence on their decision. But the passage where he insisted on the individuality of expression would in time become a reference point for copyright advocates, especially after it was reproduced in full in Robert Maugham's 1828 treatise on copyright as an authoritative statement "on the practicability of ascertaining the right of literary property."[50] The passage is worth quoting and discussing at length since Hargrave was clearly doing more than affirming that literary properties can be differentiated by their language. He took the notion of individuation as far as he could in upholding the idea–expression dichotomy but stopped short of suggesting that characteristics of expression can serve to identify a work's ownership:

The subject of literary property is a *written composition*; and that one written composition may be distinguished from another, is a truth too evident to be much argued upon. Every man has a mode of combining and expressing his ideas peculiar to himself. The same doctrines, the same opinions, never come from two persons, or even from the same person at different times, cloathed wholly in the same language. A strong resemblance of stile, of sentiment, of plan and disposition, will be frequently found; but there is such an infinite variety in the modes of thinking and writing, as well in the extent and connection of ideas, as in the use and arrangement of words, that a literary work *really* original, like the human face, will always have some singularities, some lines, some features, to characterize it, and to fix and establish its identity; and to assert the contrary with respect to either, would be justly deemed equally opposite to reason and universal experience. Besides, though it should be allowable to suppose, that there *may* be cases, in which, on a comparison of two literary productions, no such distinction could be made between them, as in a competition for originality to decide whether both were really original, or which was the original and which the copy; still the observation of the possibility of distinguishing would hold in *all other* instances, and the Argument in its application to them would still have the same force.[51]

Mark Rose has closely interrogated Hargrave's fast-sliding analogy between the written work, the mind, and the face. That people differ physically does not mean that they think differently nor that their compositions are necessarily distinctive. The analogy, as Rose suggested, collapses the categories of work and author without establishing a definitive link between the former's identity and the latter's singularity. That this link may not be discernible in all cases or that the same person may write differently "at different times" would likewise seem to obviate any correlation, let alone causation, between bodies, minds, and texts.[52]

Rose sees Hargrave's argument as a dubious attempt to naturalize literary property by fixing it to the transcendental signifier of original genius. This overlooks its import and historical significance. If Hargrave is naturalizing anything, it is not originality or genius but difference. That people thought and spoke differently was heretofore seen as the regrettable consequence of error, Babel, and the Fall, but Hargrave was dispensing with this cosmology and instead positing diversity of speech and thought as a natural justification for both the practicality and rightfulness of a common-law copyright. In so doing, he rejected as irrelevant the rhetorical principles that had till then guided arguments for and against literary property. Under these principles, the purpose of speech and learning was to help people to overcome their differences through adhering to the received verities and a determining order of address. Variations in expression were tolerated if they enhanced the persuasive efficacy of truth and if they were available for others to refine in the furtherance of harmonizing society and human thought. Individuation of expression may have been more highly prized under the new rhetoric, with perfection of style hailed as the inimitable manifestation of an author's naturally distinctive manner of thought. Yet perfection, the new rhetoricians insisted, could never be achieved by pursuing expressiveness for its own sake but could result only from a masterly harmony of mind with prevailing stylistic norms.

Hargrave, by contrast, was unconcerned with rhetorical standards or qualitative distinctions between modes of address and thought. It does not matter, he suggested, how people think and write. What matters is that copyright protects and rewards their natural inclinations to think and write differently. This was an extraordinarily prescient argument. Though it was far from his intention to set out a political rationale for copyright, Hargrave essentially defended copyright in democratic terms. He may have supposed that diversity of thought and expression was an indisputable fact of life. Yet in addition to being both unverifiable and conceptually flawed—if everyone writes differently, then no one does—the claim can act as a justification for copyright only within a framework of democratic beliefs. Outside of that framework, there is nothing compelling about the idea that people are predisposed to thinking and writing differently, nor is there any reason to conclude from that idea that the law ought to encourage this diversity and serve, as the US Supreme Court famously put it, as an "engine of free expression."[53] As more recent advocates of so-called democratic theories of copyright have proposed, the law should be understood in the first instance not as a regulatory mechanism of trade or property but as a social instrument that serves liberal self-governance by providing economic incentives for "expressive diversity," the kind of vibrantly heterogeneous discourse that is seen as vital to deliberation in a public sphere.[54] Hargrave may have been unaware of the ideological implications of what he was saying, but he was evidently the first legal theorist to contemplate the possibility, at least, that copyright serves the common good by promoting the public's expressive diversity.

There remains a problem, one that is apparent from Hargrave's loaded comparison of texts to faces, though in fact it impairs his argument at a deeper level. The problem has to do with the role of expression in evincing not merely difference but the self-determination that constitutes freedom in a democratic polity. To provide a natural basis for copyright, Hargrave had to assume that there exists a connection between how people think and how they write. Without this connection, there would be no cause to embrace expressive diversity as a democratic good. With it, Hargrave could suggest that the law, in encouraging this diversity, accorded with a fundamental freedom of mind. Yet the connection placed a significant evidentiary burden on expression, which had to seem both freely invented and as naturally determined as the singularities of human physiognomy. This explains Hargrave's seemingly disabling admission that the same person may write differently "at different times." There can be no free exercise of mind if the same person is incapable of writing differently at different times. But that a person is capable of writing differently at different times means that expression cannot serve as conclusive proof that people think in intrinsically different ways. Similarly, Hargrave had to allow that it may not be possible in every instance to tell one work from another since positing the utter impossibility of two persons creating identical works would preclude the necessary indeterminacy of free speech. Yet that such a perfect coincidence in expression had to remain within the realm of possibility equally appeared to undermine any attempt to naturalize intellectual property by maintaining that "every man has a mode of combining and expressing his ideas peculiar to himself."[55]

Like later theorists of copyright, Hargrave sidestepped this problem of evidence by treating the law as a formal arrangement that imposed no normative requirements on the discourse it regulated other than it be diverse. As he cautiously suggested in a closing apology for the hastiness of his argument, "the *practicability* of *deriving a title*" to a literary property may be sufficient to justify copyright as a working principle that would ensure predictable judgments in a wide variety of disputes "without the aid of any *positive law* to *create* the *right* or to *regulate* its *enjoyment*."[56] The law of copyright, in this account, was a procedural instrument that was both content neutral and style neutral with regard to the free expression it was designed to promote. As long as a work could be differentiated from others on the basis of its expression, so the argument went, the law could rely on a system of formal registration, rather than any mark within the work, to certify its ownership.[57] More broadly, as long as the law fulfilled its social purpose in maximizing the plurality of public discourse, it did not have to assess or confirm the quality of this diversity.

Hargrave, like later democratic theorists of the law, focused on copyright's relation to content while paying scant attention to style and its role in expression. He did not quite suggest that copyright was indifferent to content, but at one point in his pamphlet, he did allow that an idea's publication was no guarantee of its originality: "The same *ideas* will arise in *different* minds, and it is impossible to establish precisely, in whom an idea is *really original*; and perhaps *most* ideas may in fact be *equally original* in the greater part of mankind; and *priority* in the *publication* of an idea is a most *insufficient proof of its originality*."[58] As noted earlier, under the idea–expression dichotomy it did not matter who originated an idea. Authors acquired a right of property in their works by publishing a set of ideas and sentiments in a particular form before anyone else did. So long as the stationers had been recording their titles in the company's register, the determining criterion of ownership had been priority. But Hargrave denied priority's relevance in certifying an idea's originality: most published ideas were not original, having occurred to others before they were first published. The identity of a literary property, Hargrave implied, cannot inhere in its ideas since many persons were likely to share the same idea before and after its publication. Works cannot be differentiated by their ideas nor can ideas be tied to an author by their date of publication.

In suggesting this, Hargrave was inverting the traditionally defined relation between ideas and their expression. Ideas and not expression were till then considered the primary component of a work's identity. Publications might be differentiated by their expression, but a work's arrangement of words was an "accident" and not its substance. Authors conveyed ideas to others in a style dictated by the nature of the subject matter, so that, as Mansfield allowed, convention might even lead different authors to express the same idea in an identical arrangement of words. Expression was a work's public clothing, the means writers relied on to render their ideas comprehensible to others. For Hargrave, in contrast, ideas were no less public than language, since they may have occurred to more than one person prior to their publication and were accessible to all once published. The only element of a work that could not be shared before or after publication was its writer's way with words, which was only partly determined by convention and whose distinctiveness was demonstrable enough, Hargrave believed, to "fix and establish" the work's identity. The upshot of this, as Hargrave appeared to recognize, was that copyright did not directly advance learning in the sense of giving special incentives for anyone to produce new ideas or knowledge. Copyright left decisions about the value of new or old ideas to the public, who were free to choose which intellectual and artistic efforts to patronize. So long as the law promoted the circulation of ideas, whether those ideas happened to be original or not, it met the end it was designed to serve of fostering public discourse.

On the question of style, Hargrave did not claim that it can or should serve as a mark of ownership. The evidence of a single work was insufficient to identify an author by his style, even if it was believed that people may write so differently that they individuate discourse to their unique way of thinking. At the same time, Hargrave, like his mentor Blackstone, strongly believed that copyright ought to be recognized under the common law as an inherent right of property because intellectual properties were the product of mental labor. "No literary work," Hargrave explained, "whether consisting of *new* thoughts and ideas, or of *old* thoughts and ideas *newly* combined and expressed, can be produced without all industrious and painful application of the mental faculties to the particular subject."[59] Authors ought to be rewarded for the fruits of their labor, even if they expended this labor on ideas that did not originate with them. These fruits were objectified in a work's expression, which could be deemed original because it would always bear traces ("will always have some singularities, some lines, some features") of the mind and sensibility that produced it.

On the one hand, then, the law as a purely procedural instrument did not require that a link be demonstrated between a work's expression and its author. It was not necessary to find evidence of an author's style in a work in order to establish its ownership; the work simply had to be expressed differently from other works. Copyright owners had title to their property whether their style of writing was demonstrably unique or not. On the other hand, the law as a system of property founded on a notion of mental labor presupposed that a natural link between author and work existed and was most readily apparent from a work's expression, if not always its ideas. Authors ought to be rewarded for their labors, whose fruits were rendered original and protectable by virtue of their expression, which always at some level evinced the author's unique sensibility.

For Hargrave, this disjuncture between the law's practical application and its underlying rationale presented no inconsistency since the latter, at least, required that works be related to authors only in accordance with a general notion of causality. A work was the fruit of an author's labor regardless of whether the work bore specifiable indexes of this labor or not. At the same time, that a work did not originate from a source other than an individual author—such as an external regime of address—could be inferred from the fact that for all intents and purposes, no two authors will produce the same work. Diversity of expression, in this way, served in Hargrave's argument as confirmation that a written work was the fruit of an individual's mental labor. That all works differed by their expression appeared to indicate that every person thought differently, and therefore the law, so it was supposed, respected this natural diversity by inhering a right of property in individual producers or their assigns. This assumption validated the law even if, conceived as a purely formal mechanism, the law did not require its confirmation.

The only occasion, perhaps, when a court may have been asked to uphold the assumption was in the case of a forgery that was passed off as another's work. Anyone could mimic another author's style even if this style had helped make its author famous; but anyone who appropriated the author's name, if not his style, was guilty of trespassing on the individuation that publicly linked the author to his work. Interestingly, it was shortly after the question of literary property was decided that creators were first granted rights of publicity: in a landmark case from 1776, an artist was awarded substantial damages against print sellers who had put his name on their work in an attempt to sell it as the artist's own.[60]

So long as copyright promoted expressive diversity, the law's application did not require that evidence of essential differences in how people think be derived from the way they write. Copyright fulfilled its purpose by making possible a democracy of expression and was indifferent to style except insofar as it prevented others from replicating any particular expression of a given style. Under expressive diversity, any style or idea would do, whether it be original or not, whereas instances of expression that too closely resembled others would not do. The indeterminacy of public discourse may have required that it remain conceivable for two authors working independently of one another to come up with identical works, but the law permitted this indeterminacy to manifest only with respect to style and ideas and not their expression. At the same time, the law rested on the notion of individuation, the principle that diversity in expression was the result of natural differences in how people think and must therefore be protected to ensure their self-determination and the robust public exchange of ideas and styles. Expression may have carried an evidentiary burden of signaling both determinacy and freedom of mind, but this evidence did not need to be demonstrated in the law for copyright to function efficiently as an engine of free expression.

At least one disputant in the literary property debate, however, warned that expression could not bear this burden without creating legal inconsistencies were copyright to be enshrined in the common law. In *An Address to the Artists and Manufacturers of Great Britain* (1774), begun before the lords' decision yet published soon afterward, William Kenrick wondered why owners of literary properties should be entitled to a permanent monopoly, as the London booksellers claimed, whereas patents for mechanical inventions should remain protected only by statute. The booksellers, Kenrick supposed, wished to convince the lords that "*authors* claim a greater indulgence of the legislature than other *artists*, because their writings tend to the improvement of the human mind."[61] Arguing that creators of all forms of intellectual property ought to be granted the same privileges, Kenrick thought that literary expression provided insufficient evidence of how differently people thought. Inventors, he objected, were original thinkers who did not rely on the written word to make their ideas public. Likewise, many of Britain's greatest intellectuals were undistinguished as writers:

> The genius of Newton was not of a *literary* cast, nor does he raise our admiration or command our respect so much as an *author*, as he does in the capacity of an *inventor* or *artist*. . . . It is Sir Isaac Newton the *mathematician*, the *experimentalist*, the *mechanic*, and not the *writer*, whose name is so highly honoured and transmitted with so much renown to posterity. . . . [S]hall the ingenuity of those talents . . . be held *very inferiour* to his literary abilities; which were at best on a level with mediocrity?[62]

Kenrick understood that copyright applied to all new published writings, no matter how stylishly or dully written. His point, rather, was that every person was capable of thinking differently without necessarily demonstrating this difference on the printed page. The law ought to encourage learning in all its forms and by extension recognize that people may individuate themselves by means other than language.

As it happened, the House of Lords' decision effectively confirmed this by allowing a similar regime of statutory protection to remain in force for both copyrights and patents. Noting the decision in an appendix to his pamphlet, Kenrick worried that it eliminated inconsistency in the law without clarifying the relation between expression and individuation. If any mode of written expression could be copyrighted, an individuated style was irrelevant as a sign of property. Yet if copyright as a legal principle was to be justified on the assumption that every person had the potential to think and write differently, then this would have the dual effect of heightening the already elevated status of the few authors who wrote in a style so distinctive as to evince an original sensibility, while also rendering problematic the work of compilers and popularizers, like Kenrick himself. As he pointed out, the advancement of learning depended not just on the productions of original genius but on publications designed to render existing knowledge accessible to the public. "In the works of original writers, such as Shakespeare, Milton, &c.," he explained, the nature of their "property is sufficiently ascertained; but for one original writer, that appears in the republic of letters, there are five hundred copyists and compilers. Their number also of necessity encreases, as books are multiplied; nor can it well be otherwise, unless all improvements in literature be precluded." By privileging an individuated style as the paradigm of copyrightable expression, the law threatened to inhibit the wide dissemination of knowledge. To avert this possibility, Kenrick concluded, Parliament ought to inform writers "how far they are authorized to abridge, copy or make quotations from the works of their predecessors."[63] Courts and legislatures have ever since grappled with the arbitrariness of any definition of fair use.

Style and Liberty

The decision of 1774 led to a lengthy ceasefire in debates over the nature of literary property, and for decades the courts continued to apply the idea–expression distinction in infringement cases without articulating it fully or commenting on its rationale. The distinction was not formally set out until 1854, when in *Jefferys v. Boosey* the House of Lords was once again asked to consider the philosophical bases of intellectual property in response to one final challenge to its earlier decision in *Donaldson v. Becket* not to enshrine copyright in the common law. The distinction was not central to the case. It was merely one of several "first principles" of copyright that Justice Erle, one of the judges advising the lords, identified as having become embedded in the legal tradition. "The subject of property," he informed the lords, "is the order of words in the author's composition; not the words themselves, they being analogous to the elements of matter, which are not appropriated unless combined, nor the ideas expressed by those words, they existing in the mind alone, which is not capable of appropriation."[64] Erle's explanation of the distinction has since been routinely cited as its first true affirmation in the law, though it was clearly derived from Mansfield's classic statement in *Millar v. Taylor*, quoted above. The principal refinement Erle made to Mansfield's opinion was to specify the things that no one could appropriate: the words that are the raw ingredients of writing, the ideas the words express, and the mind that contemplates those ideas.

This emphasis on the mind's autonomy was the one crucial alteration that brought Mansfield's rhetorical account of the idea–expression dichotomy into line with modern notions of individuation and the self's freedom. Erle's understanding of the dichotomy owed even more to Hargrave's account than to Mansfield's, as is obvious from what he went on to say in its defense:

> [T]he claim is not to ideas, but to the order of words, and that this order has a marked identity and a permanent endurance. Not only are the words chosen by a superior mind peculiar to itself, but in ordinary life no two descriptions of the same fact will be in the same words, and no two answers to your Lordships' questions will be the same. The order of each man's words is as singular as his countenance, and although if two authors composed originally the same order of words, each would have a property therein, still the probability [of] such an occurrence is less than that there should be two countenances that could not be discriminated. The permanent endurance of words is obvious, by comparing the words of ancient authors with other works of their day; the vigour of the words is unabated; the other works have mostly perished.[65]

Almost all of this was paraphrased from Hargrave, including most notably the analogy between words and faces. Aside from the joke about no two answers to the lords being the same, the only claim in this passage that did not originate with Hargrave was the bizarre final point about the permanence of expression. Not only was the point contradictory—words can hardly be said to endure if works from antiquity have perished—but it was utterly irrelevant to the question of what was protected under copyright. Erle nonetheless saw fit to make the point because it confirmed for him Hargrave's linking of words and the mind. Works may be easily differentiated by their expression, but for Erle, the clearest evidence that a work was the creation of "a superior mind peculiar to itself" was not its expression, not any choice of words, but the individuation of its style, the "vigour of the words" that the best authors used to express and immortalize their thoughts.

Erle's comment suggests something important about the role of style in a democratic society. It is style rather than expression that has come to assume the evidentiary burden posed by the notion of individuation, the burden of showing that people think differently. As I said above, the notion of individuation legitimizes the law of copyright by assigning it the valuable function of encouraging self-determination and diversity of expression. In the law, the burden this notion poses is given to expression, but it presents no consequences for the law's application: judges can observe the idea–expression dichotomy and differentiate works by their expression without ever having to test whether people write differently because they think differently. Individuation in expression need not be verified for the law to work efficiently. It need only be embraced as a foundational tenet of democracy.

Treating the evidentiary burden posed by this tenet as irrelevant to the law's application does not eliminate it, however. It merely assumes that the burden is shared equally by all forms of discourse. Public expression, the tenet presupposes, is diverse by virtue of the different ways people think. Yet outside of the narrow parameters of the law's application, evidence of this diversity cannot be inferred solely from expression: a work might differ from others in its arrangement of words without bearing any sign of the individual sensibility that created it. It is therefore style rather than expression that carries the burden of signifying individuation. Public discourse in a democratic society depends on expressive diversity, which in turn rests on a notion of individuation, the ability of every citizen to write in a manner that corresponds to his or her natural or chosen way of thinking. The word for this corresponding manner of expression is "style," the verbal individuation that all persons have the potential to perfect as confirmation of their own self-determination.

This means that style has equally to bear the further burden posed by individuation, that of appearing to be both an expression of the mind's free agency and the product of ingrained differences in the way people think. People write differently because they think differently, whether by will or impulse. The paradoxical implications of this burden—that thought and discourse are both invented and determined, both free and not free—renders the status of style deeply ambivalent in modern democracy. On the one hand, style can be imitated and reproduced by other writers in accordance with the idea–expression dichotomy, which treats style as equivalent to ideas. It can likewise be abstracted as a set of rhetorical techniques and be shared as such, in which case it is no longer individuated, determinate, or readable as evidence that people think differently. On the other hand, the notion of individuation implies that how people think influences how they write throughout their works and not just in any single expression of their style. Individuation determines style, even if it must remain possible for authors to vary their styles by choice. The notion of individuation essentially conflates a person's distinctive way of thinking and speaking—that person's style—with its expression in any given work.

Moreover, whereas the same idea can be expressed by different authors in different words, there can be no other form of a style—no other style of a style, as it were. There can be only applications of the style, each of which cannot be legally replicated by another. According to the logic of individuation, there can be no direct transfer of a personal style from one author to another. Any author who adopts another's technique necessarily reindividuates it to his or her way of thinking. As one later nineteenth-century legal theorist explained, summarizing Erle's paraphrase of Hargrave, "No second author could express himself in the same order of words on any subject, however shortly treated, as another author, though they may deal with the same fundamental ideas. This order of words is therefore necessarily individualised and ear-marked, and incapable of being mistaken for any other man's product."[66] Like ideas, then, style in the abstract is public, indeterminate, replicable, and transferable. Unlike ideas, style in the particular is private, determinate, nonreplicable, and nontransferable, and, in principle, it legitimizes by its inimitability the law's assumption that people think differently. Style both is and is not free.

One consequence of this ambivalence is that copyright is grounded on a notion of individuation yet is indifferent to individual achievements in style. If style expresses the individual, then one author's style is no better than another's. Nor is there any need for the law to present authors with financial incentives to write in a personal style since they are already naturally inclined to do so. Conversely, the idea–expression dichotomy requires that the creation of a new style cannot be legally protected since every author ought to be free to adopt or refine another's style and to profit from its use in expressing an idea. Under the law, any style will do, since authors must be free to write in whatever style they wish, whether personal or impersonal, lively or nondescript, stock or Shakespearean. The law assumes that authors are capable of being original whether they write in an unknown language or in a language really used by men, but it does not reward stylistic originality since, the potential for individuation being realized only in exceptional instances, it cannot treat stylistically inventive authors differently than it does the generality of writers who follow conventional models of address. The law fosters expressive diversity, the right and ability of all citizens to think and write differently, while also respecting the indeterminacy of public discourse by neither requiring nor rewarding tangible evidence of stylistic distinctness. In sum, the law has neglected style because it is founded on an incoherent account of its value.

This incoherence may pose no difficulty for the law's application, but it does present a problem for democratic society in general: the evidentiary issue of how style can serve to show that people think and write in diverse ways when in fact much public expression is not stylistically distinctive. Individuation supposes that everyone thinks and writes differently, but as the new rhetoricians recognized, not everyone manages to perfect a style that can be appreciated by others. Johnson, who endorsed the idea, felt that someone with a keen critical eye might spot the singularities of any writer's style. But as he told Boswell in 1778, few authors produced enough work for their style to become widely recognizable: "I think every man whatever has a peculiar style, which may be discovered by nice examination and comparison with others: but a man must write a great deal to make his style obviously discernible. As logicians say, this appropriation of style is infinite *in potestate*, limited *in actu*." An author's style could not provide evidence of the public's expressive diversity if it bore no obvious signs of its own uniqueness. Belief in individuation had therefore to be sustained only on the evidence that *some* authors had managed to perfect a personal style that was obviously discernible. For Johnson, this evidence was readily at hand: "Those who have a style of eminent excellence, such as Dryden and Milton, can always be distinguished."[67] Canonical authors, however few in number, were the paradigms of inviolable individuality that confirmed the potential in all persons to realize a style fully attuned to their particular way of thinking. Their styles were marks of difference, if not ownership. They were individuation's proof.

Kenrick had predicted that canonical authors would enjoy even greater stature once individuation put a premium on stylistic uniqueness. Yet this was not exactly what happened. Quite aside from the fact that copyright did not reward a style of eminent excellence any more than it did a pedestrian one, authors were as likely to be canonized for their styles under a rhetorical tradition as under later aesthetic norms. What occurred instead was that stylistic distinctiveness became a quality primarily identified with literary works, with literature coming to occupy a special role among discourses: supplying the clearest proof that some authors could accommodate language to their sensibility. Before then, the compositions of any rhetorically adept writer, regardless of genre or subject, were deemed suitable models for imitation and their styles remained amenable to refinement. The idea of individuation made it difficult, however, to see how an author's personal style could advance the refinement of culture. Johnson, though drawn to the idea, was still a firm enough exponent of rhetorical principles to see some pedagogical value in imitating the styles of canonical poets, however much he regretted the bad blank verse that Milton's style had inspired in his day. What Johnson could not abide was any attempt at refining these styles. Dryden and Milton were the best at what they did and could not be surpassed. And even if it were possible to refine a well-known poetic style, the results would have a cramping effect on literary production. As Johnson warned of Pope's style, "to attempt any further improvement of versification will be dangerous."[68]

This did not mean that the project of refinement was abandoned. As I noted earlier, the project was to a degree internalized: the new rhetoricians advised students to master the plain style fully, adapt it to their personality, and "make what we write our own."[69] But while students were still taught to hone their skills by imitating literary and other forms of writing, the objective of refining prose to attain greater discursive conformity and efficiency continued to be seen as desirable in most public, professional, and scientific genres other than literature. Since the evidence of only a handful of literary authors was thought sufficient to establish that all persons were capable of thinking and writing differently, there was no need to dispense with the many rhetorical conventions and standards of verbal competence that governed writing styles in the discourses of knowledge. It is in fact debatable whether to this day these discourses actually tolerate all styles of writing, let alone one that is distinctive. Just as Hargrave apologized in his pamphlet's postscript for its imperfections of expression, as if these were not to be read as reflecting his own peculiar train of thought, so the current leading theorist of expressive diversity acknowledges, almost as an afterthought, that participation in the public sphere requires citizens to possess "discursive skill."[70] While copyright is presumed to enable diversity of expression, the reality is that in much public writing, not any style will do and rarely is the style of a composition read for signs of its author's sensibility. As a result, then, of neither encouraging nor discouraging innovations in style, the law has allowed the market to sustain and arguably promote a high degree of stylistic uniformity in most forms of public discourse.

The one enabling exception to this modern regime of expression is literature, among whose principal public roles since the eighteenth century has been to serve as confirmatory evidence of democracy's expressive diversity. Standards of verbal competence, desirable though they may be in facilitating public discourse and the circulation of knowledge, must inevitably circumscribe and therefore undermine the indeterminacy of public discourse. Only in literature is this indeterminacy presumed to manifest itself as fully as the public will allow. In not being answerable to any determining order of address, literature helps to sustain the belief that citizens are free to think and write as they wish, even though in virtually all other speech situations they will not be taken seriously if they fail to observe multiple intersecting norms of address, decorum, and intellectual preparedness. All citizens are free to create works of literature on any topic, in whichever style they please, with or without formal training, and in accordance with the autonomous exercise of their mental powers, the dictates of their temperament, or, as many believed during the later eighteenth century, the promptings of their unlettered genius. Any style may qualify as literary, from the most conventional to the most idiosyncratic. Undoubtedly the advent of copyright gave legal purport to the depreciation of rhetoric, as the modern literary author, eager to display a personal style, learned to do without the old rhetorical formulas while continuing to share with other authors the less obviously stylistic features of genre, theme, and allusion. Yet just as works in any genre can now be read for signs of literariness, so literary authors can make use of any stylistic or rhetorical feature, including the most commonplace forms of other discourses.

Literariness is, in this sense, not a special attribute of the language used by literary authors. It is rather, as Rancière has suggested, "the radical democracy of the letter that anyone can grab hold of."[71] Since it can take any form and be practiced by anyone, there can be no pragmatic criterion for distinguishing literary art from other discourses. The only condition that is felt to set literary discourse apart from other forms of public speech is that it cannot be refined—"art never improves," in Eliot's dictum.[72] All persons, the notion of individuation assumes, are capable of developing a personal style and applying it to any subject. Yet outside of literary writing, this style must be made to accord with prevailing standards of discursive competence in order to ensure its communicative efficacy. Literary art, by contrast, is felt to be impervious to improvement because it is assumed that literary authors do the obverse of what is expected in other genres: no matter how extensively they might imitate or borrow from other discourses, they are not required to answer to existing norms of address but may instead accommodate those norms to their own style and sensibility. Literature presents a democratic public with evidence of its own expressive diversity, paradoxically by honoring an aristocracy of singular stylists, like Shakespeare, Milton, Pope, Johnson, Keats, Browning, Joyce, Hemingway, and Faulkner. Yet it does so at the price of its own specificity among public discourses, its ancient role in refining the persuasive and signifying powers of public speech, any normative certitude about how excellence in literary style is to be achieved, and a persistent undecidability as to whether the individual expressiveness it enables mediates the mind's free agency or the determining compulsions of temperament and personality.

Few of the contestants in the literary property debate gave much thought to the role of style in defining intellectual property. Most believed that copyright fulfilled its purpose by directing human creativity toward the production of knowledge and ideas. The law, they felt, could be indifferent to style without either impairing the advancement of learning or denying poets the opportunity to profit from their art. As a result of this indifference, the law has since led us from an age of imitations to an information age, and it is now inconceivable that it could have been otherwise. At the same time, once the protection the law afforded to differences in expression began to be justified on the grounds that these variations proceeded directly from more fundamental differences in how people felt and thought, it equally became possible to believe that style did not require protection or encouragement because it was already private property prior to the moment of its expression. For the authors who had perfected a personal style, it could be henceforth imagined, their property in their works would remain secure well after other authors' ideas had been dispersed among the public. As Isaac D'Israeli put it at the end of the eighteenth century, "[I]t is Style alone by which posterity will judge of a great work, for an author can have nothing truly his own but his Style; facts, scientific discoveries, every kind of information may be seized by all, but an author's diction cannot be taken from him."[73]

DEFAMATION AND PRIVACY

CHAPTER THREE

What Does Literature Publicize?

Among literature's most important social uses prior to the eighteenth century was as a medium of publicity. Poetry's verbal energy and ease of retention made it the preeminent genre for immortalizing heroes, honoring patrons, transmitting divine truth to new generations, and giving durable expression to communal hopes. Its suasive reach could be extended through performance in plays, masques, recitals, and songs. Its allegories and fictions could help its makers evade the censor as they sought to spread scandal, abuse enemies, and engage in controversy. Poetry could be read in public houses, bring coteries together, mobilize a crowd, and make its authors famous.

By the early eighteenth century much literary production still served the ends of publicity, with the periodical essay, in particular, contributing greatly to the public's self-conception as a body brought together through discourse. At the same time, many of literature's traditional uses as a vehicle for publicity had begun to seem antiquated or corrupt. The image of the Grub Street hack who dreamed of poetic immortality became a staple of satire. Memorializing patrons and ministers was dismissed as mercenary business, the laureateship as selling out to party, and the writing of heroic verse as the nadir of dullness. Satirists made a show of their contempt for the public sphere even as they prided themselves on revealing the secrets of state.[1] Commentators hailed English society as too polite for panegyric and condemned it as too refined for epic.

These conflicting attitudes augured a decline in literature's medial role in the face of growing competition from other forms, above all newspapers and prints. By the end of the century, it was obvious that these other forms had eclipsed literary compositions as organs of publicity: they were easier and cheaper to obtain, appeared with greater frequency and regularity, conveyed more information and detail, presented a wider range of content, disseminated this knowledge to more people, and did so with greater uniformity and efficiency in a rhetorically accessible and more or less verifiable form. "Newspapers," one wag enthused, "are confessedly the best vehicles of political information" and, more generally, "the best registers of fact relative to the progress of civilization, arts, and sciences."[2] Just as significant, the ascendancy of the periodical press led to crucial epistemic adjustments in what was expected from public discourses in terms of their truth content and modes of expression. For its part, literature remained hugely popular, reaching more readers than ever before thanks in part to new venues, like the periodical press, and it was still prized as a medium for recording personal observations, giving bite to protest, and voicing society's aspirations. But it was no longer thought of as a major conduit of public information or opinion.

The question I address in this chapter, then, is this: what, if anything, does literature in a modern world *publicize*? That the question may seem crudely functionalist while inviting no ready answer is evidence, I maintain, of a fundamental change in literature's fortunes as a public discourse. Since the mid-eighteenth century, literary writing has gone from being one of the most versatile media of publicity to being another kind of medium altogether, one no less vital to democratic society but serving the aims of expression and invention rather than publicity. To describe the change in this way, however, only points up a deep ambiguity in what is expected of literature, for how is any expressive act, to be grasped as such, not ultimately public in its import? After all, literary writers as ever write for a public and for many of the same civic-minded or personal reasons that have long motivated poets and storytellers. Literature may be now valued primarily as a mode of expression or fiction making, but this has hardly entailed its exile from the public arena. Literary productions are publicly circulated, bought and sold, and often read or performed in public. They may deal with public concerns, dramatize the spirit of the age, and be used to sensitize the public to matters of common interest. And they are themselves the frequent subject of publicity, being cited, criticized, taught, and celebrated in public. There is no reason that literary works cannot be made to serve the ends of publicity. And yet we do not normally think of literary works as serving these ends. Some believe that using literature as a publicizing medium cheapens it. Literature, it seems, expresses without publicizing; it is and is not public.

To be precise, literature has always been valued as a creative and expressive art, but from the mid-eighteenth century onward its verbal and fictive inventiveness was felt to put it at odds with conventional modes of public address. By then, another of literature's traditional uses, as a vehicle for articulating personal experience, was becoming one of its most popular functions. In direct correlation to the rise of the periodical press as the most ubiquitous medium of public knowledge, literature's expressiveness was felt by many to be best suited to the representation of private speech, perception, and behavior in novels, lyric poems, life writings, and domestic dramas. The change, it is commonly supposed, reflected a heightened cultural fascination with the realm of the subjective and a more fundamental shift in ideological values toward prioritizing the humanizing influence of private over public life. At the least, the change was a response to the increasing impersonality of public communication, as epitomized by the quotidian prose of the periodical press, and to the view promulgated by moral philosophers that public life was a theater of sociability where strangers developed mutual sympathy by witnessing each other's experiences from a spectatorial distance.

Literary works would henceforth be valued as a corrective to the normative strangerhood that otherwise preserved personal liberty in the public sphere. They permitted autonomous individuals to overcome the hermeneutic divisions that separated them by encouraging them to imagine what life was like from the point of view of others without infringing on their autonomy. One of literature's public roles would thus be to maintain public recognition and respect for a private realm of inner lives, individual styles, and personal choices, feelings, and fantasies. It permitted the public to know what went on in the private moral spaces where individuals exercised their liberty and to know perhaps whether it was doing its job of ensuring similar spaces for everyone, but to know this without seeming to encroach on those spaces.

To the extent that it is still perceived to fulfill this role, literature occupies an exceptional position among public discourses. By definition, the public cannot intrude upon the private without making it public, without publicizing it. At the same time, it is the public that decides what it has a right to know, which means that the public must be able to possess knowledge about anything in order to make decisions about what lies within its purview. The public's access to knowledge cannot be restricted without undermining its unbounded authority. As one late eighteenth-century defender of the press put it, "The most capital advantage an enlightened people can enjoy is the liberty of discussing every subject which can fall within the compass of the human mind; while this remains, freedom will flourish."[3] Yet while a public is sustained by the unrestricted exchange of speech among its members, it also defines itself by deeming certain forms of speech and behavior as private and outside its immediate jurisdiction. Public deliberation over private experiences cannot be done without violating the self's autonomy and compromising the public's self-imposed task of safeguarding individual freedoms. More than this, without a realm of the private against which it can be defined, public discourse would encompass anything and everything, leaving it without a way of making meaningful distinctions. In a self-imposed limitation, then, the public requires that certain areas of experience cannot be treated in public unless they are mediated through modes of discourse that are sufficiently generalized, impersonal, or scientific to address those experiences without rendering all their dimensions public.

Literature is exempted, conceptually if not always legally, from this requirement. One of the principal functions of literature in modern democracies is to enable members of the public to experience forms of speech and behavior that otherwise could not be treated in public unless mediated through generalized, impersonal, or scientific language. Literature serves the public by furnishing it with knowledge it cannot otherwise obtain without infringing on personal liberty—in effect, by articulating dimensions of the self without publicizing them. In doing so, it ensures the public's supreme right to know and keeps its discourse free and indeterminate by making it possible for its members to write about anything in expressive, even indecent language without fear of being ejected from the public sphere. Literary works enable the public to experience its own freedom from determination, including the legal norms it imposes on itself to ensure that respect is maintained for personal liberty and property. Works of art and literature, as the ideology of the aesthetic would have it, are objectifications of human freedom; splendidly autonomous of any external authority that might dictate the form and nature of their being, they provide both the public and the self with compelling models of their own sovereignty.[4]

Of course, the public has often sought to contain the indeterminacy of its own discourse by censoring literary writings for offenses of speech and representation. Only since the 1920s, in fact, has the exceptional status of literature among public genres come to be formally recognized in Anglo-American law, and then somewhat tenuously, using the principle that "serious" works ought to be exempted from any legal definition of obscenity and, in some jurisdictions, blasphemy. The trouble is that it is difficult to make sense of this exemption under the norms governing public speech. If literature cannot fulfill its role of keeping public discourse free and indeterminate unless it is exempt from these norms, it is not possible under these norms to say why this role is a good thing without rendering the rationale for these norms incoherent.

Lawmakers, faced with this problem, have argued that while art and literature do not work in the same way as other public discourses do, they are to be valued on moral grounds for the special insight they provide into experience or the imaginative sympathy they foster in encouraging us to see that experience from the point of view of others. Versions of this liberal argument, however, end up doing one of two things: either they stress the primacy of the ethical as the determining criterion of legitimate speech and hence deny the indeterminacy of discourse while leaving unprotected many forms of art and literature that are not expressly moral in their import, or they so abstract the source of moral value that it becomes unclear whether art and literature serve any public purpose. An example of the latter is Alexander Meiklejohn's claim that works of art and literature ought to be accorded First Amendment protection because they "lead the way toward sensitive and informed appreciation and response to the values out of which the riches of the general welfare are created."[5] It is impossible to tell from this statement whether the values of sensitivity and informed appreciation are themselves part of the values out of which the riches of the general welfare are created, or whether they are somehow antecedent to those foundational values in the sense that we are incapable of assenting to these values unless art and literature have already rendered us sensitive to them.

A more common response to the problem has been to insist in Kantian fashion that works of the imagination should not be judged by the same criteria used to evaluate utilitarian speech. This response exempts the aesthetic on grounds that are beyond rational interrogation and thus implicitly acknowledges that the norms governing speech cannot be made fully coherent.[6] Yet this acknowledgment gives rise to two problems. First, the indeterminacy of public speech is such that the criteria for distinguishing literary from nonliterary speech can never be definitively established, so the choice of works that are felt to be entitled to an aesthetic exemption will always seem to some degree arbitrary. Second, the exemption can be applied only to select branches of the law regulating speech. Since the exemption is commonly claimed in defense of works considered obscene, and justified on the grounds that it safeguards the right of individuals to choose their tastes and beliefs, it protects literature principally as it is experienced by private persons and thus does not pertain to the social dimensions of literary production. Hence it does not free literary writers from all regulation: no matter how aesthetically expressive or serious their writings might be said to be, literary authors cannot defame, steal another's intellectual property, commit fraud, or detail aspects of anyone's private life without permission. Writers in other public genres may be permitted to violate these restrictions if they can demonstrate legal justification—an example is the truth defense in libel—which is itself rationalized on the assumption that infringing on personal autonomy may sometimes be necessary for the greater good of society. Literary authors, by contrast, cannot conceivably obtain such permission on the same grounds while also seeking special dispensation for their writings as works of artistic expression and imagination.

While the advent of aesthetic philosophy in the late eighteenth century may have been concomitant with the birth of modern democracies, the law during the period treated literature no differently than it did other discourses. All writings were subject to the same restrictions, and all writers could draw on the same few justifications to defend themselves at trial. Over the course of the period, I argue, greater press freedoms entailed newer types of restriction, such as greater prohibitions on the use of copyrighted material. These freedoms equally led to new justifications for breaches of public decorum. In chapter 4, I consider the origin of one such press freedom, the principle of fair comment, which provides a qualified privilege from charges of defamation for satirists who ridicule public figures. Copyright and fair comment, however, were the period's only legal innovations that were discussed specifically in terms of their bearing on literary production. Otherwise, no lawmaker at the time felt that literature was exceptional as a public genre or entitled to special dispensation from existing laws and moral norms.

There were nonetheless implemented other legal changes that, in altering expectations for public speech, had an indirect effect on literature's public status, such that literature began to seem not as serviceable to the public as other discourses of knowledge that were eclipsing it as a medium of publicity. It was not that literary writers renounced matters of public concern in favor of talking only of their feelings. Rather, the norms of legal justification had changed. In the past all writers defended their activities by showing how they upheld the faith, the kingdom, and eternal truth; these were among the functions that literary writings were felt to perform supremely well. By the late eighteenth century, however, authors were expected to defend what they wrote by showing how it served the "public interest," conceived as an order of values whose legitimacy depended on the fact that it pertained to all citizens while benefiting no one in particular—neither king, state, church, nor private person. In this new depersonalized order, it was not clear how literature, with its peculiar expressivity and imaginativeness, was entitled to the same legal justification as other discourses. Public authors in general might not always observe standards of rationality and impersonality, but to the degree they were expected to do so, literature's purpose and rationale as a public discourse became ambiguous.

As already noted, the change would not be formally recognized in the law until much later, nor, other than in relation to copyright, were eighteenth-century lawmakers moved to debate literature's public value. The change can all the same be inferred from emerging expectations about how public speech was to be conducted. In this chapter, I consider these expectations and what they suggest about literature's utility as a medium of publicity in relation to changing legal attitudes over defamation and privacy. Specifically, I examine how these attitudes bore upon an obscure libel case from 1783. The case itself was inconsequential, the court dismissing it without its proceedings or opinion being reported. But it is the material that provoked the action, a series of poems alleging a sexual crime, and the ensuing press coverage of the crime that interest me. What began as a subject for poetry quickly became a media event fought over in prose, its factual details examined with forensic closeness, its tit-for-tat accusations challenged according to norms of falsifiability, and its contestants judging each other on how soberly they presented their cases to the newly imagined "bar of the public." In a series of extended notes on the scandal's legal context, I suggest that this shift from poetry to prose was representative of a broader change in the nature of public discourse and a growing ambivalence over the normative status of literature within it.

A Seduction in Shropshire

In October 1782 the London bookseller Thomas Becket published a pamphlet containing two anonymous verse epistles.[7] The first, *A Letter in Verse, from a Married Man to His Own Wife*, was an exercise in extended metaphor that analogized wedded life to gardening. The second, *A Poetical Epistle from an Unfortunate Young Lady at Portsmouth to Her Lover*, purported to be a woman's farewell letter to a young man, in which she relates her desire for early death after having been sexually assaulted by an older man. This second poem, with its Shakespearean allusions tagged for readers and its requisite curtsy to John Denham's über-couplet ("Confus'd tho' guiltless, tho' enamour'd cold; / Timid through shame, through conscious honor bold"), was no less conventional than the first. The poem was nonetheless advertised as having a claim on the public's attention less for its literary merit than for its being based on fact and written with the aim of reporting a crime that had gone unprosecuted.

As the alleged incident had only recently occurred, the poet could risk presenting only oblique details about the assault. The speaker reports that the victim had been removed from her native land, "where Palmettos their cool umbrage shed," to live with an English guardian who treated her well enough until shortly after she turned fourteen when he, aroused "with Tarquin-flame," robbed her of her honor. Though intimating that the guardian had threatened his victim with a "ruffian hand," the poet refrains from calling him a rapist, since no form of defamation was considered more indisputable than the act of accusing someone of the commission of a felony. Other poets who were shortly to write on the same incident would call it a seduction, a term that could be a euphemism for rape since "seducing" a girl over ten years of age was not considered a criminal offense.[8] The speaker of *A Poetical Epistle*, however, nowhere uses the term, though she relates at length her confusion over whether, as her guardian alleged, she was complicit in "foul wrongs." She tells her lover that she was too ashamed to say anything about the assault for months afterward. Only now, on the eve of her departure from England, has she decided to reveal her secret to him after learning that her guardian has been spreading lies about her in public.

In writing to absolve a former suitor from the odium cast upon her, the poem's speaker does share one feature with the seduced maidens who were a mainstay of the period's popular fiction: they all worry that what has befallen them has tarnished the reputations of the people close to them. Parents and suitors were often depicted in seduction narratives as the victims of the woman's errant behavior, with fathers in particular shown bemoaning the disgrace to their families. The epistle's speaker emphasizes her father's innocence in putting her under the guardianship of someone whom he could not possibly have known would betray him. It is her father's absence, however, that is a cause of much distress to her, and she grieves on his behalf, to the point where she hears her own "funeral knel."[9] Pleading with her lover not to avenge the crime, the speaker insists that she would rather die unknown than have her story brought to light: "To die is all I ask.—The silent Grave / Yields a safe refuge." In a note, the poet assures readers that he is not exaggerating his subject's despair: "These excruciating feelings in the lovely Victim are not an imaginary description, but are well known to have been real."

Reviewers of the poem were not so sure. The *Monthly Review* could say little about the events in question beyond conjecturing that readers in Portsmouth knew something about them: "The poetical epistle is, it seems, founded on some recent fact, which, we suppose, is well known at the place from whence it is dated." Unable to confirm the poem's factual basis, the reviewer could only quote its account of the attack to "give some idea of the story on which the poem is founded." The reviewer for the *Critical Review* could likewise muster only tepid praise for the poem's claim to authenticity. "[C]onsidering that poetical writers have been thought to succeed best in fiction," he declared, the poem's story "is related with at least as much energy as might be expected."[10]

A few months later the epistle was reprinted, this time by the Shrewsbury bookseller Philip Sandford, and bore an attribution to the Reverend Samuel Johnson, a local schoolmaster. This second edition offered no new information on the alleged rape, though it included the statement "Truth has already most wonderfully made its way to light, and the Clouds are beginning to be dispersed."[11] As it happened, readers in Shrewsbury, if not London or Portsmouth, were by then well apprised of the events. Johnson, to whom the victim had told her story prior to leaving England from Portsmouth, was not the only Salopian poet who believed that verse could be used to elicit sympathy to her cause. By the time his epistle appeared in its second edition, the subject had occasioned at least four other poems plus an extensive series of exchanges conducted through prose pamphlets, in the pages of the *Shropshire Chronicle*, and in notes posted at a local coffee shop. Yet by that point, the poetry had served its purpose. Once details of the scandal had begun to emerge, its disputants no longer believed they could win their case before the tribunal of the public unless they discussed the details with a degree of referentiality and specificity that they felt could be achieved only through the medium of prose.

One poem, "The Trusty Guardian," was likely a squib, being advertised but never published.[12] Two others, which appeared within days of each other in late November 1782, were more substantial. One was called "The Seducer's Distracted Confession, in a Poetical Rhapsody." Later revealed as the work of another Shrewsbury poet, Joseph Williams, the poem took the form of a dramatic monologue spoken by a self-styled "Brother of the Knife" who has been driven mad with guilt over assaulting his young ward and then soiling her reputation to protect his.[13] Williams's account of the assault is more elliptical if more metaphorically violent than Johnson's:

> Lust, that rank mildew, seiz'd my ev'ry sense,
> And in black hour I blasted innocence,
> Down at my feet the vanquish'd victim fell,
> But in that struggle rous'd the fiends of hell.[14]

Reluctant to enter into the particulars of the crime, both poets emphasize the damage it has caused to their respective speaker's state of mind: like the victim in Johnson's poem, Williams's seducer spends most of his time laying bare his anguish and shame. The "Confession" is nonetheless making a different kind of emotional claim than the epistle since it is a work of pure fantasy of a type familiar to contemporary readers. Katherine Binhammer, in her study of seduction narratives, cites Williams's verse as an example of a minor poetic genre then enjoying a *Clarissa*-inspired vogue, a genre she calls the "male confessional narrative" in which one libertine tells another of his regret over his sexual crimes.[15] Williams's poem includes just enough detail to indicate that he was referencing actual persons. Its speaker twice names his victim as "F——r" and tells of his military career in India, where, he boasts, "in one night, a thousand slaves I slew."[16] But rather than attempting to generate sympathy for the victim, to whose grief his fictional seducer is oblivious, Williams is encouraging readers to indulge in moral wish fulfillment. And at least one did: after the poem's appearance, a correspondent to the *Chronicle* expressed the hope that while lampoons would have little effect on the accused, "perhaps a Ballad *bawled* in his ears every day, in Milk-Street, or wherever he walks, might at length realize the 'Rhapsody' of the 'Seducer's Confession.'"[17]

On the face of it, the longest of the poems, *Seduction; or, The Cause of Injured Innocence Pleaded*, was making a similar appeal, its poet emphatically warning the seducer that the hour of justice is near. Yet the effect of the work as a whole was rather different. Published anonymously, the poem was later acknowledged to be the work of another local cleric, Richard de Courcy, the vicar of St. Alkmond's.[18] Unlike Johnson and Williams, de Courcy does not rely on fiction to veil his accusations against the alleged seducer, whom he identifies by innuendo as a retired colonel. De Courcy's is an old-fashioned satiric performance in which the poet proclaims the accused's bad character as forcefully as possible to raise a presumption of his guilt. It does not matter in such an exercise whether the claims presented are factually accurate or rigorously argued. The colonel might have complained that de Courcy's poetic case against him was circular: as one author later put it, the poet assumes the colonel's guilt to prove the girl's innocence "and then makes use of her innocence to prove his guilt."[19] But the complaint was beside the point. De Courcy aims to work up a sense of conviction so potent that, from the reader's perspective, it simply overmatches the colonel's credibility. His poem is a thundering, 770-line vilification of an "inhuman monster" who, after plundering the Orient's riches during years of mercenary service with the East India Company, brought the imperial violence home to Britain by plundering the virtue of the Indian-born daughter of a fellow officer, who had entrusted him with her care.

Throughout, de Courcy appeals to all manner of literary, moral, and religious authority. Writing in the late Augustan mode of high abstraction, de Courcy accuses the colonel not merely of assaulting a young woman but of perpetrating crimes against Virtue and Truth. He loads the poem with allusions and exempla, and he takes advantage of coincidence by rendering the woman's name as "Miss F——r" and so linking her in the reader's mind to an earlier victim whose rape had been memorialized in verse. He includes panegyrics on the "honest zeal" of the several men, Williams among them, who brought her story to the public's attention. And he ends his poem with a vision of Christian redemption, as the angel of mercy descends from heaven to tell the colonel that were he to repent his sins, she would wash them off with her "sacred SPONGE."

Bathos aside, there is a problem with de Courcy's performance, which is that he doubts it will work on a man like the colonel. What galls de Courcy most about the colonel's behavior is his refusal to own up to any wrongdoing or to cease blaming the victim. Not content to extort secrecy from her, the colonel let it be known that her debauched ways got her thrown out of school and that he tried in vain to salvage her reputation by encouraging a match between her and a young gentleman of the town. Now, with the victim's story coming to light two years later and despite mounting public opprobrium, the colonel has redoubled his offensive by announcing that he has obtained corroboration of the girl's guilt and that, with the news that she has come into a large fortune, he is seeking to recover the expenses he incurred from paying for the maintenance of the child she bore as a result of a liaison with his footman George. In de Courcy's view, the colonel, even if he is not guilty of a crime, is behaving as if he were. He has never admitted any responsibility for the alleged sinfulness of a girl committed to his care nor extended her the least compassion. As de Courcy suggests in the poem's preface, the colonel may be "called a gentleman, because he has acquired a few hundreds a-year in the East Indies, keeps a coach, and wears a cockade," but he has not acted with honor.[20]

Sensing that it may not be possible to shame the colonel into an admission of guilt, de Courcy tries a different approach in the preface and in notes appended to the poem. In these, de Courcy abandons epideictic for forensic rhetoric and addresses his readers rather than the colonel. Claiming to set out "the melancholy, but Authentic Facts" of the case, he casts himself as the public's prosecutor, informing them of things few could have known while insisting that he never met the victim. The colonel, he writes, feigned illness on the day of the assault so as to be left alone with his prey, paid servants to spread rumors about her, and "often mentioned in company, that a tape-worm, of an enormous length, was extracted from his leg."[21] He disputes assertions the colonel has already made by citing rebuttal testimony from George the footman and others. He points out the inconsistency in how the colonel had originally discouraged contact between her and the young gentleman but then, following the assault, tried to persuade the gentleman's father to marry his son to a woman whom the colonel had accused of seducing his footman. And he contends that the colonel's few allies have undermined their credibility by resorting to an "illiberal dialect" by castigating her as a woman of the "pertest, grossest, coarsest" character. "When people inveigh," he avers, "they should at least learn to do it decently."[22]

He also writes as the victim's defender, boldly suggesting that a fourteen-year-old girl could hardly be supposed to have submitted to the advances of a man "above fifty years of age" and without "a single accomplishment of body or mind," unless she was coerced.[23] He is especially concerned to refute any suspicion that her story is unfounded because she is telling it only after it has become "impracticable" for any legal action to be initiated.[24] The "peculiar infelicity of her situation under the seducer's roof," he writes, initially "induced her to conceal the deed and the author of it."[25] Soon enough, her situation changed as she was ordered back to India—by the colonel himself, according to his later account. Unfortunately, her return to India was cut short since the ship that was taking her there, the *Mountstuart*, was part of a convoy of sixty-three vessels that were captured by Spanish and French forces during the action of August 9, 1780. The capture was Britain's greatest naval loss of the American Revolutionary War and the worst disaster ever for the East India Company. Taken captive, Miss F——r was eventually transported to London, where she was met by the colonel, who promptly housed her at a family friend's in the city.

According to the colonel, this friend was being attended at the time by the celebrated "man-midwife," Dr. William Osborn, who discovered Miss F——r's pregnancy just as the colonel was about to take her back to Shrewsbury. The colonel thereupon met with the girl's uncle, a Mr. Deveil, to inform him of her pregnancy, telling him that she had identified the footman as the child's father. Yet, according to de Courcy, "[s]ome very visible confusion having been observed in THE MANNER in which the dreadful secret was disclosed . . . excited strong suspicions in [Deveil's] breast . . . that [the colonel] was himself the guilty man."[26] However, Deveil did not meet with his niece to confirm his suspicions until he was later invited to Shrewsbury to assume guardianship over her. Deveil, sparing his niece from further humiliation while also arranging his family's relocation to India, did not initially challenge the colonel on his version of the events and only did so months later in response to the colonel vowing to sue the family for expenses. It was only then, on the eve of her return to India, from where it would have been impossible for her to answer the colonel's ongoing attacks on her reputation, that Miss F——r broke her silence.

De Courcy's ultimate aim in both his poem and its prose apparatus may be the same, but the methods he adopts in each work presuppose two different moral orders. In the poem, he is waging a verbal contest of honor, deploying the power of words and received authority to impeach the colonel's character. In the preface and notes, he supplies evidence and the testimony of witnesses, rebuts the colonel's claims, and declares that he has no personal stake in the case. His verse invites readers to imagine the colonel submitting to divine justice whereas his prose appeals to their rational judgment as a public tribunal. Either approach is legally risky. The potential consequences of accusing the colonel of rape were the same regardless of the manner in which the accusation was made. The colonel, as de Courcy later confirmed in a reply to his counterargument, was shortly to seek an indictment against the vicar's publisher, charging him with criminal libel, a charge that precluded the defendant from mounting a truth defense at trial. A person convicted of criminal libel, no matter the truth of his claims, was deemed to have acted with malice by making accusatory statements without going through established procedures and had thereby breached the peace by inviting retaliation from the injured party. This was the old order. De Courcy, however, knew that a Wilkesite campaign to recognize truth as a valid justification for libel was fast gaining momentum.[27] By 1800 judges were recognizing truth as a complete defense in civil cases.[28] And while the criminal law would be formally amended only in 1843, British juries in a series of high-profile cases, de Courcy was keen to report, had insisted on their right to determine the truth of an alleged libel.[29] This was the new order. And while the risk of prosecution was high under either, these orders presented prospective libelers with starkly different means of avoiding conviction. Under the old, an allegation could be at once veiled and affectingly conveyed in poetry and fiction. Under the new, an allegation could be justifiable only if it were verifiable and presented credibly enough in a tone of unbiased civic-mindedness for it to withstand cross-examination and be proven in court.[30]

The appearance in quick succession of three poems accusing him of rape was ample provocation for the colonel to take action. His first inclination, like de Courcy's, was to do things the old way. He demanded that Johnson sign a statement retracting his poetical epistle, and he posted a note at the Lion Coffee Room offering a reward of fifty guineas to anyone who could provide information leading to the discovery of the author of *Seduction*. Ominously, the note declared that the poet could avoid legal reprisal by granting the colonel "that satisfaction that a gentleman, aspersed in such a manner, cannot but require."[31] The note was not posted long before someone struck out its references to the colonel as a gentleman and man of honor.[32] Incensed, the colonel turned to the law and the press. He hired a phalanx of lawyers to bring his cause to the Court of King's Bench, he obtained affidavits from his servants testifying to having seen Miss F———r "embracing and kissing" his footman and performing "many other such feats,"[33] and he engaged the services of a ghostwriter to compose a twenty-eight-page prose rebuttal to de Courcy's claims. In it, the colonel comments sarcastically on de Courcy's rhetorical excesses in "his most beautiful Poem," saying that his "poetical fiction" merely disguises his ignorance about Miss F———r. His own pamphlet's "publication of that young Lady's real character," he scoffs, "will doubtless be 'ycleped horrid cruelty by her champion Poet."[34]

The colonel nonetheless takes the accusations set out in the "prose-part" of de Courcy's pamphlet seriously enough that he presents a competing narrative of the facts. In doing so, the colonel is implicitly granting that truth is a defense at least in the court of public opinion. Yet his argument wavers dramatically in tone and manner. He opens by dismissing de Courcy's accusations as merely ill informed but later denounces him as an "assassin" and "noxious vermin." At first, he refers to Miss F———r as "the very lewdest of her own lewd breed, the Parya," but later he describes her as an innocent child who was spoiled by his wife's overindulgent parenting, and then in a postscript he exonerates her as the "involuntary instrument" of a conspiracy by the Deveils to take control of her inheritance and blackmail him by charging him with her child's paternity.[35]

The colonel says he "wishes to be tried at the tribunal of the public" and insists that, unlike his detractors, he is following established rules of evidence. He offers his previous conduct as proof of his good character by telling of how "[w]hilst he was a bachelor in the East Indies, it was his fortune, as it is that of most European bachelors in that country, to have a child born to him by a native woman," but unlike those other European bachelors he had made ample provision for the child's education. He tells readers to ask experts whether he could have fathered Miss F――r's child since "deflowering and impregnating a subject so young as she is described to have been, by one and the same act, must appear a point at least problematical to many." He claims to possess the Deveils' transcript of their interview with their niece, a transcript that, he insists, contains material that de Courcy has "sedulously omitted" from his account so as to present as prejudicial a case as possible. Notably, he contends that the transcript proves he knew nothing of the girl's pregnancy because it reports that on learning the news, his first words were "Good God, I hope it is not by me!"[36]

The colonel's pamphlet, far from silencing his accusers, provoked them into taking bolder steps. In late November the *Shropshire Chronicle* published a forty-eight-line poem praising the author of *Seduction* for his courage in exposing a crime.[37] This would be the last work of poetry inspired by the scandal. From then on, the matter would be treated exclusively in prose. It is likely that de Courcy, a friend of the *Chronicle*'s publisher, Thomas Wood, had a hand in a series of articles that appeared in the paper over the next three months.[38] With increasing forwardness, the writer challenged the colonel's credibility. By mid-December, he was acting in the role of cross-examiner, posing direct questions to the colonel about his allegations against Miss F――r and the Deveils, and casting him as both dishonorable and desperate in his attempts both to sue the publisher of *Seduction* and to bring "his Cause to the Bar of the Public, by the Medium of the Press."[39]

Chastened, the colonel replied that he would willingly answer all questions but only in person at his home, a proposal that his interrogators read as an invitation to suffer "a *stroke* of his cane, (for we hear he carries one, as well as a sword) or a *bullet*."[40] A week later, a correspondent reported that the colonel had disgraced himself by threatening an esteemed seventy-year-old former county sheriff who had taken up his invitation.[41] By his actions and his failure to substantiate his charges against Miss F――r, the colonel, the *Chronicle* concluded in its final report on the scandal, was "most uncontrovertibly convicted of such a concatenation of offences against truth, honor, and decency as no history or record, perhaps, can parallel."[42]

In condemning others without proof or decency, the colonel had incriminated himself. This was the conclusion de Courcy reached in his final contribution to the controversy, a sixty-five-page point-by-point refutation of the colonel's claims entitled *The Seducer Convicted on His Own Evidence*, published in March 1783. The colonel may have had a team of eight lawyers working for him, de Courcy suggested in the pamphlet, but he was a poor advocate for his cause. The evidence he presented in his defense, particularly his admission of having fathered an illegitimate child in India, and his attributing of false statements to Dr. Osborn and others all reflected badly on his character.

The only time the colonel could be credited with honoring the truth, de Courcy remarked, was in choosing *Calumny* as his pamphlet's title, since the work was nothing more than a libel on Miss F——r and the Deveils. "How can he answer it to the public," de Courcy wondered, "thus to have transgressed the laws of honorable society, by infringing one of its principal bonds, that of an adherence to truth?"[43]

That de Courcy felt compelled to set out the truth in an argument that was more than twice the length of the colonel's may suggest that he was as keen to make a pariah out of the colonel as he was anxious to justify his own behavior. Though no correspondent to the *Chronicle* was willing to come to the colonel's defense, there was one anonymous contributor who, without naming names, condemned the whole business as an affront to decency. Anyone who published false reports about a neighbor, this correspondent maintained, was driven to do so out of a "disease of the mind."[44] De Courcy did not acknowledge the criticism but did devote several paragraphs at the start of his argument to affirming "the rectitude of his motives." Insisting that he had no personal interest in the case, he claimed that he got involved in the controversy because he was unable to "resist the call of humanity and compassion, to throw my poetic mite into the scale." Though he hoped his earlier pamphlet would "engage the public in a close examination" of the colonel's behavior, his principal design in addressing his poem to the colonel, he said, was "to make him FEEL."[45]

In this design, he was frustrated. If his poem managed to make the colonel feel anything, it was scorn for de Courcy's literary pretensions. De Courcy claimed that the colonel's sarcasm on this point had no sting. Yet in a revealing plea, de Courcy asked the public to make allowances for his poetic enthusiasm: "even if I had indulged a little poetic licence, when lamenting the misfortunes of an injured young Lady, in strains a little elegiac, . . . methinks, when the sex, the tender age, the peculiar situation, and various trials of the party that is the subject of the panegyric, are taken into consideration, . . . even excess here might be pardoned." The verbal coloring he used in painting Miss F——r's virtues, he added, was far more excusable than the "gross falsehood" that the colonel had attempted to foist on the public with his "prosaic fiction."[46] In any event, he insisted, the extent of his poetic license was no longer relevant. The controversy had long since evolved from making poetic appeals to readers' sensibilities to submitting evidence for their dispassionate consideration, evidence of the kind that the colonel had failed to provide in his efforts to blame the victim and of the kind that de Courcy contended he had provided in sufficient measure to protect him from a conviction for libel.

De Courcy knew he had nothing to fear. On February 12, 1783, the colonel's case against the publisher of *Seduction* had been dismissed by Lord Mansfield, who also "laid the Costs upon the Colonel."[47] By then, the colonel's identity had entered the public record. He was Ralph Winwood, a former artillery man with a record of distinguished service in Bengal who, since returning to Shropshire, had worked as the East India Company's chief recruiter in the region.[48] In a notice placed in the *Worcester Journal* in 1771, he presented himself to potential recruits as one "who has got a large Fortune" in the service but who would not enlist any man married or "disguised in Liquor."[49] According to the *Shropshire Chronicle*, Winwood was known to parade in the local Soldiers Field, but following the scandal he retreated to his house, having failed to convince even his friends to believe his version of the events.[50] The *Chronicle*'s report on the failure of Winwood's suit would be the last time his name appeared in the press, though it did appear again in legal documents, notably a 1790 lease agreement for a new Georgian townhouse on London's Upper Mall.[51] He died in late January 1800 in Chiswick, followed "a few days after" by his wife, Elizabeth.[52]

Miss F——r's identity was never revealed. One library notation lists her as Miss Fraser.[53] A search of other archives has suggested a more likely possibility. Annotations added to baptismal records from Bengal report that in 1761 Captain Christian Fischer, a Swiss officer serving in the East India Company, married a woman identified as Elizabeth Diveil, whose surname is a near match for Deveil, the name of Miss F——r's uncle.[54] The annotations describe the Fischers as having two daughters. Only the youngest is identified by name, Helena Frances, though from a family member's obituary we learn that the Fischers' eldest daughter was named Ann.[55] The annotations in the archive report that the Fischers sent Ann to live in England in the same month that Helena Frances was born, December 1770, which is about the time Colonel Winwood retired from service and returned to Shropshire. Fischer was by then a major and, according to de Courcy, Miss F——r was "the daughter of a Major in the army, who wished her to have the benefit of an English education."[56] Later documents reveal that Fischer had risen to the rank of lieutenant colonel by the time of his death in October 1781,[57] and he had accumulated sufficient wealth to leave Ann an inheritance of 50,000 rupees. Having returned to India, Ann was married in 1784 to George Gordon. Their marriage produced three children, two sons and a daughter named Helena Frances. As a condition of her marriage, Ann's inheritance was placed in trust under the guardianship of, among others, a "John De Veil, of Calcutta."[58] She died on December 29, 1806, in Leith, Scotland.[59]

No one writing on the scandal offered information on the fate of the child Fischer bore as a result of her seduction. The scandal itself, however, would not be soon forgotten by the people of Shropshire. As late as 1837, one local historian reported that the circumstances were still "fresh in the recollection of many of my readers."[60]

"To Make Him FEEL": Defamation and Publicity

Johnson and the other writers who initially came to Ann Fischer's defense did so using the traditional publicizing mechanism of poetry, behind whose indirectness they hoped to shield themselves from legal action while still appealing to readers' sympathies. But as the scandal grew, poetry seemed of decreasing utility in prosecuting the case against Winwood. In the remainder of this chapter, I consider the scandal's legal dimensions to suggest why this was so. I have already mentioned the campaign to have truth recognized as a defense in libel proceedings, and I indicated that a requirement of that defense was that it could be invoked only in relation to statements that were verifiable in a court of law. This valuing of fact did not deter people from using verse to slander others, and there are cases well into the nineteenth century of poets being tried for libel. Yet the campaign was one of several legal developments that reflected a broader ideological change in what was expected of public discourse. Under these new expectations, the purpose of public debate, like that of the jury trial, was as ever to arrive at a determination of truth, but now this determination involved a deliberative process of sifting and testing evidence of a kind that met standards of rationality and falsifiability. For matters of common concern to be dealt with legitimately in the public sphere, they had to be presented in a manner and detail that, as de Courcy put it, engaged the public in their close examination.

I survey these developments as they related to laws of libel in this section and the next, and then I move to privacy in the subsequent section before returning to the question of what these developments entailed for literature. Many of the most significant changes, it should be said, involved other branches of the law as well. Especially relevant in this regard are the procedural changes that came about as a result of what John Langbein has called the "lawyerization" of the criminal trial.[61] Before the mid-eighteenth century, the criminal trial operated on an oath-based method of investigating truth, in which the accused spoke in self-defense without counsel in response to the prosecution's case. By the end of the century, this method had been replaced by an adversarial system based on cross-examination, in which the accused remained largely silent while defense counsel probed and tested the prosecution's case. Under the new system, the rules of evidence were firmed up, and much testimony that could formerly be introduced at trial (forced confessions, hearsay, evidence of the accused's bad character, etc.) was henceforth excluded as a matter of principle.[62] Such testimony was seen as impairing the investigation of truth since it was prejudicial to the accused and could not be interrogated under cross-examination. Yet while the range of admissible evidence was narrowed, the role of the jury in interpreting the evidence grew. Instead of following a judge's opinion, jurors were left to decide for themselves between the competing prosecution and defense narratives and to apply the law according to a newly affirmed "beyond a reasonable doubt" standard of proof.

There was one exception to this exiling of prejudicial discourse from the courtroom. The Libel Act of 1792 confirmed the right of juries to rule on whether a work was libelous.[63] The act presupposed that jurors could be sufficiently immune to a work's libelous tendencies to rule on those tendencies with dispassion; this assumption in turn allowed for the possibility that the public at large could resist those tendencies as well, a possibility that would effectively nullify the need for the law of seditious libel. More important, the act appeared to suggest that the import of alleged libels could be rationally interrogated. Whereas the new rules excluded prejudicial testimony because it could not be properly contested in court, both the truth defense and the Libel Act treated libel as evidence that was amenable to verification.

Another change in defamation law was the gradual obsolescence of the centuries-old offense of scandalum magnatum (the defamation of peers). Both a tort and a crime, scandalum magnatum differed from libel and slander in its broader scope. "Words spoken in derogation of a peer, a judge, or other great officer of the realm," Blackstone explained in 1768, "though they be such as would not be actionable in the case of a common person, yet when spoken in disgrace of such high and respectable characters, they amount to an atrocious injury."[64] A century earlier, the Crown had relied on frequent prosecutions for the offense to make up for the inefficiencies of the licensing system. Yet since the crime had originally been defined as the spreading of false news, the truth defense was available to the accused; as a result, later governments grew wary of engaging in courtroom disputes over the accuracy of press reports about the king's ministers. Peers, meanwhile, were less likely to pursue their own actions following a 1687 ruling that disallowed successful complainants from recovering court costs.[65] By the time Blackstone was writing, actions for scandalum magnatum were rare.[66] Members of the nobility, one legal theorist supposed, had grown disinclined to seek redress under the statutes because they no longer felt their reputations merited special consideration.[67]

Behind this change may lie a broader transformation in the social conditions of speech. It may be that actions for defamation had declined in frequency since the previous century because an ongoing "civilizing process" had taught people to refrain from using ill-mannered words or from taking offense at them;[68] then again, it would be some time before men of honor ceased to regard dueling as a respectable alternative to legal redress. But the transformation had equally to do with a changing sense of the audience for defamation, the public in whose eyes a person's reputation might suffer as a result of being libeled. What I have described as the emergence of a modern conception of the public—an anonymous body, independent of the state, indefinite in its composition, and incontestable in its authority—necessitated an adjustment to the idea of defamation and the harm to dignity it inflicted. The first significant manifestation of this adjustment was the legal innovation introduced in *Rex v. Curll* (1727) whereby the prosecution of obscenity was brought into the temporal courts by treating it not simply as a public order offense but as a libel on the public itself. Previously, the courts had resisted attempts at criminalizing obscene publications as a form of libel, in part because it was difficult to see how an obscene work could be considered libelous if it did not target any particular person or institution.[69] The judges in Curll's case acknowledged the difficulty, noting that the offending publication, *Venus in the Cloister*, contained no direct reflection on religion or government, while allowing that the harmful effects of "a general immoral tendency" were of a different order than an injury to an individual's reputation. Yet the common law of libel was the only mechanism the court had to prosecute Curll, whom the judges clearly wanted to punish. They therefore proposed the novel argument that since his "book goes all over the kingdom," Curll had endangered the peace, essentially by making the public both the audience and the victim of his publication. The presumptive harm of his pornography was that it had damaged the public's reputation among itself, an argument that could be made compelling only by abstracting both the harm and the public.[70]

Abstracting the public from the institutions that represented it laid the groundwork for the liberal counterargument that the public was made up of individuals whose beliefs and values, including possibly a private taste for pornography, were to be protected under the laws the public enacted. The counterargument, first essayed in pleas for religious tolerance, configured the public not merely as an autonomous and authoritative body but as one so various in its composition that no individual set of beliefs could conceivably damage the whole unless, in acting on his beliefs, a person threatened this diversity. Yet this modern conception of the public, once it began to take hold in the social imaginary during the second half of the eighteenth century, appeared to pose a difficulty for the law of defamation—as much for its rationale as for the prosecution of cases. The difficulty lay not so much in the distinction between words and acts, where only the latter were actionable. As Montesquieu well knew in making the distinction, the law had always recognized that the uttering of libelous statements was a performative act of speech that violated the peace by inviting retaliation from injured parties or by inciting revolt among the populace.[71]

Rather, the difficulty was in assessing the effect of this performativity. To the degree that the public was seen as indeterminate, defamatory words were henceforth felt to have a less immediate and appreciable impact on public sentiment, and possibly little at all. An insult might offend a private individual, but a satiric slur on a government official neither defamed the office nor disturbed the public peace but was instead understood as the expression of a difference of opinion. Or, as its modern defenders insist, free speech involves a form of autonomous self-expression where the individual makes known an outlook on the world that the public is free to take up or reject in its deliberations on the common good.[72] As I suggest below in relation to seditious libel, a fundamental assumption of the right of free speech is that the effect of words can never be so great as to impair the public's freedom of mind.

For legal theorists during the eighteenth century, the idea that the public did not react in predictable ways to defamatory statements was a good reason for individuals not to seek legal redress for such statements. Thomas Hayter, in his 1755 treatise on press freedoms, warned that anyone feeling the sting of a libel ought not to seek sympathy among the public, for its members "will immediately see, that the Slander is only personal, and, therefore will either contemptuously forbear to examine it; or they will suspect it to be true."[73] Hayter was underestimating the popular fascination with scandal; newspapers of the day were stocked with gossip as well as letters from private individuals retracting insults or defending their honor.[74] But his point was clear: pursuing an action for defamation might seem to the public to reflect poorly on the claimant's character.

In actual defamation cases, this problem translated into having to convince juries that claimants had suffered dignitary harm. Juries were, it seems, becoming less willing to believe that libels damaged reputations. This posed a challenge especially for claimants in actions for spoken defamation, since they were required to show proof of damage beyond their own testimony. Before the mid-eighteenth century, bystanders who heard a defendant insult the claimant consistently avowed that the insulting words had hurt the claimant's reputation; this was despite their not having any previous association with either party. Yet after midcentury, bystanders were much more likely to say that the same insulting words had *not* hurt the claimant's reputation. By then, Robert B. Shoemaker reports, "prosecutors in all courts had difficulty proving that defamatory words destroyed reputations."[75] Strangers, it seems, no longer found defamatory words compelling. Slander might hurt a person's reputation in specific circumstances; the courts had long recognized a handful of contexts in which damage could be presumed to occur. Yet for unfounded accusations uttered outside of these contexts, not only was the injury becoming a matter requiring confirmation, but the accusations themselves were more and more seen by bystanders as reflecting negatively on the accuser. Winwood's critics appealed to an emerging sense that defaming an opponent was a strategy likely to backfire in attempts to win over public opinion. The colonel, they believed, was at the very least guilty of presumption in thinking that he could undermine Fischer's credibility merely by maligning her.

Since the effect of words could no longer be assuredly established at any given moment, the attention in defamation cases turned from the force to the content of offending statements: unlike the effect, the truth of an allegation could be subject to demonstration. It was only once words were felt to have lost some of their affective force that the truth defense could become compelling justification. Yet as a condition of the truth defense, alleged libels could be justified only if they bore no rhetorical signs of malice on the utterer's part. The malign import of the words might have little demonstrable effect on the public, but any sign that the utterer had wanted to produce such an effect could be read as evidence of his lack of commitment to the truth. Though it might not be possible to verify whether a statement could have any effect on anyone, the affectivity of its style could be examined as a form of knowledge about its author's state of mind.

Words had not lost all force, however. As I already noted, defense lawyers by the end of the period had managed to have several older forms of testimony excluded from the range of permissible evidence on the grounds that they were prejudicial and unamenable to cross-examination. Words could undermine judgment by virtue of their direct affectivity or by the difficulty they might pose for anyone seeking to test their signification. Judges similarly began for the first time to express concern over the effects of pretrial publicity. Chief Justice Ellenborough warned that even an impartial report of preliminary hearings on an alleged rape could be prejudicial: "No one, with the feelings of a man, can read it without being roused to indignation.... Jurors and Judges are still but men; they cannot always controul feelings excited by such inflammatory language."[76] Much as norms were developed to govern debate in the public arena, so rules were put in place in the courtroom to contain language's potential to impair the trial's truth-adducing function. It could be said that the use of verbal force was taken away mainly from plaintiffs, defendants, and witnesses; lawyers, by contrast, exercised ever more rhetorical control in framing their narratives of the facts. Yet there had equally occurred a more fundamental change in perception wherein the force of words had become indeterminable, such that some words could be felt to have an inflammatory effect whereas other offending words might not or at least could be read with a measure of detachment.

Being indeterminable, the force of words had become in some respects more difficult to challenge. The poets who brought Fischer's story before the public clearly hoped to ignite a scandal, elicit sympathy for her, and put Winwood on the defensive. Their poems did not merely serve a reporting function but worked to impugn the colonel's character. Their words were prejudicial. Johnson's poem was akin in a way to what is recognized today in US courts as victim impact evidence, that is, statements made in court by victims relating the psychological injuries they have suffered from a crime. These statements may be presented in the sentencing portion of a criminal procedure, but they cannot be introduced at trial because they are considered prejudicial, not amenable to cross-examination, and immaterial to the determination of the accused's guilt. Johnson's poem told only the victim's side of the story, referred to few facts of the case, and consisted almost entirely of the speaker describing the emotional damage she had suffered. It offered Winwood too little in the way of direct allegation for him to contest without making himself look foolish, and too much private feeling for him to challenge its credibility. Most important, the poem had an emotional and publicizing effect, which Winwood sensed sharply enough that he demanded a public retraction from Johnson. Yet it was equally an effect that Winwood could not conclusively prove had damaged his reputation.

Words, it seems, had lost some of their power to hurt. Johnson and the other poets could not go any further with their allegations against Winwood without assuming the legal risk of making their claims actionable or the rhetorical risk of appearing merely prejudicial. De Courcy, who went furthest in accusing Winwood of a felony, felt he could do so only by ultimately abandoning poetry for prosaic fact in order to stage a credible truth defense and by distancing himself from the poetic license he had earlier indulged to paint Fischer's virtues. His poem's rhetorical "excess," he hoped, was pardonable under the circumstances. Yet he conceded that his poem could only do so much with a man like the colonel: despite its elegiac strains, his poem failed "to make him FEEL." More important, de Courcy also believed that in the view of the public, rhetorical excess could ultimately weaken credibility. The case against Winwood, according to de Courcy and the correspondents to the *Shropshire Chronicle*, was decided on the basis of his failure to meet the burden of proof in support of his ill-tempered allegations against Fischer and her family. Exposing the colonel's "deep revenge" on Fischer in all its verbal indecency, de Courcy maintained, "must be of eventual advantage to her cause, and tend to fix an indelible odium on that of her Calumniator."[77]

"In Time to Come": The Libel–Slander Distinction

This sense that words possess a force that is nonetheless not readily demonstrable accounts for the most significant innovation introduced to the law of defamation during the eighteenth century: the distinction between the torts of slander and libel, between defamatory words that are spoken and those that are written and published. Both libel and slander expose the claimant to "hatred, ridicule, or contempt."[78] But of the two, libel is the greater offense and is actionable without the claimant having to show damage. Slander is not actionable unless proof of damage can be established or damage can be presumed to have occurred because of the specific nature of the allegation. Since the early modern period, statements that disgraced a claimant in his trade, accused him of committing an indictable offense, alleged misconduct in his performance of an office of trust, or imputed to him a loathsome disease have all been recognized as actionable without proof of damage.[79] Otherwise, libel and slander may involve merely two different means of committing the same wrong, but it seems that uttering is not as bad as writing a wrong.

Ever since its introduction, the distinction between libel and slander has baffled jurists. Legal historians have found no impelling cause for its development, philosophers of jurisprudence point to its lack of rationale as a glaring example of how defamation law remains an "intellectual wasteland,"[80] and even the presiding judge in the case that is now cited as having enshrined the distinction into modern law could make no sense of it. "It has been argued," Sir James Mansfield explained in his decision in *Thorley v. Kerry* (1812),

> that writing shews more deliberate malignity; but . . . the action is not maintainable upon the ground of the malignity, but for the damage sustained. So, it is argued that written scandal is more generally diffused than words spoken, and is therefore actionable; but an assertion made in a public place, as upon the Royal Exchange, concerning a merchant in London, may be much more extensively diffused than a few printed papers dispersed, or a private letter. . . . These are the arguments which prevail on my mind to repudiate the distinction between written and spoken scandal; but that distinction has been established by some of the greatest names known to the law.[81]

By then, Mansfield felt, it was simply too late to go against precedent, even though the legal distinction was less than a half-century old and rested on one decision and the commentary of legal scholars who had misconstrued the import of opinions expressed in a few earlier cases.

Before the eighteenth century, "slander" denoted any form of civil defamation, spoken or written, while "libel" was used to refer to either civil or criminal defamation in written or published form. The civil offense was the same, and the same rules—the rules now limited to oral defamation—applied to both spoken and written words. It was in the criminal courts of the seventeenth century that the distinction first took hold: libel was an indictable crime whereas slander was not.[82] These courts were responsible for protecting the peace and so were concerned that libels might incite violence among the populace to a greater extent than was possible through spoken utterances—what the justices in *Rex v. Curl* had in mind when they noted that a publication could go "all over the kingdom." A libel's potential damage extended both spatially and demographically—hence the prosecutions for seditious libel of the dean of St. Asaph (1784) and

Thomas Paine (1792), who had published works that were accessible in language and cost to poorer readers. The damage was assumed to be possible at any given time and therefore did not require proof.

A different set of assumptions informed the distinction's initial mention in a civil case. In *King v. Lake* (1670), the court ruled that the defendant's scandalous words would not have been actionable had they been spoken because they were too vague to have a specific bearing, but in publishing them the defendant had shown "more malice": the act of publication was evidence of a more definitive intent to defame the claimant.[83] A similar logic operated decisively in a 1683 case and another in 1732.[84] In these cases, libel was not necessarily a greater offense than slander but was the only one in which the meaning of words could by their publication become determinable enough to be damaging.[85]

In choosing to characterize publication as evidence of greater "malice," the judges in these cases opened the door for later jurists to see written defamation as a worse offense because it was performed with premeditation. For the justices in *Villers v. Monsley* (1769), it was evidently a small step from there to viewing the offense as analogous to criminal libel. The case involved a defendant who had published a poem accusing the claimant of smelling of the "itch." The court could have simply ruled that the poem, in imputing a loathsome disease to the claimant, belonged to one of the categories of actionable words for which no proof of damage was required. Instead, the court chose to apply the rules for criminal libel to the tort of defamation. "[A] libel is punishable both criminally, and by action," Justice Gould insisted, "when speaking the words would not be punishable in either way." Monsley's verses would not have been actionable had he recited them but that he chose to "publish them maliciously" rendered them actionable.[86] Gould did not appear to realize that his argument effectively rescinded the offense of oral defamation.

That decision set the precedent for distinguishing oral from written defamation. One further refinement to the law was needed, however, to anticipate objections, like Mansfield's, that words spoken in specific situations could do as much damage as written texts. The refinement was not set out in any opinion but proposed by commentators, who evidently believed that a judge's instructions in a 1676 case had implied different degrees of offense for actionable words.[87] Like the decision in *Villers v. Monsley*, the refinement conflated the tort with the crime but went further in attributing to written defamation the same kind of demographic reach that made criminal libel a threat to public peace. John Rayner, in a 1765 handbook on libel law, offered one of its fullest elaborations. Citing only one criminal case, he explained that libel "receives an Aggravation, in that it is presumed to have been entered upon with Coolness and Deliberation, and to continue longer, and propagate wider and farther than any other Scandal."[88] Or, as he explained in a passage on why the truth of a slander might mitigate the offense but not so in the case of a libel, "this Tenderness of the Law is not to be extended to written Scandal, in which the Author acts with more Coolness; and Deliberation gives the Scandal a more durable Stamp, and propagates it wider and further; whereas in Words, Men often in an Heat and Passion say Things which they are afterwards ashamed of, and tho' they seem to act with Deliberation, yet the Scandal sooner dies away and is forgotten."[89]

There were two dimensions to the refinement Rayner proposed. The first was psychological. The premeditation involved in writing a libel, he suggested, was characterized by rational deliberation, unlike the thoughtless passion that provoked a person to insult another in the heat of the moment. The contrast was by then a legal commonplace, but it was susceptible to one of Mansfield's objections, namely that defamatory words were actionable on the grounds not of their author's intent but of the injury they produced. Furthermore, in equating premeditation with cool deliberation, the argument echoed the kind of claim that at the time was being put forward by political radicals in their own defense. Writing in "a cool deliberate manner," Paine believed, was evidence that he was not acting out of a malign compulsion and therefore ought not to be prosecuted for libel.[90] Rayner may have supposed that the deliberation involved in writing was evidence that libelers put their reason at the service of their malice. Yet it was now equally possible to contend that the deliberation involved in the act of writing signaled an absence of malice.

The second dimension, and the more important one from a legal perspective, was temporal. For the criminal courts, libels were an immediate threat: a publication that defamed a powerful family could incite retaliation; a libel on religion could lead to sectarian discord; a seditious tract could stir popular discontent. Time made a difference only in making things worse. If left unchecked, the effects of a libel could snowball into violence. In the seventeenth century, having to deal with localized quarrels was bad enough. The durability of the libel was in this way immaterial to the crime. In cases of civil defamation, meanwhile, time was a consideration only if claimants were required to show they had suffered damage from the time that the scandalous words were first disseminated. In the case of oral defamation, this period of time could be very brief: before the mid-eighteenth century, as I already noted, an insult could be felt to harm a person's reputation even among passersby. Scandalous words, it was believed, had an appreciable effect at all times. They were a clear and ever-present danger.

Rayner's claim that writing made a defamation more durable could seem a compelling explanation for why libel was worse than slander only if it was assumed that a libel's injurious effects could escalate over time. That assumption seemed to accord with the fear that time could only make things worse. However, the assumption itself could not stand up to Mansfield's objection that it was entirely conceivable that the damage caused by slanderous words uttered in the right context could be worse than the effects of a libel. This is why Rayner, perhaps anticipating the objection, offered the additional point that the scandal from a slander dies away once the heated episode is over. Yet this explanation is based on the quite different assumption that, rather than making things worse, time heals the wounds of oral defamation, including the injuries inflicted in situations like the one Mansfield envisaged—an assumption that would seem to provide another reason for rescinding the law of slander. What time could not do, the explanation further assumed, was heal the wounds of written defamation because in this persistent form the scandal remained in public memory. The wounds of slander would heal, but the harm from libel would not unless legal action was taken. The harm may not get worse over time, but it may become more difficult to counteract. This, at least, is the rationale commonly given today on behalf of treating libel as the greater offense than slander. As Justice Cardozo wrote in his restatement of the rationale, a restatement that is widely cited largely because so few have been attempted, the distinction "has its genesis in evils which the years have not erased. . . . What gives the sting to the writing is its permanence of form. The spoken word dissolves, but the written one abides and 'perpetuates the scandal.'"[91]

If libel was the greater offense by virtue of its permanence of form, it merited penalties not merely for any injury already sustained, as was the case with slander. This was the view of some eighteenth-century commentators, who insisted that damages in an action for libel were to be computed on the basis of the injury that, if action had not been taken, the claimant would likely "sustain in Time to come."[92] No sooner was this proposed than critics objected that the future could be a very long time. One of the interlocutors in James Adair's dialogue *Discussions of the Law of Libels* (1785) proposed that libel of any kind ought to be classed as a crime because "the *materialisation* of the language" in written form "gives a consistency and permanency to the scandal." His respondent insisted that any libel action not requiring special proof of damage already "proceeds upon the presumption of its effects on the minds, not of one or more individuals, but of all individuals, of mankind in general"—that is to say, its effects at a given time. Yet if this presumption were changed so that libel was recognized as the worse offense because of its greater publicity *over time*, then the courts would either have to project an arbitrary moment in the future when the private offense becomes equivalent to a crime or face the absurd prospect of having to measure this publicity into an indefinite posterity: "You indeed pursue the circle till it vanishes."[93]

The solution to this problem has been ever since to regard written defamation as an offense comparable in degree of presumptive harm to criminal libel and hence an offense for which an action does not require proof of damage. In this way, the idea that libel inflicts injuries extending into futurity operates in defamation law similarly to how the concept of the public domain works in copyright legislation: both notions serve to justify the law by projecting the normative effects of published writings to a time when, it is presumed, these effects will be most fully realized. The rationale in both cases depends on the assumption that the effects are real but not wholly demonstrable in the present. Yet unlike the public domain, which is both the ground and the effect of the law, the purpose of libel laws is to obviate the effect. If these effects were measurable at any given time, the rationale would be unnecessary since libel would be no greater an offense than slander. But if the effects are not readily demonstrable but assumed to be permanent, then the rationale is mooted by the law it justifies: a successful action for libel would prevent the harm from propagating. Either the action puts a stop to the libel so that no future harm will occur, or no action is taken, in which case the law is redundant.

The law of libel serves to prevent injury from happening "in time to come." But as the injury cannot be specified nor will it ever happen if the law works as it is intended, it remains only a hypothetical possibility that abstracts the effects felt by individuals in the present into damages sustained over time by society in general. Abstracting harm over time in this way makes it possible for the law to take account of the indeterminacy of discourse—not just the errancy of the word in the Derridean sense but its unpredictable potential to effect change—while it equally makes the legal case for containing this indeterminacy seem all the more urgent. In the past, oral or written defamation was felt to injure society no less than its victim because it devalued the codes of honor and deference that sustained the prevailing order. By the mid-eighteenth century, lawmakers felt they could credibly say that slander had so little social impact that its scandal died away before any real damage was inflicted on the public. By contrast, libel presented the greater threat to society by virtue of its permanence, a potential for damage so great that it needed to be prevented before any damage occurred. The victim of libel may have as ever suffered an injury to his reputation, but clearly the lawmakers were extrapolating from this injury a different kind of potential social harm than the devaluation of honor, a type of harm that could not be proven because, in effect, once it had been sustained it might no longer be recognizable as harm. What they feared was perhaps the most troubling possible consequence of discourse's uncontrollability: the possibility that a falsehood might eventually become accepted as fact.

The law's rationale notwithstanding, the newly defined threat that libel appeared to pose had arguably little to do with the duration and degree of publicity and much to do with indeterminacy. After all, words did not become capable of a permanence of form only two and a half centuries ago. Poets since time immemorial had been proclaiming the time-defying power of their verses, whether uttered or written. Besides, the poets who brought Fischer's story to the public were hardly writing for posterity. Theirs was a poetry of occasion, designed to have an immediate effect on its readers. Their verses publicized a scandal, but they had limited demographic reach: readers outside of Portsmouth had no idea whom the poems were about. The poets may have entertained a hope that their message might be propagated beyond Shropshire, but this message involved less a report of the particulars of Winwood's crime than, as de Courcy's dedication would have it, a warning to all "Affectionate Parents" about the evils of seduction.[94] Had the poems anything of merit to recommend them, they might have continued to compel generations of readers, but that was not their point. They were meant neither to endure nor to go throughout the kingdom, which may be why Winwood felt that whatever injury to his honor he may have sustained from Johnson's poem was not so serious that it could not be remedied with a retraction.

Winwood was so offended, however, by the "prose-part" of *Seduction* that he initiated legal action against its publisher and answered its allegations at length in his own prose pamphlet. It is true that de Courcy went further in the preface than in the poem in accusing the colonel of having committed a crime, but he concealed personal identities behind ellipses and alluded to many particulars only indirectly, as if he were writing for readers already familiar with the case. The preface was not written in a way that would broaden the poem's demographic reach or increase the degree of publicity surrounding the scandal. And certainly, the words of de Courcy's preface were no more permanent than the verses they introduced. Yet while Winwood was merely dismissive of de Courcy's poem, he was sufficiently alarmed by the preface that he felt he had to produce pages of evidence to answer its allegations.

No doubt Winwood felt threatened by the evidence set out in de Courcy's preface, yet he seemed equally confident that the counterevidence he presented in his pamphlet would compel readers to disbelieve de Courcy. Evidence in itself, it appears, was not what so worried the colonel that he felt he also needed to take legal action against the pamphlet's publisher. It might seem bizarre to suggest that Winwood felt threatened by the way de Courcy expressed his accusations in his preface, but it appears de Courcy's demeanor in prose was part of what Winwood was reacting to. That demeanor was one of soberly presenting the facts of the case to a tribunal of the public. To be sure, de Courcy was prosecuting the case, interpreting the evidence at every turn, and doing everything he could to lead readers to a verdict against the colonel. Yet unlike his poem, which simply commanded the colonel to obey virtue and decency, the preface accorded the public the ultimate authority to judge the case. The same was true of Winwood's pamphlet, though it would not have been so at a criminal trial, where the only matters jurors would have been permitted to consider were the facts of publication.

Upon reading the accounts of the case, the people of Shrewsbury may have believed one or the other, or neither, though by de Courcy's reckoning most had decided against the colonel. Yet such a consensus would not have been known to Winwood or his accusers before they made their respective appeals. The judicial system may have been only slightly less unpredictable in its outcomes than the public tribunal, and we may never know the court's reasons for dismissing Winwood's case, but the law was and remains a mechanism for managing if not eliminating the indeterminacy of the public. So it is that libel came to be regarded as a greater offense than slander at the historical moment when the public began to be perceived as an indefinite body, independent of the state, incontestable in its authority yet unpredictable in its choices.

Oral defamation would henceforth be considered a lesser offense because it did not seem to be a deliberate attempt at public engagement but rather a form of personal insult that, to an impartial public, revealed more about the defamer's moral character than the claimant's. By contrast, an intemperate libel, like the offending verses in *Villers*'s case, might not seem so intemperate to readers once publication had unmoored it from the private circumstances that had provoked it. The most dangerous written defamation, however, was the kind that seemed least connected to any private dispute because it presented allegations of fact in an impersonal, dispassionate manner in accordance with prevailing norms of public discourse. Such a manner appealed to the public's judgment while exploiting its indeterminacy, the fact that reputations like Fischer's or Winwood's could be tarnished by unfounded allegations even if only some members of the public took the allegations seriously. In a modern world, the effects of a libel are real but cannot be conclusively demonstrated because the public is hardly ever conclusively settled in its discourses and opinions—except, that is, in long hindsight, which is the "permanence" that lawmakers fear will turn a libel into truth if it is left unchallenged. By not requiring proof of damage, the law of libel circumvents the public's indeterminacy even as it assumes it unto perpetuity.

Privacy and the Public Benefit

Under the Libel Act 1843, defendants in criminal libel cases were permitted to prove the truth of their allegations, but for this defense to be deemed valid, they had also to demonstrate that they had published these allegations for the "Public Benefit."[95] The latter section had been inserted to provide a rationale for allowing the press to inform the public on important matters without disarming the law of its power to deter publications that defamed private persons. Its inclusion in the act was a belated victory for the campaign begun a century and a half earlier to have the press recognized as a truth-adducing institution that served the public's right to know no less legitimately than the common-law jury trial. At the same time, the provision also presupposed a distinction between public and private information that was nowhere defined in the law. The distinction had long been assumed by defenders of the press whenever they upheld the public's "undubitable Right to canvass publick Affairs."[96] Yet, as the 1843 act appeared to confirm, the distinction between private and public could never be definitively settled so long as the public benefit of allegations made against private persons could always be contended at trial.

Privacy has ever since been one of the principal sites of tension between, on the one hand, democratic ideals of equality and popular sovereignty and, on the other, liberal norms of personal freedom and the rule of law. The former require that the public enjoy the supreme right of overseeing everything, including the realm of the private, whereas the latter require that this realm be protected from intrusions by the state, the public, or the prying eyes of a neighbor. Notoriously, British lawmakers have resisted the adoption of either statutory protections for private fact, like those recognized under US law, or the provisions of Article 8 of the European Convention on Human Rights, which provides respect for "private and family life."[97] Likewise, British lawmakers have until recently been reluctant to reform the nation's libel laws, which, in placing the burden of proof on the defendant, offered plaintiffs terms far more favorable than those of comparable laws in other Western jurisdictions.[98] Their reluctance in both cases is not coincidental. A right of privacy differs from the law of defamation in protecting against the disclosure of true personal information rather than punishing the dissemination of false information. But the law of defamation has been used in Britain to defend private reputations, whereas in the United States the tort of privacy has been thought by some to have eliminated the need for the law of defamation.[99]

Privacy as a legal concept, however, did not come into being with the development of the common law of defamation. "Privacy," Fernand Braudel famously suggested, "was an eighteenth-century innovation."[100] Before then, an invasive act like eavesdropping could be tried in ecclesiastical courts, where it was punishable as a sin, but privacy as such was not recognized as a defensible good. The concept first entered the common law in areas unrelated to defamation, while the value of privacy began to be affirmed only after the idea had been assimilated to a regime of property. Its first mention was in a 1709 court decision barring a new construction from blocking the windows in an adjoining structure on the grounds that "privacy is valuable."[101] The following year, the value of privacy in matters of "Trade, Commerce and Correspondence" was affirmed in the Post Office Act, which criminalized the unauthorized opening of letters, and then again in 1711 in the important case of *Mitchel v. Reynolds*, which set the terms for extending civil protection to trade secrets.[102] Shortly thereafter, the criminal courts began to punish blackmailers who sought to extort money by threatening to reveal information about individuals' private lives. In doing so the courts appeared to recognize the right of individuals to keep aspects of their private behavior secret. But they treated blackmail as a form of robbery, chiefly because robbery convictions brought a substantial statutory reward, and ever since it has been designated as a crime against property.[103]

That privacy was a form of protectable property was the idea behind two of the period's most important legal contests, both of which I have discussed already. The first was the Wilkesites' effort, capped off by their victory in *Entick v. Carrington* (1765), to limit the executive power to conduct sweeping searches of the private papers of individuals suspected of having written libels on the government. The Wilkesites had argued for recognizing privacy as an inherent freedom. "We can have no positive liberty or privacy," one typically complained, so long as writing in solitude can be done only "at the will and pleasure of the ministers."[104] What they won instead from the court was a dual affirmation of the principle that governments are not above the law and of the traditional right of all persons "to secure their property" within the confines of their own home.[105] In linking privacy to specific conditions of use and ownership, the court effectively sidestepped the problem of having to differentiate private from public information, and in so doing left it open to the government to contend in a series of later cases that individuals could have no expectation of privacy outside of any space they owned.[106]

The second major development was the literary property debate, which, as Brandeis and Warren noted in their seminal 1890 essay, "The Right to Privacy," occasioned the period's most searching legal discussion of the competing claims of private, commercial, and public interests.[107] To Brandeis and Warren's disappointment, the participants in the debate did not see fit to recognize privacy as an inherent right but rather measured the value of private information solely as a form of alienable property rather than as an essential good that defined the core of a person's individuality. At most, the courts acknowledged the right of all persons not to disclose or publish their thoughts: as Justice Yates put it in *Millar v. Taylor* (1769), "every man has a right to keep his own sentiments, if he pleases."[108] Yet this formulation did not prevent private information from being reproduced once it had been disclosed unless it was in a form that could be subject to copyright. Information about oneself could be fully controlled only within the mind. Outside that, control was limited to the same conditions of use and ownership that defined the order of private property.

What was left undefined, then, was the status of private information beyond relations of property and exchange. Compared to the multiple legal battles over the publication of state information, notably the contents of parliamentary debates, there was remarkably little direct consideration in the courts of what might constitute a legitimately public use of private information or of how the public stood to benefit from the disclosure of such information. This lack is all the more surprising given that the public sphere was increasingly inundated during the period with publications about private experiences—biographies, editions of letters and journals, reports of divorce trials, romans à clef—not to mention the increasingly common spectacle of private persons, like Winwood, putting their conduct on trial before a public tribunal.

The flood of information was met with repeated complaints about the press overstepping its bounds by targeting the reputations of private persons. "The Liberty of the Press," said one typical complainant, "is no where violated more *glaringly* or more *audaciously* than in our *public papers*." This writer went on to acknowledge that "the public may in some degree share the blame with the publisher," but like other commentators he could neither propose remedies for reining in the press nor envisage where a line might be drawn between the public and private.[109] In the absence of such a line, individuals had little to gain from initiating actions for libel against the press for intruding on their privacy. They could neither fight these intrusions without calling attention to matters they wanted to keep private nor demonstrate specific damages from them if the information happened to be true and if its disclosure posed no direct threat to property.

With few means of legal recourse available to them, celebrities, then as now, took it upon themselves to convince the public that their private lives were none of its business.[110] Goldsmith threw a fit when an attack in the *London Packet*, appearing shortly after the debut of *She Stoops to Conquer* in March 1773, mocked his "grotesque orang-outang's figure" and unsuccessful courtship of Mary Horneck.[111] Enraged, Goldsmith confronted the newspaper's editor and struck him with his cane, only to have the blow returned and be threatened with an assault charge. The episode was duly played up in the press, prompting Goldsmith to attempt to vindicate himself in a letter to the *Daily Advertiser*. "What concerns the public," he wrote, "most properly admits of a public discussion. But, of late, the press has turned from defending public interest to making inroads upon private life; from combating the strong to overwhelming the feeble." There was no way, however, for Goldsmith to generalize from his own experience while equally appealing to the public's authority without thereby sounding incoherent. He implored the public to create new laws against the press's "licentiousness, by which we are all indiscriminately abused," on the grounds that remaining silent in the face of this abuse was unacceptable because it did "not pay a sufficient deference to the opinion of the world," as if the public were at once the victim of the abuse, its regulator, and its patron.[112]

Goldsmith's rant was inconsequential, but it provoked a memorable response from Dr. Johnson. The letter, Johnson told Boswell, was "a foolish thing well done. I suppose he has been so much elated with the success of his new comedy, that he has thought every thing that concerned him must be of importance to the publick."[113] Johnson was being unfair; Goldsmith had not asked to have his love life ridiculed in the papers. Yet in projecting his embarrassment onto the public, Goldsmith was guilty of the self-importance that Hayter advised the victims of slander to avoid. It was foolish for Goldsmith to dictate what concerns the public while calling on the public to enforce limits on what "most properly admits of a public discussion."

The episode suggests something about how expectations about the public exposure of private information were then changing. Defenders of the press proclaimed the value of an informed populace, but no one had yet proposed criteria for deciding whether or when private information ought to be made public. Just as complaints about press intrusions were increasing, so commentators were also pointing out the possible moral benefits of having private details publicized. In his *Rambler* essay, Johnson encouraged biographers to get beyond the tinsel of celebrity and instead record their subjects' "domestic privacies," which, in teaching virtue, "are more important than publick occurrences."[114] And he told Boswell that he was against any legal restrictions on writing about the lives of the dead. "[I]t is of so much more consequence," he said, "that truth should be told, than that individuals should not be made uneasy."[115] Other commentators hailed the power of publicity as a mechanism of control. "A newspaper," said one, "is indeed a tremendous inquisitorial instrument, and the most abandoned character in high life would tremble at the idea of being publicly exposed through its magnifying medium."[116] Writers of very different inclinations than Johnson's, meanwhile, were championing the social benefits of sympathizing with the private experiences of others. It had also become possible for critics to suggest that certain public writings, in particular literary works, offered the greatest moral and psychological benefits when read in private—as a refuge from "the thronged walks of public Life," as Young put it.[117] To the degree that literary works were experienced privately, they may not have seemed to disclose their representations of private life to the same degree of public exposure as other discourses might.[118]

Then again, it would never have occurred to a writer like Goldsmith that his literary representations of private experiences were equivalent to the press's reporting on the affairs of individuals. He may have depicted intimate scenes of family life in *The Vicar of Wakefield* (1766), which included one of the period's best-known stories of a seduced maiden, and he may have made comedy out of secret romances in *She Stoops to Conquer*, but no one would have accused these works of indiscriminately exposing private lives to public view. These works, it bears emphasizing, were insulated from such accusations *not* by virtue of their protagonists being fictional inventions. It was not their status as fiction that rendered literary works tolerable as forms of public discourse. It was rather that they were not seen to involve depictions of *merely* personal experience. These works were understood to belong to highly conventional genres where the characters, incidents, and dialogue were to be taken as representative behavior and speech. Moralists may have worried that novels encouraged impressionable readers to escape their social responsibility and to indulge in fantasy, but for them the problem was not that novels were fictions per se but rather that their stories and characters were insufficiently representative of common experience and proper conduct. Even Lady Sarah Pennington, in admonishing young women to avoid the genre, made an exception for *The Vicar of Wakefield* as the one novel that was "equally entertaining and instructive."[119]

That said, the status of fiction was changing in Goldsmith's time. The change reflected a larger aesthetic campaign to valorize the imagination as a good in itself, but it also had certain ramifications for fiction's relation to privacy. It had been until then conventional practice to include in fictions a kind of alibi to signal that they were neither falsehoods nor unrepresentative of common experience. These alibis included the familiar disclaimers that the fictions were dream visions or found manuscripts, as well as gestures of denial, such as Richardson's refusal to acknowledge *Clarissa* as a fiction.[120] According to its long title, *The Vicar of Wakefield* was "Supposed to Be Written by Himself" as a first-person memoir, an act of autonomous self-disclosure that merited public attention because of the exemplarity of its protagonists' conduct. Arguably, these gestures served to authenticate the fiction's realism as much as its representativeness, its ability to float free of fact without being any less applicable to the lives and deportment of actual readers. At the same time, neither the gestures nor fiction more generally could provide their authors with legal deniability. "Pointing out any Person under a Character," Rayner explained, "and then abusing and reviling the Name and Character so fixed, is certainly a Libel."[121] It was only later, when the offense began to seem uncommon, that lawyers would begin to designate it as a special category: "defamation by fiction."

By then, the gestures had been transformed, their emphases reversed. Jurists today do not take novelists' rote denials—about resemblances between characters and actual persons being purely coincidental—any more seriously than their early modern predecessors did the old disclaimers.[122] Yet instead of being framed by gestures that served as alibis for their fictiveness, fiction itself has become an alibi, a legitimate public discourse for describing private life whose fictiveness is not merely acknowledged but sets it apart as a special kind of discourse that does not have to answer to a world of reference. Novelists may deal with intimate experiences without having to disavow their fictiveness, insist on the exemplarity of the experiences in relation to the actual world, or specify how the public stands to benefit from having the experiences publicized. A novel's significance may still depend on its universality of theme and characterization, but its fictiveness also insulates it to a degree from the charge that it is invading private lives and spaces.

This change has as much to do with the normalization of imagination as it does with the reduction of privacy to matters of fact, the recognition from a public standpoint that what is controlled under a right of privacy has mostly to do with particularizing information about an individual's identity rather than with the qualitative dimensions of subjective experience. The value of fiction, realist or otherwise, remains inseparable from its representativeness. But for an early novelist, like Goldsmith, this representativeness meant that all readers could relate to the commonality of his novel's characters and situations, whereas for modern novelists it means that the fiction is not necessarily referring or applicable to anyone in particular.

The change may explain the curious observation in the *Critical Review*'s note on the Reverend Johnson's poem about Fischer that "poetical writers have been thought to succeed best in fiction."[123] On the face of it, the comment is absurd: the history of poetry provides plenty of examples of powerful, nonfictional if highly rhetorical expressions of private sentiment. Besides, Johnson's poem *is* a fiction, an imaginative reconstruction of a young woman's departing words to her lover and of the emotional trauma she has suffered. Johnson may have based this reconstruction on actual testimony, but his epistle was no less fictional in presentation than the poem it took after, *Eloisa to Abelard* (1717), which was itself a fictionalization of an actual person's intimate thoughts and was, in Johnson's time, celebrated as one of Pope's finest exercises in imaginative pathos. That the *Critical Review* could seriously claim that poetry was better suited to fiction than fact was nonetheless understandable in the light of fiction's altered status. The claim implied, in the first instance, that being based on fact did not make a poem valuable as a representative depiction of human experience. And in the second, it suggested that what made literature compelling as a fictive art was that it was not beholden to the world of reference and no longer had to appear to belong to that world.

What the reviewer was actually saying, however, was that there had by then arisen the perception that poets did better at inventing fictions than reporting fact. Fiction could engage an affective public sphere by encouraging readers to sympathize with the plight of a despondent young woman. In this design, Johnson's poem, as a fictional transcription of what Fischer might have written to her lover, was a rhetorical success since it inspired others to write further poems on her behalf. It was also a literary achievement inasmuch as it furnished the public with knowledge of a private world of sexual violence and an emotional realm of personal anguish, knowledge whose subjective dimensions readers could not experience were it communicated in any other form. But what poetic fictions, like Johnson's, could not do was demonstrate the truth of an accusation.

In an earlier era, the publication of a poem charging a man with a crime would have been thought sufficient to harm his reputation. It would have had rhetorical force. By the later eighteenth century, the same poem might still perform a publicizing function in encouraging the public's imaginative identification with the victim. Yet whatever accusations the poem may have put forward were no longer as compelling an indictment of the accused's character as the presentation or misrepresentation of factual evidence. Likewise, the poems by Williams and de Courcy might have, by the force of fiction and satire, motivated the accused to feel remorse over his actions or, failing that, suggested his culpable lack of sympathy for the victim. None of the poems, however, *proved* anything. Williams's poem, especially, contained so few details of the case and so much imaginative fabrication that it seemed designed less to convict Winwood of a crime than to evoke pity for its conscience-stricken seducer.

There was another, more profound consequence to the perceptual change the *Critical Review* had identified. If poetry was now felt better suited to fiction than fact, then as a corollary it must have begun to seem less legitimate as a vehicle for informing the public of important matters than the discourses of knowledge, which under the emerging norms of public deliberation were thought to facilitate more readily the public's close examination and evaluation of information. Johnson and his allies believed that the colonel's sexual abuse of his ward was a crime or at least a moral evil that was of genuine public concern. To have let the secret die would, in their view, have rendered them complicit in the silence Winwood had extorted from Fischer; even if she, like the speaker of Johnson's poem, was loath to be the subject of scandal, the poets felt that in disclosing her story they were acting in the public interest.

Their publicizing efforts may have been effective, but under the law as it then stood, their intentions hardly constituted justification for libeling the colonel and violating his privacy. They may have felt they had no choice in introducing the scandal into the public arena by unofficial means, given the impossibility of any formal proceeding being launched against the colonel in Fischer's absence. In raising a presumption of his guilt by circulating highly prejudicial verses that presented little verifiable evidence of this guilt, their actions were ethically dubious and may have seemed all the more so in view of the fact that they had couched their allegations in fiction and poetic indirection, devices that had long been supposed to allow authors a measure of deniability. Spreading accusations against an opponent through verse had never been a legitimate way of carrying out justice, but it was a very old method of doing so. The question was whether this traditional way of doing things had come to seem obsolete and therefore more illegitimate now that, first, the public had the right of final determination in the truth of accusation and, second and arguably by extension, poets were thought to succeed better at fiction than fact.

Of relevance here is the final court decision I consider in this chapter, one of the few decisions from the period setting out the conditions under which the press might lawfully inform the public of a crime prior to it being reported through official means, such as a declaration before a grand jury. On September 17, 1760, the *Edinburgh Caledonian Mercury* printed a letter reporting that "one John Finlay a shoemaker was taken into custody for committing a rape on a servant-maid" that precipitated her death. Not long after, the paper's publishers learned that the report was false, and they duly printed a retraction and apology to Finlay, a prominent Glasgow merchant. Finlay, not satisfied, sought damages against the publishers. At the ensuing trial, the court found against the defendants, yet acknowledged that there was

> no slight difficulty to ascertain the boundary betwixt that liberty which must be indulged to a newswriter, in order to inform or divert the public, and that licentiousness which, without any evil intention, may do mischief. One thing is clear, that the writer of a news-paper is not privileged to communicate to the public any private transaction, however certain his information may be. He must confine himself to what is publicly transacted, and what must spread of course without a news-paper; in which case, a news-paper has no other effect but to quicken the intelligence. The article challenged is of that nature; for nothing can be more public than a man's being taken into custody in a great city to be tried for a crime. News-writers, however, are not privileged to defame a person by characterizing him a worthless fellow, deserving punishment adequate to his atrocious crimes. This was certainly rash and unguarded, and the less excusable, that such virulent expressions are by no means necessary for carrying on the purpose of a newspaper.[124]

What rendered a private into a public transaction was the knowledge that a public act had taken place, in this case the act of taking a person into custody, and that this knowledge could justify news reports of the act even if it was later discovered to be groundless. In effect, the press could circulate only information that it believed was already the subject of a public transaction, even if this belief happened to rest on no more than hearsay. By this standard, intelligence might spread with or without a newspaper and outside of official mechanisms, and this rendered it public but not lawfully so. It was only once intelligence was perceived to be of legitimate public concern that the public as a body could be deemed to possess the authority to deliberate over it openly. At the same time, once information had become a legitimate subject of public discourse, then it was a newspaper's responsibility to make sure its reporting of it was not cast in "rash and unguarded" language that defamed the persons identified.

The poems by Johnson, Williams, and de Courcy brought a private conflict into the public arena, but there had not been an official act to sanction the publicity. Though they believed that their actions were of public benefit, they knew their allegations against the colonel were not defensible in a court of law, while the manner in which they expressed their accusations in verse did not render them any less excusable as libels. De Courcy, in setting out corroborating evidence in his poem's notes and preface, appeared to realize that the license he had indulged in the poem may have seemed less excusable to readers than the prosaic exposition of fact. Yet in his view, the conflict became a public transaction the moment that Winwood, stymied in his efforts at contending privately with his critics and not content simply to seek legal redress, presented his own prose account of the events before the tribunal of the public. At that moment, de Courcy and his allies felt confident that the case had become a matter they could discuss openly, without mediating their allegations against the colonel through poetic indirection.

In taking up the medium of prose, Winwood and his accusers implicitly affirmed the public's right to debate the case. While statements in prose no less than in verse could be deemed libelous, the use of expository prose was by then signaling to members of the public that they possessed the authority to debate its contents. Poetry remained as ever a public genre, but prose, it seems, had become a *more* public one, the primary medium of public deliberation. Just as significant, once the conflict had become a matter for open discussion, the fact that Winwood had laced his account with virulent expressions, which were by no means necessary to achieving his purpose in defending himself, could be held against him as evincing his lack of commitment to truth, decency, and civil procedure. Poetry may have lost a measure of its rhetorical power such that it could not conclusively injure Winwood's reputation even as it brought public attention to his private behavior and his victim's pain. And while poetry remained as expressive a medium as ever, the public value of all expressive speech had become ambiguous. Winwood's accusers may have used poetry to express outrage, make readers feel for Fischer, and turn the tide of public sentiment against the colonel. Yet once they felt that the scandal had become a subject for legitimate public deliberation to be discussed without poetic license, they felt justified in declaring that the rhetorical excesses of the colonel's own public prose were not merely inexcusable but incriminated him.

Literature in the modern world may deal with any subject, from the actual world and beyond, while its modes of expression are no longer governed by a hierarchy of styles and genres linked to the dignity of their subjects. All literary works publicize their subjects. They may introduce new knowledge into the public sphere, dramatize or fictionalize existing knowledge, and render public or personal knowledge more affecting and memorable. But they publicize their subjects in forms and styles that do not strictly follow prevailing norms of publicity. To this degree, they may seem to disseminate knowledge as much about their subjects as about their own peculiar inventiveness. This inventiveness varies in the degree and kind of influence it exerts on public life inasmuch as literature can be either a fictive or a verbal art, or both.[125] As a fictive art, literature is not accountable to the world of reference and so does not necessarily have to apply to any person in particular. This makes it possible for literary writers, whether in narratives, lyrics, or dramas, to bring private experiences and perceptions into the public world and to explore their relation to historical events, moral and intellectual questions, political and economic orders, or any other dimension of public life and thought. Yet since it can never be entirely divorced from the world of reference, the fictional nature of a work in itself cannot ensure that its authors are safe from prosecution for obscenity, defamation, invasion of privacy, or other offense.

As a verbal art, literature has real effects on individuals. It can make them feel. But there can be no assurance that these effects will be felt by all members of the public at any given time, though in long hindsight it may be possible to see literature's greatest achievement as having transformed the public into a people. Because literature's effects cannot be readily demonstrated, its authors may transgress the norms of public speech and deal with intimate or controversial material while being relatively immune to prosecution for offenses of speech and representation. Yet as long as literature's effects remain indeterminable and the knowledge it presents remains unverifiable, it will not seem to have as direct an influence on public life as the discourses of knowledge that follow conventional norms. It may seem as compelling as these other discourses, but it is not as public, and certainly not as public as it used to seem in the past. Using poetry and fiction to publicize a scandal, like the one that engrossed the people of Shropshire in the early 1780s, was once utterly commonplace. Now it seems the stuff of poetry and fiction.

CHAPTER FOUR

How Criticism Became Privileged Speech

The Case of *Carr v. Hood* (1808)

The 1843 Libel Act allowed the truth defense only in the case of publications that could be shown to benefit the public. Well before the act's passage, however, speakers in certain formal settings could claim the common-law defense of privilege, or protection from actions for defamation, without having to demonstrate how their statements served the public interest. The Bill of Rights of 1689 accorded an absolute immunity from defamation charges to proceedings of Parliament. Statements made in the course of judicial proceedings had been similarly granted protection in a series of decisions beginning in the sixteenth century, such that by 1772, when Lord Mansfield declared the comprehensive rule, the privilege was considered absolute: "neither party, witness, counsel, jury, or Judge, can be put to answer, civilly or criminally, for words spoken in office."[1]

The type of dispensation that is the subject of this chapter is the principle of "fair comment."[2] Citizens may comment on the conduct of public figures and express their opinions in pointed and even scurrilous language without fear of defamation claims provided they do so "fairly," that is, without demonstrable malice. The author of a letter to the editor may go so far as to presume motives on the part of the person whose actions are being criticized, provided only that the imputation of motives is reasonable under the circumstances. Nowadays, we hear the fair comment defense being invoked chiefly on behalf of satires on public figures. These works, it is believed, deserve special consideration because they are the hard cases that help to mark the boundary between the public's interest in open and robust debate and the individual's claims to autonomy and dignity. The question that concerns me in this chapter is how these cases became hard to decide. Another way of putting the question is to ask why it was originally felt necessary to affirm fair comment as a legal principle. If laws are created to manage social problems, then what was the nature of the problem that the principle of fair comment was intended to address? And why did this problem become recognized as such only when it did? I address these questions by examining the case that established the fair comment defense and what the case suggests about how the public's interest in discourse has come to be defined.

Of all the genres of public speech, the first to be granted privilege as fair comment was literary criticism.[3] It happened in the case of *Carr v. Hood*, heard before Chief Justice Lord Ellenborough and a special jury at the Court of King's Bench on July 25, 1808.[4] The plaintiff, Sir John Carr, was a travel writer who had achieved moderate success with his accounts of touring through places like France and Ireland, where recently political conflict had kept English visitors away. He styled himself the "stranger abroad" who surveyed these regions with a fresh eye and with a genial, tolerant attitude on social issues. His "tourifications," as they were later derisively called, were designed to make travel seem once again a safe and politically innocent activity.[5] As Carr assured readers in *The Stranger in Ireland* (1806), "upon those unsettled subjects which have too long excited *party animosity*, I have advanced nothing which can have the remotest tendency to inflame the public mind."[6] Recent conflicts became in his hands topics for chatty satire, as in his remark that the recently erected Martello towers along Dublin Bay served only to lend "picturesque beauty" to the area since their placement far from ship channels could not possibly provide any military advantage. Otherwise, Carr's works were undistinguished compilations of anecdotes, trivia, hefty borrowings from other books, and indiscriminate praise for nearly every person and place he encountered. As the *Edinburgh Review* put it, Carr "seems to be an amiable, inoffensive, extremely good-natured man, who has no more right to publish quartos than to govern empires."[7]

Despite mixed reviews, Carr's books sold well enough to earn him name recognition. The publisher of *The Stranger in Ireland*, the notoriously parsimonious Sir Richard Phillips, had paid Carr £600 for the manuscript; the book sold "very nearly 1500 copies," according to Phillips, who then gave Carr an advance of £100 for a second edition.[8] The book's popularity also earned Carr the honor of being knighted by the lord lieutenant of Ireland. Yet Carr soon owed his celebrity to another, less agreeable event. In late 1807, there appeared an anonymous pamphlet entitled *My Pocket Book; or, Hints for "A Ryghte Merrie and Conceitede" Tour*, which purported to be the working notes Carr had taken during his Irish travel. It was in fact a clever burlesque of Carr's methods of gathering and recycling his materials. In it, the fictive Carr repeatedly instructs himself on where to find suitably hackneyed expressions: seeing Dublin Bay, he tells himself to "[l]ook into Ossian when you get home for something about *mountains* with *grey heads* and *ocean smiling with a blue face*."[9] Much of the parody is built around extracts from Carr's narrative, whose relentless glibness is distilled into a series of sublimely fatuous statements like this: "Ireland is not cursed with English poor-laws: there are no pauper-houses there, into which a child, in the full vigour of life and health, can cast the hoary-headed infirm author of his days."[10] Yet *My Pocket Book* also contains gratuitous mischief: whereas Carr had strenuously maintained a bland neutrality, the parody tries hard to suggest that Carr had other designs, insinuating, for example, that his remark about the Martello towers was a veiled attack on the previous Tory administration. As the conservative *British Critic* noted, plenty of what Carr had written was ripe for mockery, but some of the "gibes and jeers he has had to encounter . . . appear to have been tinged with the venom of personal animosity."[11]

My Pocket Book was an instant hit and quickly passed through two English editions and another in America. Though its authorship was never acknowledged, it was no secret that it had been written by Edward Dubois, the editor of the *Monthly Mirror*, who had undertaken the satire at the behest of the journal's publishers, Thomas Hood and Charles Sharpe. Dubois's authorship was certainly assumed by Carr's allies, one of whom produced a countersatire supposedly written by Dubois entitled *Old Nick's Pocket-Book; or, Hints for a "Ryghte Pedantique and Mangleinge" Publication to Be Called "My Pocket Book."*[12] Yet the gesture was not enough to satisfy Carr, who believed that Hood and Sharpe had "attempted personally to degrade me in a point of view that had no reference to my travels in Ireland."[13] Carr felt especially insulted by the parody's illustrations, in particular the frontispiece, which depicted him traveling with a light wardrobe, suggesting how little time he had actually spent in Ireland, and pockets filled with pages torn from travel guides whose contents he had pilfered. Carr believed that the satire hurt his relationship with his publisher, Phillips, who chose not to proceed with a second edition of *The Stranger in Ireland* and subsequently turned down Carr's latest manuscript, a tour of Scotland. In retaliation, Carr hired William Garrow to represent him in an action against Hood and Sharpe for damages in the amount of £2,000. The trial was the literary event of the season, with reviewers crying it up as an important test of press freedoms. However serious the test, those reviewers fully expected Carr to lose, which he did. He was widely derided as a fool who had been ill advised to pursue the complaint. The popularity of his writings declined rapidly following the loss, and within a few years, his writing career was over.[14]

Contrary to what commentators assumed, the verdict was not necessarily a foregone conclusion. Libel actions against caricaturists were rare, but the courts were not unsympathetic to the victims of graphic satire. In 1792 the print seller Joshua Kirby Baldrey was convicted of libeling Zachariah Button, an Essex magistrate, in a print that depicted Button standing in the pillory.[15] Eight years later, Thomas Erskine filed a criminal complaint against S. W. Fores for having sold a caricature ridiculing a prominent London surgeon. Visual satires had become "the most dangerous of all libels," Erskine explained, since they were easy to comprehend but not easy to refute.[16] Lord Kenyon, the presiding judge, agreed, noting that a complaint of visual defamation "is a very proper application to the Court and I am extremely glad the motion has been made! and I do hope similar applications will be made."[17]

Carr claimed, after his trial, that he had wished only to contest the unfairness of the illustrations accompanying Dubois's parody: "If there was any press that I wished to obtain a victory over, it was not the literary press, but the caricature press."[18] The images, he felt, impugned his moral character by distorting the meaning of what he had written. As an example, he noted how in his book he had refuted the myth that the Irish poor tied their plows to the tails of their drawing horses, yet in one of the parody's plates he was shown making a sketch of the practice as if it were commonplace.[19] The print, Carr alleged, misled Irish readers into thinking that he had "thrown odium upon the character of their peasantry."[20] Sir Walter Scott, in reply, scoffed at the idea that anyone might mistake caricatures for the truth: "that any human being upon either side of St. George's Channel could seriously draw a conclusion, as a matter of fact, from a caricature print, is one of the most whimsical inuendos which a declaration ever attached to a libel."[21] Scott's point was that even if the illustrations had insulted Carr, malice was insufficient grounds for maintaining an action for libel. Carr had to show that the caricatures had harmed his reputation, but according to Scott, no one took graphic satire seriously enough to believe it defamed its subjects.

As a claimant in a libel action, Carr was not required to provide proof of damage. It might have also been possible for him to maintain that, in disgracing him in his writing trade, Dubois's parody belonged to one of the four traditional categories of slanderous statements for which no proof of damage was required (discussed in chapter 3). Carr, however, felt that the parody was purposefully written to damage his reputation among the public and not just within the book trade. It aimed to sully his good name, he believed, by misleading readers about the nature of his reportage and opinions. To make his case compelling, then, Carr needed to establish that the parody had libeled his credibility, even if it was next to impossible to know how seriously readers took the parody. "[N]o one," Garrow acknowledged, "can know every individual who may have been influenced by such a publication."[22] Carr therefore adduced the loss of profit he sustained when his publisher refused a second edition of his book and rejected his latest submission as a special damage that could be taken as evidence that his broader journalistic reputation with the public had also been hurt. This meant that Carr had to establish that the parody's illustrations led directly to Phillips's decision to drop Carr from his list.

On this point, his case faltered. There were several problems. For one, Carr could hardly pretend that Phillips had turned against him as a result of being deceived by the caricatures' misrepresentations of fact. Instead Carr had to allow that Phillips was reacting not to the images themselves but to the bad publicity that the parody had generated for Carr's writings. Phillips, Garrow argued, felt he had to distance his name from Carr's to protect his firm's reputation. In direct testimony, Phillips confirmed that the parody's success had soured him on Carr's newest effort. Introducing Phillips's motives into the case, however, opened the door for a vigorous cross-examination of the publisher by the attorney general, Sir Vicary "Vinegar" Gibbs, acting for the defendants. To the delight of reporters, Phillips boxed himself into one corner after another. Asked whether he had read Dubois's parody, he insisted that he did not tolerate abuse of any kind—but was then confronted with a scurrilous pamphlet he had published. Asked whether he read the *Edinburgh Review*, he declared that he had no respect for "*anonymous* criticism"—but was forced to retract the statement after acknowledging his ownership of the anonymous *Oxford Review*. Asked finally whether he had told John Murray that Carr was "worn out" as an author, he denied it but then admitted that "in tenderness to Sir John Carr," he had lied to other publishers to conceal how it was, in fact, the success of Dubois's parody that had led him to end his relation with the author.[23]

Phillips's performance reflected badly on the plaintiff, but a greater liability of Carr's complaint was that in broadening his case's focus from the parody's caricatures to the effect of the text as a whole, Carr gave his opponents the opportunity to defend this effect as beneficial to society. The public, they suggested, had "an interest in the discouragement of bad books," and this interest was adequate justification for Dubois's parody, which, "although severe, was published in the spirit of fair criticism." Anticipating this defense, Garrow tried to argue that Dubois's pamphlet was not genuine criticism since it did "not give a true narrative of the work, which it professes to review." Yet the defendants never claimed that their publication was anything other than a satire, and they were happy to stipulate that their publication was a work of ridicule rather than a sober critique. It may not have provided an overview of Carr's book but, they claimed, it used humor to expose its "true character."[24] Besides, the parody incorporated many of Carr's own words, so much so that Carr thought it had invaded the market for his writings. It was, he claimed, "presented to the Public under the imposing mask of fair *quotation*," but since it was not "announced as a travesty," many readers assumed the work was authentic.[25] Carr did not go so far as to suggest that the parody violated his copyright, though the courts at the time were beginning to limit what producers of derivative works could do with other authors' writings. All the same, the decision in *Carr v. Hood* would subsequently be seen as anticipating the development of fair use exemptions, which permit critics and parodists to quote freely from other authors' publications without infringing on their intellectual property.

Although the case would also be later cited as having established the fair comment defense, it is striking that its disputants all seemed to feel that the law already protected the right to criticize. Carr and his counsel knew that they could not win their case if Dubois's parody were deemed equivalent to a critical review. To have any chance of getting the jury on their side, they had to show that the parody could not be considered fair criticism because it maligned Carr's person and integrity. Their opponents, meanwhile, did not have to do much to win their case other than to insist that their parody performed the same valuable service as works of criticism in advising the public on which books to avoid. They were never challenged to explain how ridiculing an author did not constitute defamation, to answer how their parody presented a fair critique of Carr's book, or even to identify a single feature of his book their parody was intended to criticize. Their premise that parody was equivalent to criticism was allowed to stand, so all the defendants had to do was rehearse high-minded arguments about how criticism served truth by correcting error and lower-minded claims about how reviews served consumers in advising them on where to spend their money.

In this, defense counsel was greatly assisted by the judge, who repeatedly lectured Garrow on how the courts "must allow a latitude to the free discussion of the merits and demerits of authors." Every citizen, the judge proclaimed, was at liberty to destroy the reputations of authors of bad books and could do so "in the most pointed language of wit, humour, or ridicule the threat; [and] the more pointed and forcible, the better."[26] Ellenborough had only a month earlier said much the same thing to Garrow in another case, *Tabart v. Tipper* (1808), where a publisher of children's books had brought suit against another publisher who had alleged that the plaintiff's books were immoral. "Liberty of criticism must be allowed," the chief justice had declared, "or we should neither have purity of taste nor of morals. Fair discussion is essentially necessary to the truth of history, and advancement of science."[27] Still earlier, in *Dibdin v. Swan* (1793), a case involving a negative review of a musical performance, Lord Kenyon similarly ruled that "the editor of a public newspaper may fairly and candidly comment on any place or species of public entertainment; but it must be done fairly and without malice." Kenyon referred to no case law but, according to the reporter, merely "stated the law on this subject," as if fair comment were settled doctrine.[28]

In both of these earlier cases, furthermore, Ellenborough and Kenyon had posited the absence of malice as the legal standard of fairness without saying what might constitute evidence of malice in a work of opinion. This standard, it seemed to them, was already sufficiently understood that it did not require elaboration. Yet not only were they the first judges to declare it into law, but they were equally the first to propose that the courts ought to protect the public's freedom to criticize. (In these two cases, the judges may have endorsed the principle of fair comment, but the cases did not actually enshrine the principle into law. No precedent was set in *Dibdin v. Swan* since its verdict was not recorded, whereas the plaintiff in *Tabart v. Tipper* successfully argued that he had been falsely accused of being responsible for the publication of an immoral book.)

The liberty of criticism had never till now been tested under the common law. Earlier commentators had asserted a right to criticize, with some even suggesting that the unfettered exchange of opinion on literary topics ought to be a model for free speech on political matters.[29] But no judge had yet been asked to recognize this right. Nor had any critic faced legal action for defamation because, prior to Carr, no author had yet applied to the courts to seek redress for an unjust review. Authors may have been averse to using the mechanism of the law because it was for them a point of honor to respond to attacks by using their pens to exact revenge or by making a display of their manly forbearance. This was the attitude Scott advocated when he reminded Carr of how earlier authors, like Dryden and Pope, had endured vicious insults on their character but had either responded in kind or laughed them off. Of course, Scott might have recalled that Dryden had been ambushed in Rose Alley and Pope relied on his dog and pistols to protect himself from his enemies. That satirists had not yet been tried for defamation did not mean that they or their targets believed that the law protected the freedom of critical opinion. It only meant that the extent of this freedom had never been established, and hence, as William Cobbett observed, no critic had a standard to follow in deciding "whether he dared criticise the works of any author."[30]

More to the point, the courts had never before extended this protection to criticism because they did not see it as their purview to guarantee speech freedoms outside of specific institutional contexts. When in 1760 Smollett was convicted of seditious libel for having written a review that castigated the conduct of the book's author, Admiral Charles Knowles, it would have been inconceivable for Mansfield to justify his ruling by setting out a standard of fairness against which criticism like Smollett's could be judged.[31] Not only would Smollett have not been permitted to propose a fair comment defense had it been available, but there was never any expectation that judges before the end of the eighteenth century were to be mindful of the possible chilling effects on public discourse of allowing prosecutions against critics.[32] The purpose of the law, it was understood, was to stamp out bad books, not to preserve a space for open discussion about those books. At most, the law, as Blackstone explained, did not impinge on the "liberty of private sentiment," but anyone who published such sentiments, about books or anything else, was no more protected from being sued than any other author. Critics had likewise no greater license than anyone else to condemn dangerous books: in Blackstone's words, the crime of publicizing bad sentiments was one "which society corrects."[33] There was nothing special about what critics did to entitle them to dispensation from the norms that governed discourse in general. Smollett had violated those norms, and any chilling effect that his prosecution might produce was entirely welcome.

Those norms appeared to have changed little by the time Kenyon and Ellenborough were enshrining the idea of fair comment into law. The defendants in the cases they were presiding over were accused of violating those norms in the same way Smollett had done—by writing criticism that defamed an author's moral character. Kenyon and Ellenborough did not have to assert the liberty of criticism to find for the defendants; they could have simply dismissed the claimants' cases for lack of cause. It is possible that in the wake of the Libel Act of 1792, which restored to juries the right to rule on a work's libelous content, the judges sensed a need to clarify the law.[34] Ellenborough may have thought that this was what he was doing when he instructed the jury at Carr's trial on the difference between a "fair and liberal" critique of a book and a libelous attack on a writer's personal character.[35] Yet in using the rhetoric of "fair and liberal" to describe licit speech, both Kenyon and Ellenborough were going beyond mere elucidations of points of law. By introducing such rhetoric, arguing for the social importance of fair discussion, and extending legal protection to public speech, they were redefining the law's ground and purpose.

That Kenyon and Ellenborough felt it necessary to proclaim the liberty of criticism indicated that, indeed, a fundamental change in prevailing norms had occurred: the potentially chilling effect of allowing actions against critics was now seen as a problem. The judges may not have considered it a new problem but merely one for which no precedent had yet been set. But merely by declaring it a problem, the judges were instituting a new reality. Henceforth, the norms regulating public discourse were to consist not just of prohibitions against bad books or, for that matter, constitutional prohibitions against the setting of laws that abridged the freedom of speech. The norms would now equally involve positive affirmations of the utility of specific public genres and of the importance of preserving free expression in those genres. The activity of literary criticism, and not just individual works of criticism like Dubois's, was by the judges' declarations formally recognized as so benefiting society that it merited legal protection.

These benefits, the judges believed, could be fully actualized only on condition of being privileged: critics could not speak their minds freely unless they were assured of relative immunity from the threat of defamation claims. As Ellenborough put it in his charge to the jury, without the freedom to criticize, "we should have no security for the exposition of error."[36] Accordingly, Ellenborough did not think it enough to dismiss Carr's suit for lack of cause. He equally felt it necessary to announce as a matter of principle that liberty of discussion was essential to criticism's fulfillment of its valuable public function. By their pronouncements, Kenyon and Ellenborough were fundamentally altering both the law's role and its rationale in governing speech. That role was no longer merely one of censoring bad books while leaving the liberty of private sentiment untouched. It was now one of defending the right of any citizen to criticize books. And it was henceforth expected that jurists would justify the law by affirming its role in keeping debate fair and open.

More than simply introducing a legal innovation by affirming the principle of fair comment, Kenyon and Ellenborough were granting official recognition to the public sphere. The judges were at once declaring the public's right to criticize and entrusting the public with greater responsibility for policing bad sentiments, a responsibility that in the past had been enforced principally through institutions like the courts and the church. "Every person who writes any book, and publishes it," Ellenborough assured the jury at Carr's trial, "commits it to the public; any person may comment upon it, upon its principle, upon its tendency, or upon its style. . . . [W]hatever character [Carr's] works merit, others have a right to pass their judgment upon them, and to censure them."[37] The public sphere, the judges supposed, was an economy of knowledge to which anyone was entitled to contribute and whose vitality depended on exchange. Allowing defamation claims against critics, Ellenborough told Garrow, had the potential to impoverish public debate: "We must really not cramp observations upon authors and their works. . . . [O]therwise, the first who writes a book upon a subject will maintain a monopoly of sentiment and opinion upon it."[38] Ellenborough, like the opponents of perpetual copyright, believed that the law ought to keep public speech free from private control, while leaving it up to the public to judge the value of this speech. Yet he and Kenyon went further than the anti-copyright free marketeers in affirming the rightfulness of the public's judgment. Though both the public sphere and the marketplace derived their legitimacy from their strict equality of participation, the public's decision-making was more authoritative than commercial transactions because it profited everyone equally.

The judges' defense of the public's right to criticize was as forceful in its unequivocalness as it was narrow in its application. The privilege of fair comment, as set out in these early cases, protected critics only from being sued for defamation by private individuals. The privilege in no way exempted them from criminal censure by the state or from libel actions launched by public figures. Only much later would the privilege be extended to criticism of politicians and church officials, when in *Turnbull v. Bird* (1861), Chief Justice Erle ruled that "[e]very person has the right to comment on the acts of a public man, which concern him as a subject of the realm."[39] Before the second half of the nineteenth century, in fact, the courts rarely permitted the privilege to be invoked in defense of comments made about subjects other than published books or artistic performances.[40] Anyone was free to attack an author for his dubious arguments but not a government minister for his dubious conduct or a petitioner to Parliament for his dubious motives.[41]

Liberty of criticism, Ellenborough suggested at Carr's trial, enabled a free press to police its own abuses; without it, a writer could get away with publishing "a book containing sentiments that are injurious to public morals; of infinite mischief to the public taste; or bad maxims of government." He cited as an example the works of Robert Filmer, whose reputation, he said, "ought to have been destroyed, and was destroyed, for which the world has been greatly indebted to *Mr. Locke*."[42] It is an open question whether the legendary pro-ministry bully Ellenborough, had he been the licenser in 1689, would have permitted Locke's *Treatises* to appear. Ellenborough was no champion of a free press. As he had insisted at Cobbett's trial for seditious libel four years earlier, any attempt "to alienate the affections of the people, by bringing the government into disesteem, . . . is exposed to the inflictions of the law. It is a crime."[43] For Ellenborough, there was no inconsistency between declaring a critic's right to ridicule an author and defending the government's efforts at punishing its detractors. Both were performing the vital function of correcting error.

Cobbett himself welcomed the apparent liberality of his old nemesis's argument in *Carr v. Hood*, while expressing concern over Ellenborough's illiberal assumptions. Calling the trial "one of the most important, nay the most important, that has taken place in my memory," Cobbett understood that its importance lay not so much in its decision, which merely confirmed a principle that had previously been introduced in the *Dibdin* and *Tabart* cases.[44] Rather, what made *Carr v. Hood* significant was Ellenborough's charge to the jury, where he provided a strong rationale for the freedom of critical opinion while also defining the standard for fair criticism. In a lengthy open letter to the chief justice, Cobbett applauded his vindication of satire and criticism, a vindication that, Cobbett predicted, would direct the nation to "a right way of thinking with regard to the use of the press."[45]

Cobbett nonetheless feared that in placing conditions on the fair comment privilege, Ellenborough had provided security to critics at a cost to public liberty. Though the judge did not expressly set out these conditions, Cobbett believed they were implicit in Ellenborough's interpretation of the privilege. The first had to do with how the judge presented his interpretation as if it were settled law. A work of criticism, according to Ellenborough's standard, was fair if it attacked an author's publications without suggesting anything about the author's personal character. Ellenborough told the jury that his interpretation of the standard represented his own opinion but did not suggest how the standard might be defined differently. Without saying anything about the contents of Dubois's parody, the judge repeatedly directed the jury to consider only the question of whether Carr had successfully demonstrated that the parody had not met the standard. He even took the unusual step of restating the standard, following the jury's decision, so that no one might misconstrue the verdict as countenancing libel. By leaving the jury no choice but to observe the standard he had set, Ellenborough seemed to Cobbett to be contravening at least the spirit of the Libel Act of 1792, which granted juries full discretion in deciding whether a work was libelous. Surely the public, Cobbett protested, ought to be "the sole judges of what is fair, or unfair, of what is just, or unjust."[46] If the public was free to decide questions of taste, truth, and morals, then it should be trusted to determine how these questions might be debated fairly. In denying the public the authority to set norms for civil debate, Ellenborough seemed, according to Cobbett, to be decreeing that henceforth "the courts of justice are to be looked to in matters of taste."[47]

Another of Ellenborough's conditions, and the most galling to Cobbett, was to restrict the privilege only to criticism of books. Ellenborough did not stipulate this restriction; doing so would have been gratuitous in a trial that involved only writers and their publishers. But he implied it by defining the value of criticism solely in terms of how it destroyed the reputations of foolish or knavish authors.[48] Cobbett had no doubt that Ellenborough wanted to limit the scope of the fair comment privilege to authors and their publications—and, as noted above, judges would for decades uphold the restriction. The judge, Cobbett protested, was willing to grant the press only the freedom "of combating *its own* vices and follies, and of doing nothing more."[49] There could be no reason for limiting the privilege to literary critics unless, Cobbett felt, the judge believed that "the act of book-writing should be more exposed to public censure and ridicule than any other act of man."[50]

In Cobbett's view, the restriction threatened to introduce a new and more insidious form of regulatory control, one in which the law protected debate on any subject but made this protection conditional on who was debating whom. Authors could freely criticize each other's ideas but could be targets for legal action if they ridiculed politicians for espousing the very same ideas. Yet if Ellenborough's rationale for the liberty of criticism was that it prevented the perpetuation of bad moral sentiments and bad maxims of government, then the fair comment defense, Cobbett declared, could not "consistently with *common sense*, with bare common sense" be denied to anyone who criticized those in office for attempting to enact those same bad maxims.[51]

Cobbett found Ellenborough's third and final condition more bizarre than troubling, yet it ultimately proved the most consequential for public discourse. Though he objected to the judge imposing his own standard of fairness, Cobbett was willing to grant that the standard itself was sufficiently clear to enable the jury to arrive at the right decision. By Ellenborough's standard, Carr lost his case because he failed to demonstrate how Dubois's parody had defamed him personally. This distinction between the public work and the private individual seemed defensible enough to Cobbett. But then Ellenborough proposed a refinement to the distinction. It was entirely appropriate, the judge declared, for Dubois to ridicule Carr's character as far as his character was "embodied in the work" or "connected with the work."[52] This refinement, which Ellenborough reiterated several times, was intended to address Carr's claim that Dubois's parody was a libel on "his character as an author."[53] Ellenborough could have simply answered the claim by saying that Carr was muddying the waters by conflating his professional credibility as evidenced in his work, which was a fair target of criticism, with his personal character, which was not. The judge could have, in other words, made the point that the standard of fairness cut both ways: critics ought not to engage in personal attacks on authors, just as authors ought not to take criticism of their writings personally, no matter how much they felt their reputations rested on their achievements as authors.

Ellenborough did not go in quite that direction. He instead suggested that it was possible to examine a work for evidence of its writer's character, and so long as this evidence was derived from the work, it was fair game for critics. Ellenborough did not say much about the nature of this evidence or how it might be "embodied in the work." At one point early in his opinion, he remarked how, at the start of his book, Carr described himself "taking his departure from Dublin," and thus he "speaks of himself in a manner that connects himself with the work."[54] Cobbett took this to mean that the judge was referring simply to Carr's first-person narration. Reading the judge's remark in this way, Cobbett was astonished that Ellenborough thought the point worth making. While a parody of Carr's work might seem to ridicule the author himself inasmuch as he had made his literary self a reflection of his person, there was no conceivable reason that the fair comment defense should apply only to a critic who mocked a writer's persona or use of the personal pronoun. A writer, Cobbett reminded the judge, had many different devices at his disposal for conveying his sentiments, and none of these devices "embodied" him any more fully in his work than any other: "He may, like the newspaper people and the reviewers, write in the style royal, and call himself WE; or, he may unite in the impersonal altogether." There were, Cobbett added, comparatively few publications like Carr's where an author described events "in which he has personally borne a part." The choice to relate these events in the first person was as open to critique as any other aspect of a writer's work, and so why, Cobbett asked in exasperation, should this particular mode of narration be "entitled to any extraordinary quantity of legal reprobation."[55]

Cobbett believed that in considering only how authors talked of themselves in their work, Ellenborough was overlooking an important consideration for critics. An author's self-presentation in a work might reveal something of his character, but it could equally disguise much that was relevant to understanding the work, including the author's motives for writing it or the party interests he was representing. There were many ways an author might be connected to his writing, and not all of them were evident from a work's form or content. Critics, Cobbett contended, ought therefore to have wide latitude in what they could say about a book and its author: "Every man, who writes and publishes, challenges the criticisms of the world. The very act of writing the book embodies him with it. It is his act. It belongs to him. It is the picture of his mind. It is a part of himself. The critic has a right to take the man and the book together."[56] Cobbett assumed that in not permitting critics to consider "the man and the book together," Ellenborough had excluded discussion of a writer's state of mind as outside the scope of the fair comment privilege. The judge, or so Cobbett believed, was proposing that it was both possible and necessary to differentiate between a writer's subjectivity, on which critics could not lawfully speculate, and the public image of the author, which critics could legitimately discuss provided that they derived this image solely from evidence in the work.

Cobbett's assumption was off the mark, but he had cause for concern. Ellenborough did not require critics to consider the book separately from the person who wrote it. On the contrary, he told the jury that a critic could lawfully take aim both "at the Plaintiff's work, and at the Plaintiff himself, [though] only as he is connected with, or embodied in, the work." More important, the judge insisted that the burden of proof lay with the plaintiff. A work of criticism was libelous only if the plaintiff managed to show that it dealt with material "wholly foreign to the work, or unconnected with the author of it, as embodied in the work."[57] Criticism was not libelous if it dealt with anything relating to the work or relating the writer to the work. Ellenborough was defining the scope of the fair comment privilege in negative terms: the privilege protected all comments about a work other than those that could be proven to have nothing to do with the work. Yet this negative definition of the privilege, as Cobbett sensed, did not resolve a fundamental ambiguity. While Ellenborough allowed that the man and the book together were subject to criticism, he offered no guidance on how the man *could be distinguished* from the book. For Carr to prove that Dubois's parody had gone too far in attacking his character, he had somehow to demonstrate that his subjectivity was wholly foreign to its embodiment in his work. He had to prove that the book was not a complete picture of his life and mind. Cobbett was thus right in thinking that Ellenborough believed it was possible to separate a writer's subjectivity from its expression in a work; at the very least, the judge was granting authors the opportunity to argue that their private selves had nothing to do with their identities as writers. Ellenborough had indeed introduced into the law a boundary between the public author and the private self. But what Cobbett failed to grasp was that, far from defining the boundary too strictly, the judge had made it a point of legal contention.

It is here that we can begin to understand the significance of the precedent established in *Carr v. Hood*. To explain this, I must step back from the case to consider why over the course of the eighteenth century there arose the expectation that critics ought to treat writers fairly. Arguably, the liberty of criticism was not a new idea but a long-observed customary right. Literary critics since antiquity had proclaimed their freedom to judge the productions of any author or performer. For their part, writers for almost as long had complained of criticism that maliciously defamed them. "[T]he Slander of a Book is, in Truth, the Slander of the Author," Fielding quipped in *Tom Jones*, "as no one can call another Bastard, without calling the Mother a Whore."[58] Yet since writers were held wholly responsible for what they wrote, there was no legal requirement that critics had to consider the book separately from the person of the writer. It was considered beyond the province of the law to enforce such a distinction, and, as I said, no author saw fit to test the distinction by taking a critic to court. Authorities might step in to put an end to bitter literary feuds that had gotten personal, such as the Harvey-Nashe quarrel of the 1590s, but they did so not by requiring the quarrelers to treat each other fairly but by banning them from publishing more books. Satirists, for their part, may have made a show of abiding by such rules and chastising each other for engaging in personal attacks or mocking human deformities. But no one would have thought to establish a legal standard of fairness that made the private lives of authors off-limits to criticism.

Critics before the eighteenth century did not feel obliged to observe any special code of conduct beyond what was expected of any person of their rank and community. In their view, what made their activity fair and legitimate was its utility. They thought of their right to criticize in moral rather than legal terms, as a responsibility they had tasked themselves with fulfilling in accordance with received authority, whether the rules and models of the ancients, the imperatives of religious faith, or the dictates of native and courtly traditions. They felt they were entitled to speak their minds because, in enforcing the rules, they were aiding the progress of learning and the correction of error. The legitimacy of their activity therefore derived from the same immemorial authority that upheld the law or any other institution. At the same time, much like the common-law courts, critics believed that their verdicts had the support of their peers, a jury of learned readers who shared their commitment to refining the indigenous culture.[59] Critics may have thought that their evaluative criteria obeyed the edicts of immemorial authority, but they were equally keen to assure themselves that they were performing a service on behalf of an audience of the like-minded.

By the end of the seventeenth century, critics had begun to think differently about both the public on whose behalf they wrote and the basis of their right to criticize. The audience to whom they addressed their work was no longer composed of a select few who subscribed to the same normative certainties. It was more akin to a modern public: anonymous, various in its composition, and indeterminate in its sentiments. This body in its totality could still be seen to represent an absolute authority or the conclusive edicts of the test of time. Yet what made the judgment of this public compelling at any given time was its independence from prevailing dogma. By the time Johnson was putting his trust in "the common sense of readers uncorrupted by literary prejudice," the public on whose behalf critics saw themselves acting had become an ideal embodiment of what Michael Warner has called a "principle of negativity."[60] The public for literary criticism was composed of no one in particular, abstracted as a body that subscribed to no specific set of evaluative norms and believed to exercise its judgment with such disinterest that none of its decisions bore traces of any individualizing traits of personhood.

Critics were initially drawn to the idea of a modern public because it offered a legitimizing story for their activity though one that did not require them to defer to established authority. Undoubtedly the reporting of trade news has as much claim as literary criticism does to being the first discourse whose self-proclaimed rationale was to supply the public with knowledge vital to its decision-making. But criticism was arguably the first discourse that was promoted not merely as serving a modern public but as entrusted to do so because it helped to preserve the public sphere as a space where people could engage in collective decision-making. Even the earliest reviewers believed that they could defend themselves by saying they aimed to uphold the equality of public debate. Jean de La Crose, the editor of John Dunton's review periodical *The Works of the Learned* (1691–1692), told his readers he had no greater right to criticize than anyone else, but maintaining this equality of right in the face of writers' and booksellers' attempts to control the reception of their wares was adequate justification for what he was doing:

> If some Authors and Booksellers pretend to damn this design, and ask by what right I take upon me to give out an impartial judgment over their Books, and erect my self into an Universal Critick, I'll answer, by the same right as they have publish'd 'em. Is not a Book common as soon as it comes into the world, and may not every Reader say, is it good or bad? Well then, since I may make use of my right as well as another, I shall deal more gently with 'em, if I don't tell it with all the Ill Nature the matter will bear, and am satisfied to give a little touch at those things that shall offend me most. Every one may without fear take the same liberty with me.[61]

La Crose did not set out his criteria for evaluating works or, as earlier critics might have done, cite the canons of ancient practice to justify the job of the reviewer. The liberty to criticize was for him founded on a principle of equality: others were free to endorse or question his opinions, just as he was free to approve or reject theirs.

Criticism may have been valued as ever for its benefits to learning, but those benefits were no longer the sole basis for the right to criticize. That right could now be assumed to exist because it was equally shared. Anyone could be a critic. At the same time, this assumption of equality meant that critics had to show respect to others by observing a code of conduct and address. In La Crose's words, the critic was not to speak with "all the Ill Nature the matter will bear" but to press only "a little touch at those things that shall offend me most." The critic had to uphold the reciprocity of critical exchange by not acting in a way that made others fearful of assuming the "same liberty" with his writings that he had taken with theirs. Authors would of course dismiss critics' claims to liberality as so many "specious delusive phrases," as one frustrated victim of the reviews put it.[62] Yet even if critics' promises of fairness were no more than gestures, they had at least to appear to play by certain rules when dealing with the works of people who were possibly unknown to them. As I suggested in the introduction, the public sphere is a social arrangement for managing debate, one that enables strangers to speak freely on any subject so long as they observe norms on how to speak to one another. For early exponents of free opinion, it was impossible to imagine why anyone would honor another's right to criticize in the absence of such an arrangement.

Habermas famously argued that free opinion in the world of letters was a precursor to collective will formation in the political public sphere, with literary criticism serving as the "training ground for a critical public reflection" in the political domain.[63] The literary public sphere was a model for political deliberation in three respects. First, it provided a model of freedom from determination, of speech no longer answerable to immemorial authority: since the legitimacy of critical activity was no longer moored to received beliefs and class privilege, private persons could gather in the literary public sphere to debate values and practices that had previously been held sacrosanct. Second, it was a model of participatory equality, of speech legitimized by a strict reciprocity of recognition: all private persons could engage in public discussion because they respected each other's right to speak and treated each other fairly by following protocols of civility and rational argument. Third, it was a model of normative abstraction, of strangers able to make decisions together because they occupied a view from nowhere: all private persons in the literary public sphere could to a degree suspend their own individuality when engaging in disinterested debate with others who were nonetheless all motivated to participate in such debate because they wished to mediate between their individual self-determination and the collective's.

Earlier in this book, I suggested that the tension between the first and second conditions, in which public speech is at once free and conducted according to certain ground rules, has led to inconsistency between the rationale and the practice of both the law and public discourse more generally. The third condition, by contrast, cannot be realized through the mechanism of the law. Laws may be enacted to protect the right of persons to speak, to safeguard their privacy, to manage the temper of their interactions, and to create conditions in the public sphere that can enable them to arrive at disinterested consensus. But what the law cannot do is preserve the indeterminacy of free speech and individual difference while also requiring individuals to overcome their differences. The very act of obligating strangers to make decisions as a group obviates their strangerhood. Consensus must come from their accord, or at least as a result of the spontaneous convergence of their preferences. The will, impulse, or fortuitousness that brings people together as a public is a fundamental source of value that, in giving rise to the law, cannot itself be subject to the law. No degree of legislated civility, fairness, and rationality in public debate can make strangers come together. And even if they do consent to come together, there is no obvious way to frame a law that mandates the self-reflection necessary (to the degree that it is possible) for them to suppress their individuality while at the same time revealing their individual preferences so they might collectively reach decisions that represent the sum and the summation of those preferences.

By the end of the eighteenth century, jurists no less than literary critics were willing to accept the diversity of individual preferences. What they were not ready to concede was the possibility that this diversity might have consequences for the setting of social norms. Garrow, in his opening statement at Carr's trial, told the jury that his client understood that not all readers could be expected to enjoy his works, "as men will differ very much in their opinions, (and necessarily must from their difference of capacity,) upon almost all subjects, certainly not less on taste than any other."[64] Garrow's soft relativism was hardly earth-shattering from the point of view of literary criticism; that divergences of taste were inevitable given the diversity of human ability and experience was already a commonplace when Hume wrote his essay on the subject a half century earlier.[65] From a legal standpoint Garrow's statement was a little more unusual since it was intended to preempt the jurors from allowing their personal opinions of Carr's writings to influence their judgment as to whether Dubois's parody had been unfair to Carr. Fairness in literary criticism was not, it seems, a matter of personal taste. On this point Ellenborough agreed, telling the jury that the right to ridicule an author's works was independent of "whatever character his works merit."[66] Garrow and Ellenborough assumed that the law, like literary criticism, operated on a principle of negativity: people as individuals might disagree over the value of Carr's books, but as a decision-making public they had to suppress their differences so that they might agree on how this disagreement might be lawfully expressed. While Garrow and Ellenborough were not being dismissive of personal preferences, neither of them could imagine how these preferences might play a role in public decision-making. For them, the function of criticism was not to air differences but to eliminate those differences through the correction of error.

Carr, by contrast, believed that differences had to be recognized before disagreement could be overcome. He presented himself to readers as the "stranger" who self-consciously set himself apart from both his countrymen and the subjects of his travels. He scrupulously refused to indulge in attention-grabbing polemics or to judge foreign cultures by the reigning prejudices of the day: "I have as much as possible avoided adverting to those points upon which the public opinion has divided *with temper.*"[67] His literary self-presentation, he maintained, was a direct reflection of himself as someone resolutely disengaged from public affairs. As Garrow characterized his client to the jury, "He does not dive into the depth of politics. He enters no list in controversy. Joins no party. Assists no faction, but he gives us the full benefit of his observations, upon the various scenes of life of which he has been a witness."[68] Carr felt he could benefit his readers by being frank and disinterested in his observations. His receptive disposition as a tourist, he supposed, equally rendered him sensitive to the distance between himself and his subjects. Only by being aware of these differences could the traveler see what people were really like. In his earlier *The Stranger in France* (1803), written only a few months after Britain and France had agreed to a tenuous peace, Carr claimed to have provided the first clear-eyed account of a people whose national character had been wholly changed by revolution—in his words, "a people who, under the influence of a political change, hitherto unparallelled, were to be approached as an order of beings, exhibiting a moral and political form before but little known to themselves."[69]

Avoiding controversy himself, Carr nonetheless insisted in his concluding remarks to *The Stranger in Ireland* that, far from undervaluing disagreement, he had made it his aim to record its manifestations among the people he visited in the belief that "the collision of opinion frequently elicits a spark by which a subject is afterwards more or less illuminated."[70]

Awareness of difference was not enough to kindle this spark into a desire for consensus, however. For this desire to be felt, Carr believed, there had to be an act of the sympathetic imagination. "I write from my feelings," he declared in his book of Baltic travels, *A Northern Summer* (1805). By relating his feelings, Carr hoped he was communicating directly to readers and enabling them to experience vicariously the highs and lows of travel: "Before we smile together in the beautiful islands of Sweden, we must be content to bear with resignation the gloom of her almost interminable forests of fir."[71] Carr believed that in making readers perceive life from the point of view of another, he could help them see beyond their political disagreements with other peoples, disagreements that, as he put it, produced an "artificial distance and separation, much wider, and more impassable, than nature ever intended."[72] In his view, Dubois's parody was unfair because it was not done in good faith. It did not express genuine disagreement but was instead a rejection of the sympathetic imagination, written solely for "the malicious purpose, of ruining him as an author; by turning every thing he has written into immoderate ridicule."[73]

Carr was a self-intoxicated dunce who could not conceive how his vapid, unoriginal writings might have merited the abuse. He lacked the self-reflection necessary to distance himself from his public character as an author, to comprehend how his subjectivity was subject to dispersal as soon as he had conveyed his feelings in language and in print, or to see how his books were no more likely to embody his identity merely because he avoided controversy or refused to acknowledge his own conservative politics. He was hopelessly confused in supposing that he could speak as a stranger while also articulating feelings and opinions derived from his personal experience. It was naïve of him, finally, to think that by providing readers with a picture of his mind, he could help them to transcend their differences. That said, he was not alone in believing that disagreement between peoples had been intensified by political change and revolution, that an awareness of difference was the first step toward overcoming disagreement, that recognition had to be henceforth accorded to the diversity of opinions in order for this awareness to become possible, that individuals had to be free to interpret their own experience so that this diversity might be understood, and that conveying these acts of self-interpretation in writing could engage the imagination and feeling of strangers sufficiently to encourage them to overcome their disagreement. Carr was a fool to believe that Dubois's parody was unfair, but he was not wrong in thinking that the point of critical debate was no longer simply to correct error but to give voice to difference.

The problem that the fair comment defense was designed to address, then, was not the chilling effect on public discourse that might result from permitting individuals to pursue legal actions against critics. Not only had this effect never been previously recognized as a threat but, more important, the decision in *Carr v. Hood* can hardly be said to have defused the threat. On the contrary, the decision, by making fairness in criticism a point of legal contention, opened the door to further court battles between authors and their critics. In the decades following Carr's trial, actions for redress were routinely sought against nasty reviews, tasteless parodies, and irreverent satires. Not all these complaints were found baseless, with the result that there now exists a sizable if not altogether coherent body of case law attempting to set out what counts as fair comment.

Ellenborough had introduced a legal boundary where none had existed before. He may have thought Carr's case an easy one to decide, but his opinion ensured that the question of fairness would henceforth become a hard one for the courts to address. Less than a year after Carr's case, in fact, Ellenborough presided over *Nightingale v. Stockdale* (1809), in which he felt obliged to revise his earlier opinion. In that case, an author of a book sharply critical of Methodism sued a reviewer who had questioned his motives and called him "obviously a knave." Garrow, joining Gibbs in the defense, argued that the reviewer's remarks were protected as fair comment. The judge, though sympathetic to the plaintiff, could not disallow the argument since doing so would have reversed the standard of fairness he had earlier proposed. He instead instructed the jurors to rule against the defendant if they believed that his comments, in attacking "the *private* and the *domestic*, as well as the literary character of the plaintiff," had gone beyond the evidence as it "only appears from" the plaintiff's book. In effect, the judge shifted the burden of proof from the plaintiff to the defendant, who had to show solely on the evidence of the plaintiff's book that his criticism was directed at the author's literary character and not his private self. The jury found for the plaintiff, awarding him £200 in damages.[74] The precedent set by *Carr v. Hood* may have formalized a space for opinion but, like all legally defined spaces, its boundaries were subject to interpretation.

What the fair comment defense was really designed to address was the more fundamental problem of how to accommodate individual preferences within public debate. For Ellenborough, the personal had no role to play in public decision-making. Criticism served only to correct the errors and prejudices of individual writers. The fair comment privilege, in the judge's mind, guarded critics from having to suffer the petty resentments of writers who were blind to their own folly. He, like the reviewers, assumed that the distinction between the person and the book was already in place as a precondition of the equality of the literary public sphere.

By the end of the eighteenth century, however, political events at home and abroad had exposed the limits to participation in decision-making and had emboldened many to claim a freedom to speak, to insist on democratic recognition of the value of their opinions, and to engage with others in the same spirit of equality that pertained in the literary public sphere. They demanded respect for themselves as individuals and for their right to express their perceptions, experiences, and understandings of the world. In response to this dissensus, theorists of moral sympathy, sensibility, and the imagination began to press for greater acceptance of the value of the sociable influence of the subjective, the affective, and the imaginative in human life. Conflicts between people, they believed, could not be fully addressed or resolved unless personal differences and experiences were taken into account. It was not for the law, however, to take these differences directly into account since there was no way for it to do so that did not involve either nullifying their indeterminacy by requiring all persons to live by the same rules, or making them fully a subject for the public to debate at a cost to autonomy and privacy, or acknowledging their diversity only so that they might be discounted in much the same way literary critics had done in relation to the diversity of personal tastes. The law could not give voice to individual preferences and opinions, nor could it mandate that people overcome their differences to achieve consensus. It could only enact rules and procedures that reflected an already achieved consensus about the role individual preferences were to play in public decision-making.

The principle of fair comment is one such rule. Its rationale may be that it ensures the vitality and openness of public discourse by preserving the liberty of criticism, even as, in practice, it deters critics from going too far. It allows people to air their differences freely so long as they refrain from making these differences merely personal. In this way, it is one of those modern legal compromises that serve to contain the indeterminacy of free speech by regulating not the topics that may be debated in public but the way these topics may be debated. The principle assumes a boundary between public and private, but this boundary is purposefully left open to interpretation so that the law can at once honor and limit liberty for both critics and private persons. Accordingly, its scope and referents must remain unsettled. Ellenborough may have believed that the principle was already understood when he instructed the jury in Carr's case on the difference between fair comment and personal slander. To him, the difference was clear. But only a few months later he changed his mind, although not about the principle, its rationale, or the standard of fairness he had earlier prescribed to keep the public and the personal separate. Rather, he changed his mind about how and where the personal was to be identified. In so doing, he confirmed that the precedent set in *Carr v. Hood* had instituted a new reality where the division between the public and the private was no longer a customary observance but a distinction that could be challenged in a court of law, debated in public, reaffirmed or revised, and ultimately applied to other discourses.

Writing in 1910, one legal historian noted that a shift had occurred over the previous century whereby literary critics lost a measure of their liberty just as political commentators saw theirs increase. "In the process of time," this historian wrote, "the dawning consciousness of the advantages of freedom of discussion in political affairs was accompanied by the realization of a conviction that the license of literary criticism should be restrained, and that the personal character of an author had claims to legal recognition as well as the public interests of the state."[75] The shift had already been under way in 1861, when Justice Erle extended the fair comment defense to statements made about the acts of public officials. Erle did not think there was anything novel about the extension. He merely told the jury that matters of politics and religion "are open to controversy, and on which opposite opinions may be fairly expressed."[76] By the end of the nineteenth century, the courts were permitting commentators to engage in vicious personal attacks on politicians provided they had the facts to support their allegations. Politics were by then seen as a subject of supreme public interest and as a wholly public subject that all citizens had a right to comment on and to do so in uncivil and indecorous language if they wished. The equality of participation that had formerly legitimized the literary public sphere was now a defining feature of debate on political matters.

By comparison with politics, books could never be as public a subject, and not simply because they might be the work of private individuals, convey authors' feelings, or deal with personal experiences. Writing, particularly literary writing, was by the later nineteenth century no longer a subject that anyone could feel entitled to comment on publicly. Literary critics had to display a requisite level of expertise, taste, and sensitivity since their task, as they saw it, was not merely correcting error for the public's benefit but defending the arts and culture in "a disinterested endeavour to learn and propagate the best that is known and thought in the world."[77] By then, legal scholars were insisting that juries ought never to be asked to decide whether a comment was fair. Common jurors, they claimed, could not be counted on to possess the required competence or to suppress their personal preferences sufficiently to judge the opinions of critics with informed disinterest. Said one, "[I]f the fairness of the criticism were to be left to the jury it would destroy our boasted right of free expression of public opinion, and make a body of untrained—often grossly ignorant—men, the censors of public taste and judgment."[78]

SEDITIOUS LIBEL

CHAPTER FIVE

Literature and the Freedom of Mind

The subject of this chapter is the law of seditious libel, which, in the decades following licensing's demise in 1695, became for successive British governments the most potent instrument of political censorship. Specifically, I deal with the debate among English jurists and lawmakers over the role of juries in trials for the offense. Begun in the 1730s and concluded only with the passage of Fox's Libel Act in 1792,[1] the sedition debate has as strong a claim as the literary property debate to being the most important British legal contest of the century. Yet unlike the fight over copyright, in which arguments over who should own public speech were fully aired, the sedition debate at its core involved a conflict between irreconcilable and largely unexamined beliefs about the effect of speech on the public's judgment. The older of these beliefs, the rhetorical account of language's power, was the basis for the law. The modern belief, which prompted the law's revision, supposed that this power could never be so great as to defeat the public mind.

The modern belief, I argue, entailed an ambivalence that pertains to this day over the place of literature in the public sphere. I can explain this ambivalence by considering one of the belief's most influential articulations—in a passage from Kant's *Critique of Judgment*, a book that originally appeared two years before the Libel Act's passage. In this section, Kant contrasts the honest power of poetry to the deceitful seductions of rhetoric.[2] Poetry, he writes, is the greatest of all arts because it "expands the mind by setting the imagination free." In presenting a theme in a form that conveys its complexity as richly as verbally possible, a poem makes us feel that we understand it fully in the moment of its utterance. The experience is a liberating one since it allows us to exercise our faculties without feeling the burdens of utility or consequence, and we are invigorated by the sense of being able to think for ourselves. Poetry, Kant argues, "strengthens the mind by letting it feel its capacity to consider and judge of nature . . . freely, self-actively, and independently of determination by nature." Poetry's power to enlarge our minds is not itself determining because it never enjoins us to do anything in particular. It neither rouses us to action nor summons us to a cause. It offers only a pleasurable opportunity to enhance our understanding. And we are assured that the opportunity it offers is free from determination because poetry, unlike all other discourses, readily "declares that it will conduct a merely entertaining play with the imagination."

Rhetoric makes no such declaration. It relies on artful devices and fictions similar to those at work in poetry, but it uses them in the service of persuasion rather than play. It takes from poetry, Kant says, "only as much as is necessary to win minds over to the advantage of the speaker before they can judge and to rob them of their freedom." Accordingly, rhetoric is of dubious value when used to influence people in settings where they meet to settle questions of law and morality: "it cannot be recommended either for the courtroom or for the pulpit. For when it is a matter of civil laws concerning the rights of individual persons, or of the lasting instruction and determination of minds to correct knowledge and conscientious observation of their duty, then it is beneath the dignity of such an important business to allow even a trace of exuberance of wit and imagination to be glimpsed." Nothing, Kant adds, can justify the "machinery of persuasion" in the public sphere, no matter how serious the subject matter or well intentioned the cause. Any attempt to coerce the public mind with oratorical displays while it deliberates over the common good violates the norms of debate, norms that the public imposes on itself to ensure the rightness of its decision-making. Rhetoric may produce an experience identical to poetry's, such that both make people feel free from determination, including the legitimizing ground of ethics. Yet the effect of this experience is utterly contingent on circumstance. Pursued for its own sake in the mere play of poetry, the experience expands the mind. In a public setting where people debate the laws, the experience may so distract them that they are rendered incapable of thinking for themselves.

Orators applied exuberances of wit and imagination indiscriminately to any matter of moment, and for this Kant exiled them from the public sphere as resolutely as Plato barred the poets from his ideal commonwealth. Neither philosopher doubted the power of poetry to loosen the mind or of rhetoric to dominate it. This power, they agreed, had to be contained lest it render rational self-governance impossible. Yet while the two philosophers argued from similar premises, their positions were the obverse of one another. For Plato, poetry was bad because it unhinged the mind. Appealing to people's passions and encouraging them to trust to their own irrational impulses, poets upset the harmony of the soul, without which agency was not possible. Rhetoric, meanwhile, was a serviceable if facile "art of ruling the minds of men," as Plato reputedly defined it.[3] Used judiciously, rhetoric could help to instill allegiance to the state. But this benefit came at a cost, in that orators who courted the people's favor inspired them to feel politically empowered. As Simone Chambers has observed, "Plato's attack on rhetoric is an attack on democratic politics because Plato assumes that, as the rule of the many, democracy must proceed through speeches that seek to persuade the many."[4] That said, poetry and rhetoric posed no real problem for Plato, since neither was so valuable to social order that they could not be banished from the polity.

For Kant, beautiful words and fictions did present a problem. As imaginative play, they performed a supreme good. Poetry enabled people to think beyond all determination, including the norms they established to render their deliberations manageable. In doing so, it provided a vital experience of freedom, without which no modern political order could be legitimate. Yet performing this role rendered poetry's relationship to that order ambiguous. If poetry was to enable people to become aware of their agency and freedom, including the freedom to define the rules of deliberation, then poetry could not answer to those rules or else its effects might seem programmed to perpetuate them. It had somehow to be exempt from the rules if the experience of freedom it promised was to be at all genuine.

Kant believed that this problem would not arise so long as poetry remained inconsequential. Poets, unlike orators, were true to the experience of freedom because they refrained from coercing people into doing anything in particular. This division between poetry and rhetoric, however, could not be enforced without compromising poetry's necessary indeterminacy. Kant hoped that it was in the nature of poetry to distinguish itself from rhetoric by declaring itself mere imaginative play. Otherwise, his only option for legislating against the problem was to recommend that exuberances of wit and imagination not be tolerated in contexts where the public met to debate what was right. This recommendation was directed at orators rather than poets. Only orators, Kant believed, would be reckless enough to disturb the achieved order of the public sphere and to use the force of words to take the power of the people away from them in the act of exploiting it to promote a cause. Orators refused to play by the rules without offering any compensating benefit, and for this Kant banished them from the polity. Yet if rhetoric threatened the integrity of public decision-making, by implication poetry's artful devices and fictions were equally out of place in the public sphere. In addition to having no determinable function in civil society, poetry could have no readily specifiable context of utterance except in isolation from all other public activities. As soon as poets stepped into the arena of public debate, they would inevitably become orators.

The eighteenth-century debate on seditious libel, I argue, represented a deeply strenuous shift in attitudes toward the public use of language, a shift from a Platonic suspicion of rhetoric as an instrument of democracy to a Kantian ambivalence about the power of words and how, depending on context, this power could be used either to free or enslave. By definition, the crime of seditious libel involved a doubly destructive abuse of this power. It consisted of speech that had both a bad tendency, in inciting a breach of the peace, and a defamatory aim of discrediting precisely the public institutions that were supposed to maintain the peace. The crime of seditious libel therefore posed a problem for the courts. It was not obvious how ordinary jurors could deal objectively with speech whose content criticized institutions, like the courts, but equally whose affective force might incite them to irrational hostility toward those institutions. Introducing seditious libels into the courtroom threatened to undermine the integrity of legal procedures given that this material was designed to do precisely that. The solution to this dilemma, judges believed, was to disallow jurors from considering a work's alleged seditiousness, preserving for the court alone the authority to rule on whether the work fit the legal definition of a seditious libel.

For reformers, this solution was worse than the problem since, so long as jurors were denied their customary right to judge a defendant's guilt, the courts could not maintain their legitimacy. Just as bad from the reformers' perspective was that the law's defenders were using a legal argument about the duties of judges and juries to disguise their investment in the political order. It was, in fact, only a couple of years after licensing came to an end that judges had reinstituted an older practice of restricting the jury's role in determining a defendant's guilt. Their rationale was that the definition of libel was a matter of law and not fact, and thus it was up to the court and not jurors to decide whether a work fit the definition. Only the courts, they felt, could ensure certainty in the law. Yet as reformers pointed out, the direct effect of this ruling was to make it much easier for the government to prosecute alleged libelers. Since juries could not rule on whether a work was libelous, the accused had little on which to build a defense. They could challenge the prosecution only on two questions: whether they were responsible for publishing an offending work, and whether the work's innuendos could be read with certainty as referring to the individuals who were the libel's ostensible victims. Defendants could not disprove that they had acted with seditious intent. According to the judges, intent was implied by the act of publication, while identifying a work's innuendos merely confirmed that the work was a libel on specific persons. As a result, then, of a ruling about the roles of judge and jury, the courts provided the government with justification to silence its critics without effectively having to show cause or damage.

From the judges' point of view, reformers were not taking the threat of libels seriously. For all their clamoring for a free press, none but the most radical of reformers objected to the law in principle, and most dutifully repeated the official view that the press ought to enjoy liberty but not license. Yet reformers, it seemed to the judges, offered no clear sense of where the line between liberty and license ought to be drawn or of how juries might be able to draw this line with any degree of consistency. Reformers were willing to sacrifice the certainty of the law by putting its interpretation in the hands of jurors, yet they failed to say how juries could be trusted to deal with material that was libelous in content and seditious in effect. A rabble-rouser like Wilkes could subvert the judicial process, opening the way for truly dangerous attacks on the government.

As the debate wore on, however, its assumptions began to change, at first on the reform side and subsequently on the government's, whose efforts at controlling the press were stymied by recalcitrant juries in high-profile cases refusing to return verdicts only on matters of fact. What had been primarily a debate about the respective roles of judge and jury became instead an argument over discursive conditions more generally in the public sphere. On the one hand, the public's legitimizing authority had become more and more inarguable. Reformers could assert without need of demonstration that the public had both the right to judge any idea and the capacity to do so without requiring supervision by the court. Particularly in circumstances like the jury trial, the public, according to reformers, could be assumed to possess sufficient freedom of mind to evaluate speech without being influenced by it. Reformers were even prepared to put forward the radical proposition that the public was free to alter its opinions utterly, such that it might condemn a work as libelous in one context yet embrace it as doctrine in another. Ultimately, by 1792, these ideas had gained wide enough acceptance that the reformers in Parliament were able to restore to juries the right to decide whether a work was libelous.

On the other hand, the problem of the coercive use of speech remained unsettled. Though Kant hoped the courtroom could be insulated from rhetoric's effects, it was not as if there was anything new in his loathing for lawyers. Distrust of rhetoric had been even more pronounced in early modern courts, where, in criminal trials, the accused were typically denied representation by counsel so as to ensure that the proceedings would remain focused on matters of fact. Judges by the later eighteenth century, by contrast, had grown not merely to tolerate defense counsel but to accept the adversarial trial system, in which lawyers for both sides challenged each other in verbal duels over the interpretation of facts.[5] That the adversarial system required jurors to sift eloquence from evidence and decide between competing narratives of the facts implied that juries were felt capable of withstanding the machinery of persuasion. Speech, as I suggested above, was assumed to have lost a measure of its force, the assumption being that in a democratic society, the effect of words could never be so great as to impair the public's freedom of mind.

At the same time, the effect of speech was undeniable, not least on jurors. Star performers like Garrow and Erskine had helped to make the late eighteenth-century courtroom as celebrated a site for nation-defining oratory as Parliament and the pulpit. More dramatic evidence of the force of words could be encountered out of doors, their mobilizing energies evident as much in the violence they incited—in the Gordon riots at home and political revolution abroad—as in the unprecedented demographic reach they could attain through political assemblies and the mass circulation of radical pamphlets. Responding in kind to this intensified public discourse, the government increased the number and frequency of sedition charges, staged show trials for treason, and imposed gagging orders that greatly upped the penalties for convicted libelers.[6] Yet, faced with legal challenges to its authority in determining libels, the government also began to adopt ideas that reformers had earlier introduced in the libel debate, ideas meant to counter the judges' claim that the certainty of the law would be sacrificed were its interpretation left to jurors. Such certainty, reformers had argued, was illusory because the purpose and force of words depended so much on context that a work condemned as libelous in one setting could be read without harm in another.

These ideas provided the government with the impetus to revise the prosecutorial case against libels. Earlier in the century the emphasis in libel trials had been on the libelous content of an offending statement. By the time the Libel Act was passed, the emphasis had shifted to a statement's bad effect, as evidenced by the circumstances of its publication. In the decorum of the courtroom, jurors could be expected to deal with a work filled with passionate appeals with the same equanimity as they did a work of sober reason. Lawyers might still attempt to sway juries with their oratory, which, contrary to what Kant advised, remained a valued skill so long as its use was restricted to official proceedings, like trials. Outside of formal settings, however, fine phrases and beautiful fictions could be dangerous things. So, following the act's passage, judges would instruct juries that if a work was designed as an intervention at a volatile moment, such that its passionate appeals could incite violence, then its publication was to be judged a criminal offense. By the same logic, lawmakers decreed that the occasions for political utterances made outside of official channels, such as at popular assemblies, could likewise be unlawful regardless of the content of those utterances. The uses and circumstances of persuasion, more so than the substance of a work's ideas, became the target of official censorship.

For much of this chapter, I rehearse the legal history of this change, with a particular focus on how evolving notions of speech's effects shaped the debate over who should decide whether a work was libelous. The change was complex, involving arguments over legal doctrine, ideological contests over public liberty, and ground-level adjustments to trial procedure. As in previous chapters, though, I am principally concerned with what the changing norms entailed for the regulation of public discourses and for the value of literary writing among those discourses. With the change, new forms of regulation on the conditions of speech replaced older prohibitions on opinion, and strongly rhetorical utterances came to be treated with suspicion not so much for what they said but for why and where they said it. Literature shared many of its constituent features with utilitarian forms of rhetorical speech. To preserve it from disfavor, literature had to be set apart from these forms on the basis, as Kant would have it, of both its promise of freedom from determination and its autonomy from utility and moral obligation.

More consequently, literature had to be removed from the occasions and settings of public deliberation. The libel debate came to an end when lawmakers felt they could trust the public to deal with forceful words in the formal space of the courtroom, where the temper of speech could be closely monitored. Outside of this space, there were fewer rules protecting the public from what one modern Kantian legal theorist has called the "empire of force."[7] Verbal coercion remained a threat to the public's freedom of mind, though it could be contained. The problem of coercion nonetheless appeared to pose a contradiction to democratic notions of public liberty. The public could be neither truly sovereign if the force of words could nullify its agency nor truly free if it had always to regulate its interactions so as to shield itself from this force. Literature was to be the one discourse that disproved the contradiction. Through literary writings, people could experience the force of words directly, without protection or protocols and without risk to public order. They could do so because, unlike the other discourses, the power and meaning of literary writings were not, or not so much, dependent on context, and so could be experienced in an indeterminable space beyond the realm of decision-making. Literature was to be recognized as centrally defining of the national culture and cherished for providing individuals with a liberating experience that was vital to their formation as members of a modern public. There could be no thought, however, of using its affectivity to lead the public in settings where it met to debate the common good. Doing so would deprive the public of its autonomy and undermine the basis for literature's legitimacy as a public discourse. Yet, I suggest in the epilogue, there could be no way of resolving this ambivalence over literature's purpose since it ultimately reflected an incoherence at the heart of modern democratic ideals.

Libel as Sedition

The English law of sedition dates from the Tudor period.[8] Developed in the Court of Star Chamber, the law criminalized works that sought to instill disaffection for the state by defaming its magistrates or other officials. It was intended as a more workable alternative to older mechanisms for policing dissent: more politically acceptable than declaring martial law, less cumbersome to prosecute than the crime of constructive treason, and broader in scope than the statutes of scandalum magnatum, which applied only to false allegations made against peers or state officers. Seditious words differed from treasonable utterances in not openly calling for violence, but they nonetheless imperiled public order by fueling factionalism, which could lead to violence. In principle, it was immaterial whether an offending work's allegations were true or false, its words written or spoken. In practice, jurists like Sir Edward Coke were more vigilant in prosecuting truthful utterances, which, they felt, were more likely to cause dissension. They were likewise keen to stop libels being disseminated in forms other than in print, which was already controlled by pre-publication censorship. Coke made a point of singling out slanders expressed in the form of rhymes and epigrams, which could be "maliciously repeated or sung in the presence of others."[9]

Coke's concern about the scandalizing power of verse suggests how deeply the law was informed by rhetorical precepts. Three ideas in particular influenced how early modern jurists conceived of seditious libel. First, for the purposes of the law, all speech was presumed to possess persuasive force. The power of rhetoric was supreme: in Jean Bodin's version of this commonplace, "there is nothing that hath more force ouer the minds of men, than hath eloquence." Coercion was the desired end of all virtuous speech, the formative instrument of civilization that, according to the foundational myth of Bodin's rhetorical culture, had enabled poets and preachers "to reduce the people from barbarisme to humanitie, to reform disordered maners, to correct the laws, to cast out vices, to maintain vertue." Yet while poets refined humanity through the power of words, libelers deployed this same power to rend the social fabric. "[A] knife is not more dangerous in the hand of a mad man," Bodin declared, "than eloquence in the mouth of a mutinous Orator."[10] Since all works were thought to produce effects, for good or ill, the prosecution in libel trials did not have to demonstrate a work's disruptiveness—unlike in trials for treason, where it had to prove an overt act. It was simply a given that slanderous words caused harm. At the same time, the danger posed by sedition made it a greater offense than common defamation. Whereas a personal insult might provoke retaliation, a libel against a public official invited "not only the breach of the peace, but also the scandal of Government," and so undermined conviction in the social order.[11]

Whether such scandal amounted to sedition was the only question left open to challenge, chiefly because it was unclear whether the concept of sedition had ever been recognized in the common law.[12] Otherwise, there was no thought of treating a statement's defamatory content or affecting style separately from its seditiousness: criticism of state officials, in whatever form, gave rise inexorably to discontent.

Second, a libel was believed to inflict damage regardless of how, where, or for whom it was published, the only requirement being that for a work to be tried as a libel, it had to have been made available in some form to someone who was not the defamed party. A work's seditiousness did not depend on the context of its reception. It was presumed to have the same effect on all people, regardless of the occasion. Auditors who overheard a scurrilous ballad being sung nearby were no more exposed to its bad influence than readers who encountered a libel in a setting far removed from its original performance. Even defamation spoken in a closed proceeding was thought to cause harm.[13] There was no setting—other than perhaps in Parliament[14]—where criticism of state policy could be safely expressed. There was even no limit to a libel's temporal context. It did not matter, Coke explained, whether libels defamed living or dead individuals, since attacks on public officials past or present necessarily reflected upon "the State and Government, which dies not."[15]

Third, and most important for the law's rationale, seditious libels were assumed to imperil liberty not because they manipulated people into embracing ideas they might not otherwise entertain but because they undermined social harmony by breeding a disabling diversity of opinion. Orators, Bodin explained, abused the coercive power of their eloquence in seeking to "direct & guide the peoples hearts & minds according to their owne pleasure."[16] Yet if their crime was in presuming freedom of speech for themselves, the injury that libelers inflicted was in freeing people from the necessary constraints of mind. According to the author of "An Aduertisement Towching Seditious Wrytings" (c. 1594), libelers were driven to vent their ire for any number of reasons from professional disappointment to a loss of faith. Yet whatever their motive, the effect of their libels was to set the people loose from the bounds of conscience. "[I]n all pollytyes," the author explained, "the strength is in multitude who are vnyted in subiection and obedyence by certayne qualytyes and affections of their myndes—which in very trewthe are the bandes and sinowes of all gouverment." These qualities of mind were in most persons not strong enough to withstand being "diversly interrupted" by the force of libelous persuasion. Their impulses released from the cordons of certitude, the people were wont to contemplate political rebellion, the thought of which "kindl[es] in men of all Callinges many wandrynge hopes of advantage by the Chaunge."[17] Sedition encouraged people to think that their interests could legitimately diverge from the will of the Crown. As Sir Nicholas Bacon, the lord keeper, declared in 1567, the evil of seditious words "maketh mens minds to be at variance one with another, and diversity of minds maketh seditions."[18]

Individuals accused of seditious libel were given no opportunity to answer the charge that their words were dissentious. Tried for libel in 1590, the Puritan minister John Udall protested that there was no evidence that his book, *A Demonstration of the Trueth of That Discipline* (1588), had sparked insurrection in the two years since its publication. In response, the judge directed the jury to ignore the claim since the seditiousness of Udall's work was a question of law for the court to decide. "Find him Author of the Book," the judge told the jurors, "and leave the Felony to us."[19] At his 1633 trial in the Star Chamber, William Prynne similarly denied ever having intended to cast aspersions on the Caroline court with his anti-theatrical diatribe *Histriomastix* (1632). The judges retorted that, whatever Prynne professed, the language of his book was so overheated as to imply a desire to foment sedition: "the very style doth declare the intent of the man, and that is . . . to work a discontent and dislike in the king's people against the Church and Government."[20] Only in trials for the greater offense of high treason was it possible—and by no means consistently so—for the accused to defend themselves on the grounds that mere words, however scandalous, did not produce the violent effects alleged against them.[21]

For most of the seventeenth century, judges did not feel compelled to provide a restatement of the law of sedition. In 1642, following the abolition of the Star Chamber, jurisdiction over libels passed to the common-law courts, where defendants were tried before a jury. The courts had almost no precedents to guide them on the jury's role in libel trials. The judge in Udall's case was among the few to address the matter, and his only comment was that "being ignorant of the law," jurors had no authority to pronounce it.[22] Sedition trials were, in any event, relatively uncommon. Most cases of alleged seditious libel during the period were in actuality prosecutions for licensing violations, where the facts of publication were the only matter that needed to be established for a jury.[23] Otherwise, in actual libel cases, judges rarely said anything about why jurors ought not to consider a work's seditious tendency. If they referred to a work's tendency at all, it was usually to express their hostility to its doctrines, as Justice Hyde did at a 1665 trial, when he prohibited the accused from attempting to defend his Nonconformist ideas lest he "seduce and infect his majesty's subjects."[24]

A restatement became necessary only after two important challenges were posed to the law's underlying principles. The first came in the wake of Justice Vaughan's ruling in *Bushell's Case* (1670), which affirmed the independence of juries.[25] The ruling lent legitimacy to a nascent reform movement that argued on behalf of the right and capacity of jurors to arrive at a collective decision that might diverge from a judge's opinion but was nonetheless authoritative because it was based on a greater range of knowledge than a single judge could bring to bear in weighing the facts of a case. In particular, as I explain below, jurors ideally had prior knowledge of the parties and circumstances of a crime, whereas judges could consider only the evidence given in court.

A corollary to this, set out influentially in John Hawles's tract *The Englishman's Right* (1680), was the claim that traditional division of responsibilities between the judge and the jury, where the former ruled on matters of law and the latter on matters of fact, could never be consistently realized in practice.[26] Jurors, Hawles argued, were often required to make a finding of law, notably when asked to consider how the circumstances of an offense might mitigate its criminality. That circumstances might have a bearing on a case argued against the judicial doctrine that a crime was to be judged solely in accordance with the normative certainty of the law. Hawles and other early reformers, though not specifically concerned with the law of seditious libel, were thus implicitly rejecting two of its three operative assumptions.[27] They could not abide its rationale as a mechanism for containing the diversity of opinion, since they could not see how a verdict could be legitimate if jurors were not permitted to disagree with a judge's opinion. And they could not see how jurors could apply the law fairly if they were not permitted to judge a crime in its context.

The second challenge, which at the time seemed more momentous than the first, was the outcome of the 1688 trial of the seven bishops. The bishops had written to King James II, objecting to his order in council requiring that his Declaration of Indulgence be read in their churches and requesting that he excuse them from carrying out the order. After their request found its way into print, the bishops were charged with publishing a libel "under pretence of a Petition." At their trial, the four judges on the King's Bench could not agree on whether the petition met Chief Justice Wright's definition of a seditious libel as a publication that "shall disturb the government, or make mischief and a stir among the people."[28] With no clear opinion to guide them, the jurors were left to make their own ruling on the petition's criminality, which they did by acquitting the bishops.

The decision subsequently took on legendary proportions as both a transformative precedent and a trigger for the revolution. Yet because the judges had not expressly tasked the jury with deciding whether the petition was libelous, it was debatable which legal principle was set or overturned by the jury's acquittal of the bishops.[29] The decision could be seen, as later reformers felt it should be, as confirming the jury's right to rule on a work's libelousness. By this interpretation the jury upheld the law in principle while altering the method of its prosecution. Conversely, the opponents of reform felt that the decision ought to be seen as an act of jury nullification: the jurors, in taking the unauthorized step of ruling on a matter of legality, had declared their disapproval of the law by returning a verdict that contravened the letter of the law. By this interpretation the jury rejected the law of sedition by altering the method of its prosecution.

While the jury's decision had unclear consequences for the law, the judges' disagreement over the criteria for determining libel was a more definitively transformative moment. For Wright, the petition disturbed the government: its seditious effect was proof of its libelousness. For Justice Allibond, the petition had defamed the king by questioning his authority: its content was evidence of its criminality. For Justice Holloway, the petition was not written with "an ill intention of sedition": the defendants' state of mind, a legal principle normally deemed irrelevant in libel trials, was evidence of the petition's legality.[30] For Justice Powell, the petition was no libel because it was neither indecent in expression nor false in substance: the evidence of its seriousness and truth, which till then had been seen as aggravating a libel's criminality, justified the petition.

The irreconcilability of the judges' opinions augured a change in the discursive order. While the law continued to be justified on the basis of rhetorical precepts, the structure of conviction that made those precepts seem compelling was diminishing in intensity. All speech was still assumed to produce effects of one kind or another. But if people could disagree over what those effects were, there was no reason to assume a causal relation between a statement's content or style and its effects. And if a work that appeared to one judge as having a seditious tendency could appear to another as having none at all by virtue of its truth or its author's good intentions, then words were beginning to lose some of their presumed force.

From Sedition to Libel

The decision in the *Seven Bishops Case* introduced ambiguities that needed to be resolved if the law was to remain serviceable for state censorship. With licensing coming to an end in 1695 and with Parliament deciding in the same year to render convictions for treason more difficult to obtain, the government had all the more reason to rehabilitate the law of sedition as a mechanism of press control.[31] It was helped in its efforts by sympathetic judges, who set precedents that made it easier to launch proceedings through indictments, lessened the prosecution's burden of proof, and broadened the category of seditious libel to include any attack on government and not just defamations of state officials.[32] Most important, the judges ignored whatever precedent may have been set in the *Seven Bishops Case* and unequivocally declared that the determination of libel was the province of the court.[33] As the defense counsel in a 1699 case conceded, "no person hath power to judge criminally of the effect of a man's words, for that must be left to the law."[34]

Jurors were less willing to make concessions. Restricted to ruling only on matters of fact, juries in the initial decades following licensing's demise contrived ways of exercising a law-finding authority. They rendered special verdicts that questioned whether a charge could be maintained against an accused who had only made a copy of a libel for himself or against another whose words had not been exactly transcribed in the information against him.[35] And while juries could not rule on a work's criminality, judges were challenged to abide by earlier precedents that gave juries some say in deciding whether a work was malicious in cases where its intent or victims were uncertain. In a 1706 case, it was left to the jury to determine whether a work was intended to be ironic.[36] Seven years later, the court affirmed an older practice of allowing jurors leeway in interpreting a work's innuendos.[37] Though both cases ended in conviction, subsequent prosecutions would be frustrated by jurors refusing to find criminal meaning in ironic or allusive writings, most notably at the 1729 trial of Richard Francklin, the printer of *The Craftsman*, who was acquitted by a jury packed with Tories.[38] As William Pulteney cheered in a ballad celebrating Francklin's acquittal, the attorney general "well knows / That *Innuendoes* / Will serve him no longer in Verse or in Prose."[39]

These assertions of jury independence did not stem from a principled opposition to the law of seditious libel. Few during the early eighteenth century questioned the law's rationale or method of prosecution.[40] Nor was there any revision to this method that might explain why trials like Francklin's were increasingly fought over the question of a publication's meaning. Officially the courts adhered to precedent in limiting the allowable evidence to the facts of a work's publication and the identity of its innuendos. As Andrew Benjamin Bricker has pointed out, nothing in the letter of the law had changed to warrant the common belief among contemporary satirists that their use of irony, allegory, and disguised names shielded their writings from prosecution.[41] If anything, judges had grown less willing to demonstrate caution about certainty, having, for example, discontinued an older practice in defamation cases of construing alleged slanders as mildly as possible in order to discourage offended parties from flooding the courts with suits.[42] Above all, the courts insisted on a hermeneutic standard for dealing with ironic or allusive texts, whereby prosecutors were to interpret their meaning "such as the generality of readers must take it in, according to the obvious and natural sense of it."[43] The standard was proposed in answer to accusations that the state was twisting the meaning of alleged libels to facilitate their prosecution, though judges also cited it to disallow defendants from attempting to show how else a work might be interpreted.

Despite judges clamping down on the rules of interpretation, the locus of contention in proceedings for seditious libel became more than ever libel and not sedition, the defamatory content of works rather than their emotional impact. This was perhaps inevitable given that the only doubts that could be formally raised in court had to do with the meaning of publications. Yet at a more profound level, the change was indicative of an altered universe of belief where, even as the courts were tightening the law's provisions, its legitimizing premises were losing their hold on the cultural imagination. The decision in the *Seven Bishops Case* had revealed a rhetorical order under stress, in which the order's normative certainties had proven ineffective at overcoming the intractable reality of political and religious division. Though no new discursive order had yet emerged to challenge those certainties, it was becoming possible for people to feel they could voice disagreement about prevailing norms and, to a degree, resist the force of words.

Indeed, what had been imagined as the principal threat posed by libels—the unleashing of a diversity of minds—was being normalized as a condition of liberty. Early advocates of free speech believed that people ought to be exposed to diverse opinions. A free press, they argued, was essential not for preserving this diversity, which was the regrettable consequence of human imperfection, but for overcoming it through the testing of ideas and the correction of error. "The examining [of] the Reasons on all sides," Tindal wrote, "is the only Method that can be taken to prevent Mistakes."[44] Freethinking was thus premised on a kind of negative equality, in which no single person could pretend to have a monopoly on the truth. As Trenchard put it, "[W]hilst all Opinions are equally indulged, and all Parties equally allow'd to speak their Minds, the Truth will come out."[45] Although only a handful of Whig radicals espoused the value of equality, their arguments signaled a change in expectations about discourse, such that disagreement in public debate was beginning to seem not merely unavoidable but useful.

The change entailed an adjustment to what was understood by sedition. The corrupting influence of libels was no longer characterized in terms of their moral or psychological effects. Far from releasing people from the fetters of conscience, libels were said to have, in Chief Justice Holt's much-cited opinion, a bad tendency toward "possessing the people with an ill opinion of government." Since judges saw the harm from libels as wholly political in nature, they felt little impelled to set out the moral basis of the law. Holt believed it was enough to say that the purpose of the law was to ensure that "government can be safe."[46]

The biggest change in perceptions had to do with the context of defamation, specifically the audience at whom libels were directed. By the 1730s, political recognition was being extended to the idea of public opinion.[47] The ruling parties believed that they could derive political capital from claiming to have the public's favor, to the point where the government's defenders expressed mock exasperation over the opposition press daring to presume "of late more especially, to write in the Name of the *Generality* of the People."[48] At the same time, neither party took public sentiment seriously. Certainly, neither trusted the consensual judgment of ordinary jurors. The Tories celebrated the "*Twelve good honest Men*" who acquitted Francklin at his 1729 trial, but only after they had achieved the result by packing the jury with their supporters.[49] The government reacted to the acquittal not by defending the integrity of the jury system but by forcing through the 1730 Act for the Better Regulation of Juries, which upped the property qualification for jurors.[50] Interestingly, the act also formalized the practice of sortation, or the selection of jurors by lot, as a preventive against jury packing, though the practice would subsequently be cited by reformers as a major reason that juries were less likely than judges to show political bias in libel trials.

If the public could not be trusted to judge libelers, the rise of public opinion prompted a revision in the prevailing sense of how libels worked. In the past, a libel caused damage regardless of the circumstances of its dissemination: in uttering words that severed the sinews of conscience, libelers threatened the entire social order. With the public gaining legitimacy as a decision-making body, the courts began to define this threat differently, as a measurable harm commensurate to a libel's impact on public opinion. The judges who convicted Edmund Curll for obscene libel in 1727, as I noted earlier, believed that the malign effects of his publication could be made worse by its dissemination "all over the kingdom."[51] Likewise, government apologists were appalled that the opposition was using organs of publicity to teach "the *lowest* of the *People* . . . to relish *Sedition*."[52] The remark was meant as a lordly putdown, insinuating as it did that the opposition demeaned itself by producing libels that the common people could understand. The comment nonetheless betrayed an awareness of the power of public opinion. The public was now a political agent, one that libelers had to win over for their libels to be effective. Public opinion was the context and object of libels, what provided them with both meaning and purpose.

The true sense of a libel had become a matter for the public to determine. This perception was the primary reason that libel trials were focused on the defamatory content of texts and, for the first time, legal commentators felt it necessary to defend the courts' interpretive procedures. The author of *State Law; or, The Doctrine of Libels, Discussed and Examined* (c. 1730) worried that with the tide of opposition satire, the public was getting frustrated at the courts' inability to stop political defamers. The people, he claimed, were becoming doubtful "[w]hether a witty Man may not write and publish Things of a scandalous import, yet so gloss'd over and disguised, so wrapp'd up in Implications and Allegories, as not to come within Reach of the Laws, nor be construed a Breach of them."[53] The public, by this account, could recognize libels for what they were. The meaning of seditious publications did not elude the public's comprehension, and their effects did not impair its judgment. The public, this writer supposed, was merely ignorant of the case law, which showed that judges had never tolerated satirists' attempts at using verbal subterfuge to evade the law. The courts had long observed a standard of certainty for interpreting defamations, and by this standard the "punishment of a libeler was never to be lessen'd on Account of the Mystery in his Satir."[54]

The standard was effective, he explained, because it followed common usage: even the craftiest of libelers could not escape the law because judges read libels the way "the World understands them." The public ought to trust in the ability of the courts to deal with verbally indirect libels since any defamation so wrapped in allegory that it was disguised from the law would be unintelligible to the public and therefore harmless as a libel: "it will pass for Nonsense with every one."[55] Libels posed a danger only if the generality understood them. The public may not have set the legal definition of libel, but it decided what words meant. It established certainty.[56] Believing this, defense counsel in trials like Francklin's began demanding that jurors be permitted to interpret the sense of offending publications. To this idea, the author of *State Law* made no objection but drew the line at allowing jurors unschooled in the case law to determine libels. While the public, he believed, set the standard for construing the meaning of libels, it was not qualified to judge the criminality of this meaning.

This distinction between interpreting and evaluating libels, and the question of the public's competence at doing either, would be the central point of contention in a heated and often highly technical debate over the right of juries to determine libel. The debate's instigating event was the 1735 acquittal by a New York jury of John Peter Zenger on a charge of having printed a "false, malicious, seditious, scandalous Libel" on the provincial governor.[57] Zenger's lawyer, Andrew Hamilton, won the case by persuading the jurors that their ability to understand libels gave them the right to judge them. To make his case, Hamilton had to convince the jurors that they could arrive at a verdict that diverged from the judge's opinion, and he did so by being the first defense lawyer at a libel trial to draw on Vaughan and Hawles in arguing for the jury's independence.[58] He then had to instruct the jurors on what was open to their interpretation. The jury, he proposed, ought to be permitted to consider the truth of the publication, but the court insisted that truth was no defense. With this line of argument closed, Hamilton next raised the question of who should decide whether a work was libelous. Addressing the conflict of opinion in the *Seven Bishops Case*, Hamilton declared that "there is not greater Uncertainty in any Part of the Law, than about Words of Scandal."[59] This uncertainty, he claimed, was especially acute in relation to works, like Zenger's, that deployed satire in criticizing their targets: judges were as informed as the public was about how words were understood, but neither had any special competence to say conclusively whether words "were spoke in a *scoffing and ironical Manner*, or seriously."[60]

Jurors, Hamilton argued, had the best claim to grasping the meaning and effect of Zenger's work because of their familiarity with the circumstances of its publication. The common courts, he told the jury, had long preferred to select jury members *"out of the Neighbourhood where the Fact is alleged to be committed . . . because you are supposed to have the best Knowledge of the Fact that is to be tried."*[61] Though by that time honored as much in the breach as in the observance, the requirement that jurors were to be drawn from the vicinage was premised on the idea that the jury's independence from the judge derived from its local knowledge of the facts at issue in a trial.[62] The requirement was an inheritance from an older, oath-based system of prosecution, in which the accused was brought to answer charges before persons who knew the character of the defendant and witnesses well enough to assess the credibility of their testimony.[63] A judge did not come to a trial possessing this knowledge. As a rule, a judge could not be a resident of the community where an offense had been committed; judges were expected to be, in Blackstone's phrase, "strangers in the county" so as to ensure their adherence to the law.[64] The judge could not know the particulars of a case other than what was given as evidence in court. Members of the jury, by contrast, were not strangers to the parties or the circumstances of a crime. As Vaughan had made clear in *Bushell's Case*, jurors could rely on their pretrial knowledge in weighing evidence and could return a verdict even if "no evidence were given on either side in court."[65] Jurors were considered akin to expert witnesses; a jury man who had particular information to impart could be sworn in to give testimony. Hamilton thus drew on an ancient legal tradition to persuade the jurors that they possessed a competence that both the judge and the generality lacked. The jurors had the right to pass judgment on the accused, he was suggesting, because they knew the circumstances of a crime better than anyone.

Hamilton's argument was effective because it muddied the waters. It at once posited and compounded several distinctions. The jury, Hamilton proposed, was representative of two overlapping but divergently skilled interpretive communities, the general public and the local populace.[66] As members of the public, the jury could confirm the meaning of any offending words, and as neighbors to the parties in the case, it could confirm the truth and legality of Zenger's particular words. Hamilton thus relied on both customary and modern assumptions. He played to an emerging sense that as the intended audience for libels, the public established certainty of meaning. But he also invoked an older belief that juries were qualified to serve by virtue of their local knowledge, which afforded them a measure of certainty unavailable to the judge or the broader public. He then encouraged the jurors to conclude, on the basis of both assumptions, that they possessed not merely a general competence to interpret libels but the authority to determine whether Zenger's work in particular was defamatory.

Hamilton won his case, but the muddle he helped to introduce into the legal discourse on seditious libel would take decades to resolve.

The Early Debate: From Libel to Sedition

The muddle was a consequence of the fact that the debate's contenders were arguing over one question, about how to limit public speech, by proposing answers to a different question, about who should be entrusted to define this limit. There were several reasons for the indirection. For one, defense lawyers believed that they stood a chance of getting their clients acquitted if they presented their case directly to juries. The latter, as I noted, had proven recalcitrant before, with a few juries managing to exercise a law-finding authority within the narrow scope of their responsibilities. The Zenger decision prompted attorneys to encourage juries to commit more brazen acts of self-assertion. They followed Hamilton in telling jurors that their understanding of what libels meant entitled them to decide what was libelous. In the next major case of jury nullification in a libel trial, the 1752 prosecution of bookseller William Owen, the defense advised jurors that they had a right to consider evidence of intent, given that the charges against alleged libelers routinely accused them of publishing material "maliciously, seditiously, scandalously, and falsely."[67] And, as happened in several later well-publicized cases, defense counsel persuaded juries in effect to work-to-rule: if the jury was permitted to judge only the facts of publication, then it was to find defendants "guilty of publishing and printing only."[68] Since defense attorneys could not confront the courts on the definition of libel, they staged indirect challenges by prevailing on juries to assume a greater role in deciding libel cases than the courts had so far allowed.

Another reason for the indirection was that the question of the jury's role was the one issue over which commentators felt they could most clearly articulate their differences. Reformers followed Hawles in criticizing the artificiality of the law–fact distinction, and they produced one pamphlet after another setting out how the court's strict application of the distinction in libel trials was indefensible since it contravened the practice in trials for other offenses.[69] What galled reformers most was the arbitrary way the courts had mapped the distinction onto the actions of interpreting and evaluating libels. Judges treated a libel's meaning as a matter of fact that could be verified at trial by referring to how the public understood the text and its innuendos. However, they equally insisted that the same text's libelous intent and tendency were not matters of fact because the public was incapable of reaching a similarly stable agreement over whether the text had defamed its victims. A work's criminality had to be a matter of law, they claimed, because the only way of ensuring consistency in libel prosecutions was to have the courts enforce a standard of defamation established by statute and precedent. Chaos would ensue, Mansfield warned, were juries free to interpret this standard according to their inclinations: "If the law was to be determined in every particular cause, what a miserable condition would this country be in.... If juries were to find according to the different impressions the different points of law have upon them, there might be no law at all upon the subject."[70] For Mansfield, the public certified the meaning of words, but when it came to setting norms of speech, it could not resolve its own diversity of opinion.

The jury that heard Mansfield deliver this admonition was not deterred. The case was *Rex v. Miller* (1770), one of three actions brought against publishers of *The Letters of Junius*. Ignoring the judge's instructions, the jury acquitted John Miller; upon hearing the verdict, the crowd outside the courtroom was reported to have "testified their joy, by the loudest huzzas."[71] The success of the Wilkesites at mobilizing public opinion had put the courts on the defensive. Indeed, shortly after the jurors returned an ambiguous verdict in *Rex v. Woodfall* (1770), the last of the *Junius* prosecutions to be resolved, the House of Lords took the unusual step of summoning the chief justice to answer questions about his interpretation of the law–fact doctrine. The Wilkesites, meanwhile, had not only taken up the campaign for jurors' rights but were actively revising its premises. Previously, in reply to the court's view that jurors could not be expected to judge libels fairly, reformers had appealed to an older sense of civic virtue in defending the moral "integrity and firmness" of the common jury.[72] By 1770 they had changed tack, setting aside moral claims in favor of more radical notions of democratic equality. In so doing they transformed the sedition debate from a dispute over the division of responsibilities between judge and jury into a battle over ideological first principles.

Rather than insisting on the jury's integrity, Wilkesite reformers allowed that public opinion was an uncertain guide to follow in judging libels. In effect, they agreed with Mansfield that juries were fallible. Where the judge erred, they argued, was in having too much faith in the normative certainty of the law. For reformers, certainty was both elusive and overrated. They pointed out that the legal standard of defamation had never been consistently applied because of the changing nature of the common law, the likelihood that politics influenced judges' decisions as much as jurors', and the fact that no definition of libel could ever anticipate all of the possible ways that writings could be defamatory. More important from the reformers' perspective, public opinion was no less indeterminate than the opinions of judges, but it was a fairer guide to follow because its fallibility was offset by its equality. A modern jury, like the public from which its members were drawn, was made up of no one in particular. There was thus no cause to assume, Junius declared, that judges like Mansfield were "more likely to be unbiased and impartial, than twelve yeomen, burgesses, or gentlemen taken indifferently from the county at large."[73] The judgment of a modern jury, reformers believed, was authoritative for reasons contrary to those traditionally claimed for common jurors and as recently as in the Zenger case. Instead of a dozen neighbors chosen for their familiarity with the circumstances of a crime, modern jurors were strangers to one another and to the parties involved in a criminal trial. Whether they could remain independent of political influence was less significant than that their strangerhood functioned as a normative condition enjoining each of them to suspend their individual preferences when weighing the facts of a case.

The indeterminacy of public opinion also meant that it was constantly revising itself, so there was less risk of its caprices being enshrined into law. The law's defenders warned that if jurors were permitted to rule on what was a libel, they might return verdicts that curtailed the freedom of the press; they might, as the lord justice clerk of the Scottish court worried, make it "dangerous either in Sermons, Satyrs, Sonnets, or Comedies, to reprove or expose any of the prevailing Vices of the Age we live in."[74] Reformers retorted that a jury was just as likely to let a vicious libeler go free, but the risk of either possibility was not a good reason to deny jurors the right to declare what was a libel. "There are seasons of epidemical madness," one Wilkesite boldly declared, "when a temperate Jury cannot be had, and when nothing will be deemed a libel upon government. Be it so. The disorder cannot last long."[75] Compared to the systemic injustice that a bad law might produce, the damage caused by a jury's unfair verdict would be limited to an isolated instance. Prejudice may influence a jury's decision, George Rous explained, but "[n]ew jurors succeed to another trial; so that the evil can extend only to a single case."[76] Whereas judges believed that fairness was achievable only within the certainty of the law, reformers believed that fairness was most possible under the law of chance, before which all citizens were equal. What had been, prior to the 1760s, a debate over legal doctrine had become a collision between starkly opposed political and epistemic philosophies.

At the same time, the principal cause of the muddle was that for much of the debate, neither side could imagine how the nature of libelous speech might be defined differently. Both professed to respect the liberty of the press, while also agreeing on the need to limit that liberty. "Our minds and pens ought to be free, but not mischievous," one reformer typically declared.[77] The two sides certainly disagreed over how much freedom was desirable, and they argued at length over whether truth ought to be always permissible to speak—and nothing appalled reformers more than Mansfield's stubborn adherence to the old dictum that "the greater the truth, the greater the libel."[78] Both sides, however, thought of libel solely as an offense of opinion. So long as actions for sedition were preoccupied with the defamatory meaning of libels, jurists could not envisage imposing limits on anything other than the substantive content of speech. They assumed that there existed general agreement on the nature of the mischief that the law was to prevent, with disagreement occurring only over which opinions were mischievous. And since they could refer only abstractly to what made an opinion mischievous, both sides argued over who should decide what was libelous as an indirect way of contending over which opinions were libelous.

The trouble was that in proposing who was best qualified to judge libels without explaining how these qualified persons were immune to the influence of libels, both sides occluded the harm from this influence almost out of existence. For example, soon after the Zenger decision turned the spotlight on the jury's competence, government supporters began to assert novel standards of interpretive expertise. The courts, they argued, had to rely on special juries in cases of political libel since "a plain Jury of Freeholders may happen not to be so well versed in the Arts of Composition, and Figures of Rhetorick, as to be able to trace out the exact Meaning of these mysterious Writers."[79] This argument was a nonstarter for the obvious reason that it precluded the possibility of libels inciting popular insurrection. If a plain jury of freeholders was ill equipped to comprehend libels, so was the broader populace. The author pretty much confirmed the point: "Men, whose Occupation is trade or Husbandry, cannot be supposed to be acquainted with the *cant Words, Exotick Phrases, Jibes, Ironies, Nicknames* and *Metaphors*, in use among the Factors of Treason and Blasphemy; all which, to Men of Education, and Knowledge of the World, are nevertheless as plain and intelligible as the most simple Proposition."[80] If only educated men could understand libels, then they were the only people these publications might spur into committing acts of sedition. And if only educated men were liable to engage in sedition, it would follow that they were the least qualified to judge libels.

Virtually the same muddle afflicted arguments from the other side. If an alleged libel, Junius proposed, "be so obscurely worded, that twelve common men cannot possibly see the seditious meaning and tendency of it, it is in effect no libel. It cannot inflame the minds of the people, nor alienate their affections from government; for they no more understand what it means, than if it were published in a language unknown to them."[81] Junius's point was identical to the one that the author of *State Law* had made forty years earlier: no libel could be effective if no one understood it. Yet the clear if unacknowledged implication of Junius's claim was that if the people *did* understand the sense of a libelous publication, it *would* inflame their minds and alienate their affections from government. The people had the capacity to comprehend seditious libels, but it would seem to follow that in the absence of any other qualification that might shield them from the effects of libels, this capacity rendered them unfit to judge libels.

A decisive refocusing of the debate was nonetheless implicit in what Junius said. Libels, he seemed to allow, could have an incendiary effect on people's minds. Though he alluded to the possibility only to make the point that libels were intended to rouse public opinion, what was significant was that he did not rule it out. Earlier reformers, in pinning their cause to the moral integrity of common jurors, insisted that the public's judgment was impervious to coercion: "The Conscience of a Jury is the supreme Law, the Law of Right Reason; over which, no Rhetorick from the Bar, no Direction from the Bench, should ever have the least Sway or Influence."[82] As with any liberal faith in the rationality of public debate, this argument gave only nominal recognition to the force of language. Rhetoric was imagined as an external threat to reason but one whose impotence rendered the law redundant. If no persuasion could sway the conscience of jurors, then libels could not have a coercive effect on the public mind. More to the point, right reason was by this account a "supreme law" that was anterior to the common law that judges might instruct juries on. Reason was binding on jurors, naturally determining them to abide by the truth. From this supreme law, they were not autonomous.

For radicals like Junius, popular sovereignty was inconceivable without autonomy. The public could never be truly free if its choices were not its own but the dictates of a transcendent determination of right. Democracy was predicated on the free agency of the public mind, its liberty to decide what was right. The only limits that could be legitimately imposed on this freedom were those the public adopted. The public was, as it were, sufficient to have stood free, though free to be unfree. That the public might choose to limit its own liberty by supporting greater restrictions on the press was a prospect that the opponents of reform believed ought to give the radicals pause. The latter had to allow for this possibility as a necessary corollary to their belief in the public's right of self-determination.

This was why Junius, if only obliquely, regarded sedition as a genuine threat to the public mind. Allowing for this threat was a way for reformers to make sense of how the people might choose to limit their own freedom. Reformers could easily imagine the government being responsible for creating a toxic situation: juries, Junius hypothesized, might let libelers escape punishment "in times of universal discontent arising from the notorious maladministration of public affairs."[83] More difficult for them was to see how, in the absence of external provocation, juries might be rationally motivated to nullify the law—such behavior could occur only in "seasons of epidemical madness."[84] Reformers hoped that the public would normally act in accordance with its own interest in preserving liberty. But they had to accept that the public might not always do so, and this was why the threat posed by seditious libels seemed to them a plausible answer as to why the public might engage in regressive behavior. This threat, as they imagined it, was different in kind from the evil of despotism, which simply suppressed liberty through violence and unjust laws. Seditious libelers did not curtail the public's authority so much as turn it on itself. They deployed the power of persuasion to get the public to sacrifice its own liberty. Rather than moral dissolution, the damage they caused was to subvert freedom by making the public override the plurality of its opinions. Instead of unleashing people from the bounds of conscience, libels had the opposite effect of erasing diversity by inducing a monologic certainty in the public mind.

In giving credence to this threat, reformers were helping to reintroduce the effects of sedition as a theme in the discourse on libels. It was not an important theme for them, since they had plenty of reasons not to dwell on the effects of seditious words. They were loath to give their opponents any ammunition by talking about how libels might inflame the minds of the people. Describing any normal situation where libels agitated the public would have confirmed the judges' fears about the fallibility of jurors. Worse yet, it might also have implied that the people were predisposed to being won over, as if a fatal psychological flaw impeded them from exercising full agency. Said one reformer, the notion that "some natural defect of rational power" rendered the public prey to a libeler's provocations was nothing more than an updated version of the old patrician excuse that the "free discussion of public subjects" had an "evil effect in unsettling the minds of the people."[85] Verbal coercion had to be seen as a serious threat to freedom but not as one the public was constitutionally incapable of resisting. Any attempt at characterizing the effect of words as a determining force—whether Plato's account of how poetry upsets the harmony of the soul or Kant's fear that rhetoric robs people of their freedom—inevitably betrayed a distrust of democracy and of the public's capacity to make right decisions.

At the same time, reformers could hardly maintain that words had little effect on audiences. Such a claim would have contravened their motivating belief in discourse as the engine of progress. As the pamphleteer known as Father of Candor remarked, "were it not for such writings as have been prosecuted by Attorney-generals for libels, we should never have had a Revolution, nor his present Majesty a regal Crown; nor should we now enjoy a protestant religion, or one jot of civil liberty." One of the primary goals of the reform movement was to legitimize political writing aimed at mobilizing public opinion into constructive action. Accordingly, reformers had to allow that publications could make people feel discontented with their government. "I do not see," Father of Candor observed, "how any writer can publish the justest and most important complaints, without tending thereby to render the people and their constituents dissatisfied with the administration, and even clamorous against it."[86] The difficulty with a claim like this was that it failed to say how anyone could escape being affected by these publications. Even if, as Father of Candor went on to propose, the truth of a publication ought to be subject to demonstration in court, it was not clear how juries could decide which complaints were just without being prejudiciously influenced by them. Either jurors had to be naturally predisposed to discerning the truth in even the most emotionally stirring of publications or they had to have the ethical sense not to let their clamorous impulses cloud their judgment.

The law's defenders were quick to seize on what seemed a crippling inconsistency in arguments for reform. The defenders had long maintained that the public was not skilled enough to comprehend the complexities of the law or was not alert to libelers' "ambiguous hints, and dark inuendos."[87] Now, with reformers conceding that publications critical of the state could affect the public mind, conservatives could posit yet another hierarchy of competence as a reason for denying jurors a say in deciding libels. The crowds outside yelling for liberty, they declared, would only get larger and unrulier were juries permitted to return verdicts on libels whose rhetorical appeals they could not withstand. Only judges had the training and temperament to remain unmoved by these appeals. Speaking against a 1770 motion to review the law, Solicitor General Edward Thurlow cited both old and new rationales: the traditional claim that juries were ignorant of the law and the newer proposition that they were susceptible to malign persuasion. The libel laws were "so complicated," he said, "that the mind of an ordinary man is distracted and confounded, and rendered incapable of coming to any regular conclusion." But, he added, "If we even suppose the jury sufficiently enlightened . . . [i]n state libels their passions are frequently so much engaged, that they may be justly considered as parties concerned against the crown."[88] The reformers, their opponents felt, were not taking the force of words seriously enough to recognize the muddle they had created for themselves. On the one hand, they contended that words could so ignite public passions as to bring about political revolution, yet on the other, they failed to say how a juror's conscience would not be enslaved to those same passions.

Judges, according to the law's defenders, observed the law–fact distinction not out of any sycophantic compliance with the wishes of party or Crown but to control the temper of discourse in the courtroom. Without this control, libelers would be free to subvert justice by exploiting jurors' weaknesses. Writing on the eve of the Libel Act's passage, John Bowles allowed that it would be ideal "if juries were to hear with great caution *all appeals to their passions.* Cool and sober reason should ever preside at the seat of judgment." But, he added, it is "difficult to hold the scales of justice steady, while the passions agitate the mind."[89] The courts, Bowles argued in a subsequent tract, enforced the distinction closely in libel proceedings because of the special danger sedition posed:

> The case of a public Libel, more perhaps than any other that comes before a court of justice, affords an opportunity for exciting the passions; and an unbounded latitude for the Jury to determine what is called the whole case, that is, law as well

as fact, would furnish an excellent occasion to defendants, by means of inflammatory addresses, to seduce the minds, or rather the feelings, of Jurymen; and to persuade them, that the most virulent and atrocious writings were not, or at least ought not to be, prohibited by any principle of law: but no such chance exists of deluding the steady and well-informed minds of the Judges (although even they are much more exposed to a popular bias than to an influence adverse to the public sentiment).[90]

The law–fact distinction, Bowles believed, kept the law safe from subversion because it reflected a hierarchy of psychological competence: being trained to abide by the law, judges were more inured than juries to verbal seduction. And even if counterexamples could be cited of judges acting more from impulse than principle, Bowles's point was that in objecting to the court's strict interpretation of the distinction, reformers overlooked the problem it was designed to address. They may have been right to think that jurors possessed sufficient reasoning ability to understand specific points of law. Yet what they did not offer was any assurance that a jury or, for that matter, the public could demonstrate an emotional resilience to the force of words. After all, if the public were capable of such resilience, then sedition would never happen.

Part of the problem reformers faced in dealing with the idea of sedition was the limited vocabulary available for talking meaningfully about the indefiniteness of public opinion. They made sense of speech freedoms principally through metaphors of mind ("Our minds and pens ought to be free"), and this made it difficult for them to keep their arguments about freedom conceptually separate from psychologically inflected claims about the rhetorical affectivity of speech. Reformers did not always keep these ideas separate. The public, they believed, arrived at its decisions free of determination, yet the only scenario in which reformers could envisage people acting against their own interests was if the public mind was under the pathological influence of libels. Admitting that defamers could imperil the freedom of mind made it all too easy, however, for conservatives to deploy the language of pathology to raise alarms about what would happen were jurors exposed to the corrupting force of seditious pamphlets. "Nothing will be published but libels and lampoons," Thurlow warned the Commons. "The minds of the people will be poisoned with vile aspersions, and misled by scandalous misrepresentations. The many-headed beast will swallow the poison, and the land will consequently be but one scene of anarchy and confusion."[91]

Significantly, jeremiads like this presented a vision of collective intoxication that was not dissimilar from the reformers' view that libelers worked to possess the public mind. Rhetorical precepts had supposed that libelous words had a uniform effect on all people, and there were plenty of ancient precedents for imagining sedition as a mass event where demagogues whipped up mob enthusiasm. All the same, the anarchy that conservatives now feared did not involve the people undergoing a dangerous liberation, whether being loosed from moral bonds or empowered to follow their own will. Libelers instead took advantage of people's impressionable sensibilities to turn them into a party against the Crown. The real danger libels posed, the archdeacon of Lincoln fulminated, was in aggravating people's susceptibility to coercion, such that a reader of political papers would eventually become "a fit instrument for the future purposes of any incendiary, that will have the courage to call him into action."[92] Libelers, on this account, used forceful words to focus discontent in the service of a cause. This was virtually the same argument that reformers, like Father of Candor, were putting forward in defense of radical opinion. To counter their opponents' claims, reformers had to find some way of conceptualizing the public's freedom of mind while also giving an account of how this indeterminacy did not render the public incapable of judging libels impartially. They had to find some way of resolving their ambivalence over the force of words because, if libelers could use this force to defeat the public's judgment, then perhaps the public's autonomy and agency were illusory.

The Later Debate: Purifying the Courtroom

The reformers had three options. The first was to insist, as the Wilkesites did, that diversity ensured fairness. The public, they suggested, was too various for anyone to believe that people reacted uniformly to libels. Juries reflected this multiplicity, so there could be no predicting how libels might affect them. "Juries," Wilkes's ally Robert Morris declared, "are a tribunal ever changing as the times; they judge of men's writings and actions by what they see and feel."[93] The problem with this position was that, like earlier claims for the moral fortitude of juries, it obscured the threat posed by libels. That readers might differ in their reactions to libels did not preclude libelers from attempting to achieve a general disturbance in the public mind. Besides, Morris himself believed that jurors were motivated to set their differences aside when deciding libel cases: "Who [is] more interested than juries (for juries are composed of the people) to preserve the peace and order of the state?"[94] The argument simply denied the indeterminacy that Morris elsewhere in his pamphlet considered a defining feature of the common jury: an interest in maintaining social order was, it seemed, so deeply felt an imperative among all mortals that no work's bad tendency could touch their sensibilities.

A second option was to project the public's indeterminacy over time. The scandal caused by inflammatory publications, reformers averred, would be temporary: "The disorder cannot last long."[95] The effects of a libel, one recent Wilkesite convert proclaimed to the Commons, were contingent on time and place: "The most famous harangues of Cicero or Demosthenes would be with us be termed infamous libels. . . . So changeable is the nature of a libel! so much does it assume the cameleon, and suit its colour to the complexion of the times!"[96] In his influential treatise on the English constitution, Jean-Louis de Lolme went further, arguing that time acted as a marketplace of ideas where the force of words would dissipate as the public debated their content over a longer period and expressed a plurality of opinion. Wrote de Lolme, when the public "perseveres in opinions which have for a long time been discussed in public writings, and from which, (it is essential to add) all errors concerning facts have been removed, such perseverance appears to me a very respectable decision; and it is then, though only then, that we may safely say,—'the voice of the People is the voice of God.'"[97] Abstracting the effects of libels over time enabled jurists to suspend their ambivalence over the force of words. The content of written defamations, jurists feared, could cause long-term damage were their falsehoods accepted as fact—hence de Lolme's proviso that opinions had to be cleansed of errors. They were less fearful that the emotional force of language would cause similar damage since they assumed it would not be felt indefinitely, though the assumption sidestepped the question of what effect this force had on public discourse. However heatedly ideas might be expressed, they could be debated in the court of public opinion, de Lolme seemed to be saying, while leaving unsettled the problem of orators and how their agitating ploys could trouble the "respectability" of the public's decision-making.

De Lolme was arguing against the concept of sedition and not for letting juries decide libel cases, whether in the fervor of the moment or otherwise. It was nonetheless on this last point, about the relation of trials to their discursive context, that later reformers began to present ideas that would congeal into a third approach for conceiving of the public's free exercise of mind, one whose assumptions, it so happened, their opponents were already beginning to embrace. The indeterminacy of public opinion, reformers argued, varied in degree of volatility depending on circumstance. In particular, the condition of discourse in trial proceedings was more stable and organized than in other public situations. The protocols of legal procedure, the rules of evidence, and the decorum of the courtroom setting all helped to ensure that juries, unlike the generality out of doors, could be exposed to libels while remaining relatively insulated from their effects. Most jurors, according to the Foxite jurist Capel Lofft, could willingly muster a "generous enlightened firmness" of mind sufficient to perform their role without being biased by what they read: "well knowing their duty and their powers, they have the prudence to let no insinuation or contrivance weaken them."[98] On this account, jurors were free agents who, as a condition of their service, disengaged themselves psychologically from the contrivances of all discourses except the rule of law.

Other reformers offered a different version of this argument. Juries, they suggested, ought to be permitted to consider evidence of a work's seditious tendency. Witnesses, Francis Maseres proposed, could be "brought to prove that [a work] has actually occasioned that disturbance which it seemed to be intended to create."[99] Maseres, like de Lolme, tried to sidestep the problem of verbal force: rather than letting juries assess a work's effects, his proposal merely downloaded this responsibility onto witnesses, while offering no explanation as to how the witnesses or the jury could be exempt from a libel's influence while other audiences were not. That said, in treating a work's tendency as a fact that could be verified by relating the work to its effects in specific circumstances, Maseres anticipated how prosecutors would soon be emphasizing that the contexts of libels made them seditious. And in working within the law–fact distinction by positing sedition as a fact that juries were entitled to consider, Maseres saw more clearly than his Wilkesite predecessors that rules of legal procedure, however artificial, served a purpose.

Unlike in the public sphere, where conditions were more fluid, in the jury room all persons were expected to follow procedure while working toward consensus. Replying to critics like Bowles, the Earl of Stanhope believed that it was highly improbable that all members of a jury could be "carried away by a sudden Impulse, as it were, from something that was said by the Witnesses or Counsel." Even if most were, those few "who were *not* carried away by such [a] wrong Impression" were assured of an opportunity to convince their peers of the rashness of their impulse.[100] Though strangers to each other, jurors were expected to make a serious attempt at resolving their disagreements. Accordingly, those who had not been swayed by a libeler's appeals were duty-bound to rebut these appeals and unhindered from doing so in the quarantined setting of the jury room. In enforcing both the equality of debate and an expectation of unanimity, courtroom procedure helped to contain the potentially subversive effects of sedition.

Stanhope was not saying anything new: Vaughan more than a century earlier had emphasized how diversity of opinion was a precondition of rightful decision-making in the courtroom. What was new was the Foxites' recognition that the sedition debate was about more than the question of who should decide which works were libelous. Their answer to the question—that all citizens had the right and capacity to take part in these decisions—seemed to them no longer disputable. Neither judge nor juror could claim any special expertise at evaluating libels. Inferring a work's tendency from the context of its publication, according to Maseres, involved "merely operations of reason, which is a talent common to all men."[101] Judge and jury drew on different experiences in arriving at their opinions, yet neither experience nor training provided judge or jury with greater competence at decision-making or a superior moral and psychological ability to withstand the effects of sedition.

The more difficult problem at issue in the debate, reformers sensed, was about how to manage speech in the courtroom and the public sphere more generally while still allowing for the open exchange of opinions. Protocols such as jury unanimity and the law–fact doctrine, as the law's defenders had long contended, were mechanisms for regularizing decisions about the common good, including decisions about the policing of speech. To the Wilkesites, these protocols seemed an impediment to equality since it was all too obvious to them how judges had applied procedural rules arbitrarily to enforce their jurisdiction over speech. To the Foxites, however, ground rules of debate could serve the public in legitimizing its decisions just as much as older versions of these rules had previously served the courts in confirming their authority. However much these rules might regulate the heterogeneity of opinion, they served as a normative arrangement for managing discourse in trial proceedings, which enabled judges and juries to feel that they could fairly decide which speech imperiled public liberty. Without such ground rules, the public could not assure itself of the rightfulness of its decision-making. The ground rules offered a kind of certainty, not a certainty of thought, fact, or legal standard but a procedural certainty for ensuring that opinions and information were exchanged in the courtroom to a more consistent and perhaps rarefied degree of discursive equality than was possible elsewhere in the public sphere.

If the public was to arrive at rightful decisions about the criminality of dangerous publications, it had to believe that the protocols observed in the courtroom were adequate to maintaining discursive equality even in cases where juries were to rule on works that deployed scandalous opinion and turbulent expression to win over the public mind. Neither the Foxites nor anyone else, as Bowles objected, could say how these protocols shielded jurors from the force of words. Nor did these protocols prohibit anyone from deploying this force in the courtroom. Even if jurors could approach the effect of a libeler's language as if this effect were a verifiable fact, they still had to contend with other verbal appeals directed at them by advocates, witnesses, and judges. The courts, as I explain below, had by the later eighteenth century grown more tolerant of lawyers indulging in oratorical displays. Such tolerance was possible because the old rhetorical fears that had formerly given urgency to the law had by then been displaced by a new set of principles, according to which the force of words, though potent enough to undermine liberty in extreme circumstances, could never be presumed so great as to defeat utterly the public's free exercise of mind. On the basis of these principles, both the Foxite reformers and their opponents agreed that it was possible to maintain a discursive environment in the courtroom where this freedom could be made reasonably certain.

Arguably, it was the emergence of this new structure of conviction rather than any particular legal argument that brought resolution to the sedition debate and to the muddle that had characterized it since its start a half century earlier. By the 1780s, it had become possible for all contenders to imagine people having a different relation to discourse in the courtroom than in the public sphere generally. Outside, seditious libels were dangerous because they might catch the public's attention at a critical moment, launch emotional assaults on people's instincts in tense situations, and galvanize their discontent into collective action. Jurists agreed that while the content of libels would remain the main evidence to be argued over, the principal threat to public liberty posed by libels was their seditious effect. At the same time, they could also agree that a strict adherence to courtroom protocol could help to hold this effect in relative abeyance. Procedure, it was felt, rendered the context of the courtroom safe from the seditious libeler's attempts to commandeer public discourse. And unlike the old doctrine barring juries from deciding libels, trust in formal procedure could be accommodated to a belief in the public's sovereign agency.

Utter Strangers: The Case of the Dean of St. Asaph

This structure of conviction was already sufficiently in place by the 1780s that the courts had begun to update the rules. That these changes would have special relevance for libel proceedings was evident from the case that reignited the campaign to amend the law, the widely publicized 1783–1784 prosecution of William Shipley, the dean of St. Asaph. Shipley had been charged with seditious libel after he had arranged for the republication in Wales of a pamphlet by the scholar William Jones that called for electoral reform and an armed citizenry to guard against tyranny. Shipley and his supporters in the Society for Constitutional Information had wanted to provoke a test case of the increasingly indefensible limits on the jury's role in trials for libel. They knew that a publication directed at a readership that had notoriously been given little exposure to radical ideas would push authorities into taking action. The target of prosecutions, they understood, was shifting from libel to sedition, from the publication of opinions critical of the government to the intent to disturb the peace by disseminating heterodox opinions in specific situations.[102] As it happened, the case came to an anticlimactic end when, on appeal, Mansfield discharged Shipley on the technicality that the initial indictment was faulty in not clearly stating that the offending pamphlet was a "libel on the king and his government."[103]

It was the case's inauspicious beginning, however, that revealed something of the altered cosmos of belief that would henceforth shape legal thinking on seditious libels. Shipley was to have been tried in September 1783 at Wrexham, but the prosecution successfully moved to have the trial put off after it was learned that Shipley's allies in the society had sponsored the local circulation of a published resolution in support of jurors' rights. Though the document did not refer to Shipley or his impending trial, it did include lengthy extracts from reformist accounts of earlier libel cases. Prosecutors charged that the society's dissemination of this material was intended "to bias and influence the minds of the jury."[104] Their ensuing exchange with Thomas Erskine, arguing for the defense, produced one of the first extended discussions in English jurisprudence of the bad influence of pretrial publicity on a jury's judgment.[105] The growth of the press over the previous quarter century had led judges to complain bitterly of the increased media scrutiny they faced, with the Mansfield court altering the law in 1765 to enable contempt charges to be brought against John Almon for having published a Father of Candor pamphlet that was critical of the judge.[106] But at no time before the 1740s, and only rarely during the ensuing four decades, were charges laid against individuals for having published material that was designed not to scandalize the court but to interfere in trial proceedings.[107] Only in one criminal case from 1758, cited by the prosecution at Shipley's trial, were proceedings delayed after Mansfield was alerted to published comments about the defendant's patron that, he believed, were meant to taint the jury's judgment.[108]

Despite the meager case history, Erskine agreed in principle with the prosecutors at Shipley's trial that adverse publicity might bias a jury, objecting only that the society's pamphlet did not do so since it referred to no facts in the case. Judge Kenyon, then chief justice of Chester, disagreed. The pamphlet's purpose, he declared, could be inferred from its context, appearing as it did "during the session, when this cause was in some degree agitating men's minds, and circulated in the place where the cause was to be tried." In his view the pamphlet was "of a pernicious tendency" whose purpose was to lead potential jurors into forming a prior opinion on the case. Jury challenges and other rules of judicial procedure, Kenyon explained, were designed to keep the courtroom free from contamination whether by the press or by a juror's private beliefs: because "evil may creep in, shut the door as close as you can; the law, I say, has done as much as human wisdom could do to keep the streams of justice pure and entire." Accordingly, the judge felt that the trial had to be put off so that "the minds of those who are to decide, may return to a proper tone."[109]

Kenyon's ruling represented a stark reversal of customary notions about what made a jury's judgment authoritative. The common law, as Vaughan had emphasized in *Bushell's Case* and as Hamilton reminded the Zenger jury at the beginning of the libel debate, had long required that jurors be selected from the locality since they were ideally acquainted with the character of the parties and the circumstances of a crime. Though jurors could not have a private interest in the outcome, they were not strangers to the case. They were expected to apply their prior knowledge in weighing its merits. This insider status was the basis for their independence from the judge, whose knowledge of the case was restricted to the evidence introduced at trial. Presumably, since jurors could return a verdict even if neither party presented evidence, it was reasonable for them to have formed a prior opinion on the case. It was likewise appropriate, as Vaughan insisted, for jurors to disagree with a judge or differ among themselves on a case's merits. They were expected to represent a diversity of perspectives. Whether or not they reached a unanimous verdict, their decision-making was rightful because it involved a full and serious attempt at overcoming their differences.

Kenyon redefined what was understood by this diversity. Reformers, as we have seen, had already begun to rethink the basis of the jury's independence. Twelve jurors chosen at random, Junius supposed, were less likely to be corrupt as a group than was a single judge. The jury's independence, according to this argument, was derived not from its local knowledge but from its condition of normative strangerhood, the fact that jurors differed enough in their preferences that no single juror's interests could determine a verdict. Kenyon's ruling greatly broadened this sense of jury disinterest. Potential jurors, he implied, were not to have prior knowledge of the facts of a case or have already arrived at an opinion on a verdict. They were to be complete strangers to a case, assuming the same position of epistemological purity that judges had formerly been expected to occupy. More than this, they were to take up their office in the "proper tone" of mind. Exposure to controversial ideas outside of court could disqualify them from serving. Yet once inside the courtroom, they could listen to counsel debating these same ideas and could do so without impairment to their judgment. Outside the courtroom they might advocate for divergent causes, but once empaneled the only differences of opinion they could entertain had to do with the evidence presented in court. Entering the courtroom, they were to abstract themselves as indifferent persons, as a body of strangers who occupied a view from nowhere.

Reformers criticized Kenyon's decision to delay the trial as a cynical attempt to punish Shipley by adding to his legal expenses, though none saw fit to question the ruling's rationale.[110] Erskine, at a later stage in the trial, would quote extensively from Vaughan's argument on the independence of juries, and he seemed unconcerned that Kenyon's account of this independence had thoroughly repudiated Vaughan's.[111] It was no longer necessary, he and other reformers believed, to follow Vaughan in arguing that juries were independent of judges because they were better or differently qualified to decide a case. A jury's independence remained the basis of its authority, but this independence no longer stemmed from any particular skill or knowledge. Its independence inhered rather in its collective freedom of mind, the fact that as an assemblage of persons chosen at random, it could in the aggregate embody the public's indeterminacy. Reformers did not oppose Kenyon's ruling because it agreed with what they said about juries. Jurors were more impartial than judges, they argued, because they could arrive at a verdict that was free from outside influence, personal preference, political bias, professional obligation, or any other interest except an overriding commitment to preserving liberty by seeing justice done.

The reformers' muted response to Kenyon's ruling was indicative of an ongoing rapprochement between the two sides in the sedition debate. Kenyon was censoring the reformers' press campaign, but he was relying on reformist principles to justify his ruling. He and other conservatives had come to accept the legitimizing utility of the once radical view that fairness could be most assuredly achieved under the equality of the law of chance. Kenyon in the next major ruling barring pretrial publicity was even more forthright about how a jury's impartiality was a consequence of the randomness of its selection, which media interference aimed to undermine:

> It is the pride of the constitution of this country that all causes should be decided by jurors, who are chosen in a manner which excludes all possibility of bias, and who are chosen by ballot, in order to prevent any possibility of their being tampered with. But if an individual can break down any of those safeguards which the constitution has so wisely and so cautiously erected, by poisoning the minds of the jury at a time when they are called upon to decide, he will stab the administration of justice in its most vital parts.[112]

On this account, the effect of adverse publicity was identical to the one that, according to reformers, was produced by seditious libels: it worked to make public opinion less diverse. It rigged the drawing of lots, nullifying the indeterminacy on whose equality the legitimacy of democratic decision-making depended. In taking steps to limit the bad influence of pretrial publicity, Kenyon hoped to impose new limits on the press, but only in a democracy could this influence be plausibly deemed a threat to the fairness of judicial procedure.

The prohibition on pretrial publicity was a remarkable innovation, not least because it was among the first legal mechanisms devised to help sustain the diversity of public opinion outside the courtroom. Other modifications that were then being implemented were intended to enhance the discursive equality of the jury trial. Many of these changes involved separating the duties of judge and jury more sharply than they had been under traditional protocols, such as the law–fact distinction. Jurors, for example, were being increasingly hindered from taking an active role in trial proceedings. Commentators as recent as Blackstone had allowed that jurors could be sworn in as witnesses, but by the 1780s no one with pertinent information on a case could serve on its jury.[113]

At the same time, judges faced increasing pressure to refrain from commenting on the merits of a case. A *Times* editorial in 1788 castigated any judge who, in giving his opinion prior to a verdict, upset the discursive balance of the proceedings: "he alters the Constitution by putting a very forcible voice more to the Jurors than the law intended."[114] Some judges in sedition cases felt that they had to be more circumspect in saying whether an offending work fit the definition of a libel. Presiding over Shipley's trial at the case's resumption after it had been removed to the Shrewsbury assizes, Justice Buller told the jury that he could not comment on whether the dean's publication was libelous because this was not a matter for the jury's deliberation. Were jurors to render an opinion on the work's libelousness, they would be making peremptory law, and as a consequence their ruling would deny the right of either side to challenge the verdict on appeal. "The law acts equally and justly," Buller announced, yet only on the condition that judge and jury stayed in their prescribed roles, whereby juries ruled on the facts and judges neutrally instructed on procedure.[115] Buller wanted to keep decisions about libel out of the hands of jurors, but he was invoking a principle of equality to justify the legal status quo. Here again the Shipley case signaled a change: a conservative judge felt he had to cite modern ideas on the law's moral basis to legitimize his ruling.

Shipley's trial was also, finally, a showcase for the most dramatic transformation of courtroom practice. Mansfield alluded to the change in his review of the trial. Unimpressed by Buller's reasoning, the jurors had returned a verdict of "guilty of publishing only." After Buller interpreted the ambiguous verdict as indicating a general finding of Shipley's guilt, Erskine appealed the decision based on a misdirection of the jury. Hearing the appeal in November 1784, Mansfield upheld Buller's ruling but, hoping to defuse the controversy surrounding the case, granted an arrest of judgment on the grounds that the indictment did not spell out how Jones's pamphlet defamed the Crown. In defending Buller's position, Mansfield reiterated his long-standing opposition to allowing juries a say in deciding libels. The problem with juries, he argued, was twofold: "they have no rule to go by but their affections and wishes," and, short of outlawing all communication, there was no constitutional way to prevent juries from being exposed to the bad influence of the press, whose licentiousness Mansfield condemned as *"Pandora's Box*, the source of every evil." He accordingly praised the efforts of prosecutors who had recently begun devoting part of their opening statements to counteracting this influence: "to remove the prejudices of a jury, and to satisfy the by-standers, they have expatiated upon the enormity of the libels." The approach taken by the prosecutors, the chief justice allowed, had none of the authority of a directive from the bench. But, he added, it did have a signal advantage over formal mechanisms in helping "to obviate the captivating harangues of the defendants' counsel to the jury."[116]

The change Mansfield was talking about was the advent of the adversarial criminal trial. In its most obvious aspect, the change was yet more evidence of the courts' acceptance of equality as a legitimizing principle since, under the adversarial system, courtroom discourse was evened up between the Crown and the defense. The system had begun to be put in place during the 1730s, when judges in felony cases hoped to guard against mistaken convictions by permitting the accused to be represented by counsel, who would test the prosecution's case in cross-examination.[117] Lawyers for accused libelers, notably Hamilton at Zenger's trial, very quickly took the lead among defense advocates in showing how their argumentative challenges could make a difference in a case's outcome. By the 1780s, defense attorneys were pressing for greater parity with the prosecution, demanding the right to address jurors directly so as to present them with alternative narratives of the facts. By then, felony trials had become occasions for verbal combat between lawyers, who found it easier to learn from each other's performances once detailed published reports of trial proceedings began to be regularly available.[118] Judges may have also found it easier to let lawyers, like Erskine, engage in oratorical grandstanding since the discursive equality of the adversarial trial ensured that rhetoric could always be answered with rhetoric.

Less welcome to judges was the lawyerization of trial procedure. Under the adversarial system, control over the conduct of trials shifted from the judges to the lawyers, whose mastery of the facts led to a reduction of the bench's role as well as the silencing of both juries and the accused. Libel prosecutions posed a special problem for defense advocates in this regard since there were few facts to contend over. Instead, ever since Hamilton's triumph, defense counsel in sedition trials had focused on matters of interpretation, encouraging juries to reject the state's construction of libelous meaning. Erskine did the same in his celebrated performance at Shipley's trial and in his 1789 defense of the publisher John Stockdale, but more rigorously and at far greater length than defense attorneys had done previously.[119] His declared strategy at both trials was to present extended courses in reading, where he schooled the juries on the need to understand a work in its intellectual context, to judge any offending passage in relation to the import of the entire work, and to discern its sense according to "the simple and natural construction of language."[120] Yet what Erskine was really doing was demonstrating his own mastery of textual interpretation.

He was not the only one at Shipley's trial giving lessons on interpretation. The prosecutor, Edward Bearcroft, told the jurors why he thought the pamphlet "has that meaning which makes it a libel." He did not have to do so, since a work's illegality was not a matter for juries to determine in libel cases. However, because he was presenting a case against Shipley for having reprinted Jones's work and not against its original London publishers, Bearcroft felt he had to explain why its republication constituted a criminal act. His strategy was to emphasize that it was not the pamphlet's meaning alone that rendered it seditious but more so the context of its intended audience: Shipley's reprint threatened the public peace because, as he put it, it was "addressed to the Multitude."[121] Both Bearcroft and Erskine argued for the importance of interpreting a work in its context, but the context Bearcroft felt was most relevant differed from the one Erskine emphasized. As a result, the jury was presented with competing accounts not only of the facts but of the circumstances in which a work's meaning and intent could be rendered determinable as fact.

The adversarial system owed its legitimacy to the principle of equality, by which all sides could be heard in a court of law. But in granting lawyers the power to monitor how any side was heard, the system also represented the coming into force of a new set of competences. Erskine and Bearcroft were not just telling the jury how to read Jones's pamphlet or how to infer the intended effect of its republication. They were demonstrating their professional expertise. By their command of the facts, interpretive skill, and careful orchestration of evidence, the lawyers made clear their authority over discourse in the courtroom. Theirs was a modern kind of authority—and I am here not speaking of the law's disciplinary power in the Foucauldian sense, its codifying of human behavior, or the specialized legal learning and jargon that jurists have always wielded as credentials of their guild. I am referring to how the arguments and interrogatory maneuvers of the lawyers came to dominate trial proceedings.[122] This was not the traditional authority of judges and juries, who made determinations of guilt or innocence. Lawyers did not make determinations. On the contrary, the adversarial system gave lawyers an incentive to intensify the indeterminacy of opinion: they confronted jurors with conflicting accounts of the facts while allowing no persuasive speech, whether a libeler's overtures or the declamations of opposing counsel, to stand without challenge.

Their authority lay in their mediating influence. In the adversarial courtroom, lawyers staged a version of public debate. Though it resembled in its vigor and indefiniteness the lively exchange of knowledge and ideas in the public sphere, this version differed in being channeled into the binary agon of prosecution and defense, conducted according to rules of evidence and procedure, and given coherence if not closure by the lawyers' competing arguments about the facts and testimony that the jury was to deliberate over. Yet the principal intended effect of the lawyers' performances was to recast local knowledge about the details of a crime into a form of public discourse through which the significance of this knowledge could be made appreciable to a jury so that it might decide what was fair and right. Under the old system, the accused answered charges before jurors drawn from the vicinage; these jurors were assumed to have an unparalleled sense of both the particulars of a crime and its gravity in their community, and this sense was so authoritative that, after being guided by the judge on matters of law, they could reach a rightful verdict even if no evidence was presented at trial. The lawyerized adversarial system, by contrast, came about in response to the rise of a modern conception of the public as a body indefinite in its composition, various in its sentiments, and autonomous in its determination of value. This public had neither prior knowledge of a case nor acquaintance with the character of the accused and witnesses. Once empaneled, a jury was to maintain a condition of strangerhood by remaining silent and anonymous as it listened to the debate that was staged in the courtroom. Only after hearing out both sides were jurors then to interact as a group in deliberating on a verdict.

The mediating influence of the lawyers facilitated this interaction in two ways. First, it kept the jury at a spectatorial remove from the debate played out before them. Jurors could be exposed to affecting testimony, heterodox ideas, and the most seditious of appeals without impairment to their judgment because the lawyers were continually interpreting this evidence in accordance with rational, critical norms of deliberation. By their mediation, lawyers could turn the most coercive of utterances into examinable knowledge. At the same time, their influence did not determine a jury's verdict since it was held in check by the adversarial system, in which each lawyer's arguments could be contested by opposing counsel. Besides, skillful lawyers knew to conceal their art: both attorneys at Shipley's trial ended their analyses of Jones's pamphlet by telling jurors to "read it by yourselves" (Bearcroft) and "to take the supposed libel with you out of court . . . to judge for yourselves" (Erskine), as if everything the lawyers had said in the courtroom was irrelevant to the jury's decision.[123]

The second way the lawyers facilitated the jury's interaction involved a greater test of their competence. Lawyers digested evidence on the jury's behalf, but their objective was to convince twelve strangers to render a favorable verdict. While the adversary system replicated something of the indeterminacy of public debate, it occluded the actual process of decision-making. A jury was impartial by virtue of its members' beliefs being so various that in the aggregate it had no positive identity. How it remained impartial while it agreed on an identity in the act of passing judgment—how it occupied the view from nowhere even as it took a position somewhere—was the paradoxical condition that lawyers had at once to sustain and resolve through their rhetorical appeals. The lawyers had to affirm the jury's independence of mind, its agency in making a determination that was free from determination, while at the same time encouraging jurors to abide by norms that might compel them to a particular verdict, whether the imperatives of reason or their obligations as a public either to stand by the law or to amend it. Lawyers had to persuade jurors to accept a common identity, and this required them to talk jurors into honoring their commitments while also insisting on their freedom as a public in realizing these commitments.

Erskine and Bearcroft filled their addresses with entreaties to the jury about how a verdict could be right and fair only if it reflected an alignment of personal and public interests. Jurors, Bearcroft insisted, were to think only "as men of honour, having regard for your oaths," whose only point of commonality was their civic duty to uphold the rule of law: "I know not your connections, your wishes, or your party; but I am confident, sitting where you do, in the character of jurymen, you will lay aside all general opinions, and all inclinations whatever."[124] For Bearcroft, the law was an absolute norm and no mere inclination. Their decision would be without moral foundation if it diverged from existing legal principle. Only by subsuming their identity to the rule of law could jurors feel assured of the rightfulness of their verdict.

In reply, Erskine reminded the jury that Shipley had been denied his customary right of being tried before a jury of his neighbors and instead faced the prospect of being judged by persons who "are utter strangers to him." The prosecution of his client, Erskine argued, had nonetheless revealed a connection between Shipley at a personal level and all citizens at a public level. Jurors had to understand that strangers, like them, had as much of a stake in the case's outcome as Shipley did, given the potential ramifications of their verdict. In its outcome, as he put it, "your own general rights, as members of a free state, are not less involved, than the private rights of the individual I am defending." And, as he announced at the end of his address, he himself aspired to embody this vital conflux of the personal and the public, being both "the friend of my client, and the friend of my country."[125] The jurors at Shipley's trial were thus either, as Bearcroft hoped, the people who obeyed the law or, as Erskine implored, the people who wrote it.

The case of the dean of St. Asaph was significant less for its outcome than for what its proceedings revealed about the altered conditions for civic deliberation. Although the judges—Buller at trial and Mansfield on appeal—affirmed their opposition to allowing juries to arbitrate speech, the case helped to introduce into the common law a new conception of the public and of the lawyer's role in relation to this public. Ever since, the legal profession has derived its legitimacy from assisting a modern public in defending the rights of individuals and the interests of communities. Lawyers perform this service by making public decision-making possible. They mediate knowledge into a form amenable to norms of public debate, and combine this knowledge with rhetorical appeals in persuading a jury to a decision. Their profession is one of a number in a democratic society—advertising and editorial journalism being others—that the public authorizes to use forceful words to help its membership of utter strangers achieve consensus. This force is not considered coercive since there are rules on its use. Lawyers have to operate in a discursive environment where equality is strictly observed.

Since the eighteenth century, the adversary trial has become the model for how coercive speech, whether a lawyer's or a libeler's, can be safely managed in a public setting, just as the deliberation of the jury has become the paradigmatic event of democracy, where a public settles its differences and becomes a people.

Liberty by Coercion

On May 21, 1792, the Privy Council issued the Royal Proclamation against Seditious Writings and Publications. The proclamation called on the public to be on guard against material calculated "to excite tumult and disorder, by endeavouring to raise groundless jealousies and discontents in the minds of our faithful and loving subjects."[126] A mere three weeks later, on June 11, 1792, the House of Lords agreed to the passage of the Libel Act, which Fox had seen through the Commons a little more than a year earlier. Though the House of Lords had resumed the second reading of the libel bill on the day the proclamation appeared, speakers in both houses said almost nothing about the relation of the bill to the proclamation, despite the obvious overlap in the subject and timing of the two resolutions. The same Whigs who were pushing for the libel law's reform decried the proclamation by saying that the law was already "sufficiently efficacious" at punishing libelers. Scant mention was likewise made of the circumstances that had alarmed Pitt's government into going ahead with the proclamation, in particular the extraordinary popularity of Paine's *Rights of Man* (1791). Speaking in support of the bill, Lord Shelburne, the former prime minister, recommended that his fellow lords not trouble themselves with Paine's book and instead seek to "preserve by all means the present good disposition of the people by acknowledging their most invaluable right to the possession of all the benefits of a trial by jury."[127] Equally absent from the discussion of the libel bill was any new rationale for defending or repealing the old legal doctrine that had barred juries from deciding libels. There was little in what the politicians said to indicate that a change had occurred to the premises of the legal debate, let alone a change profound enough to bring about a resolution. Only the note of political expediency in Shelburne's speech suggested that it had become publicly unacceptable for lawmakers to continue supporting the legal doctrine that barred juries from deciding libels.

The government knew it could no longer defend the doctrine, which had by then become an impediment to successful prosecutions in big-name cases. At some point during the debate on the bill, the government, anxious to contain the radicalist surge, decided to change strategy. The proclamation was the political counterstroke to the Libel Act. Without mentioning the act's bestowal of new responsibilities on juries, it strongly implied that the public now had an obligation to join the fight against sedition. While the government was to seek more indictments against the disseminators of sedition, it needed the public's cooperation in identifying these disseminators, discouraging public assemblies, and frustrating the recruitment drives of associations being run by people who were in correspondence "with sundry persons in foreign parts."[128] The proclamation, like the act, presupposed that the public could recognize and resist sedition. Yet while the Libel Act enshrined the right of juries to rule on libels, the proclamation warned that seditious opinions continued to pose a threat to the public mind because they were being circulated in conditions where their bad tendency was difficult to counteract.

Previously in this book, I argued that one of the consequences of speech being liberalized was that jurists and lawmakers had to learn to suspend if not resolve their ambivalence about the public, its indeterminacy of opinion, and the effect of words on its judgment. One way they did so was by projecting this ambivalence over time, such as in the idea of the public domain or the distinction between libel and slander. The proponents of reform may have been doing the same in relation to the law of libel: no jury or public, they presumed, could at any one time overwrite the law or redefine the offense of sedition, but the people could do so over the long course of the common law and the democratic process. Certainly, too, many of the men who debated the Libel Act projected their ambivalence onto the social order: the public that voted and served on juries, they assumed, was not the contrarian multitude that read Paine.

There was another reason, I suggest, that parliamentarians could overlook the ideological inconsistency between the act's reform of the libel law and the proclamation's call for an expanded campaign of suppression against seditious writings. By then, public discourse had been sufficiently reorganized that the effect of words could be seen as contingent on the circumstances of their utterance, and lawmakers could as a result project their ambivalence over the different sites of public speech. They could accept that the public was capable of the free exercise of mind and entitled to define the terms by which it deemed its deliberations fair and just. Yet, as reformers had conceded, accepting that the public's judgment was free meant also allowing for the possibility that the public might choose to act contrary to its own interest in preserving liberty. The only way to make sense of this possibility was to presuppose that the public mind was susceptible to coercion. The public, reformers and lawmakers agreed, might make irrational choices if it were manipulated, whether by a libeler's agitating ploys or a ministry's alarmist decrees. Recognizing, then, that the public deliberated across a variety of sites where there existed divergent safeguards against coercion made it possible for lawmakers to externalize their ambivalence over popular sovereignty.

The public, they believed, could be trusted to protect liberty in settings like the courtroom presumed by the act. The "People of England," Lord Camden said in its defense in one of his final addresses to the House of Lords, "should have the care of the liberty of the press" because, in the courtroom, they would "always be sufficiently inclined to protect the . . . government against the licentiousness of sedition."[129] Courtroom procedure enabled the public to conduct a relatively secure form of decision-making. Forceful speech in the courtroom did not impair the jury's free exercise of mind since its effect was defused within strictly observed discursive protocols.

Sedition instead happened beyond the courtroom, in situations that were not so closely monitored, such as the popular assemblies targeted by the proclamation. The public, the proclamation supposed, could with prior warning rebuff attempts at coercion in these other spaces. But it might not always do so since outside the courtroom discourse was not organized or equally distributed as it was in the courtroom. Outside, there was little to prevent the promulgators of seditious ideas from using verbal force to appeal to popular prejudices or from developing extensive networks of dissemination to overwhelm the public with their message. Sedition, lawmakers now emphasized, involved more than the mere publication of noxious doctrines. It involved the organized effort to undermine the plurality of public opinions. As the attorney general declared, Paine's ideas were bad enough, but his pamphlets would hardly have corrupted the populace if it had not been for the uncommon labors "taken to circulate them, and even children had scraps, in the form of extracts, put into their hands."[130] The proclamation, its defenders could believe, was the only way to redress the balance of public debate, which the radicals had upset by putting tens of thousands of copies of Paine's book into the hands of the populace.

The Whigs who denounced the proclamation shared their opponents' ambivalence over the force of words. Leading the charge, the future prime minister Charles Grey declared that "there ought to be a perfect liberty for the circulation of all opinions upon public affairs," but the government was making a mockery of this liberty by pretending that it could be decreed through an edict from the throne. The proclamation was coercion by the state, whose alarmist force, Grey predicted, would itself lead to "nothing but tumult." Yet if coercion by sedition or proclamation could spur the public into acts of violence, it would seem that the public could not be relied on to keep a cool temper in the open forum where opinions were to circulate. The only place safe from coercion was the courtroom where, Grey believed, the government ought to be using existing legal means to censor publications "that ought really to be suppressed."[131] The public could be trusted to do in the courtroom what it could not be trusted to do outside.

Implicit in this ambivalence over language was an assumption that there was a qualitative difference between persuasion and coercion. Under the old rhetorical precepts, all speech was presumed to have persuasive power, with all public statements tending in one partisan direction or another. What rendered an utterance unacceptable was not the coerciveness of its language but its content or the ends to which it was directed. With popular sovereignty, verbal coercion became a problem. Persuasive rhetoric could be valued in some public genres and discouraged in others, yet so long as writers played by the rules their words posed no danger to the public's judgment. And even if authors did not respect the rules, the public could always interrogate their prejudicial speech at trial. In the courtroom, the public could see how a libel violated rational, critical norms. In other contexts, however, people might lack the opportunity to test a libeler's message or see how it bent the rules. It might seem to them perfectly intelligible and no more forceful than any other oratorical display. They might not realize how much it affected their thinking. What made an utterance coercive was not simply that it violated discursive norms but that it masked this violation.[132]

This assumption entailed another adjustment to the idea of sedition, the last one I consider here. With the law being revised to allow the public to decide libels, sedition began to be seen as involving an element of coercion. Sedition, in this view, worked by manipulating people into embracing opinions they would not otherwise assent to. The purveyors of sedition might, as ever, seek to agitate the public. But their principal means of doing so was slanted or distortive speech whose tendentiousness was not readily apparent in all situations because it was delivered in distractingly expressive language, deceitfully presented as reasonable and nonpartisan, or so aggressively disseminated as to drown out opposing points of view. Seditious arguments, the proclamation's defenders averred, were disseminated in various forms and venues, but what they all had in common was that they were "covertly aimed at the destruction of our form of government."[133] The public, on this account, was not necessarily incompetent at seeing through libelers' dissimulations. But in a charged environment, like a political rally, an audience might sense the power of a libel's words without being fully alert to the libel's manipulations and misrepresentations. The public enforced the rules of discourse, but it could be misled by those who bent the rules.

There was already by 1792 a new usage for an old word to denote this kind of coercion: "propaganda." Since the seventeenth century, the word had designated the Roman Catholic Church's directorate of foreign missions. In 1789 La Propagande was adopted by a group of moderate leaders of the revolution as the nickname for a society they had founded to promote their constitutional principles in other nations. The society lasted barely a year, though this did not deter loyalists from appropriating "propagande" as a term of derision, mocking the revolutionaries' hope of converting all peoples of the world. By the end of 1790, what had been a joke had been transformed into a counterrevolutionary myth, as rumors began to spread in other European capitals of "the disciples of the propaganda" being sent from France to foment insurrection abroad.[134] There was little basis for the rumors—at least not before November 1792, when the National Convention pledged its support for democratic movements in other nations.[135] The myth nonetheless caught on quickly, such that by the time it was issuing its proclamation, Pitt's government could tap into a full-blown panic over political associations being infiltrated by foreign incendiaries who "were in this country propagating the principles that had brought wretchedness on France."[136] The "corrupting emissaries of the Propagande," an editorial in the *Times* warned, were conspiring "with all the Dissidents of all the nations" to form "a fanatical league against all Crowns."[137] Soon enough, the word was being adapted to describe not a specific body of revolutionaries but the proselytizing activities of any partisan group.[138] "We know not a class of more turbulent individuals," one critic wrote in 1799, looking back on a troubled decade, than "sticklers for the whole propaganda system," who "would impose even liberty by coercion."[139]

The idea of propaganda provided the government with justification for stepping up its censorship of the press even as the Libel Act acknowledged the public's right to decide what ought to be censored. This was apparent from the first case of seditious libel tried wholly under the terms of the act, the 1793 prosecution of the proprietors of the *Morning Chronicle* for having published an advertisement for a reform society that contained a declaration of the society's principles. Judge Kenyon, in summation, argued that the advertisement was not defensible as news since it was for a meeting held several months earlier. The timing of its publication, Kenyon contended, was proof of ill intent since much had happened in the months since the society had met. Following the National Convention's November decree, the country was, as the judge put it, "torn to its centre by emissaries from France. It was a notorious fact—every man knows it—I could neither open my eyes nor my ears without seeing and hearing them." Under these circumstances, reformist ideas like those set out in the advertisement were bound to take on a subversive meaning since "the minds of the people of this country were much agitated by these political topics." Since the advertisement was published in the midst of the *propagandistes*' assault and had no relevance as either news or publicity, it could serve no purpose, the judge concluded, other than "to infuse into the minds of his majesty's subjects a belief that they were oppressed."[140] Unlike most libel prosecutions during the wave of Pittite repression in 1793–1794, the case ended in acquittal.[141] Kenyon's opinion nonetheless confirmed that in the wake of the Libel Act, the courts were no longer defining sedition as a species of libel whose evil inhered in its defamatory content. They were instead treating sedition as a context-dependent act of coercion that aimed to subvert the public's judgment.

Jurists could now claim that in the right venue, people could debate the common good while being resistant to bad ideas or fiery words. Neither the substance nor the language of seditious publications was sufficient to induce people to revolt against the state. What made these publications dangerous was that through a combination of distortion and the intensity with which they were disseminated, they created conditions in which the public was unable to enforce its own deliberative norms. Propagandists, it was assumed, were unlikely to succeed at inducing conformity of thought among a broad public, but their agitating ploys could undermine the rationality of public agency in charged circumstances. Writing at the end of the propaganda scare in 1794, Cobbett blamed the Priestley riots that had broken out in Birmingham three years earlier on the Dissenters who had preached for the revolution: "Nothing was neglected by this branch of the Parisian *Propagande* to excite the people to a general insurrection. Inflammatory Hand bills, Advertisements, Federation Dinners, Toasts, Sermons, Prayers; in short, every trick that religious or political Duplicity could suggest, was played off to destroy a Constitution which had become the Test, and attracted the Admiration of ages; and to establish in its place a new system fabricated by themselves." The propaganda failed to make any converts and instead provoked a "convulsive moment" as the people of the city turned on the Dissenters, destroying their houses and property. The people's instinctive reaction, Cobbett believed, had been to preserve the constitution from the Dissenters' attacks, and in this respect the Dissenters' coercion was ineffectual at enslaving the public mind to a set of ideas. The Dissenters nonetheless achieved their ends since, in inciting acts of mob violence, they led the people to violate the law "whose cause they thought they were defending." Priestley may have lost his possessions, Cobbett remarked, but "the rioters did nothing that was not perfectly consonant to the principles he had for many years been labouring to infuse into their minds."[142]

Propaganda, Cobbett appeared to intuit, presupposed a new relation of the public to language. Under rhetorical precepts, all speech was considered persuasive in support of one cause or another. No one was exempt from the power of the word, though persons of faith could repel attempts at using it to break their conscience. Those persons had the authority to judge a libeler's appeals because they had subsumed their judgment to a transcendent order of providence and truth. Propaganda, by contrast, was not simply biased speech that exerted a motivating force on audiences in the way all utterances had formerly been thought to do. It was a mode of discourse designed to co-opt public opinion by subverting agreed-upon norms of decision-making. Its illegality was to be judged not on the basis of any transcendent principle of right but by its divergence from commonly approved protocols of deliberation. The public might not be able to resist propagandists' assaults on its judgment in extraordinary situations, but otherwise it was capable of following the rules enough to repel their coercion.

The idea of propaganda was thus inseparable from democratic notions of popular sovereignty because it was a way of dealing with if not resolving the incoherence of the modern conception of the public. "There can be no liberty," Cobbett said of the riots, "where a ferocious mob is suffered to supersede the law."[143] Yet as he would later assert on very different occasions, there could be no liberty where the law was used to supersede the will of the people. With popular sovereignty, the public was free to define the laws to which it had to answer, choose which determinants of right it was to observe, and enforce the rules by which it could deem its choices as rational or wrong. Popular sovereignty presented an inescapable circularity of legitimation, in which the public was free to be wrong and free to decide what was wrong.

The idea of propaganda seemed to offer an enabling exception to this circle in that it allowed for the possibility that the public was not free when it was being wrong. Under the influence of propaganda, the public might not be able to choose wisely. This idea permitted commentators, like Cobbett, to feel justified in contesting the public's choices without requiring them to reject the public's sovereign authority or its freedoms of speech, assembly, and the press. The idea even made it possible for commentators to suppose that the public might be misled into thinking that it was acting freely and justly when in fact it was not. Propaganda could be powerful enough, Cobbett felt, to induce a crowd to violate laws it believed it was defending, as if the public had no self-correcting mechanism, not even the rule of law, sufficient to counteract propaganda at its most effective. Indeed, the idea of propaganda would eventually displace the concept of seditious libel not as a legal category but as the primary cultural explanation in democratic thought for why the public might not always act in its own best interests or by the norms it set for itself.

"Propaganda" was more than a derogatory term for any ineffective or incomplete effort at shaping public opinion. It was the name for the defeat of the public mind, and thus it was the negative analogue to law and knowledge as the conceptual antitheses to the public's indeterminacy of opinion. Commentators might feel they had grounds for distrusting the public because its decisions might at times go against settled law and proven knowledge and appear instead to be unthinking responses to coercion. The difficulty with this position was that there was no coherent way to justify the grounds of dissenting from public opinion without also rejecting the public's right to define the bases of its decisions. Commentators could not lament the failure of the public mind while also professing belief in its sovereign authority. They could only ever assert such grounds as abstract projections, which, they hoped, the public might yet embrace as a set of determining norms.

For most jurists since the eighteenth century, this projection involved segregating the law from propaganda on the basis of its rules and sites of deliberation. The public sphere, they imagined, encompassed multiple venues in which the public interacted, and within each the public recognized specific conditions for its interaction. It exchanged knowledge and opinion freely through the press at the price of allowing the medium to be equally a vehicle for propaganda. In the courtroom the public managed speech more closely to protect itself from coercion. It observed a standard of discursive equality and rationality in trial proceedings and required its representatives on juries to adhere to a condition of strangerhood throughout. As the poet George Dyer made clear in 1799, now that jurors were to be the censors of seditious speech they had to think of themselves collectively not as an audience, like at other public events, but as the mind of the public:

> When jurors, therefore, are preparing *well* and *truly to try* a charge of public libel, where are they going? Are they hastening like the heroes, described by the poet [Dyer's note: Homer, *Iliad* 2.85], proceeding in disorder from the assembly? Or are they going, as it were, into a public theatre, to hear some tender tale, and to be charmed with fascinating periods? Or are they going to a debating society, where the greatest blusterer may triumph over the fairest reasoner, and the confidence of the speaker is only in proportion to the plaudits of those who surround him?—No—they are going to a court where coolness and moderation, truth and justice should invariably reside; where, indeed, they must hear, and ought patiently to hear, because they must *try*, well and truly try, and impartially decide. But they are not to be borne away with the rhetoric of a counsellor, or overawed by the gravity of the judge.[144]

There could be no rule preventing jurors from being transported by a lawyer's eloquence or cowed by a judge's tirade. It was up to them to resist the force of words. By their agency, the courtroom was to be secured as a site of fair and just deliberation.

Literature at the Precipice

Implicit in Dyer's contrasting of juries to audiences at other events was an important corollary to the quarantining of the courtroom. Members of the public were to keep a cool temper when serving as jurors, and they were to be on guard against propaganda disseminated out of doors. At the same time, they could not be truly free if they had to remain always and everywhere vigilant against coercion. There had to be other spaces where the public was free to let itself be borne away by language, even encouraged to do so as a confirmation of its freedom of mind. The examples Dyer provided of settings where people could give in to the force of words were the theater, the debating society, and the political assembly—Dyer was alluding to Homer's simile of Greek soldiers stirred up like bees from the hive after being roused into waging war against Troy. On Dyer's account, drama's tender tales and fascinating periods were as much of an occasion for the public to indulge the affective power of speech as the stage debater's bluster or the demagogue's battle cries. On this point, Dyer disagreed with Kant, for whom poetry offered readers an enabling experience of autonomy whereas the use of rhetoric in any setting was an affront to the public mind. Yet while Kant hoped to preserve poetry from its potentially delegitimizing similarity to rhetoric, Dyer's argument suggested that the public had to maintain a more fundamental distinction for the sake of ensuring the legitimacy of its decision-making. However much poetry's charming tales and periods might seem benign beside oratory's dubious triumphs over reason, the public, it seemed, had to understand that the one discourse to which both poetry and rhetoric were to serve as operative contrasts was the law.

It is thus no historical coincidence that, at about the same time when the meaning of "propaganda" was being expanded to encompass forms of political coercion, another old word was also given a new usage as the term for what we now think of as imaginative writings, including poems, plays, and prose fiction. The word was "literature." Before the late eighteenth century, eloquent writings in verse or prose had belonged to the rhetorical category of "poetry," a term that, being derived from the Greek word for "making," pertained to invention and imitation. The word "literature," meanwhile, originally had to do with reading, either the condition of being well read or the books that were available to read. The shift, I have argued elsewhere, from "poetry" to "literature" as the collective noun for imaginative works reflected a change in how these works were valued, a shift from production to consumption, from valuing the social benefits that poets produced to valuing the personal benefits readers might derive from experiencing literary works.[145]

I argue here that this change, in tandem with the emergence of the idea of propaganda, was necessitated by the advent of modern democracy. Imagining that the public was free to think whatever it wanted, write its own laws, and reinvent itself continually entailed having to accept the indeterminacy of free speech and its imperviousness to legal definition. As Erskine proclaimed in 1793, the "extent of the genuine Liberty of the Press on *general* subjects, and the boundaries which separate them from licentiousness, the English Law has wisely not attempted to define; they are, indeed, in their nature undefinable."[146] Yet it was not only the subject of speech that could never be definitively bounded. Speech could never be entirely free if restrictions were everywhere maintained on its form and effects. At the same time, those effects, unlike the content of speech, posed a problem since there was no readily identifiable way to reconcile a belief in popular sovereignty with a recognition of the power of words to change people's minds. For advocates of political reform, the public's freedom of mind was supreme, its judgment capable of overcoming any attempt at subjugating it, and therefore it was no longer tenable to subscribe wholly to the old rhetorical certainties about the efficacy of persuasion as an instrument for controlling thought. Those same advocates nonetheless had to allow that the impact of one person's words on another could be so forceful as to enable democracy itself. Words could inspire a public to come together and achieve consensus, incite people to action, and move them to tears, anger, joy, faith, or rebellion.

The problem was addressed if not resolved by reorganizing public discourse. With the public entitled to debate any subject, most prohibitions on the content of speech were lifted, to be replaced by norms of discursive rationality, civility, and truthfulness. Formerly, all words were assumed to exert persuasive force in the service of one belief or another. Now, this force was regarded as varying considerably in degree and effect depending on the form and context of an utterance. While expressivity and oratory were still valued at specific occasions, the machinery of persuasion began to be frowned on within the genres of knowledge, notably journalism and the professional discourses. In some situations, the use of forceful words could, it was feared, endanger public liberty. Coercive or extreme speech became something that a modern public could define itself against, something it could legally proscribe without restricting the substance of its thinking.

In the courtroom, the public could be entrusted to make just decisions because it protected itself from coercion by adhering to protocols of debate. The public could not, however, apply these protocols to *all* its interactions without limiting its freedom of mind. Outside the courtroom, the public permitted itself to be more indeterminate in the opinions it held and in how it arrived at them. On the one hand, this meant that the public had to allow that those opinions could have less legitimacy than the verdicts it returned in the courtroom because there were fewer safeguards against unscrupulous persons or tyrannical governments deploying forceful words to upset the rationality of public decision-making. "Propaganda" became the name for the inappropriate use of rhetorical speech to influence public opinion.

On the other hand, the public could have no real freedom of mind unless it could also experience the force of words directly and without safeguards and could enjoy this experience without impairment to its judgment or autonomy. Under the new name of "literature," poetry was divided from rhetoric as a category of affective and imaginative speech that any person was free to create without regard for rules and free to experience without threat of coercion. If the idea of propaganda implied the potential defeat of the public mind, literature was to serve in a democracy as testimonial evidence of the public's diversity, indeterminacy, and freedom to think anything, in any form and style, and conceivably in any circumstance. In fulfilling this function, literature would be unlike all other discourses in being more than simply a medium of free public expression. More fundamentally, it was proof of the freedom of mind from the power of words. It was thus the complement and enabling exception to the rule of law, and it provided an answer, if one that could never be definitive, to the incoherence of the modern conception of the public.

So it was that by the end of the eighteenth century, it had become possible to believe that literature offered an enabling experience of freedom whereas the public world, the realm of propaganda and the law, demanded only constraint. Literary writers, some even proposed, could not be true to themselves unless they refused all public commitments. The "concerns of mere literature," Isaac D'Israeli insisted in 1796,

> are not very material in the system of human life. They are objects, however, more innocent to discuss, than topics more prevalent. . . . A writer on literary topics, is now placed on a sharp precipice between politics and religion; and the public reward of all his anxieties, and all his toils, consists in the mutual denunciations of two dishonest factions. Literary investigation is allied neither to politics nor religion; it is a science consecrated to the few; abstracted from all the factions on earth; and independent of popular discontents, and popular delusions.[147]

Claims like D'Israeli's or Kant's for literature's sublime autonomy from utility and consequence can seem compelling or necessary only within a structure of conviction in which the rule of law is felt to protect freedom without ultimately circumscribing it. Literary writings contribute vitally to this structure by attesting to individual and public liberty and to how this liberty will always be anterior to the laws the public may set for itself. Yet literary writings can do this only at a remove from the purview of law and other sites and discourses of decision-making. This interval between law and literature, in turn, can never be established as a rule without vitiating the experience of liberty that literature offers. It can only ever be an indeterminate and unverifiable projection, one that Kant hoped it was in the nature of literature to declare.

EPILOGUE

Unacknowledged Legislators

More than any other purpose that literature has been assumed to serve, its role in public life underwent radical revision at the levels of both theory and practice during the transition to democracy. Over the course of the change, we went from a world where Sidney could proudly assert that poets make the world golden or where Milton could confidently believe that his epic would vindicate the ways of God, to one where commentators, like D'Israeli, were imploring literary writers to spurn both politics and religion as detrimental to their art. Many writers since then, of course, have resisted this seeming erasure of literature's public functions. It is not that literature was ever exiled from the public sphere or lost its power to define or change a people. Rather, as I have argued throughout this book, its public purpose and rationale became indeterminate in direct reflection of the incoherence of the modern conception of the public. Like the public, literature and what literary works did in public life became difficult to define because, as a condition of liberty, literature as much as the public had to be perceived as always at once changing and not.

By way of summation, I offer an overview of a few of the ways literature's public functions have been transformed. Poetry's early modern defenders could cite any number of classical authorities in support of their claims for the civic utility of literary production. One of the loftiest of these assertions held that civilization was itself the offspring of the poets. In Puttenham's version of the claim, "Poesie was th'originall cause and occasion of [men's] first assemblies," and because poets "were from the beginning the best perswaders," they acted as "the first lawmakers to the people, the first polititiens, devising all expedient meanes for th'establishment of Common wealth, to hold and containe the people in order and duety by force and vertue of good and wholesome lawes, made for the preservation of the publique peace and tranquillitie."[1] That it was poets who first laid down the law was a commonplace myth—Puttenham was channeling Cicero here—and we find variations on the theme being dutifully trotted out by the likes of Horace, Sidney, and Jonson. Bodin, as I noted in chapter 5, could cite the myth as a rationale for taking the law out of the hands of orators lest they use their power for bad ends.

In later variations, the myth was updated from society's origins to the present, when poets were no longer writing the laws. In exile during the nadir of royalist fortunes in 1650, Davenant insisted that his epic *Gondibert* could morally profit only men "who become principall by prerogative of blood" since its precepts were taken from the "Courts and Camps." Sidney had made a similar claim in poetry's defense, but Davenant, impelled by the altered political context, was more strenuous in restricting his poetry's beneficial influence to the highborn. As for the English commoners who had abandoned civilization for civil war, there was no hope of poetry redeeming them. "The common Croud," Davenant said, is "rather to be corrected by laws (where Precept is accompany'd with Punishment) then to be taught by Poesie."[2] Poetry, it seemed, may have once brought the people out of the wilderness, but it could not stop them from returning. Since it could give shape to laws only for those who already obeyed them, poetry was of limited use to the law, which was now to be enforced through violence.

This disjuncture between poetry and the law was even more pronounced in eighteenth-century revivals of the myth. In these versions, poetry acted as a supplement to the law, operating separately from it even as it provided the moral basis on which the law rested. Bevil Higgons, writing in 1701, conjured up a fictive Shakespeare to assure the public that "[t]he Law's Defect, the juster Muse [poetry] supplies, / Tis only we [poets] can make you good and wise."[3] It was no longer plausible to pretend that poetry could make people abide by the law: the original strong form of the myth was no longer available as legitimation for the literary activity. Instead poets now maintained that what they did was useful because it taught a sense of right and wrong more fundamental to social order than was the letter of the law.

In a related version of the claim, widely espoused by the satirists of the period, literature helped to maintain order by exposing those whom the law could not police. Pope defended his attacks on obscure individuals in *The Dunciad* by insisting, "Law can pronounce judgment only on open Facts, . . . so that for secret calumny, or the arrow flying in the dark, there is no publick punishment left, but what a good writer inflicts."[4] Pope knew firsthand that his self-appointed role as vigilante scourge would eventually set him at odds with those who wielded the law—"Libels and Satires," he mockingly exclaimed, are "Lawless things indeed!"—and in much of his late work he engaged in defining for himself an authority that was greater than if not quite outside the law: "the last Pen for Freedom let me draw, / When Truth stands trembling on the edge of Law."[5]

Within a generation, poets could imagine themselves stepping over that edge: Gray's Bard opted to throw himself off a cliff rather than submit to an unjust law even as he proclaimed his death to be a triumph for poetry. Whereas formerly, poets believed that they had proven their worth by having assisted at society's birth, now they saw themselves at its periphery, answerable to no authority but their own. And few expressed regret that this new freedom for literature may have been bought at the cost of its political efficacy. By the later eighteenth century, even satire was said to have "seldom answered its ostensible end of reforming the age. Yet allowing it to be of little use, it is often composed with such evident marks of genius as renders it interesting to men of taste."[6] Being purposive without purpose would soon be considered a good thing for art, of course. At the same time, poets continued to insist that they contributed fundamentally to the public good in spite or perhaps because of their indifference to public law.

So in the two most famous late articulations of the original myth, what had once been a form of self-justification in which poetry was equated with law giving became a prescription to poets to resist the pull of any particular law or ideology. In Johnson's *Rasselas*, Imlac insisted that the poet "must divest himself of the prejudices of his age or country; he must consider right and wrong in their abstracted and invariable state; he must disregard present laws and opinions. . . . He must write as the interpreter of nature, and the legislator of mankind, and consider himself as presiding over the thoughts and manners of future generations; as a being superior to time and place."[7] Imlac's "enthusiastic fit" was undercut with Johnsonian irony: a legislator who disregarded present laws was doomed to reinvent them endlessly. Irony or no, Johnson unaccountably changed the story. Instead of a myth about civilization's origins, Imlac's version had the poet exerting a powerful influence that would be realized only later, among future generations. By implication, the substance of the poet's influence would remain indeterminate until such a time as it could be recognized in hindsight, and even then it may well appear indistinguishable from its actualization in that future era's thoughts and manners.

Shelley told much the same story in his *Defence of Poetry*, albeit with notably less irony. Poets were "the unacknowledged legislators of the world" because the upshot of their efforts cannot be fully apprehended in the present, even by the poets themselves. Poetry can inspire great social transformation. It was, Shelley wrote, the "most unfailing herald companion, and follower of the awakening of a great people to work a beneficial change in opinion or institution." But the poet must equally resist the temptation to advocate for such a transformation. He "would do ill," Shelley insisted, "to embody his own conceptions of right and wrong, which are usually those of his place and time, in his poetical creations which participate in neither." The poet must simply make it possible for others to see themselves "in the place of another and of many others," for it is through acts of imaginative sympathy that we can be "greatly good." Yet once again, the substance of the poet's influence can take determinate form only later, once those whom Shelley called the promoters of reason and utility, who "follow the footsteps of poets," have absorbed enough of poetry's sympathizing influence to revise the law. Hence poets are, in Shelley's words, "the mirrors of the gigantic shadows which futurity casts upon the present."[8]

In all versions of this myth, literature plays an essential role in the development of civil society. In the earliest versions, literature establishes and preserves social order. It moves people to obey the law and, just as important, legitimizes the law's supporting moral economy by testifying to its immemorial origins. In the later versions, literature promotes social progress: it encourages individuals to think beyond themselves and their own time, and so makes it possible for them to imagine and work toward a more just society. Yet aside from their obvious ideological contrasts, the several versions of the myth disagreed about how literature performs its essential role. In Puttenham's version, poets are the first politicians, whose work inspires public consciousness and virtue. Once the myth is transposed to the present, however, doubts begin to be felt about literature's effectiveness at controlling behavior. At most, literature may extend the law's moral reach, yet this role may equally place the poet in a troubled relation with official authority. In later versions, literature must stand apart from social norms in order to enable their long-term revision. It operates unlike other discourses in that its effects may be neither immediately appreciable nor translatable into those other discourses, except perhaps retrospectively. And that it can perform its essential role at a remove from prevailing norms is what defines its singularity as a public discourse.

What I wish to emphasize is that the history I have just described, in which literature remains valuable even as its purpose becomes less easy to define, is apparent not just from the several versions of the myth in which poets fancied themselves the world's lawmakers. It is also apparent from the changes to most claims made for literature's public value between the seventeenth and nineteenth centuries and beyond, not least in the transition from ancient rhetorical theories that stressed literature's utility to modern aesthetic arguments that insist on its autonomy.

Consider as another example the notion that poetry could best serve a people by promoting its language. As I explained in chapter 2, for centuries the highest praise bestowed on poets was that they had opened the native word hoard and demonstrated that their language was comparable in expressiveness to other vernaculars or the languages of antiquity. To his successors Chaucer was the father of English poetry because he had opened the way for more poets. More crucially, he had "perfected" the rhetorical efficacy of the language, and so had made it possible for the Lancastrian court, which sponsored the copying of his works, to present itself as a center of vernacular culture to rival other European cultures. By the early modern period, poets were expected not simply to furnish the language with rhetorical adornments but to engage in a broader project of refinement. This project, I noted, provided poets with an essential public role in helping to reinforce the social order by enhancing the persuasive effectivity of language and by heightening class-based distinctions of speech and manner.

It was not long before the project became drastically reduced in scope. The obsolescence of Chaucer's English led some to doubt whether the language was capable of the staying power of Latin. Dryden was happy to concede that the restored court had done more to polish speech and manners than his fellow poets had. Others proposed that the task of perfecting the language should be left to a national academy. And far from aiding the effectiveness of public speech, the project of refinement was eventually restricted to aspects of the poetic craft, notably the goal of achieving metrical correctness. Even this goal would ultimately seem like a dead end, as Johnson implied when he remarked that Pope had taken correctness as far as it could safely go.[9] By then, many believed that the English language had already reached perfection or had begun to decline under the corrupting influence of foreign imports and modern manners. Poets, for their part, no longer justified their work by saying it aided the reformation of manners. Shaftesbury suggested that modern poets were fortunate to have shed this responsibility. "[I]n early days," he wrote, "*Poets* were looked upon as authentick *Sages*, for dictating Rules of Life, and teaching Manners and good Sense. How they may have lost their Pretension, I can't say. 'Tis their peculiar Happiness and Advantage, not to be obliged to lay their Claim openly."[10] Within a few decades, educators were telling students that poetry could never "be made subservient to any *important* Purpose of Life," while poets were being celebrated for their natural unsuitability for participating in public life.[11]

The value of the poetic art was to be measured by its divergence from conventional discourse. Instead of refining public speech, poetry was to be the occasion for writers to exercise their liberty to think and write as their individuality inclined them. Imitating the accepted styles of public "[p]rose-reason," Edward Young declared, "destroys all mental individuality," whereas poetry allowed writers to discover their otherness and to "contract full intimacy with the Stranger within." The individuality of literary style was to be the signifier of liberty, of a democratic public's diversity. With poets freed from the burden of having to perfect the language of the day, anyone could take up literary composition as a revitalizing refuge from obligation. "While we bustle thro' the thronged walks of public Life," said Young, "it gives us a respite, at least, from Care; a pleasing Pause of refreshing Recollection."[12] At the same time, poetry was no mere private effusion. To the most idealizing of its defenders, its value lay not in its diction but in its power to invest signification with feeling in a way that was impossible in other public discourses: "Poetry is the breath and finer spirit of all knowledge; it is the impassioned expression which is in the countenance of all Science."[13]

This history is almost identical in outline to the one I related earlier. As ever, poetry was said to perform an essential public role. That role was at first clearly defined and directly productive of social relations. Then, doubts began to be aired about poetry's effectiveness in performing this role. As its benefits to society appeared to grow more limited, poetry was increasingly set in opposition to prevailing manners or modes of speech. Finally, even as its divergence from other discourses was strongly affirmed, poetry's value in enabling social relations was described in terms that greatly abstracted its former direct social utility.

I have focused so far on the claims made in poetry's defense. When we examine the actual public uses that literary works served during this period, a similar history emerges, even though many residual writing practices remained in place even as their sustaining rationales began to be questioned. Until well into the eighteenth century, poetry continued to perform its traditional rhetorical role as a vehicle of praise or blame, commemoration or complaint, political declamation or religious devotion. Its ease of retention made it the most widely used medium for disseminating opinion and scandal, and its wide affectivity ensured its ongoing presence in social ritual and ceremony. Some poetic genres, like satire and heroic verse, were determinedly public in orientation, while entire forms, like drama, were public events and often intended as public statements. That literature was effective in all these roles was attested throughout the period by the repeated attempts by authorities to suppress it.

Yet the same pattern of change is evident from the several ways that literary works were expected to fulfill specific practical purposes. In keeping with the tenor of this book, I focus for the remainder of this epilogue on one of the oldest of these uses: furnishing writers with devices for evading censorship. Authors since antiquity have cloaked charged meanings under fiction and metaphor, although Annabel Patterson, extending Leo Strauss's seminal argument on the subject, argued that it was the deployment by Renaissance writers of what she called "functional ambiguity" that led directly to the modern view of literature as a form of writing that makes creative use of the "indeterminacy inveterate to language."[14] It is certainly the case that English writers into the nineteenth century relied on indirection to protect themselves. Poetry comprised much of this clandestine material: lampoons and ballads were the most popular form of propaganda at least until licensing's demise in 1695. In addition to aiding oral dissemination, verse provided rhetorical subterfuge in the form of blanks, loaded allusions, and oblique allegories. Ambiguity also served writers who hoped to hide their meaning less from authorities than from unlearned readers. It had long been assumed in allegorical hermeneutics that authors secreted their truths to prevent them from being distorted. "[T]here are many mysteries contained in Poetrie," Sidney announced to no one's surprise, "which of purpose were written darkly, least by prophane wits it should be abused."[15]

What is less clear is whether this practice of rhetorical dissimulation gave rise to the idea that the creative use of indeterminacy is a defining element of literature. That writers relied on dissimulation to afford themselves a measure of deniability did not necessarily mean that they wanted their works to be infinitely polysemic. If anything, they deployed indirection to get very determinate statements of discontent past the censors. More to the point, by the turn of the eighteenth century writers were beginning to have doubts about the functionality of ambiguity. For one thing, allegorisis had fallen into disrepute and become a target for satires in works like Swift's *Tale of a Tub* (1704), while poets like Dryden, who continued to employ allegory, did so less to conceal their meaning than to sharpen it with the force of irony and historical exemplarity. For another, the more writers felt compelled to comment on public affairs, the more they attempted to shed the veil of ambiguity in favor of identifying their targets with as much directness as possible. Balancing deniability with accessibility was tricky and occasioned much self-conscious talk about what Swift called the several ways "of abusing one another, without incurring the Danger of the Law."[16] The courts, as already noted, had by then made it more difficult for writers to get away with libeling the government under the cover of ambiguity or gutted names. In law, as Defoe discovered, irony was no defense. Besides, the government did not have to proceed with formal prosecutions in order to intimidate writers; merely the threat of arrest silenced the satirist Paul Whitehead.[17] At the same time, the legal stakes were not as high as they had been in previous centuries, when a wit could lose his life over a squib. Pope was not risking much when he filled in *The Dunciad*'s blanks a year after its initial appearance. There was no real legal incentive for satirists to continue playing their game of taunts and feints with innuendos.

Their incentive was political. So long as politics remained a closed shop, literature had a recognized role to play in sustaining the exclusivity of a ruling coterie that recognized its own members behind the anonymous fronts and verbal indeterminacies. Once licensing had lapsed, however, parties seized on the press's power of dissemination and in so doing accorded legitimizing authority to public opinion. In response, poets became more assertive about the rhetorical utility of their art to political discourse. Pope made a show of addressing his writings to an elite who knew how to decipher libelous intent beneath any rhetorical subterfuge, while lesser wits joked about how the quickest route to Parnassus was a crooked one. Said one, "[Y]ou'll merit everlasting Fame / If you can quibble on Sir *Robert*'s Name."[18] Writers enticed readers with the lure of becoming part of an in-crowd. The obscurity of *The Dunciad*, Pope teasingly wrote, "*partakes of the nature of a Secret, which most people love to be let into.*"[19] One of the dunces, James Ralph, similarly claimed, "If every Thing was set down plain, and at full length in any Work; no Words to be guess'd at or no Obscurity in the Sence, it would be thought only proper for the perusal of a School-boy."[20] None of these solicitous gestures would have had ironic force in the era of direct censorship, when the value of ambiguity and the force of words had been taken for granted.

The gestures were a defensive reaction. Verbal indirection, the poets feared, was of little use in courting the favor of a public that was increasingly assumed to be varied in its sentiments and indefinite in composition. Political writers were feeling the pressure to adapt their styles to a new regime of mass publicity sustained by an increasingly extensive press. Swift urged Pope to annotate *The Dunciad* because, as he put it, the poem was a mystery to readers "twenty miles from London"; when *The New Dunciad* finally appeared, it was greeted with the complaint that it was "too *allegorical*, and the Characters . . . too *conceal'd*."[21] By then, Pope had himself concluded that the times were so corrupt that satirists had no choice but to forgo ambiguity and start naming names. A similar doubt about the declining effectiveness of literature marked familiar Tory complaints about how Walpole had impoverished letters. "In all former Reigns," a contributor to *Common Sense* remarked, "the Wits were on the side of the Ministers," but "[h]as there been an Essay, in Verse or Prose, has there been even a Distich, or an Advertisement, fit to be read, on the Side of the Administration?"[22] Insults like this cut both ways, for they implicitly acknowledged that ministers had no use for wits anymore. The bland pamphlet anonymity by which ministry hacks signed their work did its job and fast became the norm for political commentary.

A generation after Walpole's fall, there was another round of press prosecutions, this time in response to the Wilkesite radicalism of the 1760s and '70s. By then, a sea change had occurred in the relationship of literature to politics. Newspapers and prints had displaced verse and drama as the public's principal source of information and opinion. Broad accessibility being then a commercial necessity, the papers helped to push the boundaries of licit speech. Poetic ambiguity seemed more a hindrance than a help to political writers seeking to influence public opinion. There was no guarantee that what innuendos remained would be understood, even by their intended targets. "[I]f they are not decyphered for me," the Duke of Newcastle admitted, "I could not in the least guess, very often, what they mean."[23] Accordingly, Wilkes's own essay sheet, the *North Briton*, eschewed all forms of ambiguity save for irony, and it appealed directly to ordinary readers with its bold language and its attacks on well-known persons whose names were spelled out in full. Wilkes, it was later said, "possessed the singular merit of writing to, and for, the people."[24]

With the threshold for licit speech progressively falling, the practical uses of literature as a vehicle for evading censors or for mobilizing audiences began to seem obsolete. The liberty of the press had rendered literature's ambiguity less functional as a mode of representation. The opposition no longer saw any advantage in boasting of its literary talent. Reformist wits, like Charles Churchill, proudly contrasted their populist art to what they contemptuously referred to as "*pacing* poesy."[25] Scholars often point out that the satire of the period seems alienated from the genre's traditions: its reliance on emblem, historical parallel, and classical shapeliness.[26] Churchill's satires consisted mainly of invective: they named names, remained fixated on current events, and had little overall order, offering a series of caricatures with no sure moral closure. In sum, they had more in common with the journalism of the day than with the poetry of Dryden and Pope.

Deprived of one of its oldest and most important social functions, literature from the 1760s onward was increasingly defined in opposition to the periodical press, which was quickly becoming the paradigm of public discourse in a modern world, much as poetry was believed to have been at the dawn of civilization. In conservative rants about the decline of letters, dullness was relocated from Grub to Fleet Street. The daily papers, wrote the young George Crabbe, were "enemies to literature."[27] Too intense a preoccupation with current affairs was seen as detrimental to poetry because it rendered it indistinguishable from the popular press. Looking back over Walpole's reign, Archibald Campbell thought that the disputes of the period had a "very pernicious effect" in concentrating public attention solely on politics, with the result that writers produced "only temporary pieces, which as soon as their turn was served, were thrown aside like so many almanacks or news-papers."[28] As Campbell no doubt knew, there had always been temporary pieces, verses of occasion. Only now, political occasions were felt too topical for poetry and better suited for the impermanent prose of the daily press, which, because of its decontextualizing of events, did more than anything else to make politics seem parochial. In contrast, there could be no occasion of a private nature, such as the death of a favorite cat, which could be regarded as too local for verse.

The press's limited focus on the present was thought to render readers too fixated on material pursuits to appreciate poetry's effects, which were now presumed to nourish the sensibility in ways not possible through other discourses. Newspaper readers were said to be incapable of experiencing the delicate beauties of poetry. As Vicesimus Knox put it, "They do not understand it. They know not its nature; they have never experienced its effects in themselves, and therefore they are unable to estimate its power on the bosoms of others. . . . What nonsense to be measuring syllables, and talking of purling streams, shady groves, and mossy banks, to a man who has no taste for anything but newspapers."[29] In a similar vein, Wordsworth famously decried how the media's "rapid communication of intelligence" had produced in readers a taste for sensation that blunted "the discriminating powers of the mind," rendered the mind unfit "for all voluntary exertion," and reduced it "to a state of almost savage torpor."[30] The purpose of such screeds was to defend the value of poetry in an age of emergent mass culture. Yet unlike what was presupposed in earlier jeremiads, like *The Dunciad*, the assumption in these later arguments was that poetry and politics did not mix. Poetry had always been touted as an elite discourse, yet once politics became a public one, the two no longer seemed of service to one another.

Lest poetry be made to seem too esoteric an activity, critics were quick to proclaim its universality, which they defined in contradistinction to the factionalism bred by democratic politics. Shakespeare is great, Johnson announced, because "his works support no opinion with arguments, nor supply any faction with invectives."[31] Johnson knew perfectly well that factions regularly enlisted Shakespeare in their cause. Yet the value of public opinion was now so accepted that Johnson could authorize his verdict simply by invoking an ideal of popular consensus, as symbolized by the common reader. This marked the entry of the language of political representation into the discourse of canon formation: great literature was universal not because it purveyed eternal truth but because it pleased many and pleased long. The canon was seen as more truly public than writings geared toward publicity because it evinced a degree of representativeness that exceeded the narrow interests of party and sect.

At the same time, poetry presented formal difficulties that set it apart from other discourses, and so, however universal its value, it could be justified only as a specialized mode of speech whose lack of accessibility was part of its appeal and prestige. The problem with Pope's poetry, Joseph Warton notoriously remarked, was that it was not difficult enough. Its meaning, he said, "lies more level to the general capacities of men, than the higher flights of more genuine poetry."[32] Pope may have thought that he was using irony and innuendo to get his libelous meaning past the censors. Now, critics were seeking to save poetry from the public by proclaiming its impenetrability to unsympathetic readers.

Wrote Knox, "Poetry, philology, elegant and polite letters, in all their ramifications, display their alluring charms in vain to him, whose head and heart still vibrate with the harsh and discordant sounds of a political dispute at the tavern. Those books, whose tendency is only to promote elegant pleasures or advance science, which flatter no party, and gratify no malignant passion, are suffered to fall into oblivion; while a pamphlet, which espouses the cause of any political men or measures, however inconsiderable its literary merit, is extolled as one of the first productions of modern literature."[33] Knox was forgetting that under the old rhetorical precepts, all speech, including poetry, aimed at vibrating the heads and hearts of people in one partisan direction or another. What was new was the division he assumed between literature and propaganda: the aesthetic was ineffectual yet valuable because it was the one code that could not be enlisted in the service of directing public opinion, whereas propaganda was at once coercive and widely intelligible, partisan in content yet insistent on its own univocality.

Knox, who wrote a brave critique of Pitt's gagging laws, was no doubt aware that the government's campaign of suppression against seditious writings was once again forcing writers to deploy rhetorical devices to protect their opinions.[34] Yet by then, Kant and others were also redefining the nature of literary indeterminacy to distinguish it more clearly from both rhetoric and the rationality of public deliberation. Later Romantic critics likewise rejected what they saw as the dull clarity of allegory and the mechanical application of metaphor in favor of the inexhaustible meaningfulness of the symbol precisely because the symbol's meaning, they believed, could not be replicated in any other form. Symbolism, Goethe explained, changes an "idea into an image in such a way that the idea always remains infinitely effective and unreachable, and remains inexpressible even if spoken out in all languages."[35] Being untranslatable, the indeterminacy of the symbol contrasted directly with the older practice of poetic indirection, which had served to disguise a local and determinate meaning that could otherwise be expressed plainly. So, in answer to Patterson's argument, it should be said that if semantic richness was now considered a defining property of literariness, this property was valued only if it was not made to serve utilitarian ends.

Literary indeterminacy in these later definitions is transcendent, time-defying, incapable of being conveyed in any form but its own, yet also able to inspire social change more profoundly than what is possible through any other discourse. What remains unclear is what exactly in public life is changed by literature. It does not help that we cannot know in what this change consists so long as literature's effects remain impervious to reformulation. Aesthetic philosophers believed that reading literary works made individuals more sensitive and sympathetic, and so prepared them for their public role as open-minded citizens debating the common good.[36] But this argument still left literature with, at best, an indirect role to play in the formation of civil society. Literature's defenders, like Shelley, clearly wanted to believe that it could help to remake society over the long term. Literature was for them a fully public discourse and not merely preparatory to public life. But this public role was and remains difficult to specify, or at least may be discerned only in hindsight.

Given this insuperable difficulty, it is tempting to dismiss the subsequent two centuries' worth of aesthetic philosophy as an attempt to mystify the source of literature's value in the wake of an apparent decline in its social utility and relevance to public affairs. But such a response overlooks the more fundamental question of how it is possible that this peculiar modern idea of indeterminacy, which is both singular in its workings and appreciable in its effects only retrospectively, should be seen as ensuring a vital role for literature in public life—how it is, in other words, that this idea, however mystifying, should be thought to legitimize literature in the modern world as plausibly as the old myth about poets being the first lawgivers had done in an earlier age.

The answer I propose to this question is that literature's indeterminacy is a kind of projection. The idea of indeterminacy makes it possible for us to think of literary writings as performing two distinct sets of vital functions whose incompatibility is consequent upon the incoherence of a modern public. In one set, literature is believed to do what it has always done in helping a community to know itself, though it does so in open-ended ways that do not impose an identity on a public whose self-identification remains indefinite. I have mentioned several of these varied purposes over the course of this book. As the changing record of a national culture and of representations of its life and manners, literature enables us to engage in the formation of cultural identities, which can only ever be defined retrospectively, but it does so without enjoining us to conform to any of them. In bespeaking personal styles and subjectivities, literature serves a democratic public in confirming its expressive diversity. As a form of self-interpretation, literary writing testifies to the range and depth of private experiences and, as Shelley claimed, allows us to perceive what life is like from the point of view of others without infringing on their autonomy. It may also, much like the old myth supposed, encourage strangers to make the imaginative and sympathetic leap of coming together to form a public and to write the laws by which they will preserve their liberty. Literature, in this set of roles, helps a public define itself as a people.

In its other set of roles, literature performs an opposite function of helping a public *not* define itself. Literature is the form of speech that the public reserves for itself to evince its own freedom of mind. Through literature, the public can reimagine everything, including itself and the norms it lives by. Poets are the unacknowledged legislators of the world because their works permit us to think beyond the laws and norms that regulate speech and behavior in the public sphere. They make it possible to keep public discourse free by permitting us to speak publicly about anything in expressive, irrational, and even indecent and uncivil language without fear of being ejected from the public sphere. Of course, writers since the eighteenth century have run afoul of the law for offenses of speech and representation. Before then, in eras of direct censorship, poets defended themselves by alleging that they nothing affirmed.[37] Since the eighteenth century, writers have insisted to the contrary that their works do aim to inspire and perhaps provoke the public. But unlike works of propaganda or pornography, theirs do not disable the mind, they claim, because they are written in ways that make beneficial demands on readers without manipulating them into doing or believing anything in particular. Literary art is autonomous in the sense that it is noncoercive, and it is this autonomy that ensures our freedom as readers. Knowing that literary works neither engage in public debates directly nor serve practical ends, we can approach them without fear of having our own autonomy undermined despite the fact that literary works often breach the codes of impersonal public meaning that we use to get along with each other.

There is no way of confirming that literature fulfills this role because, in principle, it is not a role that can be formally acknowledged. At most, the role can be described only abstractly or in negative terms by suggesting what literature does not do. Literature, we are told, is not designed to intervene directly in public debate and cannot be made to serve utilitarian ends. It is not fixated on the present, observes no limits on expression or subject matter, and ignores norms of discursive rationality by conveying its truths with a distracting affectivity and penchant for making stuff up, yet it does not mask its divergence from these norms even as it presents no typical or consistent formal features to distinguish it from other discourses. Above all, literature, perhaps even more than the other arts, has no particular context of utterance and reception. Literature can be written by anyone, read or heard by anyone, without any legal, institutional, or professional restriction on where, when, or how one may do these things. All persons can produce literary works, whether to articulate an identity, imagine other worlds and experiences, or make themselves heard in the public sphere. Literature can give individuals and communities a voice, mobilize them, or allow them to escape the public world of obligation and consequence. And it can do these things because it occupies no recognized site of deliberation within the public sphere. Through literature, everything can be contemplated, from any perspective, and in any form, and nothing is decided.

Literature is and is not public because a modern public is always both itself and other. If the rule of law is the public's most performative set of determinations, the most stable and organized objectification of its consensual identity and civil norms, literature is the public's freest self-projection of its own indefiniteness and autonomy. As much as literary writings may help the public to know itself, they also serve the public in conveying a sense of what lies beyond any identity or self-defining law it might choose for itself. Accordingly, literary works may be thought to speak personal or communal identities, at least potentially, but they cannot be imagined to speak the voice or opinion of the public, to direct this opinion, or to have a definable role to play in the occasions and sites where the public makes decisions on the common good.

Literature nonetheless remains a public discourse, thanks in large measure to the fact that it has been made a major subject of public discussion. Indeed, it is no historical coincidence that at the moment in the eighteenth century when commentators began to doubt literature's public utility, literary writings were made the focus of a burgeoning industry of public discourse, in professional criticism, literary histories, teaching anthologies, tourist sites, and museum displays. This discourse was the public's way of telling itself what to do with literary works since the works themselves did not appear to declare any specific purpose. This discourse mediated literature for public consumption precisely by interpreting its valuable knowledge in public language. And so vital was this discourse to the public's self-formation that in *Carr v. Hood*, literary criticism became the first public genre, before literature or even journalism, to be granted protection as privileged public speech. So long as they observed the decencies of disagreement required of any participant in public debate, all persons were entitled to present their opinions on literature, even though, unlike in the cases of the law and other discourses, there were no longer any formal rules and procedures in place to guide them on how literary works were to be written, read, and judged.

Derrida once argued that literature is "a modern invention" that emerged hand in hand with "the unlimited right to ask any question, to suspect all dogmatism, to analyze every presupposition, even those of the ethics or the politics of responsibility." Literature, he said, is not obligated to refer to the world as it is, but instead enjoys the right to say anything. With it, we can rethink everything. There can be, he added, "[n]o democracy without literature; no literature without democracy."[38] Rancière has likewise explored how the advent of democracy revolutionized the function of literature, transforming it from a political instrument for maintaining the social order into a mechanism of "self-interpretation," whose world-making and expressive powers can be taken up by anyone, even those contesting their exclusion from decision-making. "Democracy," he argues, "is first and foremost the invention of words by means of which those who do not count make themselves count."[39] Thus literature, endlessly inventive and inventing, is as indeterminate as the public whose self-reinvention it serves. This is a modern belief, a legitimation story, whose truth is impossible to verify. But we can at least begin to trace its history.

NOTES

Abbreviations
ER   *English Reports: Full Reprint*, ed. A. W. Renton et al., 178 vols. (Edinburgh: William Green and Sons; and London: Stevens and Sons, 1900–1929)
PH   *The Parliamentary History of England, from the Earliest Period to the Year 1803*, 36 vols. (London: T. C. Hansard et al., 1806–1820)
ST   *A Complete Collection of State Trials*, ed. T. B. Howell and T. J. Howell, 33 vols. (London: Longman et al., 1809–1826)

Introduction · Writing in Public

1. Thomas Babington Macaulay, *The History of England from the Accession of James the Second*, 8 vols. (London: Longman, Green, 1860–1862), 7:169. On the circumstances and immediate aftermath of the Licensing Act's demise, see Raymond Astbury, "The Renewal of the Licensing Act in 1693 and Its Lapse in 1695," *Library*, 5th ser., 33 (1978): 296–322; and Michael Treadwell, "1695–1995: Some Tercentenary Thoughts on the Freedoms of the Press," *Harvard Library Bulletin*, n.s., 7.1 (1996): 3–19.

2. *A Dialogue between a Country Farmer and a Juryman, on the Subject of Libels: The Liberty of the Press, and the Rights of Jurymen, Are the Bulwark of the English Constitution* (London: W. P. Flexney, 1770). Ralph Courteville, one of Walpole's apologists, was among the first to defend a free press as "the Palladium of all other Liberty," in the *Daily Gazetteer*, no. 104 (28 October 1735), though the phrase would be popularized by Junius and other Wilkesite authors later in the century. See Eckhart Hellmuth, "The 'Palladium of All Other English Liberties': Reflections on the Liberty of the Press in England during the 1760s and 1770s," in *The Transformation of Political Culture: England and Germany in the Late Eighteenth Century*, ed. E. Hellmuth (Oxford: Oxford University Press, 1990), 467–501.

3. Jürgen Habermas, *The Structural Transformation of the Public Sphere: An Inquiry into a Category of Bourgeois Society*, trans. T. Burger and F. Lawrence (Cambridge, MA: MIT Press, 1989), 28; Michel Foucault, "What Is an Author?," in *Textual Strategies: Perspectives in Post-Structuralist Criticism*, ed. Josué V. Harari (Ithaca, NY: Cornell University Press, 1979), 148–49; Jacques Derrida, "Passions: 'An Oblique Offering,'" in his *On the Name*, trans. David Wood (Stanford, CA: Stanford University Press, 1995), 28; Jacques Rancière, *Dissensus: On Politics and Aesthetics*, trans. Steven Corcoran (London: Continuum, 2010), 167.

4. Pierre Rosanvallon has described how "democracy" had strongly negative connotations throughout the eighteenth century. Even those who loudly espoused the principle of equality were apt to think of democracy as the illiberal and anarchic rule by the multitude.

Only gradually during the next century did the term begin to denote not a type of political regime but a form of society in which equality and personal liberty could be most fully realized. Rosanvallon, *The Society of Equals*, trans. Arthur Goldhammer (Cambridge, MA: Harvard University Press, 2013), 60–61.

5. E. P. Thompson, *The Making of the English Working Class*, rev. ed. (Harmondsworth, England: Penguin, 1968), 135.

6. Helen Small surveys recent varieties of the "democracy needs us" claim, or what she calls the "gadfly theory" of the liberal arts and humanities. Small, *The Value of the Humanities* (Oxford: Oxford University Press, 2013), 125–50. For a restatement of the claim applied specifically to the public value of literature and the creative arts, see Caroline Levine, *Provoking Democracy: Why We Need the Arts* (Malden, MA: Blackwell, 2007). As I note in the epilogue, Jacques Derrida thought that the modern inventions of "literature" and "democracy" developed symbiotically; see Derrida, "Passions," 28.

7. Jacques Rancière, *The Politics of Aesthetics*, trans. Gabriel Rockhill (London: Continuum, 2004), 23.

8. Søren Kierkegaard, *Two Ages: The Age of Revolution and the Present Age*, in *Kierkegaard's Writings*, 26 vols., ed. H. V. Hong and H. E. Hong (Princeton, NJ: Princeton University Press, 1978–2000), 14:261–63; Walter Lippmann, *The Phantom Public* (New York: Macmillan, 1927).

9. J. A. Downie offers a standard historicist dismissal of Habermas's account. Downie, "Public and Private: The Myth of the Bourgeois Public Sphere," in *A Concise Companion to the Restoration and Eighteenth Century*, ed. Cynthia Wall (Oxford: Blackwell, 2005), 58–79. Craig Calhoun summarizes the principal claims and deficiencies of Habermas's theory of the public sphere. Calhoun, "Introduction: Habermas and the Public Sphere," in *Habermas and the Public Sphere*, ed. Craig Calhoun (Cambridge, MA: MIT Press, 1992), 1–48. On the current sociohistorical research on the public state, see Andreas Koller, "The Public Sphere and Comparative Historical Research: An Introduction," *Social Science History* 34 (2010): 261–90.

10. A democratic society, Claude Lefort suggests, is one that has undergone "the dissolution of the markers of certainty." Within this society, power may be imagined as vested in a public, but the public's body, unlike the sovereign's, consists of an "empty space" of radical indeterminacy. Lefort, *Democracy and Political Thought*, trans. David Macey (Oxford: Polity, 1988), 19.

11. See Post's collected essays on definitions of public discourse in US jurisprudence: Robert Post, *Constitutional Domains: Democracy, Community, Management* (Cambridge, MA: Harvard University Press, 1995). Stanley Fish suggests that Post shies away from the radical implications of his argument in presupposing a normative vantage point outside the law from which it is possible to judge the law as incoherent. Fish, "The Dance of Theory," in *Eternally Vigilant: Free Speech in the Modern Era*, ed. Lee C. Bollinger and Geoffrey R. Stone (Chicago, IL: University of Chicago Press, 2002), 199–209.

12. Adam Smith, *An Inquiry into the Nature and Causes of the Wealth of Nations*, 2 vols. (London: W. Strahan and T. Cadell, 1776), 1:17.

13. Kierkegaard, *Two Ages*, 14:261–63; Habermas, *Structural Transformation*, 54. Michael McKeon suggests that Habermas, unlike his critics, avoids identifying the early public sphere's universality with later principles of equality:

> The public sphere's impulse toward universality bespeaks not a (bad-faith) claim to equality of access and representation (which most contemporaries would have dis-

missed frankly as neither possible nor desirable) but rather the will to make tangible the notion of a discursive and virtual calculus capable of adjudicating between an indefinite number of inherently legitimate interests. For this reason, the impulse to correct Habermas either by pointing out the non-egalitarian nature of the public sphere or by adducing "counter-publics" to supplement his partial version of it misunderstands its "rationality," which entails not a claim to liberal-democratic practice but a nascent cultural skepticism about *arcana imperii* and "reason of state"—about the age-old assumption of ruling elites that public policy goes without saying.

McKeon, "Parsing Habermas's 'Bourgeois Public Sphere,'" *Criticism* 46 (2004): 275. I agree generally with McKeon's defense, though it seems to me that the phrase "liberal-democratic" obscures the historical timeline. The public sphere, I would argue, did grow out of efforts to liberalize political discourse in the sense of attempting to render the state answerable to the rule of law. But only during the later eighteenth century did these liberal emphases begin to be enmeshed, if imperfectly so, with emergent democratic notions of equality and popular sovereignty as embodied in the public that was imagined to occupy the public sphere.

14. Michael Warner, *Publics and Counterpublics* (New York: Zone, 2002), 75–76.

15. Carl Schmitt provocatively argued that democracy could never be utterly squared with liberal individualism since the equality presumed by the former cannot be achieved without imposing a homogeneous identity on those who belong to the demos. Schmitt, *The Crisis of Parliamentary Democracy*, trans. Ellen Kennedy (1926; Cambridge, MA: MIT Press, 1988). As critics have noted, it is Schmitt himself who discounts the plurality of the demos by essentializing the public as "the people." His account of the conflict between liberal norms of human rights and democratic ideals of equality and popular sovereignty has nonetheless been taken up by theorists of democracy's indeterminacy, for whom this conflict permits a space of enabling undecidability where freedom may be exercised. See, for example, Chantal Mouffe, *The Democratic Paradox* (London: Verso, 2005).

16. On the legitimizing functions performed by public opinion, the market, and the nation in modernity, see Charles Taylor, *Modern Social Imaginaries* (Durham, NC: Duke University Press, 2004).

17. John Durham Peters briefly surveys the changing usages of the word "public" in "Historical Tensions in the Concept of Public Opinion," in *Public Opinion and the Communication of Consent*, ed. Theodore L. Glasser and Charles T. Salmon (New York: Guilford Press, 1995), 6–8. See also Lucian Holscher, "Offentlichkeit," in *Geschichtliche Grundbegriffe: Historisches Lexikon zur politisch-sozialen Sprache in Deutschland*, ed. Otto Brunner, Werner Conze, and Reinhart Koselleck (Stuttgart, Germany: Klett-Cotta, 1978), 4:413–67.

18. On how Locke used "consent" to refer to both an ongoing process of political legitimation and the originary act of creating a social matrix from which legitimation can derive, see John Dunn's classic essay "Consent in the Political Theory of John Locke," *Historical Journal* 10 (1967): 153–82.

19. Sophie Rosenfeld offers a detailed investigation of the stages of "revalorization" whereby the public's common sense became accepted during the eighteenth century as a new "epistemic authority." Rosenfeld, *Common Sense: A Political History* (Cambridge, MA: Harvard University Press, 2011).

20. On the varieties and activities of publics during the period, see James Van Horn Melton, *The Rise of the Public in Enlightenment Europe* (Cambridge: Cambridge University Press, 2001).

21. As Clare Brant has noted, an important genre of personal complaint during the period was the published letter, in which complainants would seek redress by shaming their opponents in public. Brant, "'The Tribunal of the Public': Eighteenth-Century Letters and the Politics of Vindication," in *Gender and Politics in the Age of Letter-Writing*, ed. Caroline Bland and Maire Cross (Aldershot, England: Ashgate, 2003), 15–28.

22. Jeremy Bentham, *An Essay on Political Tactics*, in his *Works*, ed. John Bowring, 11 vols. (Edinburgh: William Tait, 1839–1843), 2:314. As Habermas suggests, the public's authority to oversee social change does not invest it with power to rule but rather precludes any possible division of power: "To the principle of the existing power, the bourgeois public opposed the principle of supervision—that very principle which demands that proceedings be made public [*Publizität*]. The principle of supervision is thus a means of transforming the nature of power, not merely one basis of legitimation exchanged for another." Habermas, "The Public Sphere: An Encyclopedia Article (1964)," trans. Sara Lennox and Frank Lennox, *New German Critique* 3 (1974): 52.

23. Edward Sayer, *Essays: Literary and Political* (London: J. Ridgway, 1791), 122.

24. Samuel Johnson, *Prefaces, Biographical and Critical, to the Works of the English Poets*, 10 vols. (London: J. Nichols et al., 1779–1781), 10:35.

25. Nicholas Hudson suggests that notions of public spirit reflected "the deeply religious and moral tenor of early eighteenth-century politics." Hudson, *Samuel Johnson and the Making of Modern England* (Cambridge: Cambridge University Press, 2003), 111–13.

26. Harold Weber describes how absolutist courts contrasted "the unitary authority of the state and the dispersed and decentered power of the press" to help them legitimize controls on the press even as they used publicity for their own ends. Weber, *Paper Bullets: Print Kingship under Charles II* (Lexington: University Press of Kentucky, 1996), 134. There is considerable scholarship on the incipient public sphere of the early modern period and the legal regimes that were developed to contain it. I can here only note the relevance to my subject of some important work that has been done on the conditions for publicity in England in the revolutionary and Restoration periods: David Zaret, *Origins of Democratic Culture: Printing, Petitions, and the Public Sphere in Early-Modern England* (Princeton, NJ: Princeton University Press, 2000); Jason McElligott, *Royalism, Print and Censorship in Revolutionary England* (Suffolk, England: Boydell, 2007); Randy Robertson, *Censorship and Conflict in Seventeenth-Century England* (University Park: Pennsylvania State University Press, 2009); and Lorna Hutson, ed., *The Oxford Handbook of English Law and Literature, 1500–1700* (Oxford: Oxford University Press, 2017).

27. Or, more precisely, a public's recognition of itself requires the circulation over time of reflexive, cross-referencing discourse. See Warner, *Publics and Counterpublics*, 90–96.

28. In his groundbreaking study of the psychological effects of mass communication, Gabriel Tarde emphasized that the sense of belonging to a public emerged well after the coming of print had enabled the transmission of thought across physical distances. It was only with the press's extensive dissemination of opinion and information at regular intervals that people began to feel part of a cohesive yet indefinite collectivity that was both "*unified in space* and *diversified in time.*" Tarde, "Opinion and Conversation" (1898), in his *On Communication and Social Influence: Selected Papers*, ed. Terry N. Clark (Chicago, IL: University of Chicago Press, 1969), 304.

29. "Habermas," Neil Saccamano writes, "wants and needs to believe that, for a brief moment in the early eighteenth century, authors and readers participated in a literary conver-

sation structurally immune to the distancing, distorting effects of power relations." Saccamano, "The Consolation of Ambivalence: Habermas and the Public Sphere," *MLN* 106 (1991): 689. See also Geoff Eley, "Nations, Publics, and Political Cultures: Placing Habermas in the Nineteenth Century," in *Habermas and the Public Sphere*, ed. Craig Calhoun (Cambridge, MA: MIT Press, 1992), 289–339; and Kevin Gilmartin, "Popular Radicalism and the Public Sphere," *Studies in Romanticism* 33 (1994): 549–57. On how historians have failed to acknowledge the complexity of the public sphere, see Harold Mah, "Phantasies of the Public Sphere: Rethinking the Habermas of Historians," *Journal of Modern History* 72 (2000): 153–82.

30. Thomas Gordon, "The Right and Capacity of the People to Judge of Government," in *Cato's Letters*, no. 38, published in *London Journal* (22 July 1721).

31. Jacques Rancière, *Hatred of Democracy*, trans. Steven Corcoran (London: Verso, 2006), 54.

32. The Levellers, Zaret notes, drew on ideas of venerable precedent as well as more modern notions of public opinion in identifying "the ultimate ground for a legislative agenda." Zaret, *Origins of Democratic Culture*, 265.

33. Equality, Rancière explains, "is not a value given in the essence of Humanity or Reason. Equality exists, and makes universal values exist, to the extent that it is enacted. Equality is not a value to which one appeals; it is a universal that must be supposed, verified, and demonstrated in each case." Jacques Rancière, "Politics, Identification, and Subjectivization," *October* 61 (1992): 60.

34. "The essence of politics," he writes, "is the manifestation of dissensus as the presence of two worlds in one," that is, the confrontation between two ways of perceiving and making sense of the world. Rancière, *Dissensus*, 37.

35. *Vox populi, vox Dei* (London: Printed by John Matthews for John Lewis, 1719), 8, cited in Paul Chapman, "Matthews, John (1701?–1719)," *Oxford Dictionary of National Biography* (Oxford: Oxford University Press, 2008), https://doi.org/10.1093/ref:odnb/72387. Chapman refers to Matthews as the "first" printer to be executed in England "for printing a seditious and treasonable libel," though this is only technically true, as the printers John Twyn (d. 1664) and William Anderton (d. 1693) were executed under an earlier law of treason.

36. Kathleen Wilson, *The Sense of the People: Politics, Culture, and Imperialism in England, 1715–1785* (Cambridge: Cambridge University Press, 1998), 115–16.

37. *Mitchel v. Reynolds* (1711), 1 P. Wms. 181, 24 *ER* 347. The case, Catherine L. Fisk reports, "established the outlines of a multifactored reasonableness rule that has been applied in trade secret cases as well as in the enforcement of restrictive covenants." Fisk, "Working Knowledge: Trade Secrets, Restrictive Covenants in Employment, and the Rise of Corporate Intellectual Property, 1800–1920," *Hastings Law Journal* 52 (2001): 457. On the knitting frame, see Herbert Heaton, *Economic History of Europe* (New York: Harper and Brothers, 1936), 390.

38. T. C. W. Blanning, *The Culture of Power and the Power of Culture: Old Regime Europe, 1660–1789* (Oxford: Oxford University Press, 2002), 181–82.

39. See Ann C. Dean, *The Talk of the Town: Figurative Publics in Eighteenth-Century Britain* (Lewisburg, PA: Bucknell University Press, 2007), 48–73.

40. Ophelia Field compares Whig and Tory propaganda styles at the beginning of the period. Field, *The Kit-Cat Club* (New York: Harper, 2008), 232–33.

41. Joseph Addison, *Free-Holder* 53 (22 June 1716).

42. On the increasingly respectful usage of the phrase in the British political context, see J. A. W. Gunn, *Beyond Liberty and Property: The Process of Self-Recognition in Eighteenth-Century Political Thought* (Montreal: McGill-Queen's University Press, 1983), 260–315.

43. Alexander Pope, *The First Epistle of the Second Book of Horace, Imitated* [Epistle to Augustus] (London: T. Cooper, 1737), 6:lines 89–90.

44. Robert Walpole, in Debate on the Printing of the Proceedings of the House, 13 April 1738, in *The History and Proceedings of the House of Commons from the Restoration to the Present Time*, 14 vols. (London: Richard Chandler, 1742), 10:287. On Walpole's attitudes toward the press, see Simon Targett, "'The Premier Scribbler Himself': Sir Robert Walpole and the Management of Political Opinion," *Media History* 2 (1994): 19–33. See also Tone Sundt Urstad, *Sir Robert Walpole's Poets: The Use of Literature as Pro-Government Propaganda, 1721–1742* (Cranbury, NJ: Associated University Presses/University of Delaware Press, 1999).

45. Jeremy Waldron makes this point in his review of Anthony Lewis's *Freedom for the Thought We Hate* (New York: Basic, 2007). Waldron, "Free Speech and the Menace of Hysteria," *New York Review of Books* 55 (29 May 2008): 42. The review appears in an expanded version in Waldron's book-length defense of hate speech regulation, *The Harm in Hate Speech* (Cambridge, MA: Harvard University Press, 2012).

46. Among the many studies of eighteenth-century uses of the ancient constitution, see J. G. A. Pocock, *Politics, Language, and Time: Essays on Political Thought and History* (1971; repr., Chicago, IL: University of Chicago Press, 1989), 202–32; and John Phillip Reid, *The Ancient Constitution and the Origins of Anglo-American Liberty* (DeKalb: Northern Illinois University Press, 2005).

47. James Pitt, *London Journal*, no. 769 (23 March 1734) and no. 740 (1 September 1733); see also William Arnall, *Free Briton*, no. 142 (17 August 1732). Isaac Kramnick's account of Walpolean apologetics, *Bolingbroke and His Circle: The Politics of Nostalgia in the Age of Walpole* (Cambridge, MA: Harvard University Press, 1968), has been supplemented by Simon Targett, "Government and Ideology during the Age of Whig Supremacy: The Political Argument of Sir Robert Walpole's Newspaper Propagandists," *Historical Journal* 37 (1994): 289–317; and Thomas Horne, "Politics in a Corrupt Society: William Arnall's Defense of Robert Walpole," *Journal of the History of Ideas* 41 (1980): 601–14.

48. Pitt, *London Journal*, no. 638 (25 September 1731).

49. William Arnall, *Free Briton*, no. 14 (5 March 1729). The contentiousness of parties in England, Pitt claimed, is "so far from being a reproach, that 'tis an honor to us; and shews, that we have a sense of liberty and public virtue." *London Journal*, no. 786 (20 July 1734), quoted in Kramnick, *Bolingbroke and His Circle*, 120.

50. Peter Lake and Steve Pincus find no evidence of "a genuinely open-ended notion of deliberately discovered truth" in the public sphere gaining widespread acceptance prior to Walpole's reign. Lake and Pincus, "Rethinking the Public Sphere in Early Modern England," *Journal of British Studies* 45 (2006): 284.

51. Arnall's suggestions hardly amounted to a full-fledged account of civil society that might compare to what Quentin Skinner has called the "neo-roman" theory of political liberty espoused by Bolingbroke and the opposition. Skinner, *Liberty before Liberalism* (Cambridge: Cambridge University Press, 1998), 5. Arnall's sense of the indeterminacy of public debate nonetheless implied, I propose, a modern liberal view of civil society "as a moral space between rulers and ruled" (Skinner, *Liberty before Liberalism*, 17).

52. 26 Geo. 2, c. 22, cited in Anne Goldgar, "The British Museum and the Virtual Representation of Culture in the Eighteenth Century," *Albion* 32 (2000): 200.

53. See Goldgar, "The British Museum," 222; and Gavin R. de Beer, "Early Visitors to the British Museum," *British Museum Quarterly* 18.2 (1953): 27–32.

54. *Poems on Affairs of State, from the Year 1620 to the Year 1707*, 4 vols. (London: Thomas Tebb et al., 1716). One notably brief collection of Whig satires would later revive the title: *Poems on Affairs of State, Collected from the Daily, Evening, and Weekly Papers* (London: J. Roberts, 1733).

55. M. Dorothy George, *English Political Caricature to 1792: A Study of Opinion and Propaganda* (Oxford: Clarendon, 1959), 111–18.

56. C. John Sommerville, *The News Revolution in England: Cultural Dynamics of Daily Information* (Oxford: Oxford University Press, 1999), 121.

57. Readers at the time were cognizant of these decontextualizing effects, as evidenced by the vogue later in the century for humorous collections of jumbled headlines derived from "cross-reading" newspaper columns (i.e., jumping horizontally from column to column). See, for example, *The Humorous Effects of Cross-Reading the News-papers* (Salisbury, England: Fowler, 1782).

58. See Peter D. G. Thomas, "John Wilkes and the Freedom of the Press (1771)," *Bulletin of the Institute of Historical Research* 33 (1960): 86–98; Arthur H. Cash, *John Wilkes: The Scandalous Father of Civil Liberty* (New Haven, CT: Yale University Press, 2006), 280–87.

59. "It is," Wilkes and his colleague Frederick Bull wrote, "one of the most glorious privileges of this nation, that our courts of justice must be always open and free, that no judicial proceeding can be had in a secret, clandestine manner, but that the conduct of the judges, juries, and witnesses, is submitted to the eye of a judicious and impartial public, without any expence, fee, or gratification whatever." Wilkes and Bull, letter to Richard Akerman, Keeper of Newgate (16 October 1771), quoted in David Hughson, *London: Being an Accurate History and Description of the British Metropolis and Its Neighbourhood*, 6 vols. (London, 1805–1809), 1:602–3. Wilkes began to pursue concrete measures aimed at enhancing the accuracy and availability of trial reports only in November 1775, after he had completed his term as lord mayor. See Simon Devereaux, "The City and the Sessions Paper: 'Public Justice' in London, 1770–1800," *Journal of British Studies* 35 (1996): 466–503.

60. *Entick v. Carrington* (1765), *ST* 19:col. 1066. The case has occasioned a recent commemorative volume but, as Timothy Endicott suggests in his contribution, its significance went largely unrecognized prior to the twentieth century. Endicott, "Was *Entick v. Carrington* a Landmark?," in *Entick v. Carrington: 250 Years of the Rule of Law*, ed. Adam Tomkins and Paul Scott (Portland, OR: Hart, 2015), 120–43.

61. *Rex v. Wright* (1799), 8 T. R. 293, 101 *ER* 1399. James Oldham quotes a comment from 1867 on how Lawrence "could never bring himself to be barely civil to advocates known to be 'upon the press'" who requested reports from him for newspaper publication. Oldham, "Lawrence, Sir Soulden (1751–1814)," *Oxford Dictionary of National Biography* (Oxford: Oxford University Press, 2004), http://www.oxforddnb.com.

62. Bentham, *Essay on Political Tactics*, 2:313, 327.

63. Warner suggests that the rise of the lyric as the paradigmatic form of poetry in the modern age is of a piece with "the polarization of poetic genres from the prosaic modes of public address" but acknowledges that the history of these changes has yet to be told. Warner, *Publics and Counterpublics*, 82.

64. For Rancière, the modern concept of literature is of "an art of speech without a place or a norm other than the common force of language [*la puissance commune de la langue*]. In this, literature is homogenous with the disorder of speaking beings characteristic of the democratic age." Jacques Rancière, *Et tant pis pour les gens fatigués: Entretiens* (Paris: Editions Amsterdam, 2009), 64, quoted in Gabriel Rockhill, "Introduction: Through the Looking Glass: The Subversion of the Modernist Doxa," in Jacques Rancière, *Mute Speech: Literature, Critical Theory, and Politics*, trans. James Swenson (New York: Columbia University Press, 2011), 182n52.

65. George Orwell, "The Frontiers of Art and Propaganda," *Listener* (29 May 1941), reprinted in *The Collected Essays, Journalism and Letters of George Orwell*, vol. 2: *My Country Right or Left, 1940–1943*, ed. Sonia Orwell and Ian Angus (London: Seeker and Warburg, 1968), 124–26.

66. Taylor, *Modern Social Imaginaries*, 191. This is not a new idea. Raymond Williams traced the origins of the modern concept of national culture to the same historical conditions that spawned industrialization, democratic politics, and market economics. Williams, *Culture and Society, 1780–1950* (London: Chatto and Windus, 1958).

67. While the first stirrings of racialist and other assertive forms of nationalist ideology were heard during the later eighteenth century, even anti-democratic movements such as these assumed at some level that, however predetermined their identity, a nation's people are free agents who are working collectively toward the utmost articulation of this identity.

68. On the construction of an English literary heritage, see Lawrence Lipking, *The Ordering of the Arts in Eighteenth-Century England* (Princeton, NJ: Princeton University Press, 1970); Howard D. Weinbrot, *Britannia's Issue: The Rise of British Literature from Dryden to Ossian* (Cambridge: Cambridge University Press, 1993); Gerald Newman, *The Rise of English Nationalism: A Cultural History, 1740–1830* (London: Macmillan, 1997), 87–118; Jonathan Brody Kramnick, *Making the English Canon: Print-Capitalism and the Cultural Past, 1700–1770* (Cambridge: Cambridge University Press, 1998); and Richard G. Terry, *Poetry and the Making of the English Literary Past, 1660–1781* (Oxford: Oxford University Press, 2001). I have argued that the English began to think highly of their own literature well before the eighteenth century. Trevor Ross, *The Making of the English Literary Canon: From the Middle Ages to the Late Eighteenth Century* (Montreal: McGill-Queen's University Press, 1998).

69. Linda Colley has noted that one important way the British elite managed to maintain its cultural dominance through the period of revolution abroad was by setting aside its historical cosmopolitanism and instead espousing a new patriotism and patronizing local goods and traditions. So successful was this ideological makeover that by the early nineteenth century, the British sense of national heritage was exceptional by comparison with Continental attitudes in encompassing not just native works of art and literature but the private possessions of its ruling elite: "Only in Great Britain did it prove possible to float the idea that aristocratic property was in some magical and strictly intangible way *the people's property also*." Colley, *Britons: Forging the Nation, 1707–1837* (New Haven, CT: Yale University Press, 1992), 191. Similar sentiments were more widely expressed about the British countryside; see John Brewer, *The Pleasures of the Imagination: English Culture in the Eighteenth Century* (New York: Farrar, Straus and Giroux, 1997), 615–61.

70. Though a people is a normative construction that a public builds for itself, a public is no less of a normative construction, one created at the moment that a group authorizes itself to establish the normative basis for constructing an identity. "Acting like a people,"

Kevin Olson explains, "can precede and create the imaginary preconditions for being a people." Olson, "Conclusion: Fragile Collectivities, Imagined Sovereignties," in *What Is a People?*, Alain Badiou et al. (New York: Columbia University Press, 2016), 130.

71. William Wordsworth, "Essay: Supplementary to the Preface," in his *Poems*, 2 vols. (London: Longman et al., 1815), 1:374–75. On the Romantics' deeply ambivalent relation toward the contemporary reading public, see Jon P. Klancher, *The Making of English Reading Audiences, 1790–1832* (Madison: University of Wisconsin Press, 1987); and Andrew Franta, *Romanticism and the Rise of the Mass Public* (Cambridge: Cambridge University Press, 2007).

Chapter 1 · Literature in the Public Domain

1. Statute of Anne (8 Anne c. 19, 1710), 5. The statute has since become known as the Copyright Act, though its actual title was An Act for the Encouragement of Learning, by Vesting the Copies of Printed Books in the Authors or Purchasers of Such Copies, during the Times Therein Mentioned. Scanned images of the act, as well as numerous other tracts and documents from the literary property debate, are available via the database "Primary Sources on Copyright (1450–1900)," ed. Lionel Bently and Martin Kretschmer, www.copyrighthistory.org.

2. The limited terms of copyright were last-minute amendments to save the original bill, which had received rough treatment in the House of Commons from Whigs and moderate Tories suspicious of both licensers and powerful London booksellers. On the history of the act, see John Feather, "The Book Trade in Politics: The Making of the Copyright Act of 1710," *Publishing History* 8 (1980): 19–44, which supersedes Harry Ransom, *The First Copyright Statute: An Essay on "An Act for the Encouragement of Learning," 1710* (Austin: University of Texas Press, 1956). Mark Rose suggests that the statute's term limits on copyright protection were derived from similar terms in the Statute of Monopolies (21 Jac. 1, 1624), which granted a term of privilege of fourteen years for new inventions and twenty-one years for existing patents. Rose, *Authors and Owners: The Invention of Copyright* (Cambridge, MA: Harvard University Press, 1993), 45. While noting the similarity of their terms of duration, Ronan Deazley points out a crucial difference between the extent of the protection each statute provided: whereas monopoly privileges on patents expired at the end of their term period, the Statute of Anne stipulated that a work's copyright would simply revert to its author if still alive. Deazley contends that this proviso indicates that however much the lawmakers of 1710 may have been keen to limit the booksellers' monopoly, they were not averse to long-term monopolies on intellectual property so long as these were "intended to benefit the author and only the author." Deazley, *On the Origin of the Right to Copy: Charting the Movement of Copyright Law in Eighteenth-Century Britain (1695–1775)* (Portland, OR: Hart, 2004), 42–43. In contrast, David Saunders maintains that granting authors ownership in their writings was "convenient rather than central to the anti-monopolistic strategy of the majority in Parliament." Saunders, "Copyright, Obscenity and Literary History," *ELH* 57 (1990): 436.

3. *Edinburgh Advertiser*, 1 March 1774, quoted in Rose, *Authors and Owners*, 96.

4. W. Forbes Gray, "Alexander Donaldson and His Fight for Cheap Books," *Judicial Review* 38 (1926): 197. Though the phrase "the public domain" entered common usage only in the nineteenth century, the idea of a common stock of intellectual goods had long been recognized in legal arguments against monopolies. It was only in the twentieth century that legal theorists began to investigate the idea's rationale and conceptual limits. See David

Lange's pioneering essay, "Recognizing the Public Domain," *Law and Contemporary Problems* 44 (1982): 147–78; and Pamela Samuelson's overview of current theories in "Enriching Discourse on Public Domains," *Duke Law Journal* 55 (2005–2006): 783–834. Robert Spoo examines how the history of the public domain in US jurisprudence became "an aggressively legislated commons." Spoo, *Without Copyrights: Piracy, Publishing, and the Public Domain* (New York: Oxford University Press, 2013), 3.

5. Martha Woodmansee, "The Genius and the Copyright: Economic and Legal Conditions of the Emergence of the 'Author,'" *Eighteenth-Century Studies* 17 (1984): 425–48; Martha Woodmansee and Peter Jaszi, eds., *The Construction of Authorship: Textual Appropriation in Law and Literature* (Durham, NC: Duke University Press, 1994); Alvin Kernan, *Printing Technology, Letters, and Samuel Johnson* (Princeton, NJ: Princeton University Press, 1987), 97–102; Rose, *Authors and Owners*; Mark Rose, "The Author as Proprietor: *Donaldson v. Becket* and the Genealogy of Modern Authorship," *Representations* 23 (1988): 51–85; and Brad Sherman and Alain Strowel, eds., *Of Authors and Origins: Essays on Copyright Law* (Oxford: Clarendon, 1994). These accounts took their cue from Foucault's suggestion that the legal institution of copyright was one of several modern developments that contributed to the "individualization" of discourse and the construction of a Romantic theory of authorship. Michel Foucault, "What Is an Author?," in *Textual Strategies: Perspectives in Post-Structuralist Criticism*, ed. Josué V. Harari (Ithaca, NY: Cornell University Press, 1979), 141, 148–49. These arguments have since been supplemented and corrected by several substantial historical studies, including John Feather, *Publishing, Piracy and Politics: An Historical Study of Copyright in Britain* (New York: Mansell, 1994); Brad Sherman and Lionel Bently, *The Making of Modern Intellectual Property Law: The British Experience, 1760–1911* (Cambridge: Cambridge University Press, 1999); William St. Clair, *The Reading Nation in the Romantic Period* (Cambridge: Cambridge University Press, 2004); Ronan Deazley, *Rethinking Copyright: History, Theory, Language* (Cheltenham, England: Edward Elgar, 2006); Adrian Johns, *Piracy: The Intellectual Property Wars from Gutenberg to Gates* (Chicago, IL: University of Chicago Press, 2009); and Peter Baldwin, *The Copyright Wars: Three Centuries of Trans-Atlantic Battle* (Princeton, NJ: Princeton University Press, 2014).

6. Trevor Ross, "Copyright and the Invention of Tradition," *Eighteenth-Century Studies* 26 (1992): 1–27.

7. The public domain, Simon Stern notes, was not yet available in 1710 as "a distinctive concept that Parliament might have counterposed against the monopoly" sought by the booksellers, but the measures set out in the statute "took a form that promoted public access to texts." Stern, "Creating a Public Domain in Eighteenth-Century England," *Oxford Handbooks Online* (August 2015), doi:10.1093/oxfordhb/9780199935338.013.39.

8. Preface to *The Cases of the Appellants and Respondents in the Cause of Literary Property, before the House of Lords* (London: J. Bew et al., 1774), sig. av.

9. For this history in an English context, see Joseph Loewenstein, *The Author's Due: Printing and the Prehistory of Copyright* (Chicago, IL: University of Chicago Press, 2002).

10. Copyright in the early modern era, Ian Parsons noted, served as "an indirect form of censorship.... [O]rdinances and Acts of Parliament designed to protect society against abuses of the press frequently achieved, as a concomitant, the protection of authors and publishers against infringement of their rights." Parsons, "Copyright and Society," in *Essays in the History of Publishing*, ed. Asa Briggs (London: Longman, 1974), 32. Jody Greene presents a forceful case for the role of copyright as a form of press regulation. Greene, *The Trouble*

with Ownership: Literary Property and Authorial Liability in England, 1660–1730 (Philadelphia: University of Pennsylvania Press, 2005).

11. Company of Stationers v. Seymour (1677), 1 Mod. 257, quoted in W. S. Holdsworth, "Press Control and Copyright in the 16th and 17th Centuries," Yale Law Journal 29 (1919–1920): 853n57.

12. William Patry reviews the history and misleading implications of this "agrarian metaphor." Patry, Moral Panics and the Copyright Wars (Oxford: Oxford University Press, 2009), 78–86.

13. James Boswell, The Life of Samuel Johnson, LL.D., 2 vols. (London: Charles Dilly, 1791), 1:421–22.

14. Lord Justice Clerk Thomas Miller, as reported in The Decision of the Court of Session, upon the Question of Literary Property (Edinburgh: Alexander Donaldson, 1774), 16.

15. William Blackstone, Commentaries on the Laws of England, 4 vols. (Oxford: Clarendon, 1765–1769), 2:406.

16. William Enfield, Observations on Literary Property (London: Joseph Johnson, 1774), 11.

17. Midwinter v. Hamilton (Court of Session, Scotland, 1748), as reported by Henry Home, Lord Kames, in Remarkable Decisions of the Court of Session from the Year 1730 to the Year 1752 (Edinburgh: A. Kincaid and J. Bell, 1766), 158. Kames, who had served as senior counsel to the Scottish booksellers, was not recording the court's decision but presenting a version of his own defense brief. See Deazley, On the Origin, 129.

18. Kames, Midwinter v. Hamilton, in Remarkable Decisions, 157.

19. It may have been assumed that authors held a property right in their manuscripts, but the right to prevent their unauthorized publication was first recognized only in the 1732 Chancery case Webb v. Rose. Before then, as Mansfield later acknowledged, "the case of piracy before publication never existed: it never was put, or supposed. There is not a syllable about it to be met with any where." William Murray, Lord Mansfield, in Millar v. Taylor (1769), 4 Burr. 2303, 98 ER 252.

20. Joseph Yates, in Millar v. Taylor, 98 ER 234, 242.

21. Yates, in Millar v. Taylor, 98 ER 231–32, 235, 244, 250.

22. Mansfield, in Millar v. Taylor, 98 ER 252. Mansfield was echoing Justice Edward Willes's earlier formulation of the principle: "It is certainly not agreeable to natural justice, that a stranger should reap the beneficial pecuniary produce of another man's work" (98 ER 218). James Henry Bergeron provides a fuller analysis of the judges' competing economic theories in Millar v. Taylor, which, he reports, "contains one of the most extensive discussions of the nature of property in the law of the time." Bergeron, "From Property to Contract: Political Economy and the Transformation of Value in English Common Law," Social and Legal Studies 2 (1993): 12–15. A labor account of property value did not necessarily enjoin its adherents to believe in permanent rights for expressive works. Locke, the theory's greatest exponent, objected to exclusive rights being maintained on works older than fifty years. His 1694 memorandum on the Licensing Act, in which he stated his objection, may have influenced the later Whig lords to impose term limits on copyright in the Statute of Anne. See Justin Hughes, "Locke's 1694 Memorandum (and More Incomplete Copyright Historiographies)," Cardozo Arts and Entertainment Law Journal 27 (2009–2010): 375–408.

23. Richard Aston, in Millar v. Taylor, 98 ER 221–22.

24. Yates, in Millar v. Taylor, 98 ER 232.

25. Blackstone, *Commentaries*, 2:2. This statement has commonly been cited as representing Blackstone's own view of property but, when it is read in its larger context, it is evident that he is exaggerating traditional perceptions of property. On this point, see Carol M. Rose, "Canons of Property Talk; or, Blackstone's Anxiety," *Yale Law Journal* 108 (1998): 601–32.

26. Yates, in *Millar v. Taylor*, 98 *ER* 244, 250.

27. Blackstone, in *Tonson v. Collins* (1762, rehearing of 1761 case), 1 Black. W. 344, 96 *ER* 189. Blackstone was rearguing the case for the plaintiff and Yates was doing the same for the defendant, because Mansfield had ruled the previous year to let the case be held over for further argument.

28. J. G. A. Pocock, *Virtue, Commerce, and History* (Cambridge: Cambridge University Press, 1985), 115, 119.

29. Pocock, *Virtue, Commerce, and History*, 121.

30. William Warburton, *A Letter from an Author, to a Member of Parliament, concerning Literary Property* (1747), in his *Works*, 7 vols. (London: T. Cadell, 1788), 7:927.

31. Yates, in *Millar v. Taylor*, 98 *ER* 232.

32. *Information for Alexander Donaldson and John Wood, Booksellers in Edinburgh, &c.*, as reported by George Brown, Lord Coalston (Edinburgh, 1773), 16–17.

33. Lord Effingham Howard, as reported in *Cases of the Appellants and Respondents*, 59. I quote this pamphlet account of the 1774 decision because it provides a fuller and evidently more accurate record of the speeches than does the later standard account. See Rose, "Author as Proprietor," 81–82n55.

34. *Memorial for the Booksellers of Edinburgh and Glasgow, relating to the Process against Them by Some of the London Booksellers* (Edinburgh, 1765?), 5.

35. See the evidence collected by the Scottish bookseller Alexander Donaldson in *Some Thoughts on the State of Literary Property* (London: Alexander Donaldson, 1764).

36. On how the metaphor has been used to obscure social limits to participation in the public sphere, see Stanley Ingber, "The Marketplace of Ideas: A Legitimizing Myth," *Duke Law Journal* 1984.1 (1984): 1–91.

37. Charles Pratt, Lord Camden, as reported in *Cases of the Appellants and Respondents*, 52–54.

38. Camden, in *Cases of the Appellants and Respondents*, 54. Milton, contrary to what Camden suggested, supported the idea of copyright, at least for stationers if not necessarily for authors. See Loewenstein, *The Author's Due*, 185–91.

39. Kames, in *Hinton v. Donaldson* (1773), as reported in *The Decision of the Court of Session, upon the Question of Literary Property*, ed. James Boswell (Edinburgh: Alexander Donaldson, 1774), 19–20.

40. Kames, in *Hinton v. Donaldson*, 19.

41. Alexander Donaldson and John Donaldson, in *Cases of the Appellants and Respondents*, 6. The Donaldsons were appealing a 1772 Court of Chancery injunction granted to the London booksellers, led by Andrew Millar's former apprentice Thomas Becket, who had purchased the rights to Thomson's *The Seasons* following Millar's death. While the Donaldsons' petition to the English lords borrowed heavily from Kames's opinion, they could not cite *Hinton v. Donaldson* as a relevant precedent since the Court of Session had ruled for them solely on the grounds that copyright was not recognized in the common law of Scotland.

42. One later US commentator expressed dismay at how Mansfield's "pure principles" in defense of a common-law copyright had been defeated "by the fallacious theories of Judge

Yates and the Sophomoric rhetoric of Lord Camden." Eaton S. Drone, *A Treatise on the Law of Property in Intellectual Productions in Great Britain and the United States* (Boston: Little, Brown, 1879), 40. See Mark Rose, "Nine-Tenths of the Law: The English Copyright Debates and the Rhetoric of the Public Domain," *Law and Contemporary Problems* 66 (2003): 80–84.

43. *A Vindication of the Exclusive Right of Authors to Their Own Works: A Subject Now under Consideration before the Twelve Judges of England* (London: R. Griffiths, 1762), 43.

44. Thomas, Lord Lyttelton, in *Cases of the Appellants and Respondents*, 56.

45. Catherine Macaulay, *A Modest Plea for the Property of Copyright* (London: Edward and Charles Dilly, 1774), 17.

46. Mario Biagioli offers a stimulating discussion of how eighteenth-century theories of original genius could be only imperfectly accommodated to a defense of copyright because they attributed originality to a providential or natural source, which in principle could be subject to neither human ownership nor agency. Biagioli, "Nature and the Commons: The Vegetable Roots of Intellectual Property," in *Living Properties: Making Knowledge and Controlling Ownership in the History of Biology*, ed. Jean-Paul Gaudillière, Daniel J. Kevles, and Hans-Jörg Rheinberger (Berlin: Max Planck Institute for the History of Science, 2009), 241–50.

47. Enfield, *Observations on Literary Property*, 45–46.

48. Macaulay, *A Modest Plea*, 18.

49. Enfield, *Observations on Literary Property*, 45.

50. Adam Smith, *An Inquiry into the Nature and Causes of the Wealth of Nations*, 2 vols. (London: W. Strahan and T. Cadell, 1776), 1:16, 401. Zeynep Tenger and Paul Trolander presented a compelling analysis of Smith's critique of genius and its repercussions for later accounts of literature's public value. Tenger and Trolander, "Genius versus Capital: Eighteenth-Century Theories of Genius and Adam Smith's *Wealth of Nations*," *Modern Language Quarterly* 55 (1994): 169–89. Paul K. Saint-Amour suggests that despite his insistence on the wealth-producing benefits of exchange, Smith "was at heart a proponent of the labor theory of value." Saint-Amour, *The Copywrights: Intellectual Property and the Literary Imagination* (Ithaca, NY: Cornell University Press, 2003), 24.

51. Willes, in *Millar v. Taylor*, 98 ER 218.

52. On the rise of an "ethic of improvement" in relation to material culture, see Sarah Tarlow, *The Archaeology of Improvement in Britain, 1750–1850* (Cambridge: Cambridge University Press, 2007).

53. Enfield, *Observations on Literary Property*, 41.

54. Francis Hargrave, *An Argument in Defence of Literary Property*, 2nd ed. (London: W. Otridge, 1774), 7.

55. Quoted in "Sketch of Thursday's Debate in the House of Commons," *General Evening Post* (26 March 1774).

56. Woodmansee, "The Genius and the Copyright," 430–31.

57. Edward Young, *Conjectures on Original Composition in a Letter to the Author of Sir Charles Grandison* (London: A. Millar and R. and J. Dodsley, 1759), 53–54.

58. Young, *Conjectures*, 78.

59. Hargrave, *Argument in Defence*, 7. I consider Hargrave's claim more thoroughly in chapter 2.

60. William Duff, *An Essay on Original Genius* (London: Edward and Charles Dilly, 1767), 260.

61. Young, *Conjectures*, 6.

62. Young, *Conjectures*, 5.

63. Smith, *Wealth of Nations*, 1:19, 130–31. The elevation of prestige over money within the cultural field is, of course, the subject of Pierre Bourdieu's sociology of art. Disavowals of the profit motive, he suggests, enable those within the field not only to distinguish themselves from other artists but to define their field in opposition to the economic world. Bourdieu, *The Field of Cultural Production*, ed. Randal Johnson (New York: Columbia University Press, 1993). Robin Valenza considers the Romantic poets' aversion to professionalization as both a reaction to and an embrace of specialization. Valenza, *Literature, Language, and the Rise of the Intellectual Disciplines* (Cambridge: Cambridge University Press, 2009), 139–72. In conceiving of their labor as the product of inner compulsion, these poets made their art seem more specialized than other activities that merely required disciplinary study: "The success of authorship as a profession depended precisely on its denying that it had anything in common with training, markets, and the like" (148). Yet they equally believed that the products of their labor transcended specialization by providing readers with a national literary language that could serve as a universalizing "alternative to vocational and conversational languages at all levels" (145).

64. Trevor Ross, *The Making of the English Literary Canon: From the Middle Ages to the Late Eighteenth Century* (Montreal: McGill-Queen's University Press, 1998), 293–301.

65. William Wordsworth, "Preface," in his *Lyrical Ballads, with Other Poems*, 3rd ed., 2 vols. (London: T. N. Longman and O. Rees, 1800), 1:xi.

66. William Duff, *Critical Observations on the Writing of the Most Celebrated Writers and Original Geniuses in Poetry* (London: T. Becket and P. A. de Hondt, 1770), 339.

67. Duff, *Critical Observations*, 361.

68. Boswell, *Life of Johnson*, 1:168.

69. "On the History of Authors by Profession," *The Bee; or, Literary Weekly Intelligencer* 3 (25 May 1791): 88–89. I owe this reference to Richard B. Sher, who surveys changing attitudes toward booksellers during the period in his magisterial *The Enlightenment and the Book: Scottish Authors and Their Publishers in Eighteenth-Century Britain, Ireland, and America* (Chicago, IL: University of Chicago Press, 2006), 194–203.

70. Hugh Blair, *Lectures on Rhetoric and Belles Lettres*, 2 vols. (London: W. Strahan, T. Cadell, and W. Creech, 1783), 1:6, 9–13.

71. Vicesimus Knox, "On the Choice of Books," in his *Essays, Moral and Literary*, 2 vols. (London: Edward and Charles Dilly, 1778), 2:303; Knox, "Of Supporting the Dignity of the Literary Republic," in his *Winter Evenings; or, Lucubrations on Life and Letters*, 3 vols. (London: Charles Dilly, 1788), 3:121; and Knox, "On the Means of Reading with the Most Advantage," in his *Essays, Moral and Literary*, 3rd ed., 2 vols. (London: Charles Dilly, 1782), 2:4.

72. I have examined how Shakespeare's editors during the period increasingly justified their efforts by arguing that competent readers needed an "authentic" text to appreciate his work's full meaning and significance. Ross, *Making of the English Literary Canon*, 231–46. Margreta de Grazia offers the Foucauldian thesis that the quest for an authentic Shakespeare was propelled by the new doctrine of original genius, which was itself born of the copyright debates. De Grazia, *Shakespeare Verbatim: The Reproduction of Authenticity and the 1790 Apparatus* (Oxford: Clarendon, 1991). In a related argument, Jonathan Brody Kramnick considered how Thomas Warton and other critics revived Spenser's reputation by presenting him as an author whose difficult works promised pleasurable rewards only to expert readers.

Kramnick, *Making the English Canon: Print-Capitalism and the Cultural Past, 1700–1770* (Cambridge: Cambridge University Press, 1998), 137–89.

73. Thomas F. Bonnell provides a superbly detailed history of these competing editions in *The Most Disreputable Trade: Publishing the Classics of English Poetry, 1765–1810* (Oxford: Oxford University Press, 2008), 97–168.

74. Boswell, *Life of Johnson*, 2:112.

75. *Information for Alexander Donaldson*, 20.

76. Adam Smith, *Lectures on Jurisprudence* (1762–1763), in *Glasgow Edition of the Works and Correspondence of Adam Smith*, ed. R. L. Meek, D. D. Raphael, and P. G. Stein, 6 vols. (Oxford: Oxford University Press, 1978), 5:472.

77. The Statute of Anne had included a proviso for regulating prices, but that section proved unenforceable and was eventually repealed.

78. Macaulay, *A Modest Plea*, 28.

79. Enfield, *Observations on Literary Property*, 50.

80. Kames, in *Hinton v. Donaldson*, 21.

81. Kames, in *Hinton v. Donaldson*, 20.

82. Edmund Law, *Observations Occasioned by the Contest about Literary Property* (Cambridge: T. and J. Merrill et al., 1770), 12–13.

83. *An Enquiry into the Nature and Origin of Literary Property* (London: William Flexney, 1762), 12–13.

84. Francis Garden, Lord Gardenston, in *Hinton v. Donaldson*, 26.

85. *Enquiry*, 4–5.

86. The idea that canonical works are as traditional as they are unique has remained central to the case for a limited copyright. In Richard Posner's words, "the more extensive copyright protection is, the more inhibited is the literary imagination." Posner, *Law and Literature: A Misunderstood Relation*, 3rd ed. (Cambridge, MA: Harvard University Press, 2009), 532. Some defenders of the public domain have felt pressed to assert the idea more loudly than ever in the face of the twentieth- and twenty-first-century dramatic expansion of copyright privileges, which rights-holders have campaigned for in response to perceived threats from digitization and electronic dissemination. See, among others, Debora J. Halbert, *Intellectual Property in the Information Age: The Politics of Expanding Ownership Rights* (Westport, CT: Quorum Books, 1999); Lawrence Lessig, *Free Culture: How Big Media Uses Technology and the Law to Lock Down Culture and Control Creativity* (London: Penguin, 2004); Christine Harold, *OurSpace: Resisting the Corporate Control of Culture* (Minneapolis: University of Minnesota Press, 2007); Michele Boldrin and David K. Levine, *Against Intellectual Monopoly* (Cambridge: Cambridge University Press, 2008); James Boyle, *The Public Domain: Enclosing the Commons of the Mind* (New Haven, CT: Yale University Press, 2008); and Neil Weinstock Netanel, *Copyright's Paradox* (Oxford: Oxford University Press, 2008).

87. Harry Levin, "The Tradition of Tradition," in his *Contexts of Criticism* (Cambridge, MA: Harvard University Press, 1958), 55–66. See also Raymond Williams, *Marxism and Literature* (Oxford: Oxford University Press, 1977), 48–54.

88. Eric Hobsbawn defined an "invented tradition" as "a set of practices, normally governed by overtly or tacitly accepted rules and of a ritual or symbolic nature, which seek to inculcate certain values and norms of behaviour by repetition, which automatically implies continuity with the past." Hobsbawn, "Introduction: Inventing Tradition," in *The Invention of Tradition*, ed. E. Hobsbawn and Terence Ranger (Cambridge: Cambridge University

Press, 1983), 1. Hobsbawn's examples include nationalist ideographs, such as flags and anthems, and fictions, such as Ossian and Rowley.

89. Alexander Boswell, Lord Auchinleck, in *Hinton v. Donaldson*, 5.

90. *Information for Alexander Donaldson*, 17–18.

91. One of Donaldson's lawyers, John MacLaurin, Lord Dreghorn, had earlier acknowledged to the Berwick printer Robert Taylor that "to give a popular turn to the Cause of the Plaintiffs, your Cause has been represented as the Cause of Scotland." But he advised Taylor to avoid any reference to national rivalries in his fight with Andrew Millar since "you stand on your own Bottom: Your Industry interferes equally with the Scots, as with the English, and your Cause is more immediately the Cause of the Bookselling and Printing of England." Dreghorn, "A Letter to Robert Taylor, Bookseller, in Berwick," in *Considerations on the Nature and Origin of Literary Property* (Berwick, England: Robert Taylor, 1768), 7.

92. Boswell, *Life of Johnson*, 1:422.

93. David Nimmer, "The End of Copyright," *Vanderbilt Law Review* 48 (1995): 1416; Neil Weinstock Netanel, "Copyright and a Democratic Civil Society," *Yale Law Journal* 106 (1996): 298, emphases added in both quotes.

94. Jürgen Habermas, *The Structural Transformation of the Public Sphere: An Inquiry into a Category of Bourgeois Society*, trans. T. Burger and F. Lawrence (Cambridge, MA: MIT Press, 1989), 23. This idea was widely prevalent during the eighteenth century. In Abbé Du Bos's definition, "the word *public* is used here to mean those persons who have acquired enlightenment, either through reading or through life in society [*le commerce du monde*]. They are the only ones who can determine the value of poems or paintings." Du Bos, *Réflexions critiques sur la peinture et sur la poésie* (1719), quoted in Joan DeJean, *Ancients against Moderns: Culture Wars and the Making of a Fin de Siècle* (Chicago, IL: University of Chicago Press, 1997), 64.

95. Mansfield, in *Sayre and Others v. Moore* (1785), cited in *Cary v. Longman and Rees* (1801), 1 East. 557, 102 *ER* 140.

96. Camden, in *Cases of the Appellants and Respondents*, 53. Analogizing knowledge to the elements has been a persistent trope in defenses of the public domain. See, for example, Lewis Hyde's *Common as Air: Revolution, Art, and Ownership* (New York: Farrar, Straus and Giroux, 2010). See Biagioli, "Nature and the Commons," on the conceptual difficulties such environmental tropes pose for arguments about intellectual property.

97. Dreghorn, "Letter to Robert Taylor," 8.

98. *Stationers Company v. Carnan* (1775), 2 W. Black. 1004, 96 *ER* 592. The stationers launched their suit in November 1773, but the case was not decided until the following May and then reported a year later.

99. Thomas Erskine, Address to the House of Commons, 10 May 1779, in *PH* 20:cols. 615–16, 610. Two years later the stationers regained most of their market by successfully campaigning to have the stamp tax on almanacs doubled, which put the cost of publishing them beyond the means of most of their competitors. See Cyprian Blagden, "Thomas Carnan and the Almanack Monopoly," *Studies in Bibliography* 14 (1961): 26–43.

100. St. Clair, *The Reading Nation*, 103–39. James Raven corrects several of St. Clair's conclusions about the defeat's financial repercussions for publishers. Raven, *The Business of Books: Bookselling and the English Book Trade, 1450–1850* (New Haven, CT: Yale University Press, 2007), 230–56. Likewise, J. E. Elliott disproves the "hypothesis" put forward by St. Clair and others that the *Donaldson* decision led to a flood of cheap books and a broad extension of read-

ing. Elliott, "The Cost of Reading in Eighteenth-Century Britain: Auction Sale Catalogues and the Cheap Literature Hypothesis," *ELH* 77 (2010): 353–84. Elliott cites my original essay as among those supporting this hypothesis. Ross, "Copyright and the Invention of Tradition," *Eighteenth-Century Studies* 26.1 (1992): 1–27. My argument is not, however, about actual retail practices but about beliefs, including the belief expressed by advocates of a public domain that the repeal of perpetual copyright would lead to a ready supply of cheap editions of the English literary classics and that having such a supply would be a good thing for the national culture. That the belief would not be realized for many decades does not diminish the fact that it proved compelling enough to help win the case for repeal.

101. John Dryden, "Preface," in his *Fables: Ancient and Modern* (London: Jacob Tonson, 1700), sig. *Ar.

102. Beyond this select group of writers, the canon as represented in anthologies from the period was not so static, while the selections from the core authors included in these collections varied considerably. See Bonnell, *The Most Disreputable Trade*, 308–16.

103. E. Thurlow et al., in *Cases of the Appellants and Respondents*, 14; Gardenston, in *Hinton v. Donaldson*, 23.

104. Boswell, *Life of Johnson*, 1:238.

105. Samuel Johnson to William Strahan, 7 March 1774, in *The Letters of Samuel Johnson*, ed. Bruce Redford, 5 vols. (Oxford: Clarendon, 1992–1994), 2:131.

106. Johnson, "Preface," in William Shakespeare, *Plays*, 8 vols. (London: J. and R. Tonson et al., 1765), 1:vi–vii.

107. Michael Garner points out that by linking the term of copyright to the writer's lifespan, the 1814 act went much further than the Statute of Anne in giving priority to authors' rights over those of publishers. Garner, *Romanticism, Self-Canonization, and the Business of Poetry* (Cambridge: Cambridge University Press, 2017), 44–45. By making it impossible, furthermore, for living writers to be anthologized unless publishers bought the rights, the act underscored the sense that the public domain canon of literature was made up exclusively of dead writers.

108. Thomas Babington Macaulay, "Literary Copyright (A Speech Delivered in the House of Commons on the 5th of February 1841)," in *Speeches, Parliamentary and Miscellaneous*, 2 vols. (London: Henry Vizetelly, 1853), 1:290.

109. Thomas Noon Talfourd, "Speech on Moving to the Second Reading of a Bill to Amend the Law of Copyright (Thursday, 28th February, 1839)," in his *Three Speeches Delivered in the House of Commons in Favour of a Measure for an Extension of Copyright* (London: Edward Moxon, 1840), 76. Catherine Seville suggests that Talfourd regarded a lengthy term of copyright "as primarily something of symbolic importance." Seville, *Literary Copyright Reform in Early Victorian England: The Framing of the 1842 Copyright Act* (Cambridge: Cambridge University Press, 1999), 19.

110. John Murray, in *Minutes of Evidence Taken before the Select Committee on the Copyright Acts of 8 Anne, c. 19; 15 Geo. III, c. 53; 41 Geo. III, c. 107; and 54 Geo. III, c. 116* (London: House of Commons, 1818), 64.

111. Lee Erickson, *The Economy of Literary Form: English Literature and the Industrialization of Publishing, 1800–1850* (Baltimore, MD: Johns Hopkins University Press, 1996), 103.

112. Thomas Carlyle, *On Heroes, Hero-Worship, and the Heroic in History* (London: Chapman and Hall, 1840), 132–33.

113. For a sample of contemporary laments, see Erickson, *Economy of Literary Form*, 170–90.

114. William Wordsworth to Richard Sharp, 27 September 1808, in *The Letters of William and Dorothy Wordsworth: The Middle Years*, ed. Ernest De Selincourt (Oxford: Oxford University Press, 1937), 1:242. Susan Eilenberg discusses Wordsworth's lifelong efforts to extend the term of copyright. Eilenberg, "Mortal Pages: Wordsworth and the Reform of Copyright," *ELH* 56 (1989): 351–74.

115. William Wordsworth, "Essay: Supplementary to the Preface," in his *Poems*, 2 vols. (London: Longman et al., 1815), 1:368.

116. Talfourd, "Speech on the Motion for the Second Reading of the Bill to Amend the Law of Copyright (Wednesday, 25th April, 1838)," in his *Three Speeches*, 63.

117. Horace, *Ars Poetica* (lines 131–35), trans. D. A. Russell, in *Ancient Literary Criticism: The Principal Texts in New Translations*, ed. D. A. Russell and M. Winterbottom (Oxford: Clarendon, 1972), 283.

118. Wordsworth, "Petition of Wm. Wordsworth, Esq." (1840), appended to Talfourd, *Three Speeches*, 114.

Chapter 2 · The Fate of Style in an Age of Intellectual Property

1. *Burnett v. Chetwood* (1721), 2 Mer. 441, 38 *ER* 1008. In this case, Thomas Burnett's brother and executor sought an injunction against the proposed publication of an English translation of Burnett's *Archaeologia Philosophica*. The defendants, William Chetwood and Richard Francklin, claimed that their translation "in some respects may be called a different work" since "the translator dresses it up and clothes the sense in his own style and expressions, and at least puts it into a different form from the original." While the lord chancellor, Thomas Parker, agreed with the defendants on this point, he granted the injunction because he felt that the work's controversial content should remain "concealed from the vulgar in the Latin language." It is not clear, however, whether the report of the case, which was set down almost a century later appended to *Southey v. Sherwood* (1817) and which misdates the case to 1720, is quoting the defendants' own words or providing a reconstruction of their arguments. See additional material on the case at "Primary Sources on Copyright (1450–1900)," ed. Lionel Bently and Martin Kretschmer, www.copyrighthistory.org.

2. For an overview of these cases, see Matthew Sag, "The Pre-History of Fair Use" (2010), http://works.bepress.com/matthew_sag/9.

3. See *Roth Greeting Cards v. United Card Co.* (9th Cir., 1970), 429 F. 2d 1106; *Steinberg v. Columbia Pictures Industries, Inc.* (S.D.N.Y., 1987), 663 F. Supp. 706. For discussions of these and other cases, see Thomas M. Sipos, "Warning All Authors! Your 'Style' May Infringe Your Own Work: Authors Can Benefit through Less Copyright Protection," *Loyola Entertainment Law Journal* 9 (1989): 359–80; Richard H. Jones, "The Myth of the Idea/Expression Dichotomy in Copyright Law," *Pace Law Review* 10 (1990): 551–607; and Michelle Brownlee, "Safeguarding Style: What Protection Is Afforded to Visual Artists by the Copyright and Trademark Laws?," *Columbia Law Review* 93 (1993): 1157–84. Siva Vaidhyanathan forcefully demonstrates how the distinction between ideas and their expression has been collapsing over the past century. Vaidhyanathan, *Copyrights and Copywrongs: The Rise of Intellectual Property and How It Threatens Creativity* (New York: New York University Press, 2001).

4. *Chicago Record-Herald v. Tribune Association* (7th Cir., 1921), 275 F. 2d 799.

5. *Norowzian v. Arks Limited, Guinness Worldwide Ltd., and Guinness, PLC* (No. 2) (1999), FSR 394; (2000), FSR 363.

6. Early modern English rhetoricians, Debora Shuger suggested, regarded "style as [a] politically significant form." Shuger, "Conceptions of Style," in *The Cambridge History of Literary Criticism*, vol. 3: *The Renaissance*, ed. Glyn P. Norton (Cambridge: Cambridge University Press, 1989), 184.

7. As John Constable, citing Quintilian, made clear, stylistic harmony ideally naturalized the relation of the signifier to the signified: "the happiest structure of Style is where the right order, and connexion, and harmony of the words, fall in the most naturally with the thought." Constable, *Reflections upon Accuracy of Style* (London: John Hawkins, 1731), 222. Constable had written his *Reflections* some three decades earlier, but the work was not published until 1731.

8. Jacques Rancière, *The Politics of Literature*, trans. Julie Rose (Cambridge: Polity, 2011), 11.

9. The royalist poet George Daniel presented the most explicit case for updating the canon along Cavalier norms. Daniel, "An Essay: Endeavouring to Ennoble Our English Poesie by Evidence of Latter Quills; and Rejecting the Former" (c. 1646), in *Poems*, 4 vols., ed. Alexander B. Grosart (Boston, England, 1878), 1:79–84.

10. Joshua Poole, preface to his *The English Parnassus* (London: T. Johnson, 1657), sig. A3v.

11. John Dryden, "Defence of the Epilogue; or, An Essay on the Dramatique Poetry of the Last Age," appended to his *The Conquest of Granada by the Spaniards in Two Parts* (London: Henry Herringman, 1672), 173.

12. Thomas Sprat, *The History of the Royal-Society of London for the Improving of Natural Knowledge* (London: J. Martyn, 1667), 113.

13. Sprat, *History of the Royal-Society*, 113.

14. Trevor Ross, "The Rules of the Game; or, Why Neoclassicism Was Never an Ideology," in *Ideology and Form in Eighteenth-Century Literature*, ed. David H. Richter (Lubbock: Texas Tech University Press, 1999), 163–84. I have taken several of the points that follow in the next three paragraphs from a related essay: Ross, "Translation and the Canonical Text," *Studies in the Literary Imagination* 33.2 (Fall 2000): 1–21.

15. "An English Play," George Farquhar insisted, "is intended for the Use and Instruction of an English Audience, a People not only separated from the rest of the World by Situation, but different also from other Nations as well in the Complexion and Temperament of the Natural Body, as in the Constitution of our Body Politick." Farquhar, "A Discourse upon Comedy," appended to his *Love and Business: In a Collection of Occasionary Verse* (London: B. Lintott, 1702), 140.

16. Dryden, preface to *Ovid's Epistles Translated by Several Hands* (London: J. Tonson, 1680), sig. A2r–A3r; Abraham Cowley, preface to *Pindarique Odes* (c. 1656), in his *Works* (London: Henry Herringman, 1668), sig. T3r.

17. Constable, *Reflections upon Accuracy*, 228.

18. Henry Felton, *A Dissertation on Reading the Classics, and Forming a Just Style: Written in the Year 1709, and Addressed to the Right Honourable, John Lord Roos* (London: J. Bowyer, 1713), 46–47.

19. Joseph Spence, *Anecdotes, Observations, and Characters*, ed. Edmund Malone (London: John Murray, 1820), 52.

20. Alexander Pope, "The Publisher to the Reader," preface to *The Dunciad: An Heroic Poem in Three Books* (London: G. Faulkner et al., 1728), v.

21. Susan Staves, "Pope's Refinement," *Eighteenth Century: Theory and Interpretation* 29 (1988): 153.

22. Hugh Blair, *Lectures on Rhetoric and Belles Lettres*, 2 vols. (London: W. Strahan, T. Cadell, and W. Creech, 1783), 1:39.

23. On how the new rhetoric stressed communicability over eloquent suasion, see Wilbur Samuel Howell, *Eighteenth-Century British Logic and Rhetoric* (Princeton, NJ: Princeton University Press, 1971); and Adam Potkay, *The Fate of Eloquence in the Age of Hume* (Ithaca, NY: Cornell University Press, 1994). John Guillory suggests that the new rhetoric's norm of plainness and clarity "arose from the *publicness* of print culture, which presupposed that written communications were addressed ideally to everyone, to the hypothetical general reader." Guillory, "The Memo and Modernity," *Critical Inquiry* 31 (2004): 129.

24. Blair, *Lectures on Rhetoric*, 1:369.

25. Adam Smith, *Lectures on Rhetoric and Belles Lettres*, ed. J. C. Bryce (Indianapolis, IN: Liberty Fund, 1985), 19, 55–56. Smith originally presented the lectures in 1748–1750 and then adapted them for his course on moral philosophy at the University of Edinburgh. Bryce's edition is based on student notes from 1762–1763, the last time Smith taught the course.

26. Blair, *Lectures on Rhetoric*, 1:368, 378.

27. Smith, *Lectures on Rhetoric*, 6, 42.

28. Smith, *Lectures on Rhetoric*, 55.

29. Fredric Jameson, *Marxism and Form* (Princeton, NJ: Princeton University Press, 1971), 334.

30. Thomas Gray, letter to Richard West, 8 April 1742, in *Correspondence of Thomas Gray*, 3 vols., ed. Paget Toynbee, Leonard Whibley, and H. W. Starr (Oxford: Clarendon, 1971), 1:192.

31. Edward Young, *Conjectures on Original Composition* (London: A. Millar and R. and J. Dodsley, 1759), 42. Young and other mythologizers of original genius may have seemed intent on replacing an older determining hierarchy of bodies and words with a new order of providentially specialized laborers in the verbal arts. At the mythology's core, however, was an assertion of the inviolability of the writer's otherness. Genius, Young advised, should avoid imitation, which "destroys all mental Individuality," and look instead to "contract full intimacy with the Stranger within thee" (*Conjectures*, 28, 53).

32. Michael Warner, *Publics and Counterpublics* (New York: Zone, 2002), 82.

33. William Wordsworth, "Preface," in his *Lyrical Ballads, with Other Poems*, 3rd ed., 2 vols. (London: T. N. Longman and O. Rees, 1800), 1:vii, xxi, xxxvii.

34. William Murray, Lord Mansfield, in *Millar v. Taylor* (1769), 4 Burr. 2303, 98 *ER* 251–52.

35. William Blackstone, *Commentaries on the Laws of England*, 4 vols. (Oxford: Clarendon, 1765–1769), 2:406.

36. Joseph Yates, in *Millar v. Taylor*, 98 *ER* 234.

37. Expression in itself, John Locke explained, could certify neither meaning nor value: "Words are offer'd to the Publick by every *private* Man, Coined in his *private* Mint, as he pleases; but 'tis the receiving of them by others, their very passing, that gives them their Authority and Currancy, and not the Mint they come out of." Locke, *Mr. Locke's Reply to the*

Right Reverend the Lord Bishop of Worcester's Answer to His Second Letter (London: A. and I. Churchill, 1699), 130. I thank Chantel Lavoie for bringing this passage to my attention.

38. Edward Willes, in *Millar v. Taylor*, 98 *ER* 216.

39. Samuel Johnson, "Considerations on the Case of Dr. Trapp's Sermons, Abridged by Mr. Cave, 1739," *Gentleman's Magazine* 57 (July 1787): 556.

40. Edward Law, Lord Ellenborough, in *Cary v. Kearsley* (1803), 4 Esp. 168, 170 *ER* 680. In his decision, Ellenborough explained that the principle of fair use allowed an author to adopt only "part of the work of another . . . for the promotion of science, and the benefit of the public."

41. Blackstone, in *Tonson v. Collins* (1762, rehearing of 1761 case), 1 Black. W. 344, 96 *ER* 189.

42. William Enfield, *Observations on Literary Property* (London: Joseph Johnson, 1774), 43.

43. *A Vindication of the Exclusive Right of Authors to Their Own Works: A Subject Now under Consideration before the Twelve Judges of England* (London: R. Griffiths, 1762), 13–14.

44. *An Enquiry into the Nature and Origin of Literary Property* (London: William Flexney, 1762), 5–6, 14.

45. *Vindication*, 9, 11.

46. James Burnett, Lord Monboddo, in *Hinton v. Donaldson* (1773), as reported in *The Decision of the Court of Session, upon the Question of Literary Property*, ed. James Boswell (Edinburgh: Alexander Donaldson, 1774), 9.

47. *Information for Alexander Donaldson and John Wood, Booksellers in Edinburgh, &c.*, as reported by George Brown, Lord Coalston (Edinburgh, 1773), 10.

48. *Information for Alexander Donaldson*, 11.

49. Yates, in *Tonson v. Collins* (1762, rehearing of 1761 case), 96 *ER* 185.

50. Robert Maugham, *A Treatise on the Laws of Literary Property* (London: Longman, 1828), 216.

51. Francis Hargrave, *An Argument in Defence of Literary Property*, 2nd ed. (London: W. Otridge, 1774), 6–7.

52. Mark Rose, *Authors and Owners: The Invention of Copyright* (Cambridge, MA: Harvard University Press, 1993), 124–26. Simon Stern rightly faults Rose for reading Hargrave's emphasis on the "*really* original" work as implying both a qualitative standard and an aesthetic understanding of creativity. Hargrave was not talking about the innovations of original genius but rather differentiating between independently created works and reproductions that are passed off as originals. See Stern, "Copyright, Originality, and the Public Domain in Eighteenth-Century England," in *Originality and Intellectual Property in the French and English Enlightenment*, ed. Reginald McGinnis (New York: Routledge, 2008), 83. Rose, I would add, anticipated my argument in suggesting that copyright since the eighteenth century has been underwritten by "our conviction about ourselves as individuals." But he and I disagree about the evidence that is thought to confirm this belief in individuation. Rose thinks that it is the figure of the original author who serves as a symbol of human uniqueness. "What stabilizes the system," he writes, "is the continuing conviction that . . . there are really such beings as original authors, and these gifted creatures will express themselves in discrete works as readily distinguishable as individual human faces" (Rose, *Authors and Owners*, 138–39). This, I respond, is misleading as an account

of individuation because it conflates originality with difference. The principle of expressive diversity on which the law is based implies no normative distinction between original and unoriginal authors, or between geniuses and hacks. The principle presupposes merely that all works will be dissimilar in their expression because all persons think differently. This difference of mind is then confirmed by the fact that some authors have crafted personal styles that are readily discernible to other persons. These writers are symbols of difference. That these authors have also been canonized as original geniuses should not confuse the issue: all persons, whether blessed with superior gifts or not, are thought capable of thinking differently.

53. *Harper and Row, Publishers, Inc., v. Nation Enterprises*, 471 US (1985), 558.

54. See Neil Weinstock Netanel, "Copyright and a Democratic Civil Society," *Yale Law Journal* 106 (1996): 283–388; Netanel, "Asserting Copyright's Democratic Principles in the Global Arena," *Vanderbilt Law Review* 51 (1998): 217–349; and Netanel, *Copyright's Paradox* (New York: Oxford University Press, 2008). For a sympathetic critique, see Christopher S. Yoo, "Copyright and Democracy: A Cautionary Note," *Vanderbilt Law Review* 53 (2000): 1933–64.

55. On a similar aporia between willed invention and natural compulsion in Young's *Conjectures on Original Composition*, see Mario Biagioli, "Nature and the Commons: The Vegetable Roots of Intellectual Property," in *Living Properties: Making Knowledge and Controlling Ownership in the History of Biology*, ed. Jean-Paul Gaudillière, Daniel J. Kevles, and Hans-Jörg Rheinberger (Berlin: Max Planck Institute for the History of Science, 2009), 241–50.

56. Hargrave, *Argument in Defence*, 54. Hargrave's apology appeared as a postscript to the second edition of his pamphlet. Despite protesting that it was possible to demonstrate the practicality of copyright without indulging in "speculative reasoning," Hargrave devoted much of his pamphlet to setting out a Blackstonian labor-theory defense of intellectual property (4).

57. There was some debate at the time whether formal registration was required to establish title to a property. In the Scottish case of *Payne and Cadell v. Anderson and Robertson* (1787), the defendants maintained that they had not knowingly infringed on the plaintiffs' copyright in Frances Burney's *Cecilia* (1782) since the novel had not been entered in the Stationers Company's ledger. The plaintiffs responded by arguing that infringers could not reasonably profess ignorance if their actions in reprinting an exact copy of a work occurred "some time" after it had been originally published elsewhere. The court ruled for the plaintiffs without commenting on the matter. See *Decisions of the Court of Session, from November 1781 to August 1787*, ed. Alexander Law et al. (Edinburgh: Bell and Bradfute, 1792), 524–28.

58. Hargrave, *Argument in Defence*, 37.

59. Hargrave, *Argument in Defence*, 21.

60. *Watson v. Sayer and Bennett* (1776), cited in John Adams, "Intellectual Property in Lord Mansfield's Court Notebooks," *Journal of Legal History* 8 (1987): 22–24. The development of copyright law, more recent scholars have contended, ought to be understood in the context of a larger cultural campaign during the later eighteenth century to deter forgery, plagiarism, and other appropriative practices that threatened to discredit the notion of individuation. See Nick Groom, *The Forger's Shadow: How Forgery Changed the Course of Literature* (London: Picador, 2002); and Tilar J. Mazzeo, *Plagiarism and Literary Property in the Romantic Period* (Philadelphia: University of Pennsylvania Press, 2007). As I suggest below,

individuation provides a rationale for copyright law, but the law does not require individuation to be evident from expression.

61. William Kenrick, *An Address to the Artists and Manufacturers of Great Britain* (London: Domville et al., 1774), 15.

62. Kenrick, *Address to the Artists*, 13.

63. Kenrick, *Address to the Artists*, 65, 68.

64. William Erle, in *Jefferys v. Boosey* (1854), 4 HLC 815, 10 *ER* 702.

65. Erle, in *Jefferys v. Boosey*, 703.

66. James Paterson, *The Liberty of the Press, Speech, and Public Worship* (London: Macmillan, 1880), 253.

67. James Boswell, *The Life of Samuel Johnson, LL.D.*, 2 vols. (London: Charles Dilly, 1791), 2:220–21.

68. Samuel Johnson, *Prefaces, Biographical and Critical, to the Works of the English Poets*, 10 vols. (London: J. Nichols et al., 1779–1781), 7:330.

69. Vicesimus Knox, "On the Means of Reading with the Most Advantage," in his *Essays, Moral and Literary*, 3rd ed., 2 vols. (London: Charles Dilly, 1782), 2:4.

70. Netanel, *Copyright's Paradox*, 38.

71. Rancière, *Politics of Literature*, 13. Citing Wordsworth's rejection of neoclassic poetic diction and Flaubert's application of a single style to divergent subjects, Rancière suggests that their "absolutization of style" served as "the literary formula for the democratic principle of equality" (11). Rancière does not consider how this formula presupposes a notion of individuation, in which it is the distinctiveness of literary authors' styles rather than, say, a common reliance on a serviceable plain style that is taken as confirmatory evidence of democratic equality.

72. T. S. Eliot, "Tradition and the Individual Talent," in his *Selected Essays*, 2nd ed. (New York: Harcourt, Brace and World, 1950), 6.

73. Isaac D'Israeli, "On Style," in his *Miscellanies; or, Literary Recreations* (London: T. Cadell and W. Davies, 1796), 57.

Chapter 3 · What Does Literature Publicize?

1. On the Tory satirists' efforts at subverting the authority of public opinion, see Christian Thorne, "Thumbing Our Nose at the Public Sphere: Satire, the Market, and the Invention of Literature," *PMLA* 116 (2001): 531–44.

2. John Corry, *A Satirical View of London at the Commencement of the Nineteenth Century* (London: G. Kearsley, 1801), 230–31.

3. Robert Hall, *An Apology for the Freedom of the Press, and for General Liberty* (London: G. G. J. and J. Robinson, 1793), 2.

4. Terry Eagleton first broached this idea in 1990 and has also more recently addressed its implications for any attempt at defining literature. Eagleton, *The Ideology of the Aesthetic* (Oxford: Blackwell, 1990); and Eagleton, *The Event of Literature* (New Haven, CT: Yale University Press, 2012).

5. Alexander Meiklejohn, "The First Amendment Is an Absolute," *Supreme Court Review* 1961 (1961): 257.

6. Kantian notions of art's autonomy, argued Sheldon H. Nahmod, have so influenced First Amendment thinking on artistic expression that legal analysts typically treat nonrepresentational art as entirely noncognitive and devoid of political or ideological import. Nahmod,

"Artistic Expression and Aesthetic Theory: The Beautiful, the Sublime and the First Amendment," *Wisconsin Law Review* 1987 (1987): 256–57.

7. *A Letter in Verse, from a Married Man to His Own Wife, Written in a Garden: Together with a Poetical Epistle from an Unfortunate Young Lady at Portsmouth to Her Lover* (London: T. Becket, 1782).

8. The age of consent was set at ten years under the Rape Act of 1576 (18 Eliz. I, c.7). For most victims of sexual assault during the eighteenth century, Anna Clark argued, "the rhetoric of seduction obscured the difference between rape and seduction." Clark, *Women's Silence, Men's Violence: Sexual Assault in England, 1770–1845* (London: Pandora, 1987), 82. Toni Bowers examines how novelists during the period insisted on distinguishing between rape and seduction even as the scenes of seduction they depicted often involved an element of coercion. Bowers, *Force or Fraud: British Seduction Stories and the Problem of Resistance, 1660–1760* (Oxford: Oxford University Press, 2011).

9. Her father was likewise not available to defend her family's honor in court. The law during the eighteenth century may have treated the seduction of girls as a licit act, but it did permit fathers to sue seducers for damages on the ostensible grounds that losing a daughter to a seducer either deprived him of her domestic services, constituted a breach of promise of marriage, or trespassed on his property. For most of the period, Susan Staves explained, these legal fictions "allowed fathers to solace their wounded feelings for the loss of their daughters." But by the end of the century, the law's limits had become readily apparent since, among other reasons, the law could not be applied to "the very class of girls most vulnerable to seduction, girls sent out to service in other people's houses, [who] were not protected because their own fathers had relinquished their entitlement as masters." Staves, "British Seduced Maidens," *Eighteenth-Century Studies* 14 (1980–1981): 109–34.

10. *Monthly Review* 68 (February 1783): 184; *Critical Review* 55 (March 1783): 233.

11. Samuel Johnson, *A Poetical Epistle from an Unfortunate Young Lady at Portsmouth to Her Lover*, 2nd ed. (Shrewsbury, England: P. Sandford, 1783), sig. Av.

12. In a letter to the *Chronicle*, the chairman of the Bridgnorth Club supposed that "as the advertisement of 'The Trusty Guardian, A Poem,' is not continued, it was nothing more than a *Squib*." *Shropshire Chronicle* 12, no. 522 (4 January 1783): 4.

13. The poem would be included in a posthumous collected edition, *The Poetical Works of Mr. Joseph Williams: Some of Which Have Been before Published under the Signature of Clio* (Shrewsbury, England: T. Wood, 1786).

14. Joseph Williams, *The Seducer's Distracted Confession, in a Poetical Rhapsody to a Brother of the Knife* (London: printed for the author, 1782), 9.

15. Katherine Binhammer, *The Seduction Narrative in Britain, 1747–1800* (Cambridge: Cambridge University Press, 2010), 180n17.

16. Williams, *Seducer's Distracted Confession*, 8.

17. *Shropshire Chronicle* 12, no. 522 (4 January 1783): 4.

18. Richard de Courcy, *Seduction; or, The Cause of Injured Innocence Pleaded: A Poem, Addressed to the Author of the Villainy: With a Preface, Stating the Melancholy, but Authentic Facts, on Which the Subject of the Poem Is Founded* (London: Printed and sold by the Booksellers in Town and Country, 1782). Though de Courcy's authorship of the poem appears to have been an open secret in Shropshire, it was not confirmed until after his death in 1803, when the poem was identified as his in lists appended to his obituary, notably the lengthy memorial printed in the *Gentleman's Magazine* 94 (November 1803): 1094–95.

19. *Calumny: Being an Answer to a Pamphlet and Poem, Entitled Seduction* (London: R. Baldwin, 1782), 2.

20. De Courcy, *Seduction*, v.

21. De Courcy, *Seduction*, 16n.

22. De Courcy, *Seduction*, 30n.

23. De Courcy, *Seduction*, v.

24. Among the difficulties that rendered a trial impracticable was the lack of surviving evidence that the colonel had used force to commit the deed. Criminal courts during the eighteenth century considered proof of coercion to be vital to any successful prosecution for rape. See Anthony E. Simpson, "The 'Blackmail Myth' and the Prosecution of Rape and Its Attempt in 18th Century London: The Creation of a Legal Tradition," *Journal of Criminal Law and Criminology* 77 (1986): 132–35.

25. De Courcy, *Seduction*, vi.

26. De Courcy, *Seduction*, vi.

27. For a version of the Wilkesite argument in response to the prosecution of John Horne Tooke, see *An Interesting Address to the Independent Part of the People of England, on Libels, and the Unconstitutional Mode of Prosecution by Information Ex Officio, Practised by the Attorney General* (London: G. Kearsley, 1777).

28. Before then, the truth defense had been inconsistently recognized as justification for civil defamation: it had been affirmed in an important 1618 case (*Lake v. Hatton*), but judges during the early eighteenth century either allowed it only in mitigation of damages or rejected it altogether. By the end of the century, however, it became established as a complete defense. See the cases and opinions cited in Francis Ludlow Holt, *The Law of Libel* (London: J. Butterworth, 1816), 271–73.

29. Richard de Courcy, *The Seducer Convicted on His Own Evidence; or, A Full Confutation of a Pamphlet Intituled "Calumny" by the Author of "Seduction; or, The Cause of Injured Innocence Pleaded: A Poem"* (Shrewsbury, England: T. Wood, 1783), 1.

30. A defense of truth, Holt emphasized in relation to its application in civil cases, "must not be pleaded in loose and general terms, but it must affirm the truth of the very point and substance of the imputed slander" (*Law of Libel*, 273).

31. *Shropshire Chronicle* 11, no. 515 (16 November 1782): 3.

32. De Courcy, *The Seducer Convicted*, 7.

33. *Calumny*, 10.

34. *Calumny*, 4.

35. *Calumny*, 3–4, 28.

36. *Calumny*, 13–14, 23–25.

37. "To the Author of a Late Poem Entitled *Seduction*," *Shropshire Chronicle* 11, no. 516 (23 November 1782): 3.

38. The reverend, a local historian noted, "was most ardently attached" to Wood and his family. Thomas Phillips et al., *The History and Antiquities of Shrewsbury*, 2nd ed., 2 vols. (Shrewsbury, England: C. Hulbert, 1837), 1:234.

39. *Shropshire Chronicle* 11, no. 519 (14 December 1782): 3.

40. *Shropshire Chronicle* 12, no. 522 (4 January 1783): 4.

41. *Shropshire Chronicle* 12, no. 523 (11 January 1783): 3.

42. *Shropshire Chronicle* 12, no. 528 (15 February 1783): 3.

43. De Courcy, *The Seducer Convicted*, 23.

44. *Shropshire Chronicle* 12, no. 525 (25 January 1783): 4.

45. De Courcy, *The Seducer Convicted*, 3–5.

46. De Courcy, *The Seducer Convicted*, 14–15.

47. *Shropshire Chronicle* 12, no. 528 (15 February 1783): 3.

48. Winwood, then a captain, was singled out for his service at the battle of Buxar and the subsequent attack on the fort at Chunar in 1764–1765. See Francis W. Stubbs, *History of the Organization, Equipment, and War Services of the Regiment of Bengal Artillery* (London: Henry S. King, 1877), 1:32–33. An 1848 article in the *Calcutta Review* claimed that Winwood resigned from the East India Company in 1768, after obtaining "an exchange into the infantry, with the rank of Lieutenant-Colonel, finding that a much more lucrative and advantageous line" (9 June 1848: 424). However, Indian marital records indicate that Winwood married his second wife, Elizabeth, on 2 July 1770 in Bengal. See the entry from the India Office Ecclesiastical Returns, Bengal Presidency, at "India, Marriages, 1792–1948," accessible in summary form through http://indiafamily.bl.uk.

49. *Worcester Journal* (14 February 1771), quoted in Huw V. Bowen, "The East India Company and Military Recruitment in Britain," *Historical Research* 59 (1986): 81.

50. *Shropshire Chronicle* 12, no. 522 (4 January 1783): 4.

51. "Kelmscott House, No. 26 Upper Mall," in *Survey of London*, vol. 6: *Hammersmith*, ed. James Bird and Philip Norman (London: London County Council, 1915), 71–73.

52. *European Magazine and London Review* 37 (1800): 174. Winwood's will, now in the Public Record Office (PROB 11/1336/113), was executed on 22 January 1800, very shortly after his wife's death.

53. The record for the copy of de Courcy's *Seduction* owned by the Cambridge University Library includes an unattributed notation indicating that the poem's subject is the "supposed seduction of Miss Fraser by Col. Winwood." The British Library's copy of the poem, which is the version reproduced in Eighteenth-Century Collections Online, contains a reader's notes identifying de Courcy as the author but incorrectly supposing that the events of the poem took place in Salisbury.

54. See "Baptisms in Calcutta: 1767 to 1777," *Bengal Past and Present* 25, pt. 1, ser. no. 49 (January–March 1923): 146n26. This source identifies her maiden name as "Devril," though in the online transcript of the India Office Ecclesiastical Returns, her name appears as "Diveil." "India, Marriages, 1792–1948," accessible in summary form through http://indiafamily.bl.uk.

55. *Scots Magazine and Edinburgh Literary Miscellany* 69 (January 1807): 78.

56. De Courcy, *Seduction*, v.

57. "India Deaths and Burials, 1719–1948," accessible in summary form through http://indiafamily.bl.uk.

58. Information on Ann Fischer's marriage to Gordon, their children, and her inheritance is from the report of *Gordon v. Hope* (1849), 3 De G. & Sm. 351, 64 *ER* 512–13. This was a suit filed on behalf of Ann's daughter, Helena Frances, who alone among the Gordons' children had survived their parents. The Gordons' marriage settlement had stipulated that at their deaths, Ann's fortune should pass to her husband's "children and issue." This wording was the point of contention in the suit since it was not clear whether other descendants of the Gordons, including two grandsons and a widowed daughter-in-law, were entitled to a share in the fortune or would inherit only at Helena Frances's death. Complicating the case was the fact that Helena Frances had been declared of "unsound mind." The suit brought

on her behalf was an unsuccessful attempt to retain control of the family fortune after representatives of the estates of her deceased brothers asserted legal claim. In 1800, the Gordons had their marriage settlement amended to provide the guardian De Veil with income from annuities from the trust. The settlement and other documents relating to *Gordon v. Hope* are now in the Public Record Office (C 104/252).

59. *Scots Magazine* 69 (January 1807): 78.

60. Phillips et al., *History and Antiquities*, 1:236.

61. John H. Langbein, *The Origins of Adversary Criminal Trial* (Oxford: Oxford University Press, 2003), 26.

62. Judges into the nineteenth century continued to exercise considerable discretion in applying some of these rules, notably the hearsay rule. See Langbein, *Origins*, 233–47. Yet well before these rules had become enshrined as a matter of law, judges had been using their discretion more and more to discount testimony that was once seen as centrally relevant. Notable in this regard was the caution that justices of the peace were increasingly encouraged to exercise in applying the legal principle of "evil fame," which authorized them to bind a defendant over merely on the testimony that he was reputed to have engaged in illegal or suspicious activity. Richard Burn, in his widely reprinted 1755 manual for justices, advised skepticism of this testimony since "it may be hard to prove such evil fame," and "in fact it is not always true, for many a good man has been evil spoken of." Burn, *The Justice of the Peace and Parish Officer*, 2 vols. (London: A. Millar, 1755), 2:448. Robert B. Shoemaker examines this and other evidence of the "judicial disapproval of defamation cases" during the period. Shoemaker, "The Decline of Public Insult in London, 1660–1800," *Past and Present* 169 (2000): 118–20.

63. 32 Geo. 3, c. 60 (1792). The act dealt only with the role of juries in criminal cases, but its provisions were soon followed in trials for civil defamation.

64. William Blackstone, *Commentaries on the Laws of England*, 4 vols. (Oxford: Clarendon, 1765–1769), 3:123.

65. *Lord Peterborough v. Williams* (1687), 2 Show. K.B. 505, 89 *ER* 1068. The decision was one of a number of measures intended to discourage this type of litigation, which had grown quite frequent under Charles II. See John C. Lassiter, "Defamation of Peers: The Rise and Decline of the Action for *Scandalum Magnatum*, 1497–1773," *American Journal of Legal History* 22 (1978): 231–35.

66. The last successful action occurred in 1773, when the Earl of Sandwich, the first lord of the admiralty, was awarded £3,000 in damages against the publisher of the *London Evening Post*, which had accused him of selling naval offices. *Earl of Sandwich v. Miller* (1773), Lofft 210, 98 *ER* 614.

67. The peers of the realm, wrote Holt, have chosen "to stand upon the same footing with respect to civil remedies as their fellow subjects" (*Law of Libel*, 165).

68. Norbert Elias, *The Civilizing Process: Sociogenetic and Psychogenetic Investigations*, 2nd ed. (Oxford: Blackwell, 2000). Much has been written about the moral panic over defamation, which provoked a flurry of legal actions, legislation, and royal edicts in the later sixteenth and early seventeenth centuries. See M. Lindsay Kaplan, *The Culture of Slander in Early Modern England* (Cambridge: Cambridge University Press, 1997); Curtis Perry, "'If Proclamation Will Not Serve': The Late Manuscripts of James I and the Culture of Libel," in *Royal Subjects: Essays on the Writing of James VI and I*, ed. Daniel Fischlin and Mark Fortier (Detroit, MI: Wayne State University Press, 2002), 205–32; and the online collection

"Early Stuart Libels: An Edition of Poetry from Manuscript Sources," ed. Alastair Bellany and Andrew McRae, *Early Modern Literary Studies Text Series* 1 (2005), http://purl.oclc.org/emls/texts/libels. In this early modern culture of slander, scurrilous mocking rhymes were among the most prevalent and widely distributed forms of personal libel. See Adam Fox, "Ballads, Libels and Popular Ridicule in Jacobean England," *Past and Present* 145 (1994): 47–83; Laura Gowing, "Women, Status and the Popular Culture of Dishonour," *Transactions of the Royal Historical Society*, 6th ser., 6 (1996): 225–34; and Martin Ingram, "Ridings, Rough Music and Mocking Rhymes in Early Modern England," in *Popular Culture in Seventeenth-Century England*, ed. Barry Reay (London: St. Martin's, 1985), 166–97. Surveying the decline of defamation suits during the first half of the eighteenth century, Ingram concludes that a variety of legal and social changes "gradually made it less necessary or less appropriate to defend aspects of reputation in the courts, [and] less desirable and perhaps less respectable to bring interpersonal quarrels into the legal arena in the guise of slander suits." Martin Ingram, "Law, Litigants and the Construction of 'Honour': Slander Suits in Early Modern England," in *The Moral World of the Law*, ed. Peter R. Cross (Cambridge: Cambridge University Press, 2000), 160.

69. John Powell, in *Regina v. Reade* (1707), Fortescue 98, 98 *ER* 777.

70. James Reynolds, in *Rex v. Curl* (1727), 2 Str. 288, 93 *ER* 851. The attorney general, Sir Philip Yorke, had argued for treating Curll's crime as an offense against public institutions: in being "destructive of morality in general," obscenity threatened "the peace of Government, for government is no more than publick order, which is morality." Chief Justice Robert Raymond, seconded by Justice Reynolds, went further in abstracting the crime, defining it as any act reflecting "on religion, virtue, or morality" in a way that "tends to disturb the civil order of society" (93 *ER* 851). See Simon Stern's important discussion of the ruling's implications: "*Fanny Hill* and the 'Laws of Decency': Investigating Obscenity in the Mid-Eighteenth Century," *Eighteenth-Century Life* (forthcoming). A similar process of abstraction had occurred earlier in relation to the crime of blasphemy. Elliott Visconti has noted how, to bring blasphemy within their jurisdiction, temporal courts during the Restoration period had to change it "from a crime against religion into a crime against public morality," and in doing so they abstracted its harm. Visconti, "The Invention of Criminal Blasphemy: *Rex v. Taylor* (1676)," *Representations* 103 (2008): 43. However, judges continued to regard blasphemy as a libel on institutions, with Christianity being "parcel of the laws of England," rather than as a libel on the public. Matthew Hale, in *Rex v. Taylor* (1676), 1 Ventris 293, 86 *ER* 189.

71. Charles de Secondat, Baron of Montesquieu, *The Spirit of Laws*, 2 vols. (London: J. Nourse and P. Vaillant, 1751), 1:275.

72. For an absolutist defense of free speech based on a principle of individual autonomy, see C. Edwin Baker, "Harm, Liberty, and Free Speech," *Southern California Law Review* 70 (1996–1997): 979–1020.

73. Thomas Hayter, *An Essay on the Liberty of the Press, Chiefly as It Respects Personal Slander* (London: J. Raymond, 1755), 10–11.

74. See Donna T. Andrew, "The Press and Public Apologies in Eighteenth-Century London," in *Law, Crime and English Society, 1660–1830*, ed. Norma Landau (Cambridge: Cambridge University Press, 2002), 208–29; and Clare Brant, "'The Tribunal of the Public': Eighteenth-Century Letters and the Politics of Vindication," in *Gender and Politics in the Age of Letter-Writing*, ed. Caroline Bland and Maire Cross (Aldershot, England: Ashgate, 2003), 15–28.

75. Shoemaker, "Decline of Public Insult," 113.

76. Ellenborough, in *Rex v. Fisher and Others* (1811), 2 Camp. 563, 170 *ER* 1255.

77. De Courcy, *The Seducer Convicted*, 5, 14–15.

78. Defamation, in Baron James Parke's canonical definition, refers to a statement that "is calculated to injure the reputation of another, by exposing him to hatred, contempt, or ridicule." Parke, in *Parmiter v. Coupland* (1840), 6 M. & W. 104, 151 *ER* 342. Parke's definition is derived from the traditional view of libel as any publication that, in William Hawkins's formulation, tends "either to blacken the Memory of one who is dead, or the Reputation of one who is alive, and to expose him to publick Hatred, Contempt or Ridicule." Hawkins, *A Treatise of the Pleas of the Crown*, 2 vols. (London: J. Walthoe, 1716), 1:193.

79. "These categories," R. C. Donnelly suggested, "were not developed on theoretical grounds or pursuant to any general principle but merely as practical expedients for extending jurisdiction." Donnelly, "History of Defamation," *Wisconsin Law Review* 1949 (1949): 111.

80. Robert C. Post, "The Social Foundations of Defamation Law: Reputation and the Constitution," *California Law Review* 74 (1986): 691.

81. Mansfield, in *Thorley v. Kerry* (1812), 4 Taunt. 355, 128 *ER* 371. In the aftermath of the *Thorley* case, parliamentarians tried on several occasions to abolish the distinction yet could not finally agree on, among other things, whether libel should be assimilated to slander or slander to libel. See Paul Mitchell, "The Foundations of Australian Defamation Law," *Sydney Law Review* 28 (2006): 478–84.

82. For historical explanations of the distinction as having resulted from a merging of different legal jurisdictions, see "The Pre-*Thorley v. Kerry* Case Law of the Libel–Slander Distinction [Comments]," *University of Chicago Law Review* 23 (1955–1956): 132–50; Colin Rhys Lovell, "The 'Reception' of Defamation by the Common Law," *Vanderbilt Law Review* 15 (1961–1962): 1051–71.

83. Matthew Hale, in *King v. Lake* (1670), Hardres 470, 145 *ER* 553. The early seventeenth-century civil courts, faced with a deluge of claims, sought to discourage potential complainants by making it a practice to interpret scandalous words as moderately as possible in the defendant's favor. See W. S. Holdsworth, "Defamation in the Sixteenth and Seventeenth Centuries: Part II," *Law Review Quarterly* 40 (1924): 406–8. Paul Mitchell suggests, however, that the practice was not consistently observed. Mitchell, *The Making of the Modern Law of Defamation* (Portland, OR: Hart, 2005), 31–35. My interpretation of *King*'s case follows Mitchell's (4–7). For a counterview of the role of malice in Hale's decision, see J. M. Kaye, "Libel and Slander: Two Torts or One?," *Law Quarterly Review* 91 (1975): 524–39.

84. *Austin v. Culpepper* (1683), 2 Show. K. B. 313, 89 *ER* 960; and *Harman v. Delaney* (1732), 2 Str. 898, 93 *ER* 925–26.

85. Mitchell, *Making of the Modern Law*, 14–24.

86. Henry Gould, in *Villers v. Monsley* (1769), 2 Wils. K. B. 403, 95 *ER* 887.

87. In *Townsend v. Hughes* (1676), 2 Mod. 150, 86 *ER* 994, Chief Justice Francis North informed the jurors that since the words in the case were actionable without proof of damage, they ought "to consider the damage which the party may sustain" when determining a penalty. Had the words been actionable only with proof of special damages, he explained, the penalty would have to be determined on the basis of "such damages as are already sustained." North was doing no more than differentiating presumptive from proven damage, but the suggestion that damage could extend into the future was enough for later commentators to argue that libel differed from slander in its enduring effects. Matthew Bacon, in his

widely consulted redaction of English law, proposed that libel was the worse offense because its effects were "so lasting as to be scarce ever forgiven." Bacon, *A New Abridgment of the Law*, 5 vols. (London: D. Browne, 1736), 4:480. Yet there is nothing in North's opinion to indicate that he was referring to libel: not only was *Townsend v. Hughes* an action for scandalum magnatum, where the rules were unlike those for common defamation, but it involved a case of spoken defamation.

88. John Rayner, *A Digest of the Law concerning Libels* (London: H. Woodfall, 1765), 2. The judges in the case Rayner cited, *Rex v. Bear* (1699), were concerned about the propagation of libels since the case involved the purchase of a copy of a libel.

89. Rayner, *Digest of the Law*, 16.

90. Thomas Paine, *Common Sense* (London: J. Almon, 1776), 29.

91. Benjamin Cardozo, in *Ostrowe v. Lee* (1931), 256 NY 39, 175 NE 506.

92. Joseph Sayer, *The Law of Damages* (London: W. Strahan, 1770), 53.

93. James Adair, *Discussions of the Law of Libels as at Present Received* (London: T. Cadell, 1785), 55–57.

94. De Courcy, *Seduction*, iv.

95. Libel Act 1843, 6 & 7 Vict. c. 96, sec. 6.

96. *The Livery-Man; or, Plain Thoughts on Publick Affairs* (London: James Smith, 1740), 2.

97. European Convention for the Protection of Human Rights and Fundamental Freedoms (drafted 4 November 1950, entered into force 3 September 1953).

98. As several public inquiries in Britain have determined, the primary legal impediment to recognizing a right or tort of privacy has been the difficulty of defining the concept of privacy. The theoretical literature on the subject is accordingly extensive and various. For a sense of this diversity, see Ruth Gavison, "Privacy and the Limits of Law," *Yale Law Journal* 89 (1980): 421–71; Raymond Wacks, *Personal Information: Privacy and the Law* (Oxford: Clarendon, 1989); Robert C. Post, "The Social Foundations of Privacy: Community and Self in the Common Law Tort," *California Law Review* 77 (1989): 957–1010; C. Edwin Baker, "Autonomy and Informational Privacy, or Gossip: The Central Meaning of the First Amendment," *Social Philosophy and Policy* 21 (2004): 215–68; Daniel J. Solove, *Understanding Privacy* (Cambridge, MA: Harvard University Press, 2008); and the compilation of existing international privacy legislation and case law in Richard Clayton and Hugh Tomlinson, eds., *Privacy and Freedom of Expression*, 2nd ed. (Oxford: Oxford University Press, 2010). The UK Defamation Act 2013 is intended to make libel claims more difficult to pursue, introducing a threshold of "serious harm" for such actions and making it more difficult for so-called libel tourists with little connection to England and Wales from initiating defamation claims in those jurisdictions.

99. This was the view taken by John W. Wade in a 1962 article arguing for the colonization of defamation by privacy. "[T]he great majority of defamation actions," he wrote, "can now be brought for invasion of the right of privacy," and by this change "many of the restrictions and limitations of libel and slander can be avoided." Wade, "Defamation and the Right of Privacy," *Vanderbilt Law Review* 15 (1962): 1121. This argument did not meet with broad assent because, among other reasons, subsuming defamation in privacy would necessitate the legal fiction of "calling false statements by a new name." Harry Kalven Jr., "Privacy in Tort Law: Were Warren and Brandeis Wrong?," *Law and Contemporary Problems* 31 (1966): 341.

100. Fernand Braudel, *Civilization and Capitalism, 15th–18th Century*, vol. 1: *The Structure of Everyday Life*, trans. Siân Reynolds (Berkeley: University of California Press, 1992), 308.

101. *Cherrington v. Abney* (1709), 2 Vern. 646, 23 *ER* 1022. David J. Seipp noted this and other early decisions that introduced legal protections for personal privacy. Seipp, "English Judicial Recognition of a Right to Privacy," *Oxford Journal of Legal Studies* 3 (1983): 325–70.

102. Post Office (Revenues) Act (1710), 9 Anne c. 11, sec. 41; *Mitchel v. Reynolds* (1711), 1 P. Wms. 181, 24 *ER* 347.

103. For an early example of a woman attempting to extort payment from a defendant charged with raping her, see *Capt. Leeson's Case: Being an Account of His Tryal for Committing a Rape upon the Body of Mrs. May, a Married Woman of 35 Years of Age; for Which He Receiv'd Sentence of Death, on the 30th of April 1715. but Has Since Obtain'd His Majesty's Most Gracious Reprieve, in Order to a Pardon* (London: J. Roberts, 1715). For other examples involving accusations of rape, see Simpson, "The 'Blackmail Myth,'" 106–28.

104. Father of Candor, *A Letter concerning Libels, Warrants, the Seizure of Papers, and Sureties for the Peace or Behaviour*, 3rd ed. (London: J. Almon, 1765), 59.

105. Charles Pratt, Lord Camden, in *Entick v. Carrington* (1765), 2 Wilson K. B. 275, as reported at greater length in *ST* 19:col. 1066.

106. See John Barrell, *The Spirit of Despotism: Invasions of Privacy in the 1790s* (Oxford: Oxford University Press, 2006).

107. Louis D. Brandeis and Samuel D. Warren, "The Right to Privacy," *Harvard Law Review* 4 (1890): 193–220.

108. Joseph Yates, in *Millar v. Taylor* (1769), 4 Burr. 2303, 98 *ER* 242.

109. *Literary Liberty Considered in a Letter to Henry Sampson Woodfall* (London: J. Johnson, 1774), 15, 23. See also C. D. Piguenit, *An Essay on the Art of News-Paper Defamation* (London: Printed for the author, 1775). Simon Burrows describes the activities of one particularly energetic group of professional defamers. Burrows, *Blackmail, Scandal, and Revolution: London's French Libellistes, 1758–92* (Manchester, England: Manchester University Press, 2006).

110. On the decisions of the European Court of Human Rights rejecting pleas by Princess Caroline of Monaco and other celebrities seeking greater protection for their privacy, see Ansgar Ohly, "Privacy v. Freedom of Expression in the ECHR," *Jurist* (3 April 2012), http://jurist.org/forum/2012/04/ansgar-ohly-privacy-rights.php. Before the mid-eighteenth century, works as varied as saints' lives and Delarivier Manley's secret histories had delved into the private worlds of their subjects to peer into the mysteries of religion or the closed shop of politics. The private in these works was an avenue into the hidden and forbidden, though not necessarily a realm of experience that was either worth studying in itself or separate from other dimensions of spiritual and worldly existence.

111. Tom Tickle, "To Dr. Goldsmith," *London Packet* (24 March 1773), reprinted in Goldsmith, *The Miscellaneous Works of Oliver Goldsmith*, 5th ed., 5 vols. (London: J. Johnson, 1812), 1:86–87.

112. Oliver Goldsmith, "To the Public," *Daily Advertiser* (31 March 1773), reprinted in his *Miscellaneous Works*, 1:89–90.

113. James Boswell, *The Life of Samuel Johnson, LL.D.*, 2 vols. (London: Charles Dilly, 1791), 1:390–91.

114. Samuel Johnson, *Rambler*, no. 60 (13 October 1750).

115. Boswell, *Life of Johnson*, 2:51.

116. Corry, *Satirical View*, 230.

117. Edward Young, *Conjectures on Original Composition* (London: A. Millar and R. and J. Dodsley, 1759), 6.

118. On how the period's novelists negotiated the competing claims of privacy and sensibility, see Patricia Meyer Spacks, *Privacy: Concealing the Eighteenth-Century Self* (Chicago, IL: University of Chicago Press, 2003).

119. Lady Sarah Pennington, *An Unfortunate Mother's Advice to Her Absent Daughters*, 5th ed. (London: J. Walter, 1770), 68–69. Pennington's comment appeared in the editions of her guidebook that appeared after the publication of Goldsmith's novel.

120. Samuel Richardson, letter to William Warburton, 19 April 1748, in *Selected Letters of Samuel Richardson*, ed. John Carroll (Oxford: Clarendon, 1964), 85.

121. Rayner, *Digest of the Law*, 8.

122. The disclaimer, Judge Posner writes, "is so often false that it is no longer widely believed, if it ever was." Richard A. Posner, *Law and Literature*, 3rd ed. (Cambridge, MA: Harvard University Press, 2009), 516.

123. *Critical Review* 55 (March 1783): 233.

124. *Finlay v. Ruddiman* (1763), Mor. 3436, as reported by Henry Home, Lord Kames, in *Select Decisions of the Court of Session from the Year 1752 to the Year 1768*, ed. H. Home (Edinburgh: J. Bell, 1780), 271. The case was conjoined with a second, *Finlay v. Neill*, for which depositions were introduced to demonstrate that word of Finlay assaulting women "was common and general in and about Glasgow several weeks before any thing like it was inserted in any News-paper." As reported in George Pringle, *Memorial for Patrick Neill, Printer in the College of Edinburgh, Defender against John Finlay, Merchant-Shoemaker in Glasgow, Pursuer* (Edinburgh, 1762), 3. Though both cases were tried under Scottish law, whose rules for defamation were more closely derived from Roman law than the rules observed in English courts, the defenders in each referred to English cases. These mentions of English examples, John Blackie notes, "are the first direct references to English case law in a Scots case in this area." Blackie, "Defamation," in *A History of Private Law in Scotland*, vol. 2: *Obligations*, ed. Kenneth Reid and Reinhard Zimmermann (Oxford: Oxford University Press, 2000), 658.

125. See Trevor Ross, "Literature," in *The Oxford Encyclopedia of British Literature*, 5 vols., ed. David Scott Kastan (Oxford: Oxford University Press, 2006), 3:314–19.

Chapter 4 · How Criticism Became Privileged Speech

1. William Murray, Lord Mansfield, in *Rex v. Skinner* (1772), Lofft 55, 98 *ER* 530.

2. The UK Defamation Act 2013 (c. 26) formally replaced the common-law principle of fair comment with a quartet of possible defenses: a statement cannot be held to defame if it is substantially true, expresses an honest opinion, deals with a matter of public interest, or has been peer reviewed for publication in a scientific or academic journal. Other Anglo-American courts continue to uphold the fair comment defense, with the Canadian Supreme Court notably diverging from the direction taken by British lawmakers in its 2008 ruling that fair comment need not include an element of honest belief. See the decision in *WIC Radio, Ltd., v. Simpson* (2 SCC 40).

3. To be precise, the fair comment defense is not a privilege but a right shared by all citizens. But since its scope is limited, it is considered a qualified defense and not an absolute right. In addition, since the principle was originally intended to enable critics to correct error

and punish folly without fear of legal reprisal, early legal theorists considered it a type of qualified privilege, that is, a special immunity from defamation claims for acts committed in the performance of a legal or moral duty. See Thomas Starkie, *A Treatise on the Law of Slander, Libel, Scandalum Magnatum and False Rumours* (London: W. Clarke, 1813), 266–73.

4. Though the case is regularly cited as having established the fair comment defense, it has been the subject of little scholarly analysis or commentary. See, however, Paul Mitchell, *The Making of the Modern Law of Defamation* (Portland, OR: Hart, 2005), 170–74. For an argument that anticipated mine about how the fair comment defense paradoxically allows for freedom of opinion while also enforcing norms of discursive civility, see Robert Post, "The Constitutional Concept of Public Discourse: Outrageous Opinion, Democratic Deliberation, and *Hustler Magazine v. Falwell*," *Harvard Law Review* 103 (1989–1990): 603–86.

5. P. Dixon Hardy, review of John Barrow, *A Tour 'round Ireland* (1836), *Dublin Penny Journal* 4, no. 203 (21 May 1836): 369.

6. John Carr, *The Stranger in Ireland; or, A Tour in the Southern and Western Parts of That Country in the Year 1805* (London: R. Phillips, 1806), v. For an analysis of the assimilationist tenor of Carr's *Tour*, see Glenn Hooper, "*Stranger in Ireland*: The Problematics of the Post-Union Travelogue," *Mosaic* 28.1 (1995): 40–46.

7. Review of John Carr, *A Tour through Holland along the Right and Left Banks of the Rhine, to the South of Germany* (1807), in *Edinburgh Review* 10.20 (July 1807): 272.

8. Richard Phillips, in *Carr v. Hood* (1808), as reported in *Liberty of the Press! Sir John Carr against Hood and Sharpe* (London: Vernor, Hood and Sharpe, 1808), 11, 14. This report of the trial, published by the defendants following their victory in court, provided a fuller transcript of the proceedings than the summary provided in the official report, *Carr v. Hood* (1808), 1 Camp. 355n, 170 *ER* 983–85.

9. Edward Dubois, *My Pocket Book; or, Hints for "A Ryghte Merrie and Conceitede" Tour*, 2nd ed. (London: Vernor, Hood and Sharpe, 1808), 16.

10. Carr, *Stranger in Ireland*, 176, quoted in Dubois, *My Pocket Book*, 122. Dubois omitted the phrase "in the full vigour of life and health."

11. Review of John Carr, *A Tour through Holland*, in *British Critic* 32 (July 1808): 59–60.

12. *Old Nick's Pocket-Book; or, Hints for a "Ryghte Pedantique and Mangleinge" Publication to Be Called "My Pocket Book"* (London: Sherwood, Neeley and Jones, 1808).

13. John Carr, "Explanatory Address to the Public," preface to *Caledonian Sketches; or, A Tour of Scotland* (London: Matthews and Leigh, 1809), vi. This address was Carr's only public statement on the trial, whose outcome, he believed, might have been different had the arguments dealt only with the parody's caricatures.

14. Carr's final publication, a tour of Spain, appeared in 1811. He died in 1832 at the age of sixty. See his obituary in the *Gentleman's Magazine* 152 (August 1832): 182–83.

15. See Tamara Hunt, *Defining John Bull: Political Caricature and National Identity in Late Georgian England* (Aldershot, England: Ashgate, 2003), 6.

16. Thomas Erskine, in *Rex v. Fores* (1800), as reported in *The Times* (9 May 1800), 3. Erskine's case against Fores foundered for lack of cause.

17. Lloyd Kenyon, in *The Times* (9 May 1800), 3.

18. Carr, "Explanatory Address," ix.

19. Carr, *Stranger in Ireland*, 186.

20. Carr, *Caledonian Sketches*, vi.

21. Sir Walter Scott, review of John Carr's *Caledonian Sketches*, in *Quarterly Review* 1 (February 1809): 179.
22. William Garrow, in *Carr v. Hood* (1808), as reported in *Liberty of the Press!*, 5–6.
23. *Liberty of the Press!*, 12–13, 17–19.
24. *Liberty of the Press!*, 3, 26.
25. Carr, *Caledonian Sketches*, iv.
26. *Liberty of the Press!*, 9–10.
27. Edward Law, Lord Ellenborough, in *Tabart v. Tipper* (1808), 1 Camp. 350, 170 *ER* 982.
28. Kenyon, in *Dibdin v. Swan and Bostock* (1793), 1 Esp. 28, 170 *ER* 270.
29. Writing in 1794, the Scottish clergyman Archibald Bruce suggested that the "liberty claimed and allowed in the republic of Letters, in matters of criticism, which extends indiscriminately to good and bad publications, may be safely allowed also in political subjects, to a considerable degree." Bruce, *Reflections on Freedom of Writing and the Impropriety of Attempting to Suppress It by Penal Laws* (Edinburgh, 1794), 12.
30. William Cobbett, in *Political Register* 14 (10 September 1808): 399.
31. See Alice Parker, "Tobias Smollett and the Law," *Studies in Philology* 39 (1942): 545–58; and Lewis M. Knapp and John Chapone, "*Rex versus Smollett*: More Data on the Smollett-Knowles Libel Case," *Modern Philology* 41 (1944): 221–27.
32. The phrase "chilling effect," as a term for the preemptive deterrence of free speech, is a relatively recent usage. It appears to have been an adaptation of similar environmental tropes first used in the 1950s to characterize the inhibiting effects of overly broad statutes. Paul A. Freund used "chill" and "cloud" to describe these effects in his influential essay "The Supreme Court and Civil Liberties," *Vanderbilt Law Review* 4 (1950–1951): 540. The sense of a chilling effect on speech, of course, has been familiar to authors since antiquity, being implicit in any act of self-censorship, though few before Milton believed that preemptive deterrence did more harm than good. See the essays collected in Han Baltussen and Peter J. Davis, eds., *The Art of Veiled Speech: Self-Censorship from Aristophanes to Hobbes* (Philadelphia: University of Pennsylvania Press, 2015).
33. William Blackstone, *Commentaries on the Laws of England*, 4 vols. (Oxford: Clarendon, 1765–1769), 4:152.
34. 32 Geo. 3, c. 60 (1792). The act applied only to criminal proceedings, but its rules soon came to be followed in civil cases like Carr's.
35. *Liberty of the Press!*, 28.
36. *Liberty of the Press!*, 28.
37. *Liberty of the Press!*, 27.
38. *Liberty of the Press!*, 9.
39. William Erle, in *Turnbull v. Bird* (1861), 2 F. & F. 508, 175 *ER* 1170. In a few earlier cases, judges allowed that writers could lawfully respond to statements made by jurists and politicians, provided their responses were respectful and constructive. In a case decided in the same year as Carr's, Justice Nash Grose allowed that a newspaper editor could "with decency and candour" comment on "the propriety of the verdict of a jury, or the decisions of a Judge," but the jury agreed with the judge's assessment that the offending passages in question "contained no reasoning or discussion, but only declamation and invective, and were written not with a view to elucidate the truth." *Rex v. White* (1808), 1 Camp. 359, 170 *ER* 985–86.
40. On the narrow scope of the fair comment defense, see Mitchell, *Making of the Modern Law*, 176–77.

41. In *Dunne v. Anderson* (1825), 3 Bing. 88, 130 *ER* 447–52, the Court of Exchequer ruled that a journalist who criticized a surgeon's petition against quacks was not entitled to the fair comment defense on the grounds that submitting a petition to Parliament did not constitute publication of the document.

42. *Liberty of the Press!*, 9–10.

43. Ellenborough, in *Rex v. Cobbett* (1804), *ST* 29:col. 49.

44. Cobbett, "Summary of Politics: Sir Richard Phillips," *Political Register* 14 (10 September 1808): 398.

45. Cobbett, "To the Right Honourable Lord Ellenborough, Chief Justice of the Court of King's Bench," *Political Register* 14 (17 September 1808): 430.

46. Cobbett, "Summary of Politics: Libel Law," *Political Register* 14 (30 July 1808): 168. As I note in chapter 5, the Libel Act included a proviso, added as a compromise amendment to Fox's bill, that recognized the duty of judges to advise juries on the law. This proviso would subsequently be interpreted by judges as granting them the authority to give an opinion on the criminality of an alleged libel, an interpretation that they quickly extended to cases of private defamation.

47. Cobbett, *Political Register* 14 (30 July 1808): 169.

48. *Liberty of the Press!*, 28–29.

49. Cobbett, *Political Register* 14 (17 September 1808): 425.

50. Cobbett, *Political Register* 14: 424.

51. Cobbett, *Political Register* 14: 424.

52. *Liberty of the Press!*, 29.

53. *Liberty of the Press!*, 10.

54. *Liberty of the Press!*, 27.

55. Cobbett, *Political Register* 14: 421–22.

56. Cobbett, *Political Register* 14: 422.

57. *Liberty of the Press!*, 28–29.

58. Henry Fielding, *The History of Tom Jones, a Foundling*, 4 vols. (London: A. Millar, 1749), 3:63.

59. I consider how critics during the early modern period imagined themselves reflected in communities of learned readers in Trevor Ross, *The Making of the English Literary Canon: From the Middle Ages to the Late Eighteenth Century* (Montreal: McGill-Queen's University Press, 1998), 64–84.

60. Samuel Johnson, *Prefaces, Biographical and Critical, to the Works of the English Poets*, 10 vols. (London: J. Nichols et al., 1779–1781), 10:35; Michael Warner, *The Letters of the Republic: Publication and the Public Sphere in Eighteenth-Century America* (Cambridge, MA: Harvard University Press, 1990), 42.

61. Jean de La Crose, "To the Reader," *The Works of the Learned; or, An Historical Account and Impartial Judgment of Books Newly Printed, Both Foreign and Domestick* 1 (August 1691). La Crose's short-lived journal stood out from other early review periodicals in providing more than digests of recent publications. As Patricia Gael notes, the journal's assessments of books anticipated later reviewing practices in offering lively synopses and sometimes sharp evaluative commentaries. Gael, "The Origins of the Book Review in England, 1663–1749," *Library*, 7th ser., 13 (2012): 77.

62. George Winter, *The Farmer Convinced; or, The Reviewers of the "Monthly Review" Anatomized* (London: E. Newberry, 1788), 4.

63. Jürgen Habermas, *The Structural Transformation of the Public Sphere: An Inquiry into a Category of Bourgeois Society*, trans. T. Burger and F. Lawrence (Cambridge, MA: MIT Press, 1989), 29. A half century before Habermas first wrote his account, the legal historian Van Vechten Veeder had come to much the same conclusion: "freedom of literary criticism, being the first subject of public interest upon which the right to comment was formulated upon rational grounds, has exercised a marked influence on the gradual recognition of similar freedom of discussion in political affairs." Veeder, "Freedom of Public Discussion," *Harvard Law Review* 23 (1909–1910): 415.

64. *Liberty of the Press!*, 2.

65. David Hume, "Of the Standard of Taste," in his *Four Dissertations* (London: A. Millar, 1757), 203–40.

66. *Liberty of the Press!*, 27.

67. Carr, *Stranger in Ireland*, v.

68. *Liberty of the Press!*, 6.

69. John Carr, *The Stranger in France; or, A Tour from Devonshire to Paris* (London: J. Johnson, 1803), sig. A2r.

70. Carr, *Stranger in Ireland*, 325.

71. John Carr, *A Northern Summer; or, Travels around the Baltic, through Denmark, Sweden, Russia, Prussia, and Part of Germany, in the Year 1804* (London: R. Philips, 1805), 2.

72. Carr, *Stranger in France*, 252.

73. *Liberty of the Press!*, 2.

74. Ellenborough, in *Nightingale v. Stockdale* (11 March 1809), as reported in *Universal Magazine*, n.s., 9 (1809): 415–18. There is no official report of the trial.

75. Veeder, "Freedom of Public Discussion," 414–15.

76. Erle, in *Turnbull v. Bird* (1861), 175 *ER* 1172.

77. Matthew Arnold, "The Function of Criticism at the Present Time," in his *Essays in Criticism* (London: Macmillan, 1865), 34.

78. Charles Cooper Townsend, "The English Law Governing the Right of Criticism and Fair Comment," *American Law Register*, 2nd ser., 30 (August 1891): 530.

Chapter 5 · Literature and the Freedom of Mind

1. An Act to Remove Doubts respecting the Functions of Juries in Cases of Libel, 32 Geo. 3, c. 60 (1792). The act was repealed and the offense of seditious libel formally abolished only in January 2010, when revisions to the criminal law under the Coroners and Justice Act, c. 25 (2009) took effect.

2. Immanuel Kant, *Critique of the Power of Judgment*, ed. Paul Guyer, trans. Paul Guyer and Eric Matthews (Cambridge: Cambridge University Press, 2000), 203–5. All quotations from this work that follow are from these pages.

3. The phrase is attributed to Plato by Plutarch in his "Life of Pericles," in *Plutarch's Lives*, 6 vols., trans. John Langhorne and William Langhorne (London: Edward and Charles Dilly, 1770), 2:24.

4. Simone Chambers, "Rhetoric and the Public Sphere: Has Deliberative Democracy Abandoned Mass Democracy?," *Political Theory* 37 (2009): 328.

5. On the history of the change, see John H. Langbein, *The Origins of Adversary Criminal Trial* (Oxford: Oxford University Press, 2003).

6. The mechanisms of Pittite repression and their consequences for literary production have been the subject of several important studies, among them John Barrell's formidable *Imagining the King's Death: Figurative Treason, Fantasies of Regicide, 1793–1796* (Oxford: Oxford University Press, 2000); Barrell, *The Spirit of Despotism: Invasions of Privacy in the 1790s* (Oxford: Oxford University Press, 2006); Kenneth R. Johnston, *Unusual Suspects: Pitt's Reign of Alarm and the Lost Generation of the 1790s* (Oxford: Oxford University Press, 2013); and Paul Keen, *The Crisis of Literature in the 1790s: Print Culture and the Public Sphere* (Cambridge: Cambridge University Press, 1999). I have drawn on these and other studies, though my focus in this chapter, as throughout this book, diverges from theirs in that I am less concerned with the policing of radical speech than with how changes in assumptions about the organization of public discourse necessitated a revaluation of literature's public role.

7. James Boyd White, *Living Speech: Resisting the Empire of Force* (Princeton, NJ: Princeton University Press, 2006).

8. On the law's early development, see Roger B. Manning, "The Origins of the Doctrine of Sedition," *Albion* 12 (1980): 99–121; and Philip Hamburger, "The Development of the Law of Seditious Libel and the Control of the Press," *Stanford Law Review* 37 (1984–1985): 661–769.

9. Sir Edward Coke, in *Case de Libellis Famosis; or, Of Scandalous Libels* (1605), 3 Jac. 1, 77 *ER* 251. Though the word "seditious" had for decades been used in Tudor legal reports to describe libels or slanders on public officials, "seditious libel" was not recognized as a separate category of criminal defamation. Coke himself evidently believed that the crime was covered under the statutes of scandalum magnatum. Yet in introducing provisions that were not part of those statutes, including the rule that an offending statement could be either true or false, Coke's account of the law would subsequently be considered to have formally defined the libeling of public officials as a distinct offense.

10. Jean Bodin, *The Six Bookes of a Common-Weale* (1576), trans. Richard Knolles (London: Impensis G. Bishop, 1606), 543–44.

11. Coke, in *Libellis Famosis*, 77 *ER* 251.

12. Sir Edward Littleton, defending Sir John Selden from a charge of "stirring up sedition," contended that the concept of sedition had never been defined by statute despite having become "mingled with some other offences." *Rex v. Stroud, Long, Selden, and Others* (1629), *ST* 3:cols. 267–68.

13. At Richard Chambers's 1628 trial, the Star Chamber judges rejected Chambers's defense that the offending words he had uttered at an earlier trial "were only spoken in the presence of the privy-council, and not spoken abroad, to stir up any discord among the people." *Rex v. Chambers* (1628), *ST* 3:col. 374.

14. The right of free speech was guaranteed to members of both houses only in 1689, though parliamentarians had asserted a privilege from prosecution since the early sixteenth century. See David Colclough, *Freedom of Speech in Early Stuart England* (Cambridge: Cambridge University Press, 2005), 120–95.

15. Coke, in *Libellis Famosis*, 77 *ER* 251.

16. Bodin, *Six Bookes*, 543.

17. "An Aduertisement Towching Seditious Wrytings," Public Record Office, State Papers, 12/235/81, folios 178r–91r, reproduced in Kenneth Cardwell, "An Overlooked Tract by Francis Bacon," *Huntington Library Quarterly* 65 (2002): 431–33. Cardwell attributes the tract

to Bacon and dates it to 1594 on the basis of this attribution, but concedes that there is little external evidence of Bacon's authorship.

18. Sir Nicholas Bacon, oration in the Star Chamber, 29 December 1567, Public Record Office, State Papers, 12/44/52, quoted in D. M. Loades, "The Theory and Practice of Censorship in Sixteenth-Century England," *Transactions of the Royal Historical Society*, 5th ser., 24 (1974): 142.

19. Robert Clarke, in *Regina v. Udall* (1590), *ST* 1:col. 1289. Udall had been indicted for the felony of having written a libel on the queen. The statute he had been charged under (23 Eliz. c. 3), originally aimed at suppressing Roman Catholic attacks on the government, was one of several antecedents to the law of seditious libel.

20. Francis Lord Cottington, in *Rex v. Prynne* (1633), *ST* 3:col. 574. Since proceedings in the Star Chamber involved neither indictment nor trial by jury, there were never concerns raised about the possible divisive effects of seditious libels within the courtroom. The judges at Prynne's trial were nonetheless quick to declare how libels made them feel. The chief justice, Thomas Richardson, averred that it "maketh my heart to swell, and my blood in my veins to boil, so cold as I am, to see this or any thing attempted which may endanger my gracious sovereign" (*ST* 3:col. 579).

21. See *Regina v. Throckmorton* (1554), *ST* 1:cols. 869–902; and *Rex v. Pyne* (1628), *ST* 3:cols. 359–68. Sir Nicholas Throckmorton's trial, as well as John Lilliburne's for treason in 1649, would be celebrated by reformers during the eighteenth century as affirming the traditional right of juries to rule on matters of law as well as fact. In both cases, though, the defendants did not propose that jurors make new law but rather that they uphold the immemorial authority of the original statute in contravention of the judges' illegitimate interpretation of the law. See Annabel Patterson, "'For Words Only': From Treason Trial to Liberal Legend in Early Modern England," *Yale Journal of Law and the Humanities* 5 (1993): 389–416. On Hugh Pyne's trial, see David Cressy, *Dangerous Talk: Scandalous, Seditious, and Treasonable Speech in Pre-Modern England* (Oxford: Oxford University Press, 2010), 115–31. In the 1619 case of an Essex barrister named John Williams, indicted for treason after he had prophesized the date of the king's death, the accused claimed that he had not committed an overt act. The court rejected Williams's argument, insisting that putting thoughts down on paper amounted to treason "for *scribere est agere*" (*ST* 2:col. 1088).

22. Clarke, in *Regina v. Udall* (1590), *ST* 1:col. 1289. The judge expressed no concern over the possibility of the jury being influenced by Udall's work, though, interestingly, Udall himself felt he would not get a fair hearing unless he were "tried by an inquest of learned men" (*ST* 1:col. 1277).

23. "Most so-called seditious libel trials before 1696," Hamburger noted, "were not for the common law offense of libel but rather for violations of specific licensing statutes or judicial declarations of the royal prerogative to license printed books" ("Development of the Law," 674).

24. Robert Hyde, in *Rex v. Keach* (1665), *ST* 6:col. 702. Benjamin Keach was accused of having written "a venomous and seditious book" entitled *The Child's Instructor* (1664), though he was tried for the offense of violating the Act of Uniformity (1558).

25. *Rex v. Bushell* (1670), *ST* 6:cols. 999–1026. Kevin Crosby has noted that while the case had little impact on courtroom practice over the short term, it did help to accelerate a process whereby the jury trial was "reimagined as something grounded in the individual conscientious judgment of each juror, independent of the wishes either of the sovereign or

of the judge." Crosby, "*Bushell's Case* and the Juror's Soul," *Journal of Legal History* 33 (2012): 289.

26. John Hawles, *The English-Mans Right: A Dialogue between a Barrister at Law and a Jury-Man* (London: Richard Janeway, 1680). Though Hawles's pamphlet was not initially cited in arguments over libel prosecutions, it was regularly reprinted from the 1730s onward, often in response to developments in the libel debate. For a discussion, see J. R. Pole, "'A Quest of Thoughts': Representation and Moral Agency in the Early Anglo-American Jury," in *"The Dearest Birth Right of the People of England": The Jury in the History of the Common Law*, ed. John W. Cairns and Grant McLeod (Portland, OR: Hart, 2002), 118–20.

27. Hawles was apparently thinking of a recent trial for seditious libel, *Rex v. Harris* (1679), when he suggested that juries had a right to question the legal basis of an action. The bookseller Benjamin Harris, tried for publishing a pro-exclusionist tract, was initially found by the jury to be "guilty of selling the Book." Rejecting this special verdict, Chief Justice William Scroggs told the jurors that it "was not their business" to revise the charge and pressed them into returning a general verdict of "barely Guilty, or not Guilty." Benjamin Harris, *A Short, but Just Account of the Tryal of Benjamin Harris* (London, 1679), 7. On the significance of the Harris case for Hawles's argument, see Simon Stern, "Between Local Knowledge and National Politics: Debating Rationales for Jury Nullification after *Bushell's Case*," *Yale Law Journal* 111 (2001–2002): 1830–33.

28. Robert Wright, in *Case of the Seven Bishops* (1688), *ST* 12:cols. 279, 426.

29. William Gibson suggests that the chief justice "made a grave error" in permitting the jury to decide on both the facts of publication and the petition's seditiousness. Gibson, *James II and the Trial of the Seven Bishops* (New York: Palgrave Macmillan, 2009), 131. Yet the report in *ST*, which followed the text of a 1689 transcript of the trial, nowhere indicated that the judge gave the jury such permission. On the contrary, the judge was reported to have informed the jury that a work's libelousness was "a point of law" on which he and his fellow judges were to give their opinions. Justice Richard Holloway, however, did tell the jury that "it is left to you" to say whether the judges had acted with "ill intent" (*ST* 12:col. 426).

30. Holloway, in *ST* 12:col. 426. Hamburger noted that in earlier libel trials, defendants were rarely successful at pleading absence of knowledge or malice ("Development of the Law," 708).

31. Among other procedural changes introduced by the Treason Trials Act of 1696 (7–8 Will. 3, c. 3), the accused were accorded the right to be represented by defense counsel.

32. See Hamburger, "Development of the Law," 726–36.

33. Hamburger ("Development of the Law," 754–56) suggested that eighteenth-century judges, in particular Lord Mansfield, based their interpretation of the sedition law almost exclusively on the rulings of Chief Justice Holt from the period 1696–1706, disregarding entirely the outcome of the *Seven Bishops Case*. Thomas Andrew Green noted, however, that "Holt did not place greater restrictions on the jury's fact-finding responsibilities than the major Restoration critics of seditious libel assumed were already part of the law." Green, *Verdict according to Conscience: Perspectives on the English Criminal Trial Jury, 1200–1800* (Chicago, IL: University of Chicago Press, 1985), 321n111.

34. *Rex v. Bear* (1699), Carthew 408, 90 *ER* 836. The statement was made in a motion for arrest of judgment, though it was subsequently affirmed by the court.

35. In both *Rex v. Paine* (1696), 5 Mod. 163, 87 *ER* 584, and the original 1696 trial at nisi prius that had occasioned the motion for arrest of judgment in *Rex v. Bear* (Carthew 408,

90 *ER* 836), the jury found the defendants not guilty of publishing the copies they had made of alleged libels. In *Regina v. Drake* (1706), 11 Mod. 78, 88 *ER* 905, the jury ruled for the defendant after it was pointed out that the word "not" in the original publication had been mistakenly transcribed as "nor."

36. *Regina v. Browne* (1706), 11 Mod. 86, 88 *ER* 911.

37. *Regina v. Hurt* (10 June 1713), as reported in William Hawkins, *A Treatise of the Pleas of the Crown*, 2 vols. (London: J. Walthoe, 1716–1721), 1:194. There is no official report of the trial. On the circumstances of the case, see P. B. J. Hyland, "Liberty and Libel: Government and the Press during the Succession Crisis in Britain, 1712–1716," *English Historical Review* 101 (1986): 866–68. Since there was no jury in Star Chamber cases, the court interpreted the import of innuendos. Once the common-law courts assumed jurisdiction over seditious libel, they followed the practice in civil defamation cases of according juries the right to interpret innuendos.

38. *Rex v. Francklin* (3 November 1729), as reported in Abel Boyer, *Political State of Great Britain* 38 (1729): 591. There is no official report of the trial. Francklin's acquittal provoked the ministry's supporters at the *Daily Courant* to question the jury's motives in returning a verdict that went "against full Evidence and common Sense" (29 November 1731), reprinted in *Gentleman's Magazine* 1 (1731): 491.

39. William Pulteney, *The Honest Jury; or, Caleb Triumphant* (London, 1729), 4. Much later, in his final contribution to the libel debate, Mansfield would cite these lines from Pulteney's poem and an accompanying couplet ("For *twelve honest Men* have decided the Cause / And were Judges of *Fact*, though not Judges of *Laws*") as confirming existing limits on the jury's role. Mansfield, in *Rex v. Shipley* (Case of the Dean of St. Asaph) (1783–1784), *ST* 21:col. 1037. Mansfield, it seemed, forgot that the poem included several ironic variations on the couplet, with the last and more earnest variation altering its original meaning completely: "If *twelve honest Men* were to judge in this Cause, / One *good Verdict* more might secure all our *LAWS*" (Pulteney, *Honest Jury*, 6).

40. One of the few who did was Daniel Defoe, who felt that the law accorded judges and prosecutors too much discretionary power. Under existing procedures, he wrote, "'tis in the Breast of the Courts of Justice to make any Book a Scandalous and Seditious Libel, and nothing is more ridiculous than the Letter of an Indictment in such Cases, and the Jury being accounted only Judges of Evidence, Judges of Fact, and not of the Nature of it, the Judges are thereby unlimited." Defoe, *An Essay on the Regulation of the Press* (London, 1704), 14.

41. Disguising their victims' names with ellipses, Bricker explains, did not enable satirists to get away with defamation from any legal standpoint. Rather, it afforded them a kind of ethical deniability: they could target individuals without appearing to be indecently indulging in direct personal attacks. Andrew Benjamin Bricker, "Libel and Satire: The Problem with Naming," *ELH* 81 (2014): 889–921. Bricker's argument about satiric naming practices during the early eighteenth century is true as far as it goes. But it ignores what I describe in this chapter and in chapter 4 as a broader change in attitudes about the force of words. Satirists may have been emboldened to risk defamation claims because the harmfulness of this force was becoming so doubtful and contingent on circumstance that mere insults no longer seemed actionable. Certainly, satirists and caricaturists later in the century had no scruples about identifying their targets.

42. Paul Mitchell notes that this practice of interpreting slanders *in mitiori sensu* (in the milder sense) was never observed consistently enough to become established as a

rule. Mitchell, *The Making of the Modern Law of Defamation* (Portland, OR: Hart, 2005), 31–35.

43. *Rex v. Clark* (1728), 1 Barn. 305, 94 *ER* 207. This standard had been followed in actions for defamation since at least the end of the seventeenth century. See Mitchell, *Making of the Modern Law*, 35–37.

44. Matthew Tindal, *Reasons against Restraining the Press* (London, 1704), 5.

45. John Trenchard, "Cato's Letters," no. 100, *London Journal* (27 October 1722).

46. John Holt, in *Regina v. Tutchin* (1704), *ST* 14:col. 1128. Once the crime of seditious libel was broadened to include any misrepresentation of government, the danger it posed was abstracted. Formal indictments described the offense in vague redundancies, like those charging Francklin at his 1731 trial with "seditiously contriving and intending to disturb and disquiet the happy state of the public peace and tranquility of this kingdom." *Rex v. Francklin* (1731), *ST* 17:col. 628. The pathological effects of publications occupied more of the court's attention in trials for related crimes. At John Matthews's 1719 trial for high treason, the Jacobite pamphlet he was charged with printing, *Vox populi, vox Dei*, was said to be so incendiary that a "more dangerous attempt to alarm and rouse up the people against the government, cannot well be." Nicholas Lechmere, in *Rex v. Matthews* (1719), *ST* 15:col. 1356. As I noted earlier, obscenity became prosecutable as a form of libel following Edmund Curll's 1727 conviction for publishing a translation of *Venus in the Cloister*, which one judge condemned as "an offence against the peace, in tending to weaken the bonds of civil society, virtue, and morality." Edmund Probyn, in *Rex v. Curl* (1727), 2 Str. 288, 93 *ER* 851. The effects of blasphemous libel, by comparison, were described in more general terms. See above on how seventeenth-century judges abstracted the harm from the crime in order to secularize its prosecution as a public order offense. Similarly, the Blasphemy Act of 1697 (9 Will. 3, c. 35) declared the offense "distructive to the Peace and Welfare of this Kingdom." By the time Thomas Woolston was tried for the crime in 1728, the presiding judge believed it necessary to point out that in matters of religious doctrine, the court would not normally "meddle with any differences in opinion" and would "interpose only where the very root of Christianity it self is struck at." James Reynolds, in *Rex v. Woolston* (1728), Fitz.-G. 64, 94 *ER* 656. Interestingly, it was by then possible for the Dissenting theologian Nathaniel Lardner to maintain that the effects of Woolston's irreverent style could be resisted: "The proper punishment of a low, mean, indecent, scurrilous way of writing, seems to be neglect, contempt, scorn, and general indignation." Lardner, letter to Edward Waddington, 22 November 1729, in Andrew Kippis, *The Life of Nathaniel Lardner, D.D.* (London: J. Johnson, 1788), cxviii.

47. See J. A. W. Gunn, *Beyond Liberty and Property: The Process of Self-Recognition in Eighteenth-Century Political Thought* (Montreal: McGill-Queen's University Press, 1983), 260–315.

48. *Liberty and the Craftsman: A Project for Improving the Country Journal* (London: J. Roberts, 1730), 5.

49. Pulteney, *Honest Jury*, 3.

50. 3 Geo. 2, c. 25 (1730). The act also permitted judges to empanel special juries.

51. James Reynolds, in *Rex v. Curl*, 93 *ER* 851.

52. *The Crafts of the Craftsmen; or, A Detection of the Designs of the Coalition: Containing Memoirs of the History of False Patriotism for the Year 1735* (London: J. Roberts, 1736), 16.

53. *State Law; or, The Doctrine of Libels, Discussed and Examined*, 2nd ed. (London: T. Wotton, c. 1730), 6.

54. *State Law*, 136.

55. *State Law*, 60, 74–75.

56. The government, opposition critics pointed out, could hardly demonstrate this certainty unless it aimed to "consult all the People in *England*, to know in what Sense they understood" every publication. *The Doctrine of Innuendo's Discuss'd; or, The Liberty of the Press Maintain'd* (London, 1731), 13.

57. Andrew Hamilton, *A Brief Narrative of the Case and Tryal of John Peter Zenger, Printer of the New-York Weekly Journal* (Boston: Thomas Fleet, 1738), 15.

58. Hamilton cited Vaughan's ruling but referred to Hawles only indirectly: "the Jury are by Law at Liberty (without any affront to the Judgment of the Court) to find both the Law and the Fact, in our Case" (*Brief Narrative*, 39). In 1732 Hawles's pamphlet was reprinted for the first time since its original appearance, likely in response to Francklin's conviction a few months earlier.

59. Hamilton, *Brief Narrative*, 34.

60. Hamilton, *Brief Narrative*, 29.

61. Hamilton, *Brief Narrative*, 27.

62. According to a later jurist, the "provision that jurors should be *next neighbours*, tho' a favourite caution of the Common Law" had not been strictly observed since the seventeenth century, in part because it was difficult to apply in trials for crimes committed at sea. Edward Wynne, *Eunomus; or, Dialogues concerning the Law and Constitution of England*, 4 vols. (London, 1768), 3:190–93. Parliament reduced the vicinage requirement for civil proceedings in 1705, though it was not until 1826 that it did the same for criminal trials. On the Anglo-Norman origins of the requirement, see Mike McNair, "Vicinage and the Antecedents of the Jury," *Law and History Review* 17 (1999): 537–90.

63. Since the old system was based entirely on testimony, a later commentator explained, the "most effectual method, therefore, of eviscerating the truth, was by a jury, who were acquainted with the parties and the witnesses, and necessarily the best judges of the degree of credit to which the evidence submitted to them was entitled." *An Examination into the Rights and Duties of Jurors with Some Structures on the Law of Libels* (London: T. Whieldon, 1785), 22.

64. William Blackstone, *Commentaries on the Laws of England*, 4 vols. (Oxford: Clarendon, 1765–1769), 3:356. "The very point of their being strangers in the county," Blackstone explained, "is of infinite service, in preventing those factions and parties, which would intrude in every cause of moment, were it tried only before persons resident on the spot, as justices of the peace, and the like. And, the better to remove all suspicion of partiality, it was wisely provided by the statutes . . . that no judge of assize should hold pleas in any county wherein he was born or inhabits. And, as this constitution prevents party and faction from intermingling in the trial of right, so it keeps both the rule and the administration of the laws uniform."

65. John Vaughan, in *ST* 6:col. 1011.

66. "The success of Hamilton's performance," Michael Warner suggests, "depended on his ability to conflate [an] implicit norm of abstract universality with the customary norm of local consensus." Warner, *The Letters of the Republic: Publication and the Public Sphere in Eighteenth-Century America* (Cambridge, MA: Harvard University Press, 1990), 56. I contend that this conflation could be compelling to jurors only in a period of transition from rhetorical to modern assumptions in the law, whereas the debate over seditious libel was decided only with the ascendancy of the latter.

67. One of Owen's lawyers, Barnard Ford, put it to the jury that "[o]nly proving the sale of the book, does not prove all those opprobrious and hard terms laid in the charge against him. If his selling and publishing this book, maliciously, with a seditious intent, scandalously and falsely, with a design to disturb the peace of the nation is not proved, then this great charge in the information fails." *Rex v. Owen* (1752), *ST* 18:col. 1225. As the facts of publication were among the few that could be contested in libel proceedings, much of the libel debate was focused on the question of whether the act of publication alone constituted evidence of criminal intent. Barrell analyzes the various arguments on the question in his account of the debate in *Imagining the King's Death*, 348–56.

68. *Rex v. Woodfall* (1770), *ST* 20:col. 903. The ambivalent verdict in this case led to an abortive attempt in the House of Commons to set up a commission tasked with reviewing the roles of judge and jury in libel trials. Similar verdicts were returned in *Rex v. Williams* (1764), one of the libel actions brought against the printers of the *North Briton*, no. 45, and in the case discussed below of the dean of St. Asaph (1783–1784), whose protracted and well-publicized prosecution led to a renewal of the campaign in Parliament to amend the libel law.

69. For a detailed analysis of how participants in the seditious libel debate variously interpreted the law–fact distinction, see Green, *Verdict according to Conscience*, 318–55.

70. Mansfield, in *Rex v. Miller* (1770), *ST* 20:cols. 894–95.

71. *Rex v. Miller*, *ST* 20:col. 896.

72. *An Address to the Jurymen of London by a Citizen* (London, 1755), 24.

73. *Junius: Stat nominis umbra* [The Letters of Junius], 2 vols. (London: Henry Sampson Woodfall, 1772), 1:xxv.

74. James Erskine, Lord Grange, *The Doctrine of Libels and the Duty of Juries Fairly Stated* (London: M. Cooper, 1752), 23.

75. *Another Letter to Mr. Almon, in Matter of Libel* (London: J. Almon, 1770), 45.

76. George Rous, *A Letter to the Jurors of Great-Britain* (London: G. Pearch, 1771), 60. A bad verdict, Rous added, could always be overturned on pardon, while in turn a bad pardon would always be greeted "with more odium than advantage." Yet, he conceded, chaos would ensue were the vagaries of public opinion to trump the authority of government pardons, if not the law of libel: "When the people are roused by injuries, and inflamed by artful leaders, without such a check, juries might proscribe the opposite party, which would cause the popular scale to preponderate, and lead us through anarchy to despotism" (61).

77. *An Interesting Address to the Independent Part of the People of England, on Libels* (London: G. Kearsley, 1777), 17.

78. The dictum was attributed to Mansfield after his death, though there is no record of the judge having phrased it in this way. The idea behind it had been considered an established rule since at least the beginning of the eighteenth century. See Hawkins, *Treatise of the Pleas*, 1:194.

79. Francis Squire, *A Faithful Report of a Genuine Debate concerning the Liberty of the Press* (London: J. Roberts, 1740), 37.

80. Squire, *Faithful Report*, 37.

81. *Letters of Junius*, 1:xxiv.

82. *Address to the Jurymen of London*, 24.

83. *Letters of Junius*, 1:xxiii.

84. *Another Letter to Mr. Almon*, 45.

85. Thomas Leach, *Considerations on the Matter of Libel* (London: J. Johnson, 1791), 28–29.

86. Father of Candor, *A Letter concerning Libels, Warrants, the Seizure of Papers, and Sureties for the Peace or Behaviour*, 7th ed. (London: J. Almon, 1771), 48–49.

87. Charles Jenkinson, speech to House of Commons, 6 December 1770, reported in *Vox Senatus: The Speeches at Large Which Were Made in a Great Assembly* (London: W. Woodfall, 1771), 49. This pamphlet was a reprint of Woodfall's transcript of the speeches in the *Morning Chronicle* and would later serve as the basis for Hansard's report of the debate (*PH* 17:cols. 1211–1317).

88. Edward Thurlow, speech to House of Commons, 6 December 1770, in *Vox Senatus*, 95.

89. John Bowles, *Considerations on the Respective Rights of Judge and Jury: Particularly upon Trials for Libel*, 2nd ed. (London: Whieldon and Butterworth, 1791), 56.

90. John Bowles, *A Second Letter to the Right Honourable Charles James Fox, upon the Matter of Libel* (London: Whieldon and Butterworth, 1792), 53.

91. Thurlow, speech to House of Commons, 27 November 1770, in *Vox Senatus*, 16.

92. John Gordon, *The Causes and Consequences of Evil Speaking against Government* (Cambridge: J. Woodyer, 1771), 13.

93. Robert Morris, *A Letter to Sir Richard Aston, Knt.* (London: Geo. Pearch, 1770), 43.

94. Morris, *Letter to Sir Richard Aston*, 42.

95. *Another Letter to Mr. Almon*, 45.

96. Alexander Wedderburn, speech to House of Commons, 6 December 1770, in *Vox Senatus*, 93–94.

97. Jean-Louis de Lolme, *The Constitution of England; or, An Account of the English Government* (1771; trans., London: G. Kearsley, 1775), 295–96.

98. Capel Lofft, *An Essay on the Law of Libels* (London: C. Dilly, 1785), 59.

99. Francis Maseres, *An Enquiry into the Extent of the Power of Juries* (London: J. Debrett, 1785), 23. Maseres was reiterating an argument he had originally set out in *Additional Papers concerning the Province of Quebeck* (London: W. White, 1776), 395–435.

100. Charles Stanhope, *The Rights of Juries Defended* (London: P. Emsly, 1792), 95.

101. Maseres, *Enquiry*, 27.

102. I am indebted to Michael Lobban's account of the case and how it led to a shift in prosecutorial priorities from libel to sedition. Lobban, "From Seditious Libel to Unlawful Assembly: Peterloo and the Changing Face of Political Crime, c. 1770–1820," *Oxford Journal of Legal Studies* 10 (1990): 307–52. Lobban pointed out that by the time of the Libel Act's passage, the courts had already begun to treat seditious libel as an offense that was "dependent on effect and context" rather than inhering in the defamatory content of a work (321). Lobban considered only in passing, however, some of the procedural changes that, I argue, facilitated this shift in priorities.

103. Mansfield, in *Rex v. Shipley* (Case of the Dean of St. Asaph) (1783–1784), *ST* 21:col. 1044.

104. *Rex v. Shipley*, *ST* 21:col. 848.

105. Focusing mainly on US cases, Joseph M. Hassett suggested that a major shift in legal thinking occurred during the later eighteenth century, in which the belief that juries were independent by virtue of their local knowledge gave way to the idea that juries were impartial by virtue of their lack of pretrial knowledge about a case. Hassett, "A Jury's Pre-

Trial Knowledge in Historical Perspective: The Distinction between Pre-Trial Information and 'Prejudicial' Publicity," *Law and Contemporary Problems* 43 (1979–1980): 155–68. Though he does not consider the legal arguments over pretrial publicity, Anthony Page describes the Society for Constitutional Information and its press campaign in support of Shipley throughout his trial. Page, "The Dean of St. Asaph's Trial: Libel and Politics in the 1780s," *Journal for Eighteenth-Century Studies* 32 (2009): 21–35.

106. *Rex. v. Almon* (1765), Wilm. 243, 97 *ER* 94–106. Before Mansfield's decision, the courts had relied on the law of seditious libel to punish their critics. See Douglas Hay, "Contempt by Scandalizing the Court: A Political History on the First Hundred Years," *Osgoode Hall Law Journal* 25 (1987): 431–84.

107. Almost all these cases involved no jury; the judges were concerned instead that bad publicity might expose the parties to public opprobrium in a way that would endanger their safety and reputation. Lord Hardwicke's ruling in the *St. James's Evening Post Case* (1742) would be cited by later commentators as having established the sub judice rule that publications tended to prejudice legal proceedings. But Hardwicke was referring to how these publications might "prejudice the minds of the public" and not to how they might obstruct justice. Philip Yorke, Earl of Hardwicke, in *Roach v. Garvan* (St. James's Evening Post Case) (1742), 2 Atk. 469, 26 *ER* 683. On the ruling and its later conflicting interpretations, see Galia Schneebaum and Shai J. Lavi, "The Riddle of *Sub-judice* and the Modern Law of Contempt," *Critical Analysis of the Law* 2.1 (2015): 185–88. Schneebaum and Lavi anticipate my argument in suggesting that the rule's development later in the century was part of a broader response by the court to the growing authority of the press and public opinion: needing to "secure its position of authority within the public sphere," the court sought to claim "for itself a new kind of legitimacy based on the impartiality of judge and jury" (192).

108. *Rex v. Gray* (1758), 1 Burr. 510, 97 *ER* 424–25 (report of the discussion on the motion to put off the trial), and *Rex v. Gray* (1758), 2 Keny. 307, 96 *ER* 1191–92 (report of the subsequent trial).

109. Lloyd Kenyon, in *Rex v. Shipley*, *ST* 21:cols. 869–72.

110. The Dissenting minister Joseph Towers criticized Kenyon's motives but, like Erskine, objected only to the judge's broad interpretation of what constituted prejudicial publicity: "whether it was in any respect just, or reasonable, or proper, thus to suspend the trial, at a great expence to the defendant, merely because papers had been dispersed in the neighbourhood, asserting the general rights of juries, but in which not a single syllable was advanced relative to the particular cause of the dean of St Asaph, must be left to the decision of an impartial public." Towers, *Observations on the Rights and Duty of Juries, in Trials for Libel* (London: J. Debrett, 1784), 118–19.

111. Thomas Erskine, in *Rex v. Shipley*, *ST* 21:cols. 991–92.

112. Kenyon, in *Rex v. Joliffe* (1791), 4 T. R. 285, 100 *ER* 1024.

113. Blackstone, *Commentaries*, 3:375.

114. *The Times* (18 September 1788).

115. Francis Buller, in *Rex v. Shipley*, *ST* 21:col. 945.

116. Mansfield, in *Rex v. Shipley*, *ST* 21:cols. 1035–40.

117. As already noted, the Treason Trials Act of 1696 granted individuals accused of that crime the right to be represented by legal counsel. In trials for other offenses, defense counsel was normally prohibited; as Hawkins explained, the accused was expected to answer the

prosecution on matters of fact "as if he were the best Lawyer" (*Treatise of the Pleas*, 2:400). The right to counsel was formally extended to other offenses in the Trials for Felony Act of 1836 (6 & 7 Will., 4 c. 114), though judges over the previous century had already lifted most restrictions on the presence and activities of defense lawyers in felony trials.

118. See Langbein, *Origins*, 305–7.

119. *Rex v. Stockdale* (1789), *ST* 22:cols. 237–308.

120. Erskine, in *Rex v. Shipley*, *ST* 21:col. 909.

121. Edward Bearcroft, in *Rex v. Shipley*, *ST* 21:cols. 886, 889.

122. The political ascendancy of the bourgeoisie during the eighteenth century, Foucault famously argued, "was masked by the establishment of an explicit, coded and formally egalitarian juridical framework, made possible by the organization of a parliamentary, representative régime." But this development had its "other, dark side" with the emergence of the intellectual disciplines, which operated as micro versions of the law, applying its general codification of behavior "to the infinitesimal level of individual lives." Michel Foucault, *Discipline and Punish: The Birth of the Prison*, trans. Alan Sheridan (New York: Vintage, 1977), 222.

123. Bearcroft and Erskine, in *Rex v. Shipley*, *ST* 21:cols. 891, 912.

124. Bearcroft, in *Rex v. Shipley*, *ST* 21:cols. 890–91.

125. Erskine, in *Rex v. Shipley*, *ST* 21:cols. 901, 929.

126. The proclamation, which was read in the Commons four days later, is reproduced in *PH* 29:cols. 1476–77.

127. William Petty, Earl Shelburne, in Debate in the Lords on Mr. Fox's Libel Bill, 21 May 1792, *PH* 29:col. 1423. Hansard's report of the debate identified Petty by his later title, the Marquess of Lansdowne.

128. *PH* 29:cols. 1476–77.

129. Charles Pratt, Earl Camden, in Debate in the Lords on Mr. Fox's Libel Bill, 16 May 1792, *PH* 29:cols. 1408–9. Forty years earlier, as counsel for the defense in *Rex v. Owen*, Pratt had been the first advocate to challenge the court's strict interpretation of the law–fact distinction in libel cases.

130. Archibald Macdonald, in Debate in the Commons on the King's Proclamation against Seditious Writings, 25 May 1792, *PH* 29:col. 1508.

131. Charles Grey, in Debate in the Commons on the King's Proclamation against Seditious Writings, 25 May 1792, *PH* 29:cols. 1486–87.

132. Jason Stanley suggests that rhetorical self-masking is a common feature of political propaganda though it is not used for all forms of propaganda. Stanley, *How Propaganda Works* (Princeton, NJ: Princeton University Press, 2015), 51.

133. Richard Pepper Arden, master of the rolls, in Debate in the Commons on the King's Proclamation against Seditious Writings, 25 May 1792, *PH* 29:col. 1478.

134. John MacPherson, letter to George, Prince of Wales (27 September 1790), in *The Correspondence of George, Prince of Wales, 1770–1812*, 8 vols., ed. Arthur Aspinall (London: Cassell, 1963–1971), 2:98–99.

135. The convention's declaration of 19 November 1792, dubbed the First Propaganda Decree by later historians, was intended primarily as a promise of assistance to collaborators in countries that were at war with the republic. After being informed that Pitt's ministers were citing the decree as confirmation that France was sponsoring emissaries from La Propagande as "secret apostles sent into England," the French minister of foreign affairs,

Pierre Henri Lebrun-Tondu, reportedly scoffed that "it would be madness to waste the treasures of the State to produce events which when they happen can only be the offspring of reason." *Report of the Committee of General Defence on the Dispositions of the British Government towards France, and on the Measures to Be Taken: Addressed to the National Convention of France, in the Sitting of January 12, 1793* (London: James Ridgway, 1793), 4.

136. Hamilton, in *PH* 29:col. 1514.

137. "A Brief Account of the Different Parties in France," *The Times* (29 August 1792).

138. In a letter dated 26 October 1793 to the former French ambassador, Bernard François de Chauvelin, Pitt's agent William Augustus Miles disputed the ambassador's denial that the republic had anything to do with the "propagandisme" of "quelques mauvaises têtes" who had "erected themselves into apostles to propagate the doctrines of equality and fraternity in England." Appended to *The Conduct of France towards Great Britain Examined* (London: G. Nicol and J. Sewell, 1793), 194. Bertus H. Wabeke offered a brief survey of how the term "propaganda" began to change "from being a concrete noun denoting a specific organization into an abstract one denoting an activity." Wabeke, "1790: A Turning Point in the Life of a Word," in *A Desirable World: Essays in Honor of Professor Bart Landheer*, ed. A. M. C. H. Reigersman-Van der Eerden and G. Zoon (The Hague: Martinus Nijhoff, 1974), 53–58.

139. "Review of Female Literature," *Lady's Monthly Museum* (April 1799), in *The Lady's Monthly Museum*, vol. 2 (London: Vernor and Hood, 1799), 313.

140. Kenyon, in *Rex v. Lambert* (1793), *ST* 22:cols. 1017–18.

141. On the number and variety of legal actions for seditious libel during the period, see Clive Emsley, "An Aspect of Pitt's 'Terror': Prosecutions for Sedition during the 1790s," *Social History* 6 (1981): 155–84; and Philip Harling, "The Law of Libel and the Limits of Repression, 1790–1832," *Historical Journal* 44 (2001): 107–34.

142. William Cobbett, *Observations on the Emigration of Dr. Joseph Priestley* (Philadelphia: T. Bradford, 1794), 4–8.

143. Cobbett, *Observations*, 9.

144. George Dyer, *An Address to the People of Great Britain, on the Doctrine of Libels, and the Office of Juror, More Particularly in Cases of Libel* (London, 1799), 88–89.

145. Trevor Ross, *The Making of the English Literary Canon: From the Middle Ages to the Late Eighteenth Century* (Montreal: McGill-Queen's University Press, 1998), 293–301.

146. Erskine, "Declaration of the Friends to the Liberty of the Press, at Their Second Meeting, January 22, 1793," in *The Resolutions of the First Meeting of the Friends to the Liberty of the Press, December 19th, 1792; Also, the Declaration of the Second Meeting, January 22nd, 1793* (London: J. Ridgway, 1793), 17.

147. Isaac D'Israeli, preface to his *Miscellanies; or, Literary Recreations* (London: T. Cadell and W. Davies, 1796), vii, xxi.

Epilogue · Unacknowledged Legislators

1. George Puttenham, *The Arte of English Poesie* (London: Richard Field, 1589), 5.

2. William Davenant, *A Discourse upon Gondibert: An Heroick Poem* (Paris: Matthieu Guillemot, 1650), 29–30.

3. Bevil Higgons, prologue to George Granville, Baron Lansdowne, *The Jew of Venice: A Comedy as It Is Acted at the Theatre in Little-Lincolns-Inn-Fields, by His Majesty's Servants* (London: Bernard Lintott, 1701), sig. b2v.

4. William Cleland [Alexander Pope], "A Letter to the Publisher, Occasioned by the Present Edition of *The Dunciad*," in *The Dunciad, Variorum: With the Prolegomena of Scriblerus* (London: A. Dod, 1729), 9.

5. Alexander Pope, *The First Satire of the Second Book of Horace, Imitated* [To Fortescue] (London: A. Dodd and E. Nutt, 1733), line 150; and Pope, *One Thousand Seven Hundred and Thirty Eight* [Epilogue to the Satires: Dialogue II] (London: T. Cooper, 1738), lines 248–49.

6. Vicesimus Knox, "Cursory Notes on Satire and Satirists," in his *Essays, Moral and Literary*, 3rd ed., 2 vols. (London: Charles Dilly, 1782), 2:228.

7. Samuel Johnson, *The Prince of Abissinia: A Tale* [Rasselas] (London: R. and J. Dodsley, 1759), 70–71.

8. Percy Bysshe Shelley, *A Defence of Poetry* (1821), in *Essays, Letters from Abroad, Translations and Fragments*, ed. M. Shelley, 2 vols. (London: Edward Moxon, 1840), 1:16–17, 42, 56–57.

9. Samuel Johnson, *Prefaces, Biographical and Critical, to the Works of the English Poets*, 10 vols. (London: J. Nichols et al., 1779–1781), 7:330.

10. Anthony Ashley Cooper, Earl of Shaftesbury, "Soliloquy; or, Advice to an Author," in his *Characteristicks of Men, Manners, Opinions, Times*, 3 vols. (London, 1711), 1:155.

11. John Clarke, *An Essay upon Study* (London: Arthur Bettesworth, 1731), 194.

12. Edward Young, *Conjectures on Original Composition* (London: A. Millar and R. and J. Dodsley, 1759), 6, 28, 42, 53.

13. William Wordsworth, "Preface," in his *Lyrical Ballads, with Other Poems*, 3rd ed., 2 vols. (London: T. N. Longman and O. Rees, 1800), 1:xxxvii.

14. Annabel Patterson, *Censorship and Interpretation: The Conditions of Writing and Censorship in Early Modern England* (Madison: University of Wisconsin Press, 1984), 18; Leo Strauss, "Persecution and the Art of Writing," *Social Research* 8 (1941): 488–504.

15. Sir Philip Sidney, *The Defence of Poesie* (London: William Ponsonby, 1595), sig. Kv–K2r.

16. Jonathan Swift, *The Importance of the Guardian Considered* (London: John Morphew, 1713), 24.

17. See John Baird, "Literary Politics and Political Satire: Paul Whitehead and Alexander Pope," *Lumen* 35 (2016): 19–36.

18. James Bramston, *The Art of Politicks, in Imitation of Horace's Art of Poetry* (London: Lawton Gilliver, 1729), 8.

19. [Alexander Pope], "Advertisement," in *The Dunciad*, 3.

20. James Ralph, *The Touch-Stone; or, Historical, Critical, Political, Philosophical, and Theological Essays on the Reigning Diversions of the Town* (London, 1728), xxiii–xxiv.

21. Swift to Pope, 16 July 1728, in *The Correspondence of Alexander Pope*, ed. George Sherburn, 5 vols. (Oxford: Clarendon, 1956), 2:504–5; "Of *The New Dunciad*," *Universal Spectator*, 3 April 1742. Catherine Gallagher described a related transformation in the period's scandal fiction. Whereas earlier practitioners, she pointed out, used the abstractness of allegory to shield themselves from the censors, later writers became less afraid of relying on particularizing detail and other "novelistic" techniques to relate the secrets of high society. Gallagher, *Nobody's Story: The Vanishing Acts of Women Writers in the Marketplace, 1670–1820* (Berkeley: University of California Press, 1994), 101–4.

22. *Common Sense* 37 (8 October 1737).

23. Thomas Pelham-Holles, Duke of Newcastle, to Philip Yorke, Lord Hardwicke, 28 September 1762, in *Memoirs of the Marquis of Rockingham and His Contemporaries*, ed. George Thomas Keppel, 2 vols. (London: Richard Bentley, 1852), 1:113.

24. "Sketch of the Life of the Late John Wilkes, Esq.," *Monthly Magazine* 4, no. 27 (January 1798), reprinted in *Monthly Magazine*, vol. 5 (London: R. Phillips, 1798), 49.

25. Charles Churchill, *The Prophecy of Famine: A Scots Pastoral* (London: G. Kearsley, 1763), line 89.

26. See, for example, Thomas Lockwood, *Post-Augustan Satire: Charles Churchill and Satirical Poetry, 1750–1800* (Seattle: University of Washington Press, 1979).

27. George Crabbe, *The News-Paper: A Poem* (London: J. Dodsley, 1785), viii.

28. Archibald Campbell, *Lexiphanes, a Dialogue: Imitated from Lucian, and Suited to the Present Times* (London: J. Knox, 1767), 159–60.

29. Vicesimus Knox, "Of the Interruption Which the Vulgar Cares of Life Give to Poetry and the Elegant Pleasures of Imagination, and of the Contempt Thrown upon Them by Men of Business," in his *Winter Evenings; or, Lucubrations on Life and Letters*, 3 vols. (London: Charles Dilly, 1788), 3:105.

30. Wordsworth, *Lyrical Ballads*, 1:xv–xvi.

31. Samuel Johnson, "Preface," in William Shakespeare, *Plays*, 8 vols. (London: J. and R. Tonson et al., 1765), 1:vii.

32. Joseph Warton, *An Essay on the Genius and Writings of Pope*, vol. 2 (London: J. Dodsley, 1782), 479.

33. Vicesimus Knox, "On the Influence of Politics, as a Subject of Conversation, on the Taste of Literature," in his *Essays, Moral and Literary*, 14th ed., 2 vols. (London: Charles Dilly, 1795), 2:171. Knox varied the selection of essays throughout the multiple editions of his two principal collections, *Winter Evenings* and *Essays, Moral and Literary*. This essay began to appear only in later editions of the latter.

34. In *The Spirit of Despotism* (London, 1795), Knox warned that Pitt would use a war against France to curtail civil liberties at home.

35. J. W. Goethe, "Maximen und Reflexionen," no. 1113, in his *Werke*, 143 vols. (Weimar: Böhlau, 1887–1919), 48:205–6, translated in Rainer Nägele, *Theater, Theory, Speculation: Walter Benjamin and Scenes of Modernity* (Baltimore, MD: Johns Hopkins University Press, 1991), 88.

36. Michael Meehan described how literary theorists of the later eighteenth century were heavily invested in attempting to define the relation between literary culture and political liberty. Meehan, *Liberty and Poetics in Eighteenth-Century England* (London: Croom Helm, 1986). That such a definition was felt desirable and, indeed, is still being attempted by commentators to this day suggests that the function of literary art in a democracy remains ambiguous.

37. Sidney, *Defence of Poesie*, sig. Gr.

38. Jacques Derrida, "Passions: 'An Oblique Offering,'" in his *On the Name*, trans. David Wood (Stanford, CA: Stanford University Press, 1995), 28.

39. Jacques Rancière, *The Politics of Literature*, trans. Julie Rose (Cambridge: Polity, 2011), 40.

INDEX

Act for the Better Regulation of Juries 1730, 189, 279n50
Adair, James, *Discussions of the Laws of Libel*, 136
Addison, Joseph, 14, 35, 37, 63; on the press, 21
"Aduertisement Towching Seditious Wrytings, An," 183, 275n17
Allibond, Sir Richard, on seditious libel, 186
Almon, John, trial for contempt, 205
ancient constitution, 17, 20, 22–23
Anderton, William, trial for treason, 243n45
Arden, Sir Richard Pepper, on sedition, 216
Arnall, William, on indeterminacy of public debate, 22–23, 244n51
Arnold, Matthew, 171
Aston, Sir Richard, on literary property, 40–42, 60
Auden, W. H., 29
authors, 1; aesthetic dispensation for, 115, 149; as specialized laborers, 53–58, 252n63; character, 161–63; incentives for, 60–61, 72–74, 77, 104, 111; liberty of criticism and, 155–61, 165, 169; national literary traditions and, 63–64, 69–70; originality and, 51–52, 56–58, 62, 259n52; property rights, 19, 35–40, 71–72, 77, 90–94, 97–102, 247n2, 248n10, 249n10, 250n38, 255n107; public role, 29–31, 79–81, 116, 242n29; refinement and, 5, 79–81; style and, 76, 79–89, 100–101, 104–8, 261n71. *See also* genius

Bacon, Matthew, *A New Abridgment of the Law*, 267n87
Bacon, Sir Francis, 44, 275n17

Bacon, Sir Nicholas, on sedition, 184
Baldrey, Joshua Kirby, trial for defamation, 153
Barrell, John, 275n6, 281n67
Bearcroft, Edward, on interpreting libels, 209–12
Becket, Thomas, 117, 250n41. *See also Donaldson v. Becket*
Bell, John, 56
Bentham, Jeremy, on publicity, 12, 28
Bentley, Richard, 50
Bergeron, James Henry, 249n22
Biagioli, Mario, 251n46
Bill of Rights 1689, 150
Binhammer, Katherine, 119
Blackie, John, 270n14
Blackstone, William, 98, 250n27; on censorship, 157; on the Crown's prerogative copyright; 68; on jurors, 207; on the literary system, 54, 59; on the nature of literary property, 38, 90–91, 94; on perpetual copyright, 41, 98; on property, 41, 250n25; on scandalum magnatum, 128; on style, 91; on the vicinage rule, 191, 280n64
Blair, Hugh, *Lectures on Rhetoric and Belles Lettres*, 55, 84–86
Blanning, Tim, 20
blasphemy (blasphemous libel), 4, 114, 195, 266n70, 279n46
Blasphemy Act 1697, 279n46
Bodin, Jean: on libels, 182–83; on the power of rhetoric, 182, 226
Bonnell, Thomas F., 253n73, 255n102

booksellers: free market for, 61–63, 71–72; idea-expression dichotomy and, 49, 75, 91; liberty of criticism and, 164–65; as monopoly, 42–43, 58–61, 247n2, 248n7; national literary traditions and, 63–65; originality and, 50–52, 56–57; property rights, 19; 35–40; role in literary system, 54–55, 252n69
Boswell, Alexander Boswell, Lord Auchinleck, on literary tradition, 63
Boswell, James, *Life of Johnson*, 54, 65, 70, 105, 143
Bourdieu, Pierre, 252n63
Bowers, Toni, 262n8
Bowles, John, on juries deciding libels, 198–99, 202–3
Brandeis, Louis, on privacy, 141
Brant, Clare, 242n21
Braudel, Fernand, 140
Bricker, Andrew Benjamin, 187, 278n41
British Critic, on John Carr, 152
British Museum Act 1753, 23
Browning, Robert, 107
Bruce, Archibald, on liberty of criticism, 272n29
Bull, Frederick, on publication of trial proceedings, 245n59
Buller, Sir Francis, on juries deciding libels, 208, 212
Burke, Edmund, 22; on defeat of perpetual copyright, 50
Burn, Richard, *The Justice of the Peace and Parish Officer*, 265n62
Burnett, Thomas, *Archaeologia Philosophica*, 256n1
Burnett v. Chetwood (1721), copyright, 256n1
Burney, Frances, *Cecilia*, 260n57
Burrows, Simon, 269n109
Bushell's Case (1670), rights of juries, 184, 191, 205, 276n25
Butler, Samuel, 57
Button, Zachariah, 153
Byron, George Gordon, Lord 72

Camden, Charles Pratt, 1st Earl: on copyright, 43–46, 57, 67–68, 250n38, 250n42; on genius, 46, 53, 58, 60; on improvement, 48; on juries deciding libels, 215; on law-fact distinction, 284n129; on privacy, 27, 141
Campbell, Archibald, on public discourse, 233
canon, literary: copyright and, 43–44, 46, 62–65, 67, 71; editions of canonical works, 35–36, 50–51, 56–57, 254n100; as national heritage, 5, 62–65, 69–73; made up of old works, 69–70, 255n107; as public domain, 12, 59–67, 74, 253n86; refinement and, 79, 85, 257n9; stylistic individuation and, 105–7; test of time and, 70–71, 234
Cardozo, Benjamin, on libel-slander distinction, 136
Cardwell, Kenneth, 275n17
Carlyle, Thomas, on national identity, 73
Carnan, Thomas, 68
Carr, Sir John, 151–63, 166–71, 271n14; on fair use, 153–54; on overcoming differences, 167–68; and strangerhood, 151, 167–68; on visual defamation, 153. Works: *Caledonian Sketches*, 271n13; *A Northern Summer*, 168; *The Stranger in France*, 167; *The Stranger in Ireland*, 151–55, 161, 168
Carr v. Hood (1808), defamation, 150–63, 166–71, 238, 271n4, 271n13
Cary v. Kearsley (1803), copyright, 259n40
Cato's Letters, on liberty of the press, 14, 188
censorship, 1–5, 237; copyright as, 37, 43, 248n10; liberty of criticism and, 157–61; political, 180, 186, 213–17, 230–35; publicity as, 12; rhetorical indirection and, 111, 230–35, 286n21; self-censorship, 272n32
Chambers, Richard, trial for seditious libel, 275n13
Chambers, Simone, 177
Chapman, Paul, 243n35
Chatterton, Thomas, "Rowley" poems, 63, 253n88
Chaucer, Geoffrey, 50, 70, 79, 229
Chauvelin, François-Bernard de, 285n138
Cherrington v. Abney (1709), privacy, 269n101
Chetwood, William, 256n1
Chevy-Chase, 63
chilling effect, 157, 169, 272n32
Churchill, Charles, on poetry, 233
Cicero, 201, 226
Clark, Anna, 262n8

Clarke, Robert, on juries deciding libels, 184, 276n19
Cobbett, William: on the character of authors, 162–63; on liberty of criticism, 156, 159–63; on popular sovereignty, 219; on propaganda, 218–19
coercion, verbal, 181–82, 196–97, 200, 214–22, 237; persuasion vs., 216, 218
Coke, Sir Edward, on seditious libel, 182–83, 275n9
Colley, Linda, 246n69
Common Sense, 232
Constable, John, *Reflections Upon Accuracy of Style*, 257n7
copyright, 1–4, 19; commons, 76; consequences of defeat of perpetual, 56, 69–74, 254n100; fair use exemptions, 101, 155; labor vs. exchange theories of value in, 40–53, 60–68, 71, 98–99, 249n22; literary canon and, 36, 43–44, 46, 50–51, 56–57, 61–65, 67, 69–74, 105, 253n86, 255n107; literary property debate, 35–69, 75, 77–78, 89–101, 107–8, 141, 175; as monopoly, 40–43, 45–46, 58–64, 68, 95, 247n2; mythology of genius and, 36, 46–54, 57–58, 67, 258n31; and nationalist sentiment, 64–65; nature of literary property, 38–41, 90–95, 98, 101–2; originality and, 36, 51–58, 62, 76–77, 95, 97–98, 104, 251n46, 259n52; plagiarism and, 260n60; Crown's prerogative, 37, 41, 50, 67–68; and privacy, 141; style and, 75–78, 89–108, 259n52. *See also* expressive diversity; idea-expression dichotomy; public domain
Copyright Act 1710 (Statute of Anne), 1, 19, 35–39, 44–45, 48–51, 67, 247n1, 247n2, 248n7, 249n22, 253n77, 255n107
Copyright Act 1814, 71, 255n107
Copyright Act 1842, 71
Coroners and Justice Act 2009, 274n1
Courcy, Richard de, 119–25, 127, 132, 138–39, 146, 148, 263n38. Works: *The Seducer Convicted on His Own Evidence*, 124–25; *Seduction*, 119–23, 138, 262n18, 264n53
Courteville, Ralph, on liberty of the press, 239n2
Cowley, Abraham, 81

Cowper, William, 70
Crabbe, George, 233, 287n27
Craftsman, The 187
Critical Review, The, 118, 145, 146
criticism: function of, 55, 154–55, 157–59, 163–71, 238; liberty of, 155–61, 163, 170–71, 238, 272n29, 274n63; public sphere and, 165–66
Crosby, Kevin, 276n25
Crose, Jean de la, on liberty of criticism, 164–65
Curll, Edmund, 129, 189, 266n70, 279n46

Daily Advertiser, The, 142
Daily Courant, The, 278n38
Daniel, George, on refinement, 257n9
Davenant, William, 226
Deazley, Ronan, 247n2
defamation, 3–4, 127–40, 265n62, 265n68, 267n78, 270n124, 273n46, 279n43; contexts of slander, 130, 267n79; dignitary harm from, 130–39; fair comment, 150–51, 155–59, 169–70, 271n2, 270n3; by fiction, 144; libel-slander distinction, 3, 132–37, 139, 267n81, 267n87; privacy and, 140, 147–48, 268n99; and the public, 28, 128–30; rhetorical indirection and, 122–23, 148, 187, 189–90, 232, 278n41; truth defense, 115, 122, 127–28, 131, 139, 263n28, 263n30; visual, 153
Defamation Act 2013, 268n98, 270n2
Defoe, Daniel, 35, 231; on seditious libel, 278n40
democracy, 2–6, 239n4; equality and, 16–18, 240n13; expressive diversity and, 96–97, 99–100, 103–7; free agency of mind and, 103, 130, 196–97, 222–23; indeterminacy of, 9–10, 16, 30, 100, 114–15, 207, 240n10, 241n15; legal profession and, 212–13; liberalism and, 8–9, 140, 240n13, 241n15; literature and, 5–6, 106–7, 114–15, 221–23, 238, 240n6, 287n36; nationalism and, 30; Plato on, 16, 177, propaganda and, 221–22; popular sovereignty, 6–15, 24–25, 140, 219, 241n15
Demosthenes, 201
Denham, John, 117
Derrida, Jacques, 2, 137, 238, 240n6

Deveil, John, 122–26, 264n58
Dibdin v. Swan (1793), defamation, 155–56, 159
D'Israeli, Isaac, on autonomy of literature, 223, 225; on stylistic individuation, 108
Diveil, Elizabeth, 126, 264n54
Doctrine of innuendo's discuss'd, The 280n56
Dodsley, Robert, *Miscellany*, 69
Donaldson, Alexander, 45, 57, 70, 93, 250n41, 254n91; on national literary traditions, 64–65
Donaldson, John, 250n41
Donaldson v. Becket (1774), copyright, 35–37, 43, 45–46, 50, 56–57, 67, 69–70, 75, 78, 94, 101, 250n41, 254n100
Donne, John, 70
Donnelly, R. C., 267n79
Drone, Eaton S., 250n42
Dryden, John, 50, 70, 105, 156, 231, 233; on refinement, 69–70, 80, 229; on stylistic individuation, 81–82. Works: "Defense of the Epilogue," 80; *Fables, Ancient and Modern*, 69–70; preface to *Ovid's Epistles*, 81–82
Dubois, Edward, 152–55, 157, 160–61, 167–69; *My Pocket Book*, 151–52, 271n10
Du Bos, Abbé, on "public," 254n94
Duff, William, on genius, 52, 54, 58
Dunne v. Anderson (1825), defamation, 273n41
Dunton, John, 164
Dyer, George, on libels in the courtroom, 220–21

Eagleton, Terry, 261n4
Earl of Sandwich v. Miller (1773), scandalum magnatum, 265n66
Edinburgh Caledonian Mercury, 147
Edinburgh Review, The, 154; on John Carr, 151
Eilenberg, Susan, 256n114
Eliot, T. S., on art and improvement, 107
Ellenborough, Edward Law, Lord, 151; on the character of authors, 161–63, 169–71; on fair use, 91, 259n40; on liberty of criticism, 155–63, 167; on pretrial publicity, 131; on seditious libel, 159
Elliott, J. E., 254n100
Endicott, Timothy, 245n60

Enfield, William: on copyright, 47–48, 57, 59, 91; on the nature of literary property, 38–39
Enquiry into the Nature and Origin of Literary Property, An, 62, 92
Entick v. Carrington (1765), trespass, 27, 141, 245n60
equality, 16–18, 24–25, 239n4, 241n13, 241n15, 243n33; of legal procedure, 202–3, 207–10; of public debate, 17, 158, 164–65
Erickson, Lee, 72
Erle, Sir William: on fair comment, 159, 171; on idea-expression dichotomy, 101–4;
Erskine, Thomas, 180, 206, 271n16; on the Crown's prerogative copyright, 68–69; on interpreting libels, 208–11; on juries, 206, 212; on the liberty of the press, 221; on pretrial publicity, 205; on visual defamation, 153
European Convention on Human Rights, 140
evil fame, 265n62
Examination into the rights and duties of jurors, An, 280n63
exchange theory of value, 40–53, 60–68, 71
expressive diversity, 96–100, 103–7, 236, 259n52

fair comment, 116, 150–51, 155–62, 167–71, 270n2, 270n3, 271n4, 272n39, 273n41
fair use, 90–91, 101, 154–55, 259n40
Farquhar, George, on English plays, 257n15
Father of Candor, on seditious libel, 197, 200, 205
Faulkner, William, 107
Felton, Henry, *A dissertation on reading the classics, and forming a just style*, 83
fiction, 123, 143–49, 176–78, 286n21
Fielding, Henry, *Tom Jones*, 163
Filmer, Robert, 159
Finlay, John, 147, 270n124
Finlay v. Neill (1762), defamation, 270n124
Finlay v. Ruddiman (1763), defamation, 147, 270n124
Fischer, Ann, 120–27, 131–32, 138–39, 145–46, 148, 264n58

Fischer, Christian, 126
Fischer, Helena Frances, 126
Fish, Stanley, 240n11
Fisk, Catherine L., 243n37
Flaubert, Gustave, 261n71
Ford, Banard, on seditious libel, 281n67
Fores, S. W., 153, 271n16
forgery, 76, 85, 99, 260n60
Foucault, Michel, 2, 36, 51, 57, 210, 248n5, 284n122
Fox, Charles James, and Libel Act, 4, 213
Francklin, Richard, 187, 189–90, 256n1, 278n38, 279n46, 280n58
freedom of mind: effect of language on, 3, 87, 130, 175–84, 188, 196–207, 214–23; literature and, 106–7, 221–23, 236–37; style as, 96–97, 100, 102–7. *See also* coercion; propaganda; seditious libel
Freund, Paul A., 272n32

Gael, Patricia, 273n61
Gallagher, Catherine, 286n21
Gardenston, Francis Garden, Lord: on literary tradition, 62; on the term of copyright, 70
Garner, Michael, 255n107
Garrow, William, 152–55, 158, 166–67, 169, 180; on John Carr, 167; on diversity of opinion, 166–67; on parody, 153–54
Gay, John, 37
genius: mythology of, 36, 44, 46–58, 60, 62–63, 67, 251n50, 258n31; originality and, 51–54, 56–58, 251n46, 252n72, 259n52; stylistic individuation and, 85–88, 95, 100–1, 106, 259n52
George III, 20
Gibbs, Sir Vicary, 154, 169
Gibson, William, 277n29
Goethe, Johann Wolfgang von, on symbolism, 235
Goldsmith, Oliver, on privacy, 142–45. Works: *She Stoops to Conquer*, 142–43; *The Vicar of Wakefield*, 143–44, 270n119
Gordon, George, 126, 264n58
Gordon, Helena Frances, 264n58
Gordon v. Hope (1849), estate, 264n58
Gould, Sir Henry, on libel-slander distinction, 134

Gray, Thomas, 69; *The Bard*, 227; on language of poetry, 88
Grazia, Margreta de, 252n72
Green, Thomas Andrew, 277n33, 281n69
Greene, Jody, 248n10
Grey, Charles, Earl Grey, on seditious libel, 215
Grose, Sir Nash, on fair comment, 272n39
Guillory, John, 258n23

Habermas, Jürgen, 2, 7, 9, 14–16, 18, 20, 66, 165, 240n9, 240n13, 242n22, 242n29, 274n63
Hale, Sir Matthew, on libel-slander distinction, 266n70
Hamburger, Philip, 276n23, 277n33
Hamilton, Andrew, 209; on juries deciding libels, 190–92, 205, 280n58, 280n66
Hargrave, Francis: on idea-expression dichotomy, 49, 52, 94–99, 102, 104, 106; on labor theory of value, 98–99, 260n56; on originality, 259n52
Harley, Robert, Earl of Oxford, 18
Harris, Benjamin, trial for seditious libel, 277n27
Harvey, Gabriel, 163
Hassett, Joseph M., 282n105
Hawkins, William: on defamation, 267n78; on representation by counsel, 283n117
Hawles, Sir John: *The Englishman's Right*, 277n26, 280n58; on juries deciding libels, 277n27; on law-fact distinction, 185, 190, 192
Hayter, Thomas, on defamation, 130, 143
Hemingway, Ernest, 107
Higgons, Bevil, on law and poetry, 226
Hinton v. Donaldson (1773), copyright, 250n41
Hobsbawn, Eric, 253n88
Holloway, Sir Richard, on seditious libel, 186, 277n29
Holt, Francis Ludlow: on defamation, 263n28; on scandalum magnatum, 265n67
Holt, Sir John, on seditious libel, 188, 277n33
Homer, 63, 220–21
Hood, Thomas, 152
Hopkins, Gerard Manley, 76
Horace, 71, 226; on literary commons, 74

Horneck, Mary, 142
Horne Tooke, John, 28, 263n27
Hudson, Nicholas, 242n25
Hume, David, 35, 167
Hyde, Sir Robert, on seditious libel, 184

idea-expression dichotomy, 39, 75–78, 89–108, 256n1, 256n3
indeterminacy: democracy and, 9–10, 16, 30, 100, 114–15, 207, 240n10, 241n15; of free speech, 97, 100, 104, 114–15, 137, 166, 170, 210–11, 221–23; literature and, 7, 29, 106–7, 176–77, 230–31, 235–38; of the market, 30, 65, 67, 71; of the public, 9–11, 15, 23, 30, 139, 194, 200–201, 214, 219, 237–38, 244n51
individuation: of discourse, 51–52; of readers, 56; stylistic, 56, 77–78, 81–89, 94–108, 259n52, 260n60, 261n71
Ingram, Martin, 265n68

James I, 68
James II, 185
Jameson, Fredric, 88
Jefferys v. Boosey (1854), copyright, 101
Johnson, Samuel, 35, 107; on abridgments, 90; on booksellers, 54; on the common reader, 12, 164, 234; on copyright, 37, 70; on privacy, 143; on public domain, 65, 71; on stylistic individuation, 105–6, 229; on the test of time, 70–71. Works: *Dictionary*, 54; edition of Shakespeare, 57, 70–71, 234; *Lives of the English Poets*, 56–57; *Rasselas*, 227
Johnson, Samuel, Reverend, *A poetical epistle from an unfortunate young lady at Portsmouth to her lover*, 117–20, 123, 127, 131–32, 138, 145–46, 148
Jones, William, 204, 209
Jonson, Ben, 57, 79, 226
Joyce, James, 107
Junius, 239n2, on juries deciding libels, 193, 195–96, 206; *Letters*, 193
juries: and adversarial trial, 127–28, 179–80, 209–13; deciding libels, 4, 178–79, 184–87, 190–215, 220, 276n22, 277n27, 277n29, 277n35, 278n32, 278n38, 278n40, 281n38, 281n76; and law-fact doctrine, 178, 184–85, 192–93, 198–99, 202–3, 207, 278n39, 284n129; and pretrial publicity, 131, 205–7,

282n105, 283n110; rights of, 12, 184–85; sortation, 189; vicinage rule, 191, 210, 280n62, 280n63

Kalven, Harry, Jr., 268n99
Kames, Henry Home, Lord: on copyright, 44–46, 60–61, 73, 249n17, 250n41; on exchange theory of value, 44–45, 48, 52; on the nature of literary property, 39
Kant, Immanuel: on the autonomy of art, 115, 223, 261n6; *Critique of Judgment*, 175; on poetry and rhetoric, 175–81, 197, 221, 235
Keach, Benjamin, trial for seditious libel, 276n24
Keats, John, 107
Kenrick, William, on copyright, 100–1, 105
Kenyon, Sir Lloyd: on fair comment, 155–58; on pretrial publicity, 205–7, 283n110; on seditious libel, 217–18; on visual defamation, 153
Kierkegaard, Søren, on the public, 7, 9
King v. Lake (1670), defamation, 134
knitting frame, 19
Knowles, Sir Charles, 156
Knox, Vicesimus, 287n33; on appreciating poetry, 234, 235; on propaganda, 235; on satire, 227; *The Spirit of Despotism*, 235, 287n34; on stylistic individuation, 56, 106
Kramnick, Jonathan Brody, 252n72

labor theory of value, 40–52, 98–99, 260n56
Lackington, James, 72
Lake, Peter, 244n50
Lake v. Hatton (1618), defamation, 263n28
Langbein, John, 127
language: competence in, 86–87, 106–7, 190–91; effect of defamatory words, 129–33, 135–39; effect of seditious words, 178–81, 183–84, 187–88, 195–204, 214–16; literary, 28–29, 88–89, 106–7, 114, 125, 148–49, 100–101, 220–23, 229–30, 236–38, 252n63; power of, 87, 175–78, 182, 186, 222; as public communication, 87, 90, 94, 212–13, 258n23; refinement of, 79–81, 229. *See also* poetry; public discourse; rhetoric; style
Lardner, Nathaniel, on blasphemous libel, 279n46

Lavi, Shai J., 283n107
Lavoie, Chantel, 258n37
Law, Edmund, on copyright, 61
law-fact doctrine, 178, 184–85, 192–93, 198–99, 202–3, 207, 284n129
Lawrence, Sir Soulden, on publication of trial proceedings, 28, 245n61
Lebrun-Tondu, Pierre Henry, on propaganda, 284n135
Lefort, Claude, 240n10
Letter in verse, from a married man to his own wife, A, 117
Levin, Harry, 63
Libel Act 1792 (Fox's Libel Act), 4, 128, 157, 175, 179–80, 213–17, 273n46, 274n1, 282n102
Libel Act 1843, 139, 150
Libellis Famosis, Case of (1605), seditious libel, 275n9
libel-slander distinction, 3, 132–39, 214, 267n81, 267n87
liberty, 3, 16–17, 22–25, 181, 239n4, 240n13, 244; literature and, 106–7, 113–14, 176–77, 222–23, 225, 229–30, 287n36; and the public, 9–12, 20, 88, 196–98, 214–19, 236. *See also* criticism, liberty of; democracy; freedom of mind; liberty of the press
liberty of the press, 1–2, 6–7, 14, 21, 26, 188, 239n2; copyright and, 68–69; and fair comment, 159–61; and juries deciding libels, 194–96, 215; and licentiousness, 147, 179, 194–95, 208, 221; and privacy, 141–42, 147; and rhetorical indirection, 232–33
licensing, 128, 184, 276n23; end of, 1, 7, 14, 19, 21, 25, 37, 67, 175, 178, 186–87, 231–32
Licensing Act 1662, 1, 19, 239n1, 249n22
Lilliburne, John, trial for treason, 276n21
Lippmann, Walter, on public, 7
literature: democracy and, 6–7, 106–7, 114–15, 221–23, 238, 240n6, 287n36; idea of, 2–3, 6–7, 29, 74, 105, 221, 246n64; indeterminacy of, 7, 29, 106–7, 176–77, 230–31, 235–38; public function of, 2, 5–8, 16, 28–31, 43–45, 53–54, 72–74, 79–81, 105–7, 113–17, 148–49, 175–78, 181, 221–38; publicity and, 111–16, 149. *See also* fiction; poetry

Littleton, Sir Edward, on seditious libel, 275n12
Lobban, Michael, 282n102
Locke, John, 11, 44, 64, 159; on consent, 241n18; on copyright, 249n22; on expression, 258n37; *Two Treatises of Government*, 159
Lofft, Capel, on juries, 201
Lolme, Jean-Louis de, on seditious libel, 201–2
London Packet, The, on Goldsmith, 142
Lyttelton, Thomas, Lord, on genius, 46

Macaulay, Catherine, on genius, 46–47; on booksellers, 59
Macaulay, Thomas Babington, 1; on copyright, 72
MacLaurin, John, Lord Dreghorn, on copyright and national literary traditions, 254n91
Macpherson, James, "Ossian" poems, 63, 152, 253n88
Magna Carta, 22–23, 36
Mandeville, Bernard, 22
Manley, Delarivier, 269n110
Mansfield, Sir James, on libel-slander distinction, 133–36
Mansfield, William Murray, Lord, 125, 156, 250n27; on adversarial trial, 208–9; on copyright, 39–40, 249n19, 249n22, 250n42; on courtroom speech as privileged, 150; on exchange theory of value, 40, 45, 58, 60, 67; on fallibility of juries, 192–93, 208; on idea-expression dichotomy, 90, 98, 102; on labor theory of value, 40, 67; on pretrial publicity, 205, 283n106; on seditious libel, 194, 204, 208, 212, 277n33, 278n39, 281n78
market: exchange theory of value and, 45, 53–54, 59–64, 71; idea of the, 10, 13, 22, 24, 29–30; public domain and, 65–68
marketplace of ideas, 43, 201
Maseres, Francis, on seditious libel, 202, 282n99
Matthews, John, trial for treason, 19, 243n35, 279n46
Maugham, Robert, *A Treatise on the Laws of Literary Property*, 94
McKeon, Michael, 240n13

Meehan, Michael, 287n36
Meiklejohn, Alexander, on freedom of artistic expression, 115
Miles, William Augustus, on propaganda, 285n138
Millar, Andrew, 250n41, 254n91. See also *Millar v. Taylor*
Millar v. Taylor (1769), copyright, 39–41, 43, 45–47, 58, 90, 102, 141, 249n22, 254n91
Milton, John, 36, 44, 50, 57, 62, 64, 69–70, 85, 101, 105, 107, 225, 272n32; on copyright, 250n38; *Paradise Lost*, 72
Mitchell, Paul, 267n83, 272n40, 278n42
Mitchell v. Reynolds (1711), restraint of trade, 141, 243n37
Monboddo, James Burnett, Lord, on copyright, 92–93
Montesquieu, Charles de Secondat, Baron de, on word-act distinction, 129
Monthly Review, 118
Morning Chronicle, The, 282n87; trial for seditious libel, 217
Morris, Robert, on juries deciding libels, 200
Murray, John, on copyright, 72

Nahmod, Sheldon H., 261n6
Nashe, Thomas, 163
nation: and language, 86, 252n63; idea of, 10–11, 20; nationalism, 29–31, 246n66, 246n67, 246n69, 254n88; national literary traditions, 5, 36, 43, 62–65, 69, 72–74, 254n91, 254n100
Newcastle, Thomas Pelham-Holles, Duke of, on innuendoes, 233
newspapers and the periodical press, 1–2, 18–19, 21, 25–26, 72, 112, 232, 242n28, 245n57; literature and, 112, 233–34
Newton, Sir Isaac, 44, 64, 100
Nightingale v. Stockdale (1809), defamation, 169–71
North, Sir Francis, on defamation, 267n87
North Briton, The, 233, 281n68

obscene libel (obscenity), 4, 27, 114–15, 129, 149, 189, 266n70, 279n46
Oldham, James, 245n61

Old Nick's Pocket-Book; or, Hints for a "Ryghte Pedantique and Mangleinge" Publication to be called "My Pocket Book, 152
Olson, Kevin, 246n70
originality, 36, 51–53, 56–58, 62, 76–77, 88, 90–91, 95, 97–98, 104, 251n46, 252n72, 259n52
Orwell, George, 29
Osborn, William, 122
Owen, William, trial for seditious libel, 192, 281n67
Oxford English Dictionary, 10–11
Oxford Review, The, 154

Page, Anthony, 282n105
Paine, Thomas, 135; *Rights of Man*, 213–15; trial for seditious libel, 133–34
Parke, Sir James, on defamation, 267n78
Parker, Sir Thomas, on idea-expression dichotomy, 256n1
Parliament, reporting of debates, 1, 26, 28, 141–42
Parmiter v. Coupland (1840), defamation, 267n78
Parsons, Ian, 248n10
Patry, William, 249n12
Patterson, Annabel, 230, 235
Payne and Cadell v. Anderson and Robertson (1787), copyright, 260n57
Pennington, Sarah, on *Vicar of Wakefield*, 144, 270n119
Phillips, Sir Richard, 151–52; on John Carr, 154
Pincus, Steven, 244n50
Pindar, 81–82
piracy, 1, 35–36, 38–39, 46, 51, 91, 249n19
Pitt, James: on Magna Carta, 22; on parties, 244n49
Pitt, William, 213, 217, 235, 275n6, 284n135, 285n138, 287n34
Plato, on democracy, 16, 177; on poetry, 176–78, 197; on rhetoric, 177, 274n3
Plutarch, 274n3
Pocock, J. G. A., 42
Poems on Affairs of State, 25
poetry: and fact, 145–46; as indirection, 122–23, 146–48, 231–33; as medium of publicity, 111–12, 137, 149, 182; poetic

profession, 53; politics and, 25, 231–34; vs. prose, 28–29, 88–89, 117, 125, 127, 132, 148, 245n63; vs. rhetoric, 5, 175–78, 221–23; share of literary market, 72; social utility of, 111, 225–31; value of reading, 55–56, 234–35

Pope, Alexander, 37, 69, 105–7, 156, 229, 233–34; on public opinion, 21, 37, 69; on satire and the law, 226–27; on style, 83–84. Works: *Dunciad*, 84, 226–27, 231–32, 234; *Eloisa to Abelard*, 145; *Essay on Man*, 84

pornography, 129, 237. *See also* obscene libel

Posner, Richard, 253n86, 270n122

Post, Robert C., 8, 133, 240n11, 271n4

Post Office (Revenues) Act 1710, 140

Powell, Sir John, on seditious libel, 186

pretrial publicity, 28, 131, 205–7, 282n105, 283n107

Priestley, Joseph, 218

prints, 25, 112, 153, 232

privacy, 3–4, 19–20, 139–49; defamation and, 139–40; literature and, 113–14, 144–45, 149, 236, 270n118; and the press, 142–43, 147; and the public, 113–14, 142–43; right of, 27–28, 140–41, 145, 268n98, 268n99, 269n110

Proclamation against Seditious Writings and Publications, Royal (1792), 213–17, 284n126

propaganda: idea of, 217–23, 284n132, 284n135; literature vs., 29, 221–23, 235, 237; origin of word, 216–17, 285n138

Prynne, William, trial for seditious libel, 184, 276n20; *Histriomastix*, 184

public, the: idea of, 7–15, 20–21, 23–25, 27, 67, 113–14, 128–29, 196, 211–13, 219, 225, 236–38, 241n17, 241n20; 242n22, 242n27, 242n28; incoherence of, 6, 8, 11–12, 15, 25, 27–28, 30–31, 219, 223, 225, 236; indeterminacy of, 9–11, 15, 23, 30, 139, 194, 200–1, 214, 219, 237–38, 240n10, 244n51; as legitimation story, 10, 12–13, 23, 241n19; and the people, 8–9, 20, 30–31, 65–66, 74, 149, 241, 246n70; public interest, 116, 150, 171, 270n2; and the public sphere, 13–18, 20, 24; public spirit, 13; as tribunal, 12, 117, 119, 122–24, 138–39, 142, 148; and vox populi, 11

publication of trial proceedings, 26, 28, 209, 245n59

public discourse: literature as, 2–3, 6–7, 16, 29, 31, 112–15, 144, 148–49, 181, 228–38; style of, 18, 21, 26, 77–78, 80–81, 86, 106–7, 231–33, 245n63, 258n23; norms of, 5, 8, 15–16, 25–29, 112–14, 127, 139, 157, 166, 170, 222; subjects of, 19, 26, 31, 146–47. *See also* expressive diversity

public domain, 4, 36–37, 65–71, 214, 247n4, 248n7, 253n86, 254n96, 254n100; and the commons, 76; and libel law, 137; literature as, 36, 69–70, 73–74, 255n107

publicity, 12–15, 18–21, 26–28, 143, 242n22, 242n26; defamation and, 136–39; literature and, 111–16, 149, 232, 234; privacy vs., 113–14, 147–49; right of, 99. *See also* pretrial publicity

public opinion: authority of, 8, 13, 21, 24 27, 188–89, 232–34, 241n16, 241n19, 243n32, 244n42, 261n1, 283n107; and defamation, 130; indeterminacy, 22–23, 193–94, 199–201, 281n76; literature and, 235, 238; propaganda and, 218–20, 222, 235; sedition as inducing conformity of, 196–97, 207, 215–16

public sphere, 2–3, 7–9, 13–20, 165–66, 177, 237, 240n9, 240n13, 242n22, 242n26–44; vs. courtroom, 203–4, 210, 220, 283n107; equality in, 16–17, 166, 170–71; and expressive diversity, 96; giving recognition to, 23, 158; and idea of the public, 13–18, 20, 24; limits on, 15–19, 24, 27; literature in, 16, 31, 113–14, 175–78, 225, 236–37; and norms of debate, 5, 15, 17, 24, 113–14, 166, 170, 176–77, 203; requirements for participation in, 66, 106

Pulteney, William: on innuendoes, 187; on juries, 278n39

Puttenham, George, on poets as lawmakers, 225–26, 228

Pyne, Hugh, trial for treason, 276n21

Quintilian, 257n7

Ralph, James, on poetic indirection, 232
Rancière, Jacques, 2, 6, 16–17, 79, 107, 238, 243n33, 243n34, 246n64, 261n70

Rape Act 1576, 262n8
Raven, James, 254n100
Raymond, Sir Robert, on obscene libel, 266n70
Rayner, John, *A Digest of the Law concerning Libels*, 134–36, 144, 268n88
readers: common reader, 12, 164, 234; of fiction, 144–45; and imaginative sympathy, 118–20, 131–32, 145–46, 148–49, 167–68; literary canon and, 70–72; of newspapers, 25–26, 234, 245n57; reading libels, 187, 200, 233; reading literature, 234–35, 237; reading as self-improvement, 42, 45, 54–58, 90, 221, 252n72; reading and style, 84–87
Regina v. Drake (1706), seditious libel, 277n35
Regina v. Throckmorton (1554), treason, 276n21
Regina v. Udall (1590), seditious libel, 184, 276n22
Rex v. Bear (1699), seditious libel, 268n88, 277n35
Rex v. Chambers (1628), seditious libel, 275n13
Rex v. Cobbett (1804), seditious libel, 159
Rex v. Curl (1727), obscene libel, 129, 133, 189, 266n70, 279n46
Rex v. Fores (1800), libel, 271n16
Rex v. Francklin (1729), seditious libel, 187, 278n38
Rex v. Harris (1679), seditious libel, 277n27
Rex v. Keach (1665), seditious libel, 276n24
Rex v. Matthews (1719), treason, 243n35, 279n46
Rex v. Miller (1770), seditious libel, 193
Rex v. Owen (1752), seditious libel, 192, 281n67, 284n129
Rex v. Paine (1696), seditious libel, 277n35
Rex v. Paine (1792), seditious libel, 133–34
Rex v. Prynne (1633), seditious libel, 184, 276n20
Rex v. Pyne (1628), treason, 276n21
Rex v. Shipley (1784), seditious libel, 133, 204–12, 278n39, 281n68, 282n105
Rex v. Smollett (1760), libel, 156–57
Rex v. Stroud, Long, Selden and Others (1629), seditious libel, 275n12

Rex v. Taylor (1676), blasphemous libel, 266n70
Rex v. White (1808), libel, 272n39
Rex v. Williams (1619), treason, 276n21
Rex v. Williams (1764), seditious libel, 281n68
Rex v. Woodfall (1770), seditious libel, 93, 281n68
Rex v. Woolston (1728), blasphemous libel, 279n46
Rex v. Zenger (1735), libel, 190–92, 195, 205, 209
Reynolds, Sir James: on blasphemous libel, 279n46; on obscene libel, 266n70
rhetoric: in the adversarial trial, 209–12, 220; depreciation of, 107; distrust of, 177–79, 181, 197; and idea-expression dichotomy, 89–95, 102; and law of sedition, 182–86; "new rhetoric," 77–78, 85–88, 94–96, 105–6, 258n23; persuasion vs. coercion, 216, 218; vs. poetry, 5, 175–78, 221–23, 235; power of, 182, 196, 199; refinement, 50, 78–83, 105, 229; and truth, 131–32, 146–48. *See also* propaganda
rhetorical indirection, 111, 122–23, 148, 230–35, 286n21
Richardson, Samuel, 51; *Clarissa*, 119, 144
Richardson, Sir Thomas, on seditious libel, 276n20
Roos, John Manners, Lord, 83
Rosanvallon, Pierre, 239n4
Rose, Mark, 95, 247n2, 259n52
Rosenfeld, Sophie, 241n19
Rous, George, on fallibility of juries, 194, 281n76

Saccamano, Neil, 242n29
Saint-Amour, Paul K., 251n50
Sandford, Philip, 118
Sandwich, John Montagu, Earl of, 265n66
Saunders, David, 247n2
scandalum magnatum, 128, 182, 265, 267n87, 275n9
Schmitt, Carl, 241n15
Schneebaum, Galia, 283n107
Scroggs, Sir William, on juries deciding libels, 277n27

seditious libel, 1, 3–4, 159, 175, 178–220, 274n1, 275n9, 275n12, 276n19, 276n23, 277n30, 277n33, 279n46, 283n106, 285n141; as breeding diversity of opinion, 183–84, 188; as context-dependent, 133–34, 180, 200–4, 214–20, 282n102; defamatory content vs. seditious tendency, 187–88, 194–98, 204, 215–16; as inducing conformity of opinion, 196–200, 207, 215–19; innuendoes in, 178–79, 187, 192, 233, 278n37; juries deciding libels, 4, 128, 178–79, 184–87, 190–215, 220, 276n22, 277n27, 277n29, 277n35, 281n67, 281n68, 281n76; and law-fact doctrine, 178, 184–85, 192–93, 198–99, 202–3, 207, 277n33, 280n58, 281n69, 284n129; and the public, 188–91, 194, 203–4, 213–19, 280n56; rhetorical ideas of, 182–86; treason and, 182, 184, 186. *See also* propaganda

Seditious Words Act 1580, 276n19

Seipp, David J., 269n101

Selden, Sir John, trial for seditious libel, 275n12

Septennial Act 1716, 25

Seven Bishops, Case of the (1688), 185–86, 188, 190, 277n29

Seville, Catherine, 255n109

Shaftesbury, Anthony Ashley Cooper, Earl of, on poets and refinement, 229

Shakespeare, William, 36–38, 50, 52, 57, 62, 64, 69, 70, 73, 81, 101, 107, 226, 234, 252n72

Sharpe, Charles, 152

Shelburne, William Petty, Earl, 213, 284n127

Shelley, Percy Bysshe, *Defense of Poetry*, 227–28, 236

Sher, Richard B., 252n69

Shoemaker, Robert B., 130, 265n62

Shropshire Chronicle, The, 118–19, 124, 126, 132, 262n12

Shuger, Debora, 257n6

Sidney, Sir Philip, 225–26, 231, 237

Skinner, Quentin, 244n51

Small, Helen, 240n6

Smith, Adam: on division of labor, 9, 47; on exchange theory of value, 47; on genius, 53, 57, 251n50; on labor theory of value, 251n50; *Lectures on Rhetoric and Belles Lettres*, 86–87, 258n25; monopolies, 59; on style, 86; on stylistic individuation, 86–87

Smollett, Tobias, trial for libel, 156–57

Society for Constitutional Information, 204–5, 282n105

Sommerville, C. John, 25

Southey v. Sherwood (1817), copyright, 256n1

Spacks, Patricia Meyer, 270n118

Spenser, Edmund, 57, 62, 70, 252n72

Spoo, Robert, 247n4

Sprat, Thomas, on style, 80

Stage Licensing Act 1737, 1, 18

Stamp Act 1712, 18

Stanhope, Sir Charles, on juries deciding libels, 202

Stanley, Jason, 284n132

St Asaph, William Shipley, Dean of, 133, 204–6, 208–9, 211–12, 281n68, 282n105

State Law: or, The Doctrine of Libels, Discussed and Examined, 189–90, 195

State Trials, 277n29

Stationers' Company v. Carnan (1775), copyright, 68–69, 254n98

Staves, Susan, 84, 262n9

St Clair, William, 69, 72

St. James's Evening Post Case (Roach v. Garven) (1742), libel, 283n107

Steele, Sir Richard, 14

Stern, Simon, 248n7, 259n52, 266n70

Stockdale, John, 209

Strahan, William, 71

strangerhood: as condition for liberty, 9–10, 113; defamatory words and, 130; and indeterminacy of the public, 9, 166, 236; individuation and, 87, 229–30, 258n31; John Carr and, 151, 167–68; juries and, 193–94, 202, 205–6, 211–13, 220; public sphere and, 14–15, 165–66; and vicinage rule, 191, 280n64

Strauss, Leo, 230

style: in copyright law, 75–78, 89–108; vs. expression, 89–92, 98–100, 103–5; and expressive diversity, 96–100, 103–7, 230, 236; harmony of subject and, 79, 81–85, 257n7; individuation, 56, 77–78, 81–89, 94–108, 259n52, 261n71; in libelous utterances, 131, 183–84, 186, 279n46; literary, 88–89, 106–8, 113, 148–49, 223,

style (*continued*)
  229–30; plain, 80–81, 86–87, 106, 258n23; of public discourse, 18, 21, 26, 80–81, 86, 106–7, 231–33; refinement, 61, 78–88, 90, 105–6, 229; rhetoric and, 78–79, 83–87. See also idea-expression dichotomy
Swift, Jonathan, 35, 37, 231–32. Works: *A Modest Proposal*, 20; *Tale of a Tub*, 231

Tabart v. Tipper (1808), defamation, 155–56, 159
Talfourd, Thomas, on copyright, 71–73, 255n109
Tarde, Gabriel, 242n28
Taylor, Charles, 241n16
Taylor, Robert, 254n91. See also *Millar v. Taylor*
Tenger, Zeynep, 251n50
test of time, 70–71, 164, 234
Thompson, E. P., 4
Thomson, James, *The Seasons*, 40, 72, 250n41
Thorley v. Kerry (1812), defamation, 133, 267n81
Thorne, Christian, 261n1
Throckmorton, Sir Nicholas, trial for treason, 276n21
Thurlow, Sir Edward, on fallibility of juries, 198; on seditious libel, 199
Times, The (London), 208, 217
Tindal, Matthew, on liberty of the press, 188
Tonson, Jacob, 38, 70
Tonson v. Collins (1762), copyright, 41, 250n27
Towers, Joseph, on pretrial publicity, 283n110
Townsend v. Hughes (1676), scandalum magnatum, 267n87
trade secrets, 19, 141, 243n37
treason, 180, 182, 184, 186, 243n35, 276n21, 279n46
Treason Trials Act 1696, 277n31, 283n117
Trenchard, John, on liberty of the press, 188
Trials for Felony Act 1836, 283n117
Trolander, Paul, 251n50
"Trusty Guardian, The," 119, 262n12
Turnbull v. Bird (1861), defamation, 159
Twyn, John, trial for treason, 243n35

Udall, John, trial for seditious libel, 184, 276n19

Vaidhyanathan, Siva, 256n3
Valenza, Robin, 252n63
Vaughan, Sir John, on rights of juries, 184, 190–91, 202, 205–6, 280n58. See also *Bushell's Case*
Veeder, Van Vechten, on liberty of criticism, 274n63
Venus in the Cloister, 129, 279n46
vicinage rule, 191, 210, 280n62
Villers v. Monsley (1769), defamation, 134, 139
Vindication of the Exclusive Right of Authors to their own Works, A, 92
Visconti, Elliott, 266n70
Von Hannover v. Germany (No 2) (2012), privacy, 269n110

Wabeke, Bertus H., 285n138
Wade, John W., 268n99
Waldron, Jeremy, 244n45
Walpole, Sir Robert, 18, 21–22, 232–33, 239n2; on libels, 21
Walsh, William, 84
Warburton, William, on monopolies, 42
Warner, Michael, 9, 164, 242n27, 245n63, 280n66
Warren, Samuel, on privacy, 141
Warton, Joseph, on Pope, 234
Warton, Thomas, 252n72
Webb v. Rose (1732), copyright, 249n19
Weber, Harold, 242n26
Whitehead, Paul, 231
WIC Radio Ltd. v. Simpson (2008), defamation, 270n2
Wilkes, John, 26–27, 179, 200, 233, 245n59; *Essay on Woman*, 27
Willes, Edward, on copyright, 49, 58; on exchange theory of value, 48; on genius, 47–48; on idea-expression dichotomy, 90; on labor theory of value, 249n22
Williams, John, trial for treason, 276n21
Williams, Joseph, *The Seducer's Distracted Confession*, 119–20, 146, 148, 262n13
Williams, Raymond, 246n66
Winwood, Elizabeth, 126, 264n48
Winwood, Ralph, 120–27, 130–32, 138–39, 142, 146, 148, 264n48, 264n52, 264n53
Wood, Thomas, 124, 263n38

Woodfall, William, 282n87; trial for seditious libel, 193, 281n68
Woodmansee, Martha, 51, 57
Woolston, Thomas, trial for blasphemous libel, 279n46
Worcester Journal, 126
Wordsworth, William, 35, 261; on copyright, 73–74; on poetic expression, 89, 230; on the press, 234; on poetic sensibility, 54; on the public vs. the people, 31
Works of the Learned, The, 164, 273n61
Wright, Sir Robert, 185–86, 277n29
Wynne, Edward, on vicinage rule, 280n62

Yates, Joseph, 250n42; on the Crown's prerogative copyright, 41; on the function of literature, 44–45, 53; on idea-expression dichotomy, 39, 90–92; on labor theory of value, 40; on monopolies, 40, 45–46, 59; on the nature of literary property, 39, 44; on perpetual copyright, 43; on privacy, 141; on property, 41, 45; on style, 94
Yorke, Philip, Earl of Hardwicke: on obscene libel, 266n70; on pretrial publicity, 283n107
Young, Edward: *Conjectures on Original Composition*, 51–52, 260n55; on genius, 53, 57–58, 258n31; on originality, 51–53, 56–58, 62; on poetic composition, 52–53, 230; on poetry vs. prose, 88, 229; on private reading, 143

Zaret, David, 243n26
Zenger, John Peter, trial for seditious libel, 190–92